CASS LIBRARY OF AFRICAN STUDIES

GENERAL STUDIES

No. 43

Editorial Adviser: JOHN RALPH WILLIS

CECIL RHODES, 1889

THE
MAKING OF RHODESIA

HUGH MARSHALL HOLE

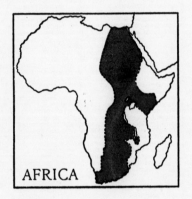

AFRICA

"All that Red—that's my dream!"
CECIL RHODES.

FRANK CASS & CO. LTD.
1967

Published by
FRANK CASS AND COMPANY LIMITED
67 Great Russell Street, London WC1

First published by Macmillan & Co. Ltd. in 1926

First edition	1926
New impression	1967

Printed in Great Britain by
Thomas Nelson (Printers) Ltd., London and Edinburgh

THIS BOOK IS DEDICATED TO

MY DAUGHTER MONICA

AND TO THE MEMORY OF

MY WIFE

BOTH OF WHOM SHARED WITH ME THE JOYS

AND ADVENTURES OF THE EARLY

DAYS OF RHODESIA

PREFACE

THE evolution of the British colonies which bear the name of Rhodes, their founder, has never, so far as I am aware, been described as a consecutive whole. Disconnected episodes have at different times excited attention and provoked controversy, but their correlation has not yet been presented to English readers and many of their details have been published in a garbled shape. My justification for attempting to piece the story together and to clear away some misconceptions lies in the fact that I lived in various parts of Southern and Northern Rhodesia for twenty-three years, and was in close personal contact throughout with the men who participated in the events of their stirring history. Many of these men have passed into the realms of silence, and before long no eye-witness will be left.

I desire gratefully to acknowledge the assistance which the Board of the British South Africa Company has rendered by allowing me to refer to early records and original reports. I wish also to record my indebtedness and thanks to Mr. E. A. Maund and Mr. Leo Weinthal, C.B.E., for some of the photographs, to Mr. H. H. Kitchen of the British South Africa Company for drawing the maps, and to Mr. J. G. MacDonald, O.B.E., and other Rhodesian friends for supplying deficiencies in my narrative. In preparing the early chapters I was greatly helped by the late Mr. Rochfort Maguire, President of the Chartered Company, who was intimately connected with many of the events recorded in them.

It is perhaps impossible for one who has served the Company from its inception to escape altogether the imputation of partiality, but I have honestly endeavoured to present the simple truth and to gloze over no shortcomings.

H. M. H.

London,
February, 1926.

vii

CONTENTS

LIST OF ILLUSTRATIONS

THE MAKING OF RHODESIA

CHAPTER I

THE GENESIS OF THE MOVEMENT

THE project upon which Cecil Rhodes embarked thirty-six years ago, of creating a British Colony in the heart of Africa, has long since passed beyond the experimental stage. Its justification is now in the hands of the small but enterprising body of settlers in Southern Rhodesia who have lately, on their own initiative, shouldered the management of the great estate provided for them by the genius of its founder and by the patient and only partially requited labours of that remarkable corporation the British South Africa Company, whose history is, in fact, the history of the country itself.

The genesis of the movement which ultimately received the sanction of a Royal Charter may be traced to two principal influences.

The first of these was the persistent tradition, handed down from remote antiquity, that vast deposits of gold lay ready for the miner in Central South Africa, and the second was the impulse which came upon Englishmen, almost suddenly, in the latter part of the nineteenth century, to acquire fresh tracts of Africa for future development, to link South with North, and to create a Tom Tiddler's ground from which other European Powers should be excluded.

In the beginning these two influences operated independently and either of them might in time have become strong enough, unaided by the other, to have inspired a British enterprise. When they were ultimately merged they advanced with a rush which swept aside all opposition, and what had at first been the dream of a few adventurers rapidly assumed the form of a solid commercial movement. It is proposed at the outset to trace briefly the history of each of these two ideas up to the point where they became united in the mind of one man, and as the gold was the earlier attraction in point of time, so it will be dealt with first in this narrative.

It is unnecessary to do more than recall the legend of wealth which, through ancient and mediæval history, has clung about Mashonaland, long thought to be the Ophir of Biblical lore. It was this that prompted the Portuguese expeditions of the fifteenth and sixteenth centuries : it was for gold that the miners of Zimbabwe, unidentified to this day, built the walls and towns, and sunk the shafts, which remain as enduring monuments to their industry, and it was the gold-glamour which made the mysterious Empire of Monomotapa a household word in Europe up to comparatively recent days.[1] The builders of Zimbabwe played their part and passed from the stage; the coast lands were occupied in turn by Arab traders and Portuguese adventurers. None of these were destined to establish themselves in the interior as a nation; the barbarous Kaffir tribes survived them all, and one is sometimes driven to speculate as to whether this virile race may not be destined to outlast even the present colonists of South Central Africa.

The history, mythical or actual, of these successive occupations belongs to another period, and has been well told by other pens. The following pages will deal with the latest phase only of Rhodesia's long history, during which the vague and doubtful rumours of hidden riches have gradually taken concrete shape in blocks of veritable gold.

The story dates back fifty or sixty years, and begins at a time when Mashonaland and Matabeleland were unknown, save to a few intrepid hunters who toiled painfully into the

---

[1] Interest in these legends and speculation as to their veracity was strangely but unmistakably revived by the publication in 1885 of Rider Haggard's celebrated romance, *King Solomon's Mines*.

interior from Durban or Capetown, and risked health and life in the pursuit of ivory. One of these, Henry Hartley, a well-known elephant hunter, whose wanderings led him more than once into the remote regions of Mashonaland, was struck by the shallow excavations and heaps of quartz which he saw in many parts of the country, and which were obviously the work of human hands. Hartley was one of the British settlers of 1820, and had his home at Bathurst in the Cape Colony, whence for many years he made expeditions into the interior for trade and hunting, but it was not until 1866 that he was able to put into practice the idea of obtaining scientific investigation of the mineral potentialities of the quartz reefs, which he knew to be so widely distributed in this part of Africa. In that year he fell in with a young German scientist named Carl Mauch, and engaged or invited him to accompany his next expedition.

On their return, in the latter part of 1867, Mauch wrote a letter to the *Transvaal Argus*, describing, in extravagant language, the result of his visit to the Northern goldfields. After narrating the discovery of two bodies of auriferous rock, one of which he traced for eighty and the other for twenty-two miles, he proceeds :—" The vast extent and beauty of these goldfields are such that at a particular spot I stood as it were transfixed, riveted to the place, struck with amazement and wonder at the sight, and for a few minutes was unable to use the hammer. Thousands of persons might here find ample room to work in this extensive field without interfering with one another." [1]

These fascinating phrases produced an immense impression in South Africa. Men began to talk about expeditions and stamp batteries; syndicates were formed, and Mauch was beset with inquiries as to the locality and accessibility of his discoveries. The reports reached Great Britain, and in the following year (1868) appeared a pamphlet by Mr. Richard Babbs, entitled *The Goldfields of South Africa*, a few sentences of which I will repeat, as they afford some explanation of the remarkable rush which followed the

[1] Letter from C. Mauch to the *Transvaal Argus*, 3rd December, 1867.

publication to the world of Mauch's reports. The writer
says that Mauch had no hesitation in asserting that the
goldfields in the interior were richer than those of California
or Australia. "When he saw the white reefs of auriferous
quartz glistening in the sun as they cropped out here and
there, he was startled by the conception of the wealth before
him. Thousands of holes some ten feet deep give evidence
of old native workings, and bear out Dr. Livingstone's
remark about the gold washing carried on in wooden bowls
by the Kaffirs in time past."

The Times also had several articles on the discoveries,
couched in hardly less glowing language, and in the same
year published an assay of some specimens of quartz from
the new fields, furnished by the Bank of England, and
showing 1185 ozs. of gold and 60 ozs. of silver to the ton ! [1]
Was it to be wondered at that amateurs from England, and
even professional diggers from Australia and California,
began to flock towards Durban, which was then regarded
as the nearest port to the new El Dorado?

Almost simultaneously with the reports of Hartley and
Mauch from Mashonaland, a discovery of gold-bearing reefs
was made at Tatin, or, as we now call it Tati, on the south-
western side of Matabeleland, and it was to that district,
as being more accessible, that the first prospecting parties
gave their attention. As it turned out, the Tati goldfields
monopolised the rush, and the disappointments met with
there, followed by the counter-attraction offered in 1870
by the diamond discoveries on the Vaal River, checked the
impulse which might otherwise have led to a thorough
exploration of the more remote regions to which Mauch
had drawn notice.

Among the earliest arrivals at Tati was Sir John Swinburne, who, as the representative of a company styled
"The London and Limpopo Company," undertook in 1869
an expedition to secure digging rights from the Matabele
chief; and about the same time another company, bearing
the familiar-sounding name of the "South African Goldfields and Exploration Company," despatched a party to

[1] *The Times*, 11th September, 1868.

Mashonaland, under the leadership of Thomas Baines, an experienced colonial traveller who had accompanied Dr. Livingstone on his then recent expedition to explore the lower courses of the Zambesi River.

Swinburne's venture resulted in the well-known " Tati Concession," which was specially excluded from the Rudd-Rhodes Concession, and exists to this day under independent management; but, of the various companies formed to develop the mines in the Tati area, only two or three survived the stress and trials of the early 'seventies, and even these led a chequered existence until, many years later, the arrival of the railway line enabled them to work on a payable basis.

Baines in his turn obtained a mineral concession from the chief, and as, later on, much will have to be said regarding the Matabele tribe and its politics, it will only be necessary here to indicate briefly the position at the time of which I am speaking.

Mziligazi, the original leader of this offshoot of the Zulus, who had conducted the tribe from Zululand to the country which they have since inhabited, died in 1868, but before his death he had by annual raids acquired sovereignty over a wide extent of country, reaching from the Gwaai River on the west to the Sabi on the east, and from the Zambesi to the Limpopo, and had reduced to subjection the various weaker tribes occupying it. During 1869 the Matabele were ruled by a regent, Um-nobata, a relative of the deceased chief, pending the removal of a doubt as to what had become of the legitimate heir, Kuruman, who had quarrelled with his father and disappeared. Some time was spent in investigating the claims of a pretender from Natal, who alleged that he was the true Kuruman, but upon these breaking down, the tribe proceeded to elect a permanent successor, and in December 1869 their choice fell upon Mziligazi's younger son, Lobengula, so well known later in connection with the occupation of Mashonaland.

His formal investiture as Paramount Chief took place in February 1870, and Baines, who had been waiting for this event to take place, immediately visited him to prefer his demands for a concession. He had just returned from an extended journey made on behalf of his company through Mashonaland, during which he had reached a point 150 miles due south of the Portuguese settlement of Zumbo on the Zambesi (*i.e.* somewhere between the modern town of Salisbury and Sinoia), and had discovered old " Mashona " workings in many parts of the adjacent country, as well as some ruined buildings, which he assumed to be the former dwellings of missionaries from Zumbo. On learning that the question of the succession had been determined, he thought to secure the grant of a mining area from the new chief. But Lobengula was not to be drawn into any rash undertakings. He informed Baines that having been so recently appointed he could neither give land nor fix boundaries, and Baines had to content himself with a verbal promise of the right to dig for gold in a district limited by the Gwailo (Gwelo) River on the west, and the Ganyana (Hanyani) on the east. This was confirmed in August 1871 by a written document under Lobengula's sign-manual —the famous " Baines Concession "—among the provisions of which were a clause stating that the chief alienated no portion of his kingdom, and an undertaking by the concessionaire to recognise his sovereignty.[1]

The next year or two were occupied by Baines in a vain endeavour to raise capital in order to develop the rights which he had obtained. The moment was unpropitious. The Franco-German War had depressed the money markets of Europe, and, when a recovery took place, the rich discoveries of diamonds on the Vaal River and in Griqualand West diverted men's thoughts from the gold so far away in the north. In spite of strenuous efforts on Baines' part to revive interest in Mauch's goldfields and his own enterprise, the necessary funds were not subscribed.

As a last resource, Baines sunk his own small means in the purchase of a quartz-crushing machine, and made

---

[1] It is interesting to note that even in those days the Portuguese claimed Mashonaland, for, immediately after the publication of the Concession, the Governor of Quilimane, Senhor Carlos è Costa, lodged a protest against the district between the Gwelo and Hanyani rivers being worked without Portuguese sanction.

arrangements to travel, almost alone, to the Mashonaland goldfields, but disappointments had told upon a constitution already impaired by many arduous journeys in unhealthy climates. His new plans were frustrated by an attack of dysentery, to which, after a long illness, he succumbed in May 1875.[1]

After Baines' death no further steps were taken to open up the Mashonaland goldfields for many years. Some of the mines in the Tati district were worked for a time in a spasmodic manner, but the more certain rewards of the diamond fields kept men away, and any attempts to prospect in other parts of the country were instantly repressed by the Matabele and their chief. Lobengula was always obsessed by a dread that his country would be overrun by gold-seekers if he once allowed them a foothold. He was ready to give encouragement to a limited number of hunters, who curried favour with him by presents of European goods, and he extended this indulgence to a few missionaries whom he found useful as business advisers in matters relating to the white men, but he was suspicious of all new-comers, and cherished a special hatred for the Boers, knowing their tendency to penetrate further and further into the interior, and the tenacity with which they clung to any ground on which they had once settled. Probably also he entertained a lively memory of the days when they had driven his father and people out of the Transvaal. His attitude towards the generality of travellers in his country was tolerant, but no more, and there was always present in the minds of the few resident Europeans an uneasy feeling as to what might happen if his young braves got beyond control, and a conviction that they were living with a sword suspended by a thread above their heads.

[1] Baines was by profession an artist, and one of no mean ability, as his well-known paintings of the Victoria Falls attest. In 1855 he accompanied Gregory's expedition to North Australia; in 1858 he travelled with the brothers Charles and David Livingstone, but separated from them owing to a quarrel; from 1861 to 1868 he was the companion of Chapman in his endeavour to reach the Zambesi from the West Coast of Africa, and in the latter year he made his first expedition to Matabeleland. Although past fifty at this time he possessed all the energy and elasticity of a young man.

No mining enterprise could have been promoted under such conditions, and for years no serious attempt was made to explore the country's resources. Had not other causes begun to operate—notably the revival of interest created by the successive discoveries of gold at de Kaap in 1883 and at Witwatersrand in 1886—the mineral wealth of Rhodesia might have remained unproved until this day.

The second influence which was an agent in the ultimate creation of the Chartered South Africa Company was the idea of British expansion.

It is a remarkable fact that the two nations which secured the earliest foothold in South Africa, and which therefore had the first and best opportunities of extending their dominion over the interior, should have allowed so many years to slip by without taking a single step towards securing the back country with its vast and unknown possibilities, and should have been stirred at length into activity by the colonising schemes of other and younger Powers.

In the case of the Portuguese this impetus came too late. They might have possessed Africa from Angola to Mozambique. It needed all the efforts of Serpa Pinto and Paiva d'Andrade to save their coast colonies from being cut up, in the general partition which followed the scramble for Africa by other European Powers. In the case of Great Britain the movement was too late to save Damara-land, and was only just in time to prevent the great inland territories between the Congo and the Cape from being appropriated by Germans, Boers and Portuguese.

Prior to Dr. Livingstone's first journey to the Zambesi in 1850, nothing was known, and little was cared, about these regions. During the succeeding twenty-three years the great explorer had the field to himself. His prodigious geographical discoveries appealed to a comparatively small section only of the British public, but the revelations which he made as to the extent and horrors of the interior slave trade, the mystery of his long disappearance, Stanley's sensational expedition for his rescue, and the pathetic circumstances of the missionary's lonely death, stirred men's feelings to their depths, and excited a wave of senti-

mental enthusiasm about those dark portions of the continent which had previously been merely the subject of
scientific speculation.

The immediate and tangible result of Livingstone's
explorations north of the Zambesi was the establishment
of a few missionary settlements on the shores of Lake
Nyasa and in the Shiré highlands. Although intense eagerness had been excited, not only in England and Scotland,
but also in France and Germany, for the further exploration
of the great Central African Lakes, the idea of colonisation
did not occur to any of these until long after Livingstone's
death in 1873, and while a number of minor expeditions
were organised and the details of Livingstone's rough outlines were gradually filled in, no overt step was taken by
Britain, or by any other Power, to assert dominion over
a single square mile of the immense area which now stood
disclosed. It was Stanley's travels in continuation of
Livingstone's great work which first kindled the spark,
and converted the academical interest of Europe into a
practical scheme of occupation.

The movement started in an unexpected quarter. In
1876, while Stanley was still investigating the sources of
the Congo, Leopold, King of the Belgians, convened a
Conference of the Powers at Brussels, to discuss the opening
up of the interior of Africa to European commerce and
industries, and to consider a united policy for the extinction
of the slave trade. The result of this Conference was the
formation of an international association for carrying out
the above objects, and national committees to collect funds
for the common cause.

Upon Stanley's return from his Congo researches in 1878
the Association assumed a new and special rôle—that of
civilising the Congo basin, and laying the foundations of
a great State, to be controlled by the Committee, with
Leopold as its President. No apology is necessary for
briefly recapitulating the salient features of this movement—
familiar as they must be to many of my readers—partly
because it was the *causa causans* of the partition of Africa,
in which Cecil Rhodes' schemes bulked so large at a later

date, and partly also because the southern border of the
Congo Free State was the wall which eventually opposed
itself to Rhodes' ideas of extending British influence
northwards.

Between 1879 and 1883 Stanley, the organiser and
administrator of this undertaking, with a view to paving
the way for the government of the Congo basin by the
International Association, had founded several European
stations and had challenged the Arab régime, which for
so many years had dominated Central Africa. There is
no need to enter into the complicated negotiations and
by-play which ensued between France, Portugal and
England, each struggling for a share in the regions watered
by the Congo, beyond pointing out that they led to the
Conference of Berlin in 1884 and the succeeding year, and
ultimately to the formation of the Congo Free State, with
Leopold as its sovereign. The boundaries of the State
were roughly sketched out at the time, but its precise
limits were not immediately settled, and were purposely
(and fortunately) left open on the southern side and towards
Lake Tanganyika in deference to British claims, although
these latter were of the most nebulous nature.

The Conference of Berlin was the starting-point in the
race for Africa. Great Britain's neglect to occupy the
territories lying ready for her grasp had for some time
been succeeded by a positive aversion from meddling with
African affairs, owing to the manner in which her fingers
had been burnt in the Transvaal and in Zululand, but even
British Ministers now became alive to the necessity for
vigorous action.

An opportunity presented itself in Bechuanaland, and as
the events which followed there had a direct and important
bearing on the northern expansion of British territory,
and the creation of the Chartered Company, they must be
considered in some detail.

Authorities for historical data in this chapter :

Missionary Travels in South Africa, by David Livingstone.
The Gold Regions of S.E. Africa, by Thos. Baines.
The Partition of Africa, by J. Scott Keltie.
Blue Book C. 4739.
Files of the following South African newspapers between 1865 and 1872 :—
Grahamstown Journal, Transvaal Argus, Natal Mercury, Transvaal Advocate, Natal Herald, Natal Witness, Natal Colonist, Times of Natal, Eastern Province Herald and *Colesberg Herald*.
The following English newspapers :—*The Times*, 1868, *Field*, 1871, and *Daily News*, 1872.

CHAPTER II

BECHUANALAND : THE CORRIDOR TO THE INTERIOR

THE recapitulation of the events which led up to the British Protectorate in Bechuanaland may seem unnecessary, and even wearisome, but it must always be borne in mind that the Royal Charter of the British South Africa Company was the crystallised result of a flux of movements and counter-movements. The Boer intrigues in Bechuanaland had behind them the shadow of a far more dangerous threat, namely, the aspiration of Germany to become the paramount Power in South Africa. Had Bechuanaland fallen into the hands of the Boers the key to the northern territories would have been lost, and British expansion, if not irretrievably thwarted, could only have proceeded with the greatest difficulty.

Properly to comprehend the series of movements which extended British influence up to the confines of Matabeleland, it is necessary to hark back to the early 'seventies. By a piece of diplomacy, which has sometimes been described in less complimentary terms, England, soon after the discovery of diamonds on the Vaal River, had acquired Griqualand West in the teeth of Boer opposition. The northern boundaries of the new province were, by design or accident, loosely defined, and it was discovered later that a strip of territory had been taken in which in reality belonged to the chief Mankoroane of the Batlapin tribe. Owing to the uncertainty as to the precise boundary, this strip became a sort of no-man's-land, and as such offered an irresistible bait to Boer adventurers from the neighbouring Transvaal.

Mankoroane had always aspired to British recognition, and, on the annexation of the Transvaal in 1877, had issued a bombastic proclamation styling himself " Paramount Chief of the Batlapin nation," and asserting his claims, " under the advice of his august ally Queen Victoria," to far more territory than he really had any rights over. These pretensions, however, were not accepted by other Bechuana chiefs, and some of them sought an opportunity to oust Mankoroane from his assumed paramountcy.

Events in Griqualand soon provided this. In 1878 serious native disturbances arose, and in fact a rebellion broke out, to quell which Colonel Charles Warren, R.E., was sent up from the Cape. The disaffection of the local Griquas found native sympathisers over the border; several white traders in Southern Bechuanaland were murdered, and some of the tribes, under the leadership of one Luka, son of Jantje, took up arms, and identified themselves with the cause of the Griqualand rebels.

In consequence of this outbreak Colonel Warren, in June 1878, led a small punitive expedition into Bechuanaland itself. For a year the country was under military occupation, and ultimately the natives were pacified, and a sort of makeshift British Administration was instituted. The Rev. John Mackenzie, a prominent member of the London Missionary Society, was recognised as the Government agent, and continued in that capacity after military operations had ceased. In this manner the way was paved for an orthodox British Protectorate, which would have been justified on far stronger grounds than have existed in the majority of similar cases.

But the Government of the day was in no mood for such a step. Its attitude, and that of the British public, may be gleaned from a remark addressed by Colonel Lanyon (the Administrator of Griqualand) to Mackenzie at this time. " The people of England dislike any more annexation, and many of them are sensitive about interfering with the inherited rights of Native chiefs and tribes." It is true that there were people at the Cape who were less complacent. There was Sir Bartle Frere, the High Commissioner, who saw further than most men into the future, and realised that the ultimate supremacy in the interior, and indeed in South Africa as a whole, lay between British

and Boer. There was also Mr. Hofmeyr, who was fully
alive to the importance of keeping the British out of any
territory which might be available for further Boer occupation. For the time being, however, the home policy prevailed. In spite of the security which the short British
occupation had produced; in spite of the vehement protests
of Mackenzie and his missionary colleagues, who urged
that the expedition had so broken down the authority of
the chiefs that they would never again be able to maintain
peace and good order among the natives; in spite too of
the strong representations of Sir Bartle Frere and of the
moral obligation resting on Britain of substantiating and
maintaining her occupation in the interests of the natives
themselves; in spite even of the entreaties of the very
chiefs, who voluntarily ceded their territories in order to
assure a Protectorate, the Little Englanders had their way,
and Southern Bechuanaland was, in April 1881, abandoned
to its fate.

What that fate might have been is well indicated in
Mackenzie's letters of the period. What immediately
happened was that, after three years of good order, Bechuanaland suddenly became an Alsatia, and was handed over
to anarchy and outrage!

This was the opportunity for the Boers. The retrocession
of the Transvaal in 1881 gave them encouragement to take
advantage of the condition of the country. Under the
pretext of settling a dispute between Mankoroane and
Masow, another chief on the Transvaal border, a number
of filibusters entered Bechuanaland. Posing as champions
of Masow, they settled down in the neighbourhood of what
is now Vryburg, and constituted themselves a Republic—
the notorious "Stellaland." Practically the same thing
happened a little further north, where the Bechuana chief
Montsioa of Mafeking was at loggerheads with a chief called
Moshete, living just over the Transvaal border. Montsioa's country was invaded and steps were taken to form
a second Republic to be called "Goshen." [1]

[1] Sometimes referred to in the records of the period as "Land Goosen,"
and in one instance, in the *Contemporary Review*, as "Goschen"!

AFRICA SOUTH OF THE EQUATOR AT THE TIME WHEN CECIL RHODES ENTERED POLITICS 1882

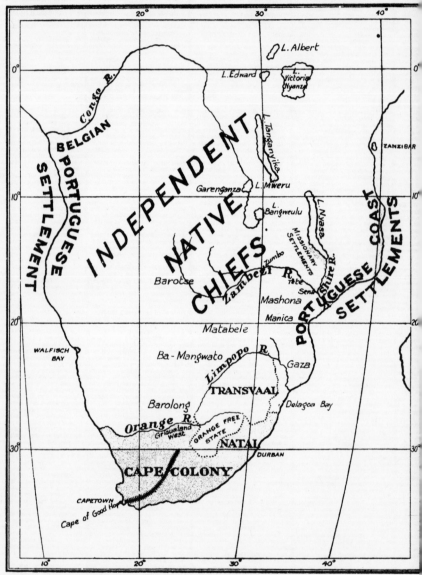

At this point Cecil Rhodes, who for many months had been keeping a watchful eye on the Bechuanaland question, which so vitally concerned his dream of northern expansion, stepped publicly into the arena.

Ostensibly to inquire into the question of the boundaries of Griqualand West, the imperfect settlement of which had left the position of Mankoroane's territory in doubt, Rhodes obtained from the Cape House of Assembly in May 1882 the appointment of a commission, and was himself selected as one of its members. On arrival in the disputed territory, he found that Stellaland included a large number of farms occupied by Transvaal Boers, who had settled within Mankoroane's limits. He had two parties on the spot to deal with, and saw that if he could secure a cession of the district from the native chief, as well as the consent of the Boers to be annexed to Cape Colony, he would obtain an indefeasible title from both disputants. In each case he was successful. Mankoroane, whose only concern was to be relieved from the Boer threat, cheerfully agreed to the cession, and the Stellalanders, after some little per- suasion, consented to annexation, and signed a petition to that end. But a third party had to be reckoned with— the Cape Parliament—and, disregarding Rhodes' repre- sentations and entreaties, it decided to reject the annexation policy. In this it was guided by Mr. Hofmeyr, whose idea was that the northern territories should be kept open for the Transvaal—the very thing which Rhodes was anxious to prevent, for he knew that Bechuanaland was, to use his own expression, the " Suez Canal to the interior," and he knew that Paul Kruger was, equally with himself, alive to this fact.

An attempt to induce the Imperial Government to step in was also unsuccessful. It is true that Rhodes extracted a conditional promise from Lord Derby to establish a pro- tectorate in Bechuanaland, if the Cape Colony would bear half the cost, but the Cape refused to meet him even to this extent, and he was once more baffled.

At this time he was convinced that there was a power behind the Boer trekkers into Stellaland and Goshen, and

that that power was Paul Kruger.   He accordingly redoubled
his efforts, and, in August 1883, made a speech in the Cape
House, which strikes so prophetic a note that some passages
are worth repeating verbatim.

The question before the House was a motion by Mr.
Scanlen, to allow the Cape Government to be represented
on the occasion of the visit to London of the delegates who
were to discuss modifications to the Pretoria Convention
of 1881, which gave autonomy to the Transvaal.   Rhodes
dragged in a characteristically irrelevant amendment, suggesting that a Resident should be placed by the Cape
Colony with Mankoroane.   He informed the House that
the real question was "Whether Cape Colony is to be
confined to its present borders, or is to become the dominant
State in South Africa—whether, in fact, it is to spread its
civilisation over the interior. . . . We want," he said, "to
get rid of the Imperial factor in this question, and to deal
with it ourselves, jointly with the Transvaal. We must
not disregard the legitimate interests of the Transvaal,
but we are bound to think first of the interests of this
Colony. . . . I respect the Transvaal, but as politicians we
have to look to our position as the future paramount State
of South Africa. . . . The question of the Union of South
Africa is bound up in this Bechuanaland question; but I
regard the question first in its consequences to the interests
of Cape Colony.   I have been favoured with reports from
Tati, and I have learned how great are the prospects of the
territory beyond the Transvaal. . . ."

Rhodes' references here to the Transvaal were exceedingly adroit.   He felt that its policy of expansion had
the sympathy of a large section of the House, and he therefore placed the Transvaal and the Cape Colony side by
side, hinting at the possibility of their union in the future
as sister States of a United South Africa.   Imperial interference in the affairs of South Africa had in the past been
a failure, and the Imperial factor was to be excluded as
far as possible.   But his words have been imperfectly
understood, some of his critics having gone so far as to
interpret this speech, and a later one made in July 1884,

as demonstrating that he was intriguing for a Transvaal annexation of Bechuanaland! In reality nothing was further from his thoughts. His object throughout was British expansion, but it was the Cape Parliament which he was addressing, and unfortunately at this time British prestige was not at its highest in Cape Colony, or indeed in any part of South Africa. Rhodes knew quite well that if he banged the big drum of Jingoism in Capetown or in Bechuanaland he would not only lose his point, but would arouse bitter opposition. He had a crafty opponent in Hofmeyr, whose policy was " Africa for the Afrikanders," and northward expansion for the Boers. Rhodes always followed the direction of least resistance, and, on the present occasion, this meant to keep the British Government in the background, and to urge the annexation of Bechuanaland by the Cape Colony, using the latter purely as a stalking-horse.

He failed, however, to carry his amendment, and in his earnest endeavour to save Bechuanaland for British interests was compelled, after all, to have recourse to the Imperial factor. Accordingly he approached the High Commissioner, Sir Hercules Robinson, who was induced by his constant importunities to make strong representations to the Colonial Office as to the urgent necessity for setting up a Protectorate, and so shutting off permanently all idea of an extension of the western border of the Transvaal.

The late Lord Randolph Churchill is said to have once exclaimed, " What an army we might have if only we had no War Office ! " Had he addressed himself to the task of expanding British influence in South Africa he would doubtless have been more comprehensive in his regrets. Rhodes' representations, even backed as they were by Sir Hercules Robinson, would have had short shrift with the Colonial Office of 1883 had not the Home Government, in the nick of time, received a severe shock owing to the annexation by Germany of Angra Pequeña.[1] This sudden

---

[1] A British warship (the *Boadicea*) which had been sent from Capetown to Angra Pequeña in November 1883, returned with the disconcerting news that she had been met there by the German corvette *Carola*, and had been informed that she was in German waters, and that Herr Luderitz had acquired rights over the coast as far as the Orange River.

blow, coupled with the repeated appeal by the Boer delegates for complete independence, roused the Government
at length from its lethargy, and Lord Derby and his colleagues began to see reason in Sir Hercules Robinson's
arguments. In February 1884 a Protectorate was proclaimed and the " Suez Canal to the interior " was saved.
At the same time the western boundaries of the Transvaal
were definitely laid down by the London Convention.

It is hardly necessary to enter into any detailed narrative
of the settlement and administration of Bechuanaland.
The Rev. John Mackenzie, who was selected as the first
Deputy Commissioner, was unsuccessful in his attempts
to induce the squatters of Stellaland, still less the freebooters of Goshen, to recognise British authority. Mackenzie, like Rhodes, was an Imperialist, but, while the
objects of the two men were identical, their methods were
diametrically opposite. Mackenzie was wholly lacking in
diplomacy, and believed that he was furthering the cause
of British expansion best by adopting a stone-wall attitude.
" The British Government has annexed you : the subject
is closed to further discussion." This was the tone which
he took up towards the land-holders of the two so-called
Republics. But what did they care about the British
Government? They had Kruger behind them, and Kruger
had just outwitted the British Government ! The Boers
had thrashed the *rooinekes* at Majuba, and they could
thrash them again !

Rhodes, who succeeded Mackenzie as Deputy Commissioner in August, found the country in a state of open
rebellion and anarchy, and although his conciliatory policy
had a good effect in Stellaland, he fared little better than
his predecessor in Goshen, where matters speedily began to
assume a serious aspect. General Pieter Joubert, appointed
by the Transvaal Government " Commissioner of the
Western Border," was despatched to Rooi-Grond (the
" Republican " head-quarters), nominally to assist in
effecting a settlement, but really to secure Goshen for the
Transvaal in defiance of the London Convention. The
utmost pitch of audacity was reached when Kruger, on

the 16th of September, 1884, " proclaimed and ordained "
the territory of the contending chiefs Moshete and Montsioa
to be under the protection and control of the South African
Republic.

This was a false move on the part of the President, and
so far from jockeying the British out of their Protectorate,
it had the unexpected effect, not only of spurring the
Government to vigorous action, but also of alienating a
good deal of the Cape sympathy. A mass meeting held
at Capetown on September the 24th passed a resolution
asserting that Imperial intervention was necessary to maintain the trade-route to the interior and to protect the
native tribes from oppression, and that failure to maintain
the boundaries laid down by the Convention of London
would be fatal to British supremacy in South Africa.

Without any further delay, Colonel Sir Charles Warren
was appointed Special Commissioner, with authority to
take a military expedition to Bechuanaland to remove the
filibusters, to pacify the country, to reinstate the natives
in their own lands, and to adopt such measures as might
be necessary to prevent further depredations. Kruger was
formally called upon to withdraw the obnoxious proclamation, and Warren was ordered to hold Bechuanaland until
a further policy was decided on. The proclamation was at
once withdrawn, and, upon Warren's arrival with a force of
4000 men, Kruger met him and Rhodes at Fourteen Streams,
on the borders of the Transvaal and Cape Colony, and
pledged himself to abide for the future by the ordained
boundaries.

The following is a quotation from a speech made by
Rhodes in the Cape House of Assembly on June the 30th,
1885, when for the first time he pointed out publicly the
danger to British interests which had so narrowly been
averted.

" Do you think that if the Transvaal had Bechuanaland
it would be allowed to keep it ? Would not Bismarck have
some quarrel with the Transvaal; and without resources,
without men, what could they do ? Germany would come
across from her settlement at Angra Pequeña. There would

be some excuse to pick a quarrel—some question of brandy, or guns, or something—and then Germany would stretch from Angra Pequeña to Delagoa Bay. I was never more satisfied with my own views than when I saw the recent development of the policy of Germany. What was the bar in Germany's way? Bechuanaland. What was the use to her of a few sand-heaps at Angra Pequeña and the interior with this English and Colonial bar between her and the Transvaal? If we were to stop at Griqualand West, the ambitious objects of Germany would be attained."

Although Sir C. Warren sought to ignore the pledges given to the Boers of Stellaland that their titles should be respected, thereby causing great umbrage to Rhodes, who protested strongly against this breach of faith,[1] his expedition was successful in re-establishing British prestige in Bechuanaland, but it cost about a million and a half sterling, which might have been saved to the Treasury had the policy advocated by Rhodes in 1882 been adopted. On September the 30th, 1886, the southern portion of Bechuanaland, *i.e.* that between Griqualand West and Mafeking (Montsioa's town), was constituted a Crown Colony. In the meanwhile Warren had concluded treaties of friendship and protection with the chiefs in the northern portion, of whom Khama was the most important, and a Protectorate was on the same date proclaimed from Mafeking up to latitude 22°, which included all territory lying on the western border of the Transvaal. President Kruger's hope of extending his boundaries on that side was now definitely at an end. There still remained, however, the northern border separating the Transvaal from Matabeleland, and we shall see later what strenuous efforts were made to keep this side open for Boer expansion.

[1] Space will not permit a more detailed account of the differences which arose over the settlement. Rhodes objected bitterly to Warren's racial prejudice against the Boers and to his adoption of the rough-shod methods which had already proved a failure under Mackenzie. The controversy was pursued for some weeks in the columns of *The Times*, and ultimately the more conciliatory policy advocated by Rhodes was endorsed by the Secretary of State.

Authorities for historical data in this chapter:

Austral Africa, Losing it or Ruling it, by John Mackenzie.
John Mackenzie—South African Missionary and Statesman, by W. Douglas
    Mackenzie.
The following *Blue Books :* C. 3419, 3841, 4036, 4194, 4213, 4252, 4432,
    4643 and 4889. The last mentioned contains an admirable sum-
    mary of the history of the various Bechuana tribes and of the events
    which led to the agreement between Mr. Rhodes and the inhabitants
    of Stellaland, 1884.

The extracts from Mr. Rhodes' speeches are copied from *Cecil Rhodes :
    his Political Life and Speeches,* 1881–1890, by " Vindex."

CHAPTER III

EARLY STEPS TOWARDS THE NORTH

IN 1886 Mr. Rhodes faced the problem of securing for Great Britain all that was left of Central and Southern Africa. As Matabeleland and Mashonaland were not only nearest to his base of operations, but were in more imminent danger of annexation by European Powers than other parts of this huge area, it was to these two countries that his initial efforts were directed. Nor was there any time to lose, for Boers, Germans and Portuguese had all turned longing eyes towards the land reputed to be so wealthy. The Boers were inspired by the lust of horizon which ever prompted them to push northwards; the Germans recalled the almost forgotten discoveries of their explorer Mauch, and the Portuguese were alarmed lest their ancient, if somewhat legendary, claim to the sovereignty of Monomotapa should be jeopardised in the general scramble for territory in which European States were indulging.

The Boers had already led a card in this four-handed game, and it is interesting to note that they began to think of Matabeleland about the same time that they were making their first encroachments in Southern Bechuanaland, *i.e.* in 1882, and less than a year from the date when the Gladstone Ministry crowned its policy of scuttle by signing the Pretoria Convention. The following letter found later at Lobengula's kraal by Mr. F. R. Thompson—one of the parties to the Matabele Concession—throws a remarkable light upon the tactics adopted by the Boers in making their preliminary overtures :

> " *Marico,*
> " *The South African Republic,*
> " *March 9th,* 1882.

" *To the great ruler, the Chief Lo Bengula, the son of Umzilikatse, the great King of the Matabili nation.*

" GREAT RULER,

   " When this letter reaches you, then you will know that it comes from a man who very much desires to visit

you, but who, being a man of the people, cannot get loose
to make such a long journey. Therefore he must now be
satisfied with writing a letter to carry his regards to the son
of the late King of the Matabili, our old friend Umzilikatse.
When I say that I desire to see you, it is not to ask for
anything, but to talk of something, and to tell Lo Bengula
of the affairs and things of the world, because I know that
there are many people who talk and tell about these matters,
whilst there are but few who tell the truth. Now when a
man hears a thing wrong, it is worse than if he had never
heard it at all. Now I know that Lo Bengula has heard
some things wrongly, and for this reason would I tell him
the real truth. Now you must have heard that the English—
or as they are better known the Englishmen—took away
our country, the Transvaal, or as they say, annexed it. We
then talked nicely for four years, and begged for our country.
But no; when an Englishman once has your property in his
hand, then is he like a monkey that has its hands full of
pumpkin seeds—if you don't beat him to death, he will
never let go—and then all our nice talk for four years did
not help him at all. Then the English commenced to arrest
us because we were dissatisfied, and that caused the shooting
and fighting. Then the English first found that it would be
better to give us back our country. Now they are gone,
and our country is free, and we will now once more live in
friendship with Lo Bengula, as we lived in friendship with
Umzilikatse, and such must be our friendship that so long
as there is one Boer and one Matabili living, these two must
remain friends. On this account do I wish to see Lo Bengula,
and if I may live so long, and the country has become
altogether settled, and the stink which the English brought
is first blown away altogether, then I will still ride so far as
to reach Lo Bengula, and if he still has this letter, then he
will hear the words from the mouth of the man who now must
speak with the pen upon paper, and who therefore cannot so
easily tell him everything. The man is a brother's child
of the three brothers that formerly—now thirty-two years
ago—were at Umzilikatse's, and then made the peace with
him which holds to this day. He still remembers well when
the first Boers, Franz Joubert, Jan Joubert, and Pieter
Joubert, came there, and when they made the peace whereby
Umzilikatse could live at peace and the Boers also, and the
peace which is so strong that the vile evil-doers were never
able to destroy it, and never shall be able to destroy it as

long as there shall be one Boer that lives and Lo Bengula also lives.

" Now I wish to send something, to give Lo Bengula a present as a token of our friendship. I send for Lo Bengula, with the gentleman who will bring him this letter, a blanket and a handkerchief for his great wife, who is the Mother of all the Matabili nation. I will one day come to see their friendship. The gentleman who brings the letter will tell you all about the work which I have to do here. Some bad people have incited Kolahing, and so he thought he would make fortifications and fight with us, but he got frightened, and saw that he would be killed, therefore I made him break down the fortifications, and pack all the stones in one heap, and he had then to pay 5000 cattle and 4000 sheep and goats for his wickedness. Now there is another chief, Gatsizibe— he came upon our land and killed three people and plundered them—he must also pay a fine, or else we will punish him or shoot him, because we will have peace in our country.

" Now greetings, great Chief Lo Bengula from the Commandant General of the South African Republic for the Government and Administration.

" P. J. JOUBERT." [1]

Whether these sycophantic protestations ever elicited a reply from the " Great Ruler " is not known. It is highly probable that they missed fire, for Lobengula was of a very different calibre from Montsioa and Mankoroane, and was not likely to be inveigled into a Boer alliance by the sorry gift of a blanket and a handkerchief. Doubtless, however, General Joubert was anxious to know something about the man he was dealing with, and sent the letter as a *ballon d'essai*, to be followed up by more definite action if its result were satisfactory. There were Boers at this time living in Matabeleland who enjoyed the chief's friendship, and spent their time in hunting and collecting ivory with his permission, and Joubert and Kruger were in communication with these, and would have found them useful as agents in subsequent negotiations. Looking at other and simultaneous attempts by the Boer leaders to " burst their kraal," and trespass beyond the limits assigned to them by the Pretoria

---

[1] The text of this letter is taken from *The Transvaal from within*, by Sir Percy Fitzpatrick.

Convention—attempts in Zululand, Swaziland and Bechuanaland—there can be no doubt that, in 1882, the Transvaal
leaders had made up their minds to secure for their own
people the rich pasturage of Mashonaland and Matabeleland.

In May 1885 Sir Charles Warren received word from a
trustworthy correspondent in Shoshong, Khama's capital
town in Northern Bechuanaland, that the Boers had by no
means abandoned their idea of getting a foothold in Mashonaland (which they knew to contain the finest agricultural land
in South Africa), and by this means of acquiring a base from
which they could make a flank attack upon Matabeleland,
and gradually by conquest overspread the whole of what is
now Southern Rhodesia. The communication went on to
refer to quiet movements on the part of both Germany and
Portugal, with a view to obtaining concessions in these
regions, and pointed out that both were only watching the
policy of Great Britain before taking definite action.[1] These
reports abundantly indicated the danger which Rhodes, a
little later, pointed out in his speech, already quoted, in the
Cape House, and although he did not then specifically allude
to Portugal, he never lost sight of the possibility of her
attempting to revive her ancient influence.

The establishment of a Protectorate over Khama's country
in August 1885 brought all territory south of latitude 22°
under British control. It also placed England on equal
terms with the Transvaal and Portugal in respect of Matabeleland. From this moment the struggle between British,
Boers and Portuguese for the upper hand in Lobengula's
country began in earnest, and it was only through extraordinary efforts on the part of Rhodes that the victory
ultimately rested with the first named.

During that year a party of three officers—Major Sam
Edwards, who had a long and intimate acquaintance with
Matabeleland and was *persona grata* with the chief, Lieut.
E. A. Maund, of Sir Charles Warren's force, and Lieut. C. E.
Haynes, of the Royal Engineers—was despatched to

---

[1] This information was confirmed about the same time by the Vicomte
E. de la Panouse in a report sent to Sir C. Warren. Both statements
appear in *Blue Book* C. 4558. Further confirmation was supplied in the
reports by Messrs. Edwards, Maund and Haynes referred to below.

Lobengula, with the object of informing him of the Protectorate over the country on his southern border, and of assuring him that our Government was well-disposed towards him.[1] Rumours had been spread about that Lobengula meditated an attack upon Khama, the bone of contention being the strip of country between the Macloutsie and Shashi Rivers, which was claimed by both chiefs, and was generally known as the " Disputed Territory." Lobengula took umbrage at Khama's action in " making the line " (22°) without consulting him, and abated not one inch of his claim.[2] The dispute was an old one, and dragged on, without any serious attempt at a settlement, until 1887. Early in that year Mr. Sam Edwards, who had returned to civil life, and another old interior hunter, Mr. John Fry, returning from a visit to Bulawayo, informed Sir Sidney Shippard, the Deputy Commissioner of Bechuanaland, that there was an evident desire on the part of Lobengula and his people to come under British protection, and that the great obstacle to its realisation was the question of the boundary. They thought, however, that Lobengula would consent to a decision being left to the arbitration of the British Government.

It is evident that the settlement of Montsioa's and Mankoroane's countries resulting from the British Protectorate, and the freedom from Boer depredations which they had since enjoyed, appealed strongly to the Matabele chief, who had an ancient grudge against the Boers. Had they not driven his tribe out of the rich Marico district, where his father, Mziligazi, had first settled, and were there not constant rumours of plots to oust them from Matabeleland in the same way? The only people who had stood up to them in South Africa were the English, and, plentiful as their mistakes had been, Lobengula knew well their reputation for just dealing with native tribes that sought to live on friendly terms with them and for stern measures against

---

[1] Each of these three officers sent in a valuable report of observations on the Matabele and subject tribes and on the mineral and agricultural potentialities of their country. Their statements constitute the first official accounts of this region. They are printed in *Blue Book* C. 4643 (Transvaal).   [2] *Blue Book* C. 5237.

SAM EDWARDS

[*To face p.* 27.

those that opposed them. True their prestige had been besmirched by the rout at Majuba Hill, and the subsequent discreditable peace, but the peace was not a matter which would appeal very forcibly to a native mind. The object lesson of Cetewayo's downfall was a far more convincing one, and this had left a lasting impression on Lobengula, as on all the great chiefs of South Africa. The Protectorate accepted by Khama was having its effect in native territories more distant than Matabeleland. The important chief Lewanika, whose country lay far to the north across the Zambesi, but marched with Lobengula's on the southern side, made inquiries, about this time, of Khama as to his relations with the British.

It is easy to understand, therefore, that, when taken in conjunction with the Boer threat, and the increasing difficulty of excluding white adventurers, the action of Khama in accepting British protection had great weight on the mind of Lobengula, whose country was now jostled by European States on three sides. Since the establishment of the Protectorate, white prospectors were finding their way into Matabeleland from Khama's country, and to cope with this immediate trouble, and in the continued absence of Sir John Swinburne, the original concessionaire, Lobengula decided to put Sam Edwards [1] in charge of the Tati district, and issued to him the following " commission " :

" *To Samuel Howard Edwards.*

" As the laws of my country are not suitable for the government of Europeans and others engaged in mining, or who may be resident within the Tati district, now I, Lobengula, King of the Amandebele nation, do hereby authorise you, S. H. Edwards, with power to delegate the authority hereby

[1] Edwards was the son of one of the pioneer missionaries who settled on the Kuruman River, in the Bechuanaland country, in the early part of the nineteenth century, but forsook missionary work for the more attractive life of an ivory and cattle trader. Robert Moffat, writing in 1842, said that he purchased a farm and slaves in Cape Colony and became a " hoary-headed infidel." The son, known to all the natives of those parts as " Samu," was born in Bechuanaland, and was one of the first hunters and traders in Matabeleland. He visited Mziligazi, in Moffat's company, in 1854, and spent his early life in expeditions into many parts of the interior. He acquired a great influence with Lobengula, who held him in the deepest regard. At the time mentioned he had just been appointed Manager of the Tati Gold Mining Company. He died at an advanced age in 1922.

granted to whomsoever you may think fit, for me, and in
my name, to make by proclamation all such laws and regulations as you may consider expedient and necessary, for
the peace, order and good government of the Tati district,
and to represent me in all matters occurring in the said
district, and further with authority to you to appoint fit
and proper persons to carry out and administer all laws
made by you for maintaining peace, order and good government. . . .[*Here follows a description of the boundaries of the
Tati district.*]

" And I engage to protect you, the said S. H. Edwards,
or whoever you may appoint in your stead, and give you
such assistance as you may require, for giving effect to the
powers hereby granted.

" Given under my sign-manual and seal at Umvangew
(? Mhlangeni) this 24th day of February, 1887.[1]

His

LO X BENGULA

Mark."

A copy of this was sent to Sir S. Shippard, the Commissioner of Bechuanaland, and another to the chief Khama,
many of whose people were at work in the Tati mines, and
about the same time Lobengula wrote to Shippard com-
plaining of the arbitrary way in which the boundary of the
Protectorate had been fixed, without his consent, and saying
that the white people were coming into his country " like
wolves," and making new roads without his permission.

On receipt of these communications, Shippard, taking the
hint from Edwards and Fry as to Lobengula's leanings
towards closer relations with the British, wrote to both him
and Khama, suggesting that the vexed question of the
disputed territory should be left to the arbitration of the
British Government, but th﹀ chief did not respond very
cordially to the proposal, wl ich was therefore dropped at
the time, to be renewed later in a different form.

In July 1887 Mr. J. S. Moffat (son of Robert Moffat the
missionary, and brother-in-law of David Livingstone) was
appointed Assistant Commissioner for the Bechuanaland
Protectorate. The British policy, as communicated to

---

[1] C. 5237,   23, 24.

him in a despatch from Sir Hercules Robinson, both as
regards the Protectorate and any extension of it which might
be possible towards the Zambesi, was to assist the native
chiefs to repel the invasion of their territories by freebooters
and others desirous of possessing themselves of their lands,
but to abstain from interference with native administration,
and to discourage for the present any tendency towards
settlement by Europeans.

Moffat was advised, after visiting the principal chiefs in
the Protectorate, to approach Lobengula with friendly
overtures, to assure him that the Protectorate implied no
hostility to him, and to acquaint him that Her Majesty's
Government was willing to assist, by every means, in the
settlement of the boundary question.   If this mission proved
successful, periodical visits, with the object of promoting
the extension of British influence and trade to Matabeleland
and Mashonaland, would be arranged.

Reference may here be briefly made to an incident which
sheds further light on the policy of the Government, which
was to avoid any direct action in the direction of annexing
Matabeleland, but to say " Hands off ! " to other Powers.

The attention of Lord Salisbury was drawn to an official
map, issued from Lisbon, which showed, as Portuguese
territory, a large part of Matabeleland.   The Prime Minister
at once wrote and informed Portugal that, under the Berlin
Act, no claim to territory in Central Africa could be recognised which was not supported by occupation.   This pro-
nouncement put a somewhat strained construction on the
Berlin Act, which referred to *coastal* territory,[1] but Lord
Salisbury adhered to his point, and stated that no foreign
pretensions to Matabeleland would be allowed, and that the
Zambesi should be regarded as the natural northern limit
of British South Africa—a dangerous admission in the light
of subsequent events.   For the time being the matter
ended with this *communiqué*, but the Portuguese did not
yield without many further attempts to substantiate their
claim to the interior.

Before describing the steps which Moffat took to further

[1] General Act of Berlin Conference, 1885, Article 35.

the policy which was outlined in his instructions from Sir Hercules Robinson, it will be desirable to give a somewhat detailed account of the Matabele people and of their chief Lobengula, whose fortunes, from this moment were so intimately interwoven with the movement towards British expansion.

Authorities for historical data in this chapter :

Blue Books Nos. C.4588 (Transvaal), C. 4643 (Transvaal), C. 5237. *The Transvaal from within*, by Sir Percy Fitzpatrick.

CHAPTER IV [1]

THE MATABELE

THE Matabele were not the original possessors of their present country, but were recent interlopers. The founder of the tribe, Mziligazi, son of Matshobana, of the Kumalo clan, was one of the principal captains of Tshaka, the Napoleon of the ama-Zulu peoples, a man of great military genius and of bloodthirsty ferocity, who built up a nation by ruthless coercion of the adjacent tribes. Originally the Zulus formed only one section of a loose congeries of tribes occupying the coast lands between the Umgeni River in Natal and the Pungwe River in Portuguese East Africa— tribes which, more or less, spoke the same language, and were known generally to their neighbours as the aba-Nguni (Angoni). Up to the end of the eighteenth century the Zulus were a small and unimportant clan of the Tetwa tribe on the River Mvolosi, near Cape Sta. Lucia, but they came into prominence through the genius of Tshaka, who, besides being a man of great bodily strength, possessed, to an extraordinary degree, the capacity for organisation. In process of time his armies exterminated practically every native tribe between Delagoa Bay and the St. John's River, the younger women and boys only being spared for absorption into the Zulu hegemony. Upon Tshaka's assassination by his brother Dingana in 1828 the tribe became somewhat disintegrated, but even before this one large section, the ama-Ndebele,[2] had broken away over the

---

[1] This chapter was read before the Rhodesia Scientific Association in 1913, and is published in the Transactions of that body.
[2] This is the Zulu form of the name. It was derived from the Suto word le-Tebele (plur. ma-Tebele), a kaffir, *i.e.* a member of any of those neighbouring tribes that did not speak the same language nor belong to the same ethnological group as the ba-Suto themselves. It was originally applied by these latter to the marauders from Zululand as a term of contempt. The usual spelling of the name is Matabele, and this will be adopted throughout the following pages.

Drakensberg mountains, following their *Induna* Mziligazi, who had incurred the wrath of Tshaka, and now sought to escape from his relentless oppression.[1] They first made a short sojourn in the ba-Khunda country near the Vaal River, and then moved to that of the ba-Kathla, northeast of Kuruman in Bechuanaland, where by employing Tshaka's methods they speedily put a wide belt of country between themselves and the Zulu headquarters, wiping out the less warlike denizens of the invaded territories.

For nearly ten years Mziligazi pursued these tactics, despatching raiding and foraging parties into Bechuanaland and other adjacent countries, and annihilating whole tribes of inoffensive natives; but always looting the cattle and reserving the young girls and boys—the former as wives for his soldiers, and the latter for slavery and subsequent incorporation into his own following.

It was not until 1836 that he received his first check. In that year some sturdy Boer *voortrekkers* from Cape Colony, sick of the British Government, and pining for the free life of the interior where no irritating laws could pursue them, journeyed over the Orange and Vaal Rivers and settled in the Orange Free State and the southern portion of the Transvaal. The Matabele were upon them at once, and had murdered several parties before the Boers could concentrate and offer an organised resistance. In the many conflicts which ensued the Boers adopted their well-known *laager* formation, defending themselves from behind the protection of ox-wagons drawn up in the form of a hollow square, and with their muzzle-loading muskets they successfully beat off the natives, who were only armed with stabbing and throwing assegais. It is possible, however, that the Boers would eventually have been compelled to give way had not an unexpected ally appeared on the scene. Dingana—Tshaka's murderer and successor—sent

---

[1] It may here be mentioned that another branch of the Zulus under Manukuza or So-shangane (father of Mzila and grandfather of un-Gungun-yana) established the aba-Gaza dominion, which was a source of perpetual trouble to the Portuguese. A third section, under u-Zwang-Endaba, migrated northwards, and founded the Angoni tribe on the confines of Portuguese East Africa, north of the Zambesi, and was the only one which retained the old national name.

an *impi* of Zulus into the Transvaal, which fell upon Mziligazi at a time when he was endeavouring to re-organise his
forces, already somewhat demoralised by the long *roers*
of the Dutch farmers.   Before this combined opposition
Mziligazi realised that the district was too hot for him.
He collected his cattle and the fragments of his regiments,
and retreated northwards, laying waste the country as he
passed through it.[1]

Mziligazi made no fresh attempt at settlement until he
had crossed the Crocodile River and reached the high veld
on the watershed of that and the Zambesi River, where
he called a halt near the hill now known as Thabas Induna,
twelve miles from the modern town of Bulawayo.   In this
locality he made his headquarters, meeting with no resistance
from the indigenous tribes, who fled, helter-skelter, at his
approach.   Mziligazi left the bulk of his tribe at Thabas
Induna, and with a few selected regiments pursued his
course of devastation towards the Zambesi, which he would
doubtless have reached and crossed had he not been baffled
by the tsetse fly.   During his absence, and probably in the
belief or hope that he would never return, some of his
headmen at Thabas Induna made up their minds to settle
down in peace, and selected one of the chief's young sons
to succeed him.   They were most grievously mistaken, for
Mziligazi was apprised of their action, immediately returned
to his head-quarters, and had the conspirators put to death
upon the hill which owes its modern name, Thabas Induna
(*Intaba yez-Induna*, "the hill of the headmen"), to
this event.

Matabeleland, up to this time, had been occupied by
various unwarlike and pastoral tribes, some being of Swazi
and others of Basuto origin, who belonged to an older
period of Bantu invasion than the Zulus and Bechuanas
of the south.   The principal of these were the ama-Kalanga,

---

[1] In undertaking this *anabasis* he was greatly influenced by the advice
of the Rev. Robert Moffat, the pioneer of the London Missionary Society,
then settled at Kuruman, for whom the savage chief to the last entertained
a strong regard.   It is worthy of note that at the next great crisis of the
Matabele nation, Mziligazi's son was advised by Moffat's son, then British
Resident in Bulawayo.

who are referred to by early Portuguese writers as having
been there in the days of Monomotapa, the ba-Tonka, found
in the north-western part of the country near the Zambesi,
the ama-Zwina (Mashona) [1] and the aba-Nyai or aba-Lozi.
None of these could make any stand against the annual
raids of the new-comers; some fled towards the Zambesi
in the north or the Sabi in the east, while others remained,
but only as slaves to till the land for their conquerors.
For thirty years Mziligazi and his people waxed fat at the
expense of their neighbours. Regularly each dry season
regiments were despatched to pillage some one or other
of the weak tribes on their borders, and these operations
extended westward as far as Lake Ngami, northward across
the Zambesi, and eastward to the villages of Lomagunda,
if not further. The Mashona natives who were nearest,
and therefore provided the readiest victims, took to building
their villages in inaccessible granite fastnesses, and led the
existence of hunted beasts rather than human beings.

During his boyhood Lobengula, who was the youngest
of the chief's three principal sons,[2] became the heir apparent,
owing to his father, in a fit of jealous rage, having caused
the murder of his two brothers, Kuruman and Ubuhlelo.
There is little doubt that these two were killed, though the
deed was concealed at the time and was only brought to
light when a person claiming to be Kuruman appeared
afterwards in Natal.[3]

---

[1] The word ama-Zwina (the dirty ones), corrupted by Europeans into
Mashona, appears to be a sort of nickname, or term of contempt, applied
generically by the Matabele to the eastern tribes. Father Torrend, in
his Bantu Grammar, suggests that the word is the Kalanga form of ama-Sena,
the people from Sena district.

[2] Lobengula's mother was not the " great " wife of the chief, but a
Swazi woman of inferior descent. The literal meaning of the name is
" He that drives like the wind," and of Mziligazi, " Pathway of Blood."
Kuruman (more correctly un-Kulumana) was called after the station of
the Rev. Robert Moffat, the celebrated Bechuanaland missionary—a compliment due to the great regard in which Moffat was held by the Matabele
chief.

[3] Mr. F. W. T. Possett, of the Native Department of Southern Rhodesia,
a recognised authority on Matabele history, has recently contributed an
interesting article to the Departmental Magazine, quoting documents
which strongly support the bona fides of this claimant. But although he
found champions in official circles in Natal, his identity with Mziligazi's
son was repudiated by the bulk of the Matabele tribe.

Mziligazi's reign of terror came to an end in 1868, when
he died at his capital town Mhlahlanhlela of an attack of
gout. Lobengula, although named by his father as successor to the kingdom, refused to assert his rights until
the death of his elder brother Kuruman had been proved
to his satisfaction. This was in January 1870, when he
formally accepted the position of Supreme Chief and was
acknowledged as such by the Council of the nation. He
had then reached thirty-seven years of age, and consequently was about fifty-five at the date of the events
referred to in the preceding chapter.

Immediately after his accession, the new chief professed
his intention of putting down the abuses which had existed
under his father's rule. At this time he was undoubtedly
influenced for good by the clergy of the London Missionary
Society, two or three of whom had settled in Matabeleland.
Among the reforms which Lobengula promised were the
cessation of the annual slave-raiding expeditions, and the
abolition of the death-sentence for suspicion of witchcraft.

Either this was vain talk, or his good impulse soon evapor-
ated. Both of these practices were so deeply ingrained in
the Matabele constitution that, even had he really so desired,
Lobengula could never have suppressed them, but it is
unlikely that he ever genuinely intended making the attempt.
Be this as it may, the slave-raids were doubled during his
chieftainship, and the cruel devastations were carried much
further westward than before, while, so far from interfering
with the capital punishment for witchcraft, Lobengula
employed this system (of which more hereafter) as the
principal means of removing his private enemies, and of
bolstering up his own despotic power.

The first event of importance in the new reign was the
defection of a portion of the nation, which included the
Zwangendaba,[1] the Induba and other powerful regiments,
and severe fighting took place, in which Lobengula and his
adherents were ultimately victorious. Their success was

---

[1] u-Zwangendaba (*i.e.* " one listening to a story being told ") was the
name of one of the regiments formed by Dingana, the murderer and successor
of Tshaka.

signalised by a revolting massacre in which the recalcitrant chiefs and their families were put to the assegai, the death-roll on this occasion being estimated by white men then in the country at ten thousand souls !

After this difficulty had been overcome, Lobengula, in accordance with Zulu custom, established a new capital. He selected a site near the Khami River,[1] and appropriately named it kwa-Bulawayo,[2] " the place of killing "; but although much of his time was spent here, he was fond of moving frequently and without notice, and had other favourite kraals, such as Mvutjwa, Umganin and Inyati.

While a general discussion of the social organisation and customs of the Matabele is foreign to the purpose of this sketch, there are three matters which should be referred to in some detail because of their direct bearing on many of the episodes of the British occupation. These are the practice of witchcraft, the military system, and the principles of land tenure and cattle ownership.

The " religion " of the Matabele, like that of all other Bantu tribes, consists in a belief in the active existence of the spirits of their departed ancestors, and finds expression in superstitious observances based on that belief. The practice of witchcraft appears to be connected with this, to the extent that it embraces the employment of occult means of propitiating the spirits so as to solicit their in-fluence, either for good or bad, in the affairs of this world, and the foretelling by secret and exclusive knowledge what that influence will be.

The superstition of the " Mlimo," a being credited with an important part in the rebellion of 1896, is not a Matabele, but a Kalanga one. The Mlimo is an invisible deity sup-posed to take cognisance of all matters affecting the natives as a body, and consulted, like the Delphian oracle, through the medium of priests, when any national danger, such as

[1] Subsequently abandoned in favour of the site on which Mr. Rhodes' house was built, near the modern township of Bulawayo.

[2] Bulawayo was the name of the military kraal near Eshowe in Zululand, which had been the head-quarters of the regiment to which Mziligazi be-longed. The syllable *kwa-*, sometimes written *gu-*, is merely the locative prefix.

war or disease, threatens, or when a common movement is on foot. The Mlimo superstition was tolerated, and to a certain extent employed, by the Matabele after their arrival in the country.

Apart, however, from the cult of the Mlimo, sorcery or witchcraft played and still plays an important part in the social economy of the natives. The fundamental idea is that natural phenomena, such as weather or the ripening of the crops, and the incidents of life, such as warfare and the health of men and stock, are favourably or adversely directed by the intervention of supernatural agencies, and may be influenced by magical means. Properly employed, that is, through the medium of the professional " witch-doctors " (*is-Anusi*), magic enables human beings to hasten the advent of the rains, and to predict the success or failure of any contemplated enterprise, from an important expedition against a neighbouring tribe down to such trivial affairs as a journey to the next village. On the other hand, all such happenings as deaths, diseases or accidents to men or cattle are the result of an illicit invocation of these secret agencies by evilly disposed laymen, who compass misfortunes against their neighbours to gratify their own ends.

The *is-Anusi* were a distinct order among the natives. They were employed by the Paramount Chief to prepare " rain-medicine " or " war-medicine," and by all classes to foretell by their magic bones the good or bad prospects of any contemplated action. This last practice was in vogue among the original inhabitants of the country and was reserved for a special class of *is-Anusi*. The " bones " were four in number and were carved on one side with symbolical designs; they were allowed to fall to the ground, and according to the position they assumed, or the side on which they lay, gave warning of good or evil fortune.

A further duty of the *is-Anusi* was to propitiate by means of sacrifices the shades of ancestors, who, as has been said, exercised some control, not precisely ascertained, over mundane affairs; but their most important, because most abused, function was the detection or " smelling out " of private individuals concerned in bringing death or misfortune to others by illicit witchcraft. Those whom the *is-Anusi* pronounced guilty of such practices were generally despatched without mercy (always so where the chief himself was the victim of the spells), their belongings being appropriated by the informers.

It may readily be understood that this detective agency was a powerful instrument in the hands of a chief, and Lobengula had no scruples in taking full advantage of it. On the pretext of sorcery, hundreds, nay thousands, of innocent people who had incurred the chief's suspicion, or who had acquired too great a popular influence, were " smelt out " and butchered.

The power of bringing rain was vested in the chief himself, who annually went through a series of disgusting rites, aided by the witch-doctors. To give reality to these ceremonies it was necessary for him to be an expert weather prophet, and to time his rain-making mysteries to coincide with the approach of wet weather.

The aid of the witch-doctors was constantly being invoked for particular occasions, but there were two annual celebrations during which their hierarchy was especially conspicuous, and which were also closely connected with the military organisation of the tribe. These were the " Little Dance " in January and the " Great Dance " in February. The former was attended only by the regiments of a few towns in the neighbourhood of Bulawayo, and was not an occasion for rejoicing so much as a warlike demonstration to signalise the brewing by the chief of " medicine " for the ensuing year. The materials for this were collected at the four important military kraals of Bulawayo, Inyati, Imbezu and Ingubo, and concocted by the chief himself, aided by his witch-doctors. The chief, however, did not attend the actual dance, in which only the selected regiments participated.

The " Little Dance " was a celebration of an expiatory character, and was the prelude to the far more elaborate proceedings which distinguished the " Great Dance " held immediately after the full moon in February. Many

descriptions of this extraordinary rite—for such it undoubtedly was—have been published, and the following
account has been compiled from the graphic narratives
of four eye-witnesses, each of whom saw the dance in a
different year.

For some weeks before the occasion great quantities of
beer were brewed and conveyed into Bulawayo in calabashes by the girls of the neighbouring kraals, while around
the chief's town temporary camps of grass huts were prepared by advance parties from the various regiments which
were to participate in the review and other ceremonies.
During the course of the festival the chief temporarily
resigned his authority in favour of a regent (who in later
days was Mhlaba, the prime minister), so as to be free to
carry on without interruption the mystic hocus-pocus
demanded by custom. At this time no Europeans were
permitted to enter or leave the country, and all in Bulawayo were expected to be spectators of the main dance,
which occupied an entire day. No violence or bloodshed
were tolerated, and red wearing apparel was strictly tabooed,
though gaudy raiment of other colours was much in evidence.
The dance being a festival of thanksgiving and purification,
every man, woman and child used to prepare for it by
bathing in the river Matje-mhlope (" white stones ") below
the town.

On the morning of the dance the proceedings were heralded
by the arrival of the three " dance-doctors " controlling
the ceremonies, one of whom was the " war-doctor," whose
special function it was to sprinkle the army with some
decoction warranted to render men invulnerable in action.
The three took up a position in the large open space facing
the royal quarters and between them and the huts of the
townspeople, and were immediately succeeded by the
soldiers, filing in, regiment by regiment, to the number
sometimes of ten or twelve thousand, and each accompanied by crowds of singing women and girls belonging to
its particular town. The soldiers deployed into a vast
crescent, from three to eight or ten men deep, facing the
chief's kraal, and in this formation their appearance was

impressive and even awe-inspiring. The younger warriors
(*ama-Tjaha*) wore head-dress and ample cape of black
ostrich-feathers, a kilt of the skins of the tiger-cat, and
fringes of white ox-hide round their arms and legs. All
carried assegais and the long ox-hide war-shield (uniform
in colour for each regiment) in their left hands, and long
wands in their right. Round their ankles were castanets
made of dried fruit-pods with the seeds rattling inside.
With perfect precision and order they marched to their
places in the half-circle, singing national songs, punctuated
by blows on the shields with their dancing sticks, and a
simultaneous stamping on the ground, the effect of so
many thousands of feet coming down together being like
a succession of claps of thunder.

Some of the regiments were composed entirely of older
men (*ama-Doda*), who had been granted the privilege of
marrying as a reward for distinction on active service.
These, instead of the ostrich-feather hoods or " bonnets,"
wore bands of otter-skin and long cranes' feathers which
left visible the distinctive head-ring (*isi-Dhlodhlo*), the
badge of their married estate.

Before coming into the presence of the chief all the
soldiers submitted to a purification by the dance-doctors,
who sprinkled medicine over them. The whole army then
made a general charge towards the sacred cattle-kraal,
within which Lobengula still remained, returning after a
short pause to the first position. At this stage the chief
emerged, duly " doctored " for the occasion, and covered
with streaks of black paint. He was dressed like the
others, except that a kilt of blue monkey-skin replaced the
cat-skins of the soldiers. In later years he used to sit in
a bath-chair, in front of the cattle-kraal, facing the centre
of the line, and any white men present would group themselves on either side of him.

The army now marched past in regiments, each as it
reached the chief shouting out the royal salute, " *Bayete
Kumalo!* " in thundering unison.[1] After an exhortation

---

[1] *Bayete* is the traditional salutation of Zulu tribes, and is only given
to royalty : *Kumalo* is the family name of the Matabele blood-royal.

by the head war-doctor the army chanted the national
song and executed a rhythmical dance, stamping on the
ground and beating time with their sticks. Occasionally
one or more would rush in front of the line and act, in
graphic pantomime, a hand-to-hand combat, stabbing with
their assegais an imaginary foe on the ground, and rattling
the sticks on their shields as they leapt into the air. A
shrill whistle would start at one end of the line, swell with
gradual crescendo to the middle, and then die away.

The next episode was a dance by fifty or more of the
chief's wives—ponderous ladies these, for the most part,
but picturesque as they waddled out of the royal enclosure,
with festoons of beads round their necks and waists, and
numerous brass bangles encircling their legs from ankle to
knee. Garbed in black goat-skin kilts open in front, be-
decked with gaudy kerchiefs, and all wearing a coronet
of blue jay's feathers, they executed an elephantine dance
up and down in front of the regiments. Next came the
witch-doctors in long single-file procession, each bearing
a calabash of some potent medicine, with which they retired
into the sacred cattle-kraal, after which the whole line of
warriors again charged furiously with lowered assegais up
to the chief, gradually closing so as to hem in the white
men as well. Indunas were stationed near to prevent their
offering any violence or indulging in any horse-play in the
excitement of the charge.

The sacred cattle were now released from the kraal gates
into the veld, and after a short gallop were headed back
by some of the young braves—a custom symbolical of the
raiding of an enemy's herds. The chief, who had retired
during this last manœuvre, re-appeared in full war-paint
and went through a *pas seul* in front of the admiring nation,
after which the day's ceremonies were brought to an end
with the solemn performance of "throwing the assegai."
The chief advanced from the main gate of the kraal and
hurled his assegai in the direction in which he intended to
despatch a raiding expedition during the coming year;
whereupon the *ama-Tjaha* rushed forward and stabbed
their own spears in the ground in the same direction as a

sign that they would obey their sovereign's orders. The assemblage was then dismissed, and once more marched past the chief before dispersing to the different camps.

On the day following three or four hundred cattle were selected from the national herds, and given to the soldiers to be slaughtered. A wild scene of carnage ensued, the excited Matabele rushing among the bullocks to stab them, and the wounded animals charging in all directions in terrified efforts to escape. The meat was not eaten at once but left for the night, so that the ancestral spirits might take what they desired, but on the third day the population gave themselves up wholeheartedly to the consumption of the enormous quantities of beef and beer provided for them.

The ceremonies throughout were of a highly symbolical character, and although they varied in detail from year to year, were generally conducted on the lines described above. The period of the annual dance was one of strong excitement among the natives, and of corresponding danger to the Europeans, and most of the crises in which Europeans were involved coincided with this time of the year.

Executions for alleged witchcraft were taking place more or less throughout the year, but after the great dance was over and the injunction against bloodshed had been removed, the witch-doctors ran riot in slaughter. These blood-hounds were the instruments used by the chief for accusing any subject who had become obnoxious to him, and no one, however influential, was safe from being " smelt out," nor was there any appeal or redress. The late Mr. D. Carnegie, who laboured for many years as a missionary in Matabeleland, gave the following terrible picture of the waste of life due to witchcraft.[1]

" It is no exaggeration to say that hundreds of innocent men, women and children were murdered every year because they were supposed, in some way or other, to be traitors to the chief, who, in order to consolidate his kingdom and extend it far and wide, never scrupled to throw the people

[1] Lecture before the Rhodesia Scientific Association, 27th July, 1906. *Transactions*, Vol. VI. Part II. p. 114.

to the wolves, whether they were of high birth or otherwise. His own seven brothers were put to death, and his own sister also was murdered at his command. . . . The people were led by the nose, deceived, burned to death, clubbed to death, driven out of the land, thrown to the crocodiles, murdered and treated in all shameful ways by the ' witch-doctors.' "

The Matabele nation was divided into three social grades, of which the first—the *abe-Zanzi* (" people from down-country ")—constituted the aristocracy, and was composed of the pure-blooded ones—those who had originally emigrated with Mziligazi, and their descendants, all of Zulu origin.

The second grade—*abe-Nhla* (" the people from above," or " from the veld ")—was originally formed out of the fragments of the Basuto and Bechuana tribes which had been attacked by Mziligazi during his devastating progress from Zululand. These were incorporated into the body of the Matabele tribe, and, together with the sons of pure-blooded Matabele by slave-women, went to make up an important class.

The third division was known as the *ama-Holi*. These really belonged to the indigenous tribes of Matabeleland—boys captured in raids, and others who were admitted from time to time into the nation. They were regarded as slaves, and as belonging to the lower orders. In a wider sense, however, the term *Holi* was used to describe all tribes between the Crocodile and Zambesi Rivers—all, in fact, who were not *abe-Zanzi* or *abe-Nhla*.

The vigour of the two superior sections had undoubtedly in later years become impaired by the frequent absorption of women of inferior local tribes, who became the wives of their captors, though the aristocracy were not supposed to marry into any but their own class.

Every male adult was a soldier, and the nation was divided into military districts, each of which furnished a regiment. These latter were composed either entirely of married men (*ama-Doda*) or of bachelors (*ama-Tjaha*), the privilege of marriage being conferred upon a whole regiment at a time as a reward for prowess in warfare. Upon obtaining the licence to marry they were also permitted and expected to build a new town—including separate huts for their wives—and to wear the *isi-Dhlodhlo*, or head-ring. Prior to this their connubial alliances were not officially recognised, though many of the *ama-Tjaha* possessed slave-wives.

A careful estimate made in 1889 put the fighting power of Lobengula's army at 11,550 of pure Matabele, or non-indigenous blood, and a further 10,000 composed of Maka-langa from the west, and Mashona and others from the north of Bulawayo, who, although supposed to be loyal, were not of much account as a fighting factor. Of the pure-blooded regiments the crack ones were the Imbezu (an *ama-Tjaha* regiment, 900 strong) and the Mhlahlanhlela (of *ama-Doda*, 500 in number).

Fighting, that is to say raiding, was the recognised and regular profession of the Matabele. The younger soldiers were braggarts, impatient of authority, and overbearing to the last degree, their one idea being to kill, and so attain the reward of marriage. They were constantly urging the chief to allow them to eject or " wipe out " the European residents, and on many occasions were with great difficulty restrained from doing so. Both old and young soldiers practically made their livelihood out of the raids on their weaker neighbours. Sir Sidney Shippard, who visited Matabeleland in 1888, stated that no less than thirteen *impis* (armies) had been sent out on forays during that year, and had left the most appalling desolation among the villages, not only of the Mashona and Banyai, but also of the tribes immediately to the north of the Zambesi. Every man, woman and infant in these villages had been killed by the stabbing assegai of the *ama-Tjaha* except a few old crones, who had been used as carriers for so long as they were required, and then tied to trees and burnt to death—a holocaust of old Mashona women being one of the favourite diversions of the high-spirited young soldiers. The little boys and girls were saved and driven as slaves into Matabeleland, where they were, on the whole, well treated. The slave-boys were fed entirely on beef, a diet which proved fatal to all the weakly ones, but the survivors became very strong, and fit to be admitted into the regiments, where they soon became as bloodthirsty as the Matabele themselves.

The land belonged to the whole nation, and the Paramount Chief had no power to dispose of it to outsiders without the consent of his Council of Indunas, though he possessed and exercised the right to allot portions to sections of the tribe to be held under communal tenure. The cattle were nominally the property of the chief and the nation, but private possession of cattle, and even the right to traffic in them, were recognised, within due limits. When an individual native became too rich in cattle he ran the risk of incurring the chief's jealousy, with the inevitable sequel of assassination on a charge of witchcraft. In every kraal there were, besides the private herds, a number of state-owned cattle, upon which the chief could draw at will for such purposes as the feast at the Great Dance. The people of the kraal were permitted to use their milk and to retain the hides of those slaughtered for the manufacture of war-shields.

Finally, it may be mentioned that the Paramount Chief was the judge of all disputes, serious or trivial, and in the days of Lobengula a great portion of his time was occupied in hearing and deciding cases, his retentive memory being a great aid to him in dispensing justice.

The foregoing account embraces so much of the constitution, customs and history of the Matabele as is necessary for a proper understanding of the relations which arose between them and the European settlers, at the time of the British occupation of Mashonaland, but a few words may be added on Lobengula himself as he was in 1889, his manner of living and his attitude towards the white men, who were then beginning to alight in his country like flies. In these later years of his life there is evidence that Lobengula's control over the people, and especially over the young braves, was weakening, and he himself complained that they were getting out of hand. But this pretext was sometimes used to excuse acts of aggression for which he wished to evade responsibility. Towards Europeans Lobengula was, on the whole, kindly disposed. The missionaries he valued as advisers because he appreciated their disinterestedness. In the British generally he may have detected some sense of honour which inspired him to tolerate, and in a few cases even to trust them, but he was never quite free from suspicion as to the ulterior objects of any white man not connected with the missions, and this feeling was quickly intensified by any action which he could not understand, and was responsible for the few acts of treachery in dealing with Europeans which can be laid at his door. The murders of Captain Patterson and his party in 1878 were undoubtedly compassed by the chief, though the crime was never actually brought home to him.[1]

On the whole Lobengula preferred the British in his dealings with white men, and recognised the policy of keeping on friendly terms with them. The fate of Cetewayo no doubt made a strong impression upon him as it did upon other great African chiefs, and, though it cannot be denied that the retrocession of the Transvaal may have shaken his confidence in the fighting capacity of the British, as compared with that of the Boer, Lobengula's aim in seeking to retain the friendship of the British was unquestionably to use them as a buffer between him and the Boers, and perhaps more indirectly the Portuguese.

Although in the later years of his life Lobengula had a

[1] Captain Patterson and Mr. Sargeant (son of a former Colonial Secretary of Natal) were the bearers of a letter from Sir Theophilus Shepstone to the chief. A Boer residing in Matabeleland spread a report that their real mission was to bring an army of white men from the north to attack the Matabele. They started for the Zambesi with a son of the Rev. T. M. Thomas and some native guides. Young Thomas was warned by the chief not to accompany them, but persisted. A fortnight after their departure from Bulawayo the guides returned with the report that the three white men had died from drinking water poisoned by the Bushmen. Some years after, David Thomas, another son of the missionary, obtained from two of these natives who were then in the Transvaal a confession that they had murdered the party by the chief's orders because he considered it necessary for the safety of his country. Mr. Thomas' son tried in vain to get the British authorities to take the matter up. He eventually returned to Matabeleland, but he, in turn, was murdered by Batonka, on an island on the Zambesi. It is greatly to be deplored that the Government of the day did not press their inquiries into the Patterson tragedy to a conclusive issue.

brick house built for him in Bulawayo, his favourite dwelling-place was a Cape bullock-wagon, in the tent of which he slept, while from the driver's seat he held interviews and sometimes settled disputes. The most sacred part of the royal precincts was the goat-kraal, and here the mysterious rites preparatory to the great dance of the first-fruits, and the brewing of potions and examining of omens, invariably took place, under the personal supervision of the chief himself. Outside the goat-kraal was the *isi-Kohlo* (court-yard), where justice was dispensed and audiences granted to white men or other suppliants. At Bulawayo, near Mr. Rhodes' house, which was built on the actual site of Lobengula's kraal, they show a tree—a species of wild plum—with gnarled roots, which is said to have been the favourite seat of Lobengula when holding his court. No one, except, of course, a white man, approached him upright on these occasions : all began their salutations from a distance, shouting out the fantastic and complimentary titles of the chief [1] with more and more fervour as they drew closer, till by gradually crouching and sidling they were able to creep into a place in the circle of courtiers. At these *indabas* immense quantities of cooked beef were consumed, being brought into the *isi-Kohlo* by female attendants for the chief, who had a prodigious appetite, and for his European guests, who were compelled by etiquette to eat with a pretence, at any rate, of heartiness. Earthen-ware pots of *u-tshwala*, or " Kaffir beer," were freely cir-culated, the girl who brought each pot being required to taste the liquor before it was offered to the chief.

As far as can be ascertained, Lobengula never allowed himself to be photographed or even sketched—a strange prejudice, for a native's vanity is usually much tickled by posing for a picture.[2] He was a man of striking mien.

[1] Some of the commonest expressions were " Eater of men," " Stabber of Heaven," " Calf of a black cow," " Thunderer," " Black Pig "—not always complimentary in the English sense, but occasionally appropriate !

[2] The late Mr. D. Carnegie's book, *Among the Matabele*, published in 1894, contains a striking portrait purporting to be that of Lobengula, but the author was assured by the late Mr. Helm that this is not a genuine likeness of the Matabele chief, but a copy of a photograph of some other native. Another portrait appears in the late M. Lionel Décle's work,

Above the middle height and of immense bulk, he nevertheless escaped unwieldiness by a carriage of great dignity. The late Sir Sidney Shippard, who journeyed to Bulwayo in 1888, in describing his first official visit to the chief, writes :

" He was completely naked save for a very long piece of dark blue cloth rolled very small and wound round his body, which it in nowise concealed, and a monkey-skin worn as a small apron and about the size of a Highland sporran. . . . His colour is a fine bronze, and he evidently takes great care of his person, and is scrupulously clean. He wears the leathern ring over his forehead as a matter of course. . . . Altogether he is a very fine-looking man, and, in spite of his obesity, has a most majestic carriage. Like all the Matabele warriors, who despise a stooping gait in a man, Lo Bengula walks quite erect with his head thrown somewhat back and his broad chest expanded, and as he marches along at a slow pace with his long staff in his right hand, while all the men around shout his praises, he looks his part to perfection." [1]

While recognising that Lobengula was an inhuman tyrant, treacherous when it suited him, brutal in his passions, and merciless to those who thwarted him, and while allowing that his extinction was inevitable in the interests of civilisation, one can yet spare a shred of sympathy with him as the victim of circumstances. His force of character was undeniable. He not only possessed the capacity of ruling his own people, but in his dealings with Europeans he displayed political skill of an unusually high order. These qualities enabled him to keep intruders at arm's

---

Three Years in Savage Africa, and this, although possibly a sketch from memory, has been authoritatively stated to be a fairly good one. Mr. E. A. Maund informed the author that the chief's objection to being photographed was due to an uneasy suspicion that the process was connected with witchcraft.

[1] Cf. Lionel Décle in *Three Years in Savage Africa* : " He held his head erect, and looked at you from his great towering height with such an air of command that it was impossible to mistake him for anyone else, and it could be seen that he was accustomed to command and to be obeyed. I have seen many European and native potentates, and, with the exception of the Tsar Alexander, never have I seen a ruler of men of more imposing appearance."

length for a time, but were powerless in the end to dam back the tide of white occupation. From the moment when gold was known definitely to exist within his territory the end of Lobengula's despotism was in sight. Better for him to disappear as he did, than living to fret in exile, or become an outlaw in his own country !

For the historical data and the account of the social life of the natives given in this chapter, reference has been made to the following authorities amongst others :

Rev. A. T. Bryant's Zulu Dictionary, which contains a concise history of the Zulu peoples.

The Wild Sports of Southern Africa, by Captain W. Cornwallis Harris (published in 1839), describing an expedition to Mziligazi's country in 1836.

Missionary Labours and Scenes in South Africa, by the Rev. R. Moffat.

Eleven Years in Central South Africa, by the Rev. T. M. Thomas (published in 1872), containing personal experiences of Mziligazi and Lobengula.

Among the Matabele, by the Rev. D. Carnegie, an account of ten years' missionary work in Matabeleland.

Three Years with Lobengula, by J. Cooper Chadwick.

From Ox-wagon to Railway, by A. Boggie.

The Amandebele and other Tribes of Matabeleland, a paper by Sir H. Taylor, Chief Native Commissioner of Southern Rhodesia.

The author has also had the advantage during a long residence in Matabeleland of verifying many of the details given by conversations with old-established missionaries, Native Commissioners and native chiefs.

CHAPTER V

THE MOFFAT TREATY

TOWARDS the end of 1887 a rumour steadily gained currency that Lobengula had entered into a treaty with the Transvaal Government, and ultimately it reached Sir Hercules Robinson through a private letter from a gentleman at Pretoria. That the Transvaal Government contemplated the annexation of Matabeleland had become an open secret, and there seems reason to believe that the Boers meant to repeat the strategy which had been employed in Bechuanaland and subsequently in Swaziland and Zululand, that is to say, a few men would have crossed the border on some plausible pretext, their numbers would gradually and stealthily have been increased, and in due course a pioneer republic would have been proclaimed. The preliminary excuse for entry might have been a hunting expedition, or a quarrel between native chiefs living on either side of the frontier. That part of Lobengula's territory which adjoined the Transvaal was not occupied by the Matabele proper, but by ba-Nyai and other tribes of greatly inferior morale. Some sort of foothold had already been gained there by Boers from Zoutpansberg (the northern district of the Transvaal), a few of whom had been accorded permission by Lobengula to enter his country for the purpose of hunting. They had taken advantage of this to squat on the northern side of the Crocodile River, and had been joined by others. The fame, however, of the fierce Matabele *impis* had no doubt deterred them from further encroachments, and to aid them in the prosecution of their plan as well as to justify it in the eyes of the world, it became necessary that it should be supported by some sort of agreement with the chief. That such an agreement existed was now the common report, and Rhodes' policy

was first to investigate this and next to establish an understanding between Lobengula and the British Government.
Accordingly, Moffat's visit to Bulawayo, which had been
included in his instructions, was expedited. He entered
Matabeleland in December 1887, and at once set to work
to find out the precise nature of the relations between the
chief and Kruger—a necessary preliminary to negotiations
for an *entente* with Britain.

It is well known that Rhodes himself was the author of
this mission. His original idea had been to work for an
extension of the Protectorate system from Bechuanaland
to Matabeleland, and it is conceivable that Lobengula,
impelled by his apprehension of Boer and Portuguese
incursions, would have consented to such an arrangement.
But would the British Government have been disposed to
make the Protectorate an effective one? Probably they
would have refused to undertake any step involving either
increased expenditure or additional responsibility, and
Matabeleland would certainly require both. This at any
rate was the view held by Sir Hercules Robinson. Direct
expansion from the Cape was, of course, out of the question,
as Khama's country intervened. Nevertheless, Rhodes
always professed a desire that whatever territory could be
obtained south of the Zambesi should become the heritage
of the Cape, and it was by continually harping on this
idea that he succeeded in weaning the Afrikander party
in the Cape House from their old conviction that the north
was for the Transvaal, and in gaining its support to his
own schemes. The northern expansion was for Cape money,
Cape trade, Cape railways. This was the idea he dinned into
them, and by 1888 they had come to believe in its reality.

Still the Imperial factor was necessary as a preliminary,
and could not this time be eliminated, so that when Sir
Hercules Robinson told him that the Government were
most unlikely to assume a Protectorate, Rhodes suggested
a new expedient—a sort of negative arrangement. Would
it be allowable to induce Lobengula to undertake that he
would make no treaty with any foreign Power without
British consent? To this Sir Hercules could see no objec-

tion, and to obtain such an undertaking was Moffat's purpose. Rhodes, however, did not stop here. He saw that if Moffat were successful, and an agreement were arrived at which should place Lobengula's territory within the British sphere of influence, the chief would be at once beset by the agents of English financiers seeking mineral and trading concessions. Simultaneously, therefore, with Moffat's visit to Matabeleland, he decided to send up an emissary of his own to anticipate possible rivals, and commissioned a Mr. Fry, one of the staff of the De Beers Mine, and a fine Zulu linguist, to make tentative proposals to the chief as soon as Moffat brought his negotiations to a successful issue. Unhappily this gentleman's health broke down under the trials of a rainy season on the road. He was forced to return to the Cape Colony without achieving his object, and his death occurred shortly afterwards.

On 30th January, 1888, Moffat had a long and important interview with the chief. He informed him of the reports that he had concluded an agreement with Kruger, and that a Transvaal consular agency was about to be established in Matabeleland, and pointed out the desirability of his declaring with his own mouth how matters stood. Lobengula in reply very gravely and emphatically asserted that he had made no engagement whatsoever with the Boer Government, that he recognised no right on their part to interfere in his country, and that he was totally ignorant of any intention on the part of Mr. Grobler to come and live in Matabeleland. He had allowed certain Boers to enter on hunting expeditions, but no more.

Having elicited this important statement, Moffat deemed it impolitic to approach the corollary of a treaty with the British Government until some time had elapsed. It was the period between the Little and Great Dances, when all the principal regiments were mustering at Bulawayo, and when the chief himself was considering his policy for the coming year. At such a season the witch-doctors were much in evidence; " medicine " had to be brewed, and Lobengula was engrossed in the mysterious rites devolving upon him as Grand Master of the Ceremonies. Moreover, during the past year or so he had been plagued by a stream of " concession-hunters," and was nervous at the advance of Europeans into the interior, some of them being at his very door. Added to all this he was suffering from an attack of gout—a complaint to which he had long been subject. Moffat therefore wisely decided to postpone the opening of his real mission—the treaty with Great Britain—until after all the fuss and excitement inseparable from the annual dances had subsided.

A little later he conceived that the moment was opportune, and in a series of conversations cautiously led up to the subject, explaining to the chief the dangers which assailed him, and the importance of securing a strong ally, in anticipation of possible aggressions from Portuguese or Boers. His negotiations were much embarrassed by the fact that previous visitors to Matabeleland had fraudulently claimed to be representatives of the British Government in the hope of currying favour. It was difficult for Lobengula to discriminate between the true and the false, but in the long run the circumstances of Moffat's arrival, the obvious importance attached to his entry by every European in the country, and the military escort of police which had attended him, convinced the chief that Moffat was the genuine representative of the " Great White Queen," and, being really anxious for an alliance, he put his signature to the document which is quoted below. It should be mentioned that Lobengula was not alone in the consultations which took place on this matter. Every point was weighed and argued by his three principal Indunas, who, in fact, carried on the best part of the discussion on the chief's behalf. These were Mlugulu, Nungu and Buzungwane—all members of the priestly order—whose presence and assent were constitutionally indispensable. As a mere matter of speculation it is hard to say whether the chief realised the full import of the document he was signing. There can be no question, of course, that he clearly understood the terms of the actual agreement, but its far-reaching possibilities must have been beyond his comprehension. To gain security from the dangers of Boers and Portuguese, this was his main idea. But to ally himself to the British—virtually to admit their protection—was a leap in the dark.

The full text of the " Moffat Treaty " is as follows :

" The Chief Lo Bengula, ruler of the tribe known as the Amandebele, together with the Mashuna and Makalaka tributaries of the same, hereby agrees to the following articles and conditions :—

" That peace and amity shall continue for ever between Her Britannic Majesty, her subjects, and the Amandebele people; and the contracting Chief Lo Bengula engages to use his utmost endeavours, to prevent any rupture of the same, to cause the strict observance of his treaty, and so to carry out the spirit of the treaty of friendship which was entered into between his late father, the Chief Umsiligaas, with the then Governor of the Cape of Good Hope in the year of our Lord 1836.

" It is hereby further agreed by Lo Bengula, chief in and over the Amandebele country with its dependencies as aforesaid, on behalf of himself and people, *that he will refrain from entering into any correspondence or treaty with any foreign State or Power to sell, alienate, or cede, or permit or countenance any sale, alienation or cession of the whole or any part of the said Amandebele country under his chieftainship, or upon any other subject, without the previous knowledge and sanction of Her Majesty's High Commissioner for South Africa.*

" In faith of which I, Lo Bengula, on my part have hereunto set my hand at Gubulawayo, Amandebeleland, this 11th day of February, and of Her Majesty's reign the 51st.[1]

his
Lo Bengula, X
mark

Witnesses : W. Graham,
G. B. van Wyk.

Before me, J. S. Moffat,
Assistant Commissioner."

---

[1] Quoted from *Blue Book* C. 5524. The word " year " is obviously omitted.

The despatch containing the news of the Moffat Treaty reached Lord Knutsford, the Secretary of State for the Colonies, on 10th April, 1888, and a fortnight later he telegraphed to Sir Hercules Robinson giving him authority to ratify the agreement, which was at once published in a Gazette Extraordinary. Its publication created a stir, not only in financial circles, but also among the foreign rivals of Great Britain in South Africa, namely, Portugal and the Transvaal. Several financiers besides Rhodes had been carefully watching events in Matabeleland, with a view to the exploitation of its supposed mineral wealth when the opportunity became ripe, but to the Boers and Portuguese the clause which shut them out from all hope of gaining a foothold in Lobengula's country was a rude shock. The first protest came from Senhor Eduardo de Carvalho, Portuguese Consul in Cape Town, who wrote to the High Commissioner strongly objecting to the inclusion of the Mashona tribes as tributaries of Lobengula, and affirming that the Crown of Portugal claimed sovereignty over the Mashona country by right of conquest and cession.

As more will have to be said later regarding the Portuguese claims in relation to various regions successively occupied by the British South Africa Company, it will be sufficient now to state shortly that while there is historical evidence of Portuguese expeditions penetrating during the sixteenth century from Sena on the Zambesi River to the Mazoe River, and from Sofala on the coast to Manica, there is also the clearest proof that these expeditions were not followed by effective or continuous occupation.

The official archives at Lisbon contained papers relating to a treaty of alliance made between the " Monomotapa " [1] and the Governor of Mozambique towards the end of the

---

[1] " Monomotapa." A separate volume might be written on the traditions and controversies which have clustered about this name. The word is applied both to a vast kingdom which formerly existed in the interior of Africa, and to its ruler. For centuries reports of the great importance and power of the successive kings of this State, and of the richness of their country, continued to excite European adventurers at home, much in the same way as did the fabulous stories of Prester John of Abyssinia. Kean's *Gold of Ophir* and Wilmot's *Monomotapa* may be consulted by those who wish to learn more on the subject.

sixteenth century, and a document, purporting to be the
original, was actually produced during the dispute between
Great Britain and Portugal over the ownership of Delagoa
Bay.   But however well-founded their original title may have
been—and the genuineness of this document is by no means
above suspicion—the Portuguese had long since suffered the
real control of the *hinterland* of East Africa to slip from
them, and it was only now, when they saw their opportunities disappearing, that they made feverish attempts to
infuse new life into their colonies.[1]

Portugal's claim to sovereignty over the Mashona tribes
was not treated very seriously by the British Government.
Lord Knutsford pointed out that Moffat's Treaty was not
the first which had been made between Great Britain and
the Matabele chief, and referred to an alliance which had
been concluded in 1836 between Sir Benjamin D'Urban,
Governor of the Cape, and Mziligazi, Lobengula's father,
in which the latter agreed that he and his people should
be regarded as the " subjects and friends of the Governor,"
and consented to the appointment of a British Resident
in his country.   Lord Knutsford mentioned that this treaty
had not been made the subject of protest by Portugal
during the fifty-one years of its existence, but the reference
was hardly pertinent, for the D'Urban Treaty was entered
into four years before the Matabele had settled in their
present territory, at a time when they were still occupying
a portion of the Transvaal.   It could scarcely be argued

[1] There are vague references by seventeenth- and eighteenth-century
Portuguese writers to expeditions into the interior, and to the establishment of trading stations and missionary work at places as far west
as Tati, but the downfall of Portugal in Europe, and the discovery of
gold and diamonds in Brazil, turned men's thoughts in other directions,
and the development of the slave trade with its easier profits, while it
sapped the vigour of the Portuguese on the coast by promoting sloth
and luxurious habits, took away at the same time all desire for the more
arduous pursuit of gold in the interior.   As early as 1789 a Portuguese
writer, Andrada, denied the existence of any real dominion in East Africa
outside Mozambique, and this was corroborated by Lameiro, writing in
1824.   Gradually during the nineteenth century the influence of the
Portuguese declined, and one by one their former outposts were abandoned, until they finally gave way before the great wave of Zulu incursions which brought Mziligazi and his following to their west and Zwangendaba and Mzila to their north and south.   Even the ancient settlements
of Sena and Tete on the banks of the Zambesi fell into decay, and would
have so remained had they not acquired a new importance in the European
scramble for Africa.

that it had any bearing on the territorial claim to Mashonaland put forward by Portugal.

Senhor Carvalho's letter of protest was followed, later
in the year, by a notice in the Press to the effect that " the
Government of His Most Faithful Majesty refused to recognise the pretended rights of Lobengula to Mashonaland and
adjacent territories, over which the Crown of Portugal
claimed Sovereignty," and the claims were repeated after
the grant of the Charter to the British South Africa Company in 1889, when they were finally dismissed by a despatch
from Lord Salisbury which will be referred to in its proper
place.

The Portuguese objections to the Moffat Treaty only
anticipated by a few days a much more active counter-effort
on the part of the Transvaal Government.   Kruger's first
step was to issue on May 4th the following Proclamation :

> " Be it hereby made known that the Government
> of the South African Republic, with the advice and
> consent of the Executive Council, has resolved, accord-
> ing to existing treaties between this Republic (con-
> cluded with the Matabele kings Moselikatse and Loben-
> gula), and on the request of the King Lobengula, to
> appoint a representative in the above country with
> the title of Consul, who will have his domicile in the
> capital of the aforesaid King.
>
> " Mr. Pieter Daniel Cornelis Johannes Grobler has
> been appointed to this post of representative of the
> South African Republic.
>
> " It is to the interests of the subjects of this Republic,
> who stay in Matabeleland, either temporarily or
> permanently, to give their names and addresses to
> the Consul aforesaid.
>
> " Everyone who wishes to go to Lobengula's terri-
> tory, either for hunting, trading or otherwise, may
> procure a permit from the Government of the South
> African Republic. Such a permit may, however, be
> refused without any reason for it being given.
>
>   .   .   .   .   .
>
> " As this system of permits has been established by

King Lobengula's own request, who also wishes to be protected in this manner against an influx of evil-doers and the like, warning is hereby expressly given to all who venture into Matabeleland without permits, that they expose themselves to danger at their own risk.

" If any dispute arise, either with natives or others or amongst one another, the subjects of the South African Republic have at once to betake themselves to their aforesaid representative."

This Proclamation entirely ignores the British Treaty, of the terms of which Kruger had without doubt been apprised, but a fortnight later a copy of the treaty was formally handed to the President by the British Agent at Pretoria, whereupon he stated that as it clashed with one which he had made with Lobengula, he would send a communication on the point to the High Commissioner. In the meanwhile Mr. Grobler as " Consul for the Republic," started for Bulawayo in accordance with his commission, and was followed by a number of Transvaal Boers, with whose assistance he placed a *pont* or ferry on the Crocodile River. The point selected was between Macloutsie and the Shashi River, and lay, therefore, on the boundary between the Transvaal and the British Protectorate of Bechuanaland. After a short sojourn in Matabeleland, Grobler was returning to the Transvaal to fetch his family, when, on the 8th of July, he and his party unfortunately came into collision with a number of Khama's men on the British side of the river, and in a fracas which followed two Boers were killed and Grobler himself so seriously wounded that he died sixteen days later. During the correspondence which was exchanged between Kruger and the High Commissioner as to this occurrence, the latter took occasion to refer to the alleged Transvaal Treaty and to question its validity, and this ultimately led to the production of the document in question. In August the President supplied the High Commissioner with the following " historical facts " :

In 1885 and again in the year following, Lobengula

sent a request to the Transvaal Government that the bonds between the two nations might be drawn closer by the renewal in an amended form of a former treaty which had been made in 1853. This request did not lead to any definite result until 1887, when a document was prepared in accordance with Lobengula's expressed wishes, and was taken to Matabeleland by Mr. Grobler with the object of ascertaining whether it correctly represented them. Lobengula and some of his Indunas intimated their full concurrence, and in proof thereof the document was signed at Omchaunien. Subsequently Lobengula sent three delegates back with Mr. Grobler to get confirmation by the Republican Government. The terms of the treaty were again explained, word for word, and were testified as correct by the native delegates, who also expressed their satisfaction at Grobler's nomination as Consul.

The terms of the Treaty are as follows :

" His Honour Stephanus Johannes Paulus Kruger, State President of the South African Republic, represented in this by Pieter Johannes Grobler, by virtue of a power furnished him under date 6th June, 1887, in the name and on behalf of the people and the State of the South African Republic, and Lo Bengula, Paramount Chief of Matabeleland, assisted by his Council and Captains, represented in this by Moluchelu, Nowcho, Postochau and Omownd, in name and on behalf of the people and tribe of Mozelekatse, wishing to confirm, ratify and renew the formerly concluded treaties, have hereby agreed as follows :

" ARTICLE I

" There shall be between both parties a perpetual peace and friendship.

" No violation of territory on either side shall take place.

" ARTICLE II

" The Chief Lo Bengula is acknowledged as an independent chief. He shall be an ally of the South African Republic.

"ARTICLE III

" The said Chief Lo Bengula binds himself at all times, whenever he is called upon by the Government or by an officer of the South African Republic to grant any assistance, either with troops or otherwise, to furnish such assistance; and his people shall then have to stand under the authority and command of the Commanding Officer, or of a subordinate officer under him, without showing the least disobedience to him or one of them.

"ARTICLE IV

" The Chief Lo Bengula shall cause all offenders who fly from the South African Republic into his country to be caught and extradited if it shall be asked.

"ARTICLE V

" The said Chief Lo Bengula shall, without charge, allow each person who comes from this Republic, and who is provided with a pass from His Honour the State President, freely to hunt or to trade in his country, and he shall afford or cause to be afforded to such a hunter, traveller or trader all protection and assistance; such hunters or travellers shall, however, have to conduct themselves quietly and properly, use no violence and also not remove anything arbitrarily.

"ARTICLE VI

" If the President shall appoint a person to live in he territory of the Chief Lo Bengula, and to have charge there as Consul of the subjects of the South African Republic, there shall be granted to such a person all necessary protection, as well for his person as for his property. He shall have criminal and civil jurisdiction over all subjects of the South African Republic. If there is a civil question between a subject of the South African Republic and a subject of the said Chief Lo Bengula or another person, then this Consul may also jointly have jurisdiction.

" Article VII

" In proof that the State President of the South African Republic and the chief approve this treaty, they shall respectively send each other as soon as possible the following presents, viz. :

" The State President of the South African Republic shall send . . . . . . and the chief shall send . . . . .

" I Lo Bengula hereby acknowledge with my Council to fully approve and to have signed this document.

his

Chief Lobengula   X

mark

P. J. Grobler.

The undersigned Indunas :

Moluchelu,	X
Nowcho,	X
Postochau,	X
Omownd,	X

As witnesses.

F. A. Grobler.

" Signed at Omchaunien, Matabeleland,
on this 30th July, 1887."

This document bears the stamp of imposture from beginning to end. In the preamble no reference is made to the former treaties by date, but merely in general terms. The only European signatures are those of P. J. Grobler (the Consul) and F. A. Grobler, his brother. To all genuine papers signed by the chief there have been appended the signatures of at least two independent European witnesses, of whom one has almost invariably been a missionary. Lobengula was by this time (1887) far too astute to affix his signature to a paper without having the assistance of one of the resident missionaries, to ensure his wishes being correctly expressed. But the pretended signatures of the Indunas are the clearest proof that the document is spurious; with the exception, perhaps, of the first, these names bear not the slightest resemblance to Matabele words, and are, beyond doubt, fictitious. The place of execution, " Om-chaunien," is not known in Matabeleland, though it may possibly be a Boer attempt at " Umganin," one of the chief's residences. To anyone familiar with the circumstances this precious treaty stands revealed as a forgery of the grossest type.

However, as was mentioned above, Moffat obtained from Lobengula on 30th January, 1888—six months, that is to say, after the date of the Transvaal document—a most explicit denial of having signed such a paper, and a disclaimer of all knowledge of Grobler's supposed appointment as Consul. This was confirmed later by a written statement, duly witnessed by the Rev. C. D. Helm, one of the oldest and most respected of the missionaries resident in Matabeleland, in which Lobengula said that all the conversation which had taken place with Grobler had reference to the old treaty of general friendship, made between his father Mziligazi and Enteleka (Potgieter), and that the words of the treaty were not his words.

A wearisome correspondence ensued between the British and Transvaal Governments, and was protracted until long after the Transvaal claims had ceased to be of any importance. The Transvaal Government cast doubt on the *bona fides* of the Moffat Treaty, and even insinuated that the murder of their Consul, Grobler, had been instigated by Mr. Moffat—a suggestion too ridiculous to need refutation. They also appealed to the London Convention of 1884, asserting that it was contravened by the declaration that Matabeleland was within the British sphere, that it had been expressly understood that the Republic was to be allowed extension and development to the north, and that the Moffat Treaty put a ring fence round it. To this Sir Hercules Robinson replied in 1889, on the advice of Lord Knutsford, that by the London Convention Her Majesty's Government had kept themselves quite free to extend British influence in that direction—that the limits of the Republic had been clearly defined, and that its Government was strictly pledged to prevent any encroachments upon lands beyond its boundaries.

The discussion had by this time become purely academic, because the Rudd Concession had been signed and the force of events had made it impossible that the Transvaal should ever be allowed a foothold in Matabeleland.

For the historical data in this chapter reference has been made to the following authorities :

Blue Books C. 5237, C. 5524, C. 5918.
The Convention of London, February 1884.
Cecil Rhodes, his Political Life and Speeches, by " Vindex."

CHAPTER VI

THE RUDD CONCESSION

THE conclusion of the Moffat Treaty checkmated the Portuguese and the Transvaalers, but other birds of prey had long been hovering over Lobengula's country, and now that the carcase lay there, ready, as they thought, to be seized, they swooped down with one accord to get their pickings. These were the concession-hunters, some of them backed by influential City men or South African financiers, while others were mere adventurers with no capital beyond a few trade goods and a bullock-wagon. All had a fair start, and it is satisfactory to reflect that success was attained by Rhodes, the only one who had a less sordid object in view than mere spoliation. It has been made clear that his aim in coveting Matabeleland was not one of personal aggrandisement, but was part of his ambitious scheme to add the northern territories to the British Empire. He had already succeeded in Bechuanaland. He had been instrumental in getting Moffat sent up to save Matabeleland from the clutches of foreign rivals; and his next task was to turn the negative agreement which Moffat had obtained into something which would make the country a tangible and useful asset for future British colonisation.

Practical experience had taught him to look for very little real assistance from either the Imperial or Cape Governments. The former lacked the inclination, and the latter the means, to maintain a living Protectorate over the huge area which now lay ready for development; moreover, Rhodes saw, from the example of Bechuanaland, that an Imperial Protectorate was by no means the most favourable way of opening up new countries. The direct rule of the Colonial Office meant dependence upon party politics in England; it meant an irritating officialdom with its narrow and blundering procedure inspired by Ministers who were either ignorant of local needs or obliged to play to the gallery of their Conservative or Liberal constituents.   In opening up Bechuanaland Rhodes had, on more occasions than one, been thwarted by Mackenzie, who was appointed to conciliate the " Exeter Hall " party, and whose policy was pro-native and anti-Dutch, and by Sir Charles Warren, whose War Office methods were too heavy and inelastic for the delicate work of balancing all parties.   He was therefore determined that the northern territories should be guided by a freer hand.

The question of finance did not for the moment disturb him, for Rhodes was by this time at the head of a powerful group of capitalists, which included Mr. Alfred Beit.   He had also acquired the controlling hand in the De Beers Company, and, in amalgamating the various elements which went to make up that Corporation, he had stipulated successfully for financial aid in furthering his ideas of northern expansion. He believed that a private syndicate, untrammelled by Downing Street restrictions, could make more rapid headway in commercial development than a coterie of officials, but he did not forget that such a private body must have Imperial sanction and support, and could not stand alone. The obvious means of achieving his purpose was to obtain a Royal Charter, and he realised that any proposals laid before Her Majesty's Government with this end in view would carry more weight if he could show that he had already secured some foothold in the regions which he sought to open up to British enterprise.

Nowadays, when the struggle for Africa is a thing of the past, the business of angling for concessions from native chiefs may at first sight appear unworthy or even degrading, and it is impossible to deny that when conducted by un-scrupulous persons, as was too often the case, it led to grave abuses.   But it is only right that the circumstances of the time should be borne in mind, and that there should be due discrimination between the many who sought concessions from purely mercenary motives and the few who had a higher object in view.   Of course there have been—and may still be—people who hold that any intrusion of Europeans into native States, except for the religious and moral improvement of the aboriginal inhabitants, is indefensible.   With such there can be no argument.   They shut their eyes to the inexorable march of civilisation.   They refuse to see that backward races must give way to progressive ones.   If, however, it be admitted that it is in itself a good thing, or a necessary thing, that native territories should pass under the control of a civilising Power, there are only three ways in which this can be accomplished—occupation by force (after the manner of the Spaniards in South America), gradual penetration (as has often been attained with missionary effort as the motive power), and occupation with the consent of the native tribes or their rulers, either under a Protectorate or by " concession."   The first of these methods is repugnant to modern, and especially to British ideas; the second is too slow to be employed except where there is no competition by rival Powers.   There remains then the last.   In the case of Matabeleland it was hopeless to rely on securing a Protectorate, and the only means by which a foothold could be obtained peacefully was an agreement with its ruler.   This was Rhodes' reason for resorting, in this and similar cases, to an expedient which, despite pharisaical or fanatical objections, was justifiable as the only course open to him.

As has already been said, he sent up an agent, close on the heels of Moffat, and some time before the British Treaty had been signed, to find out how the land lay, but unfortunately this emissary was obliged to return through ill-health, and Rhodes, knowing that if any time were lost others would step in, at once arranged to despatch a more ambitious expedition, composed of Messrs. Charles Dunell Rudd, James Rochfort Maguire and Frank Thompson, for the purpose of securing a concession for the mineral rights of all Lobengula's territories.

The first named was an English public-school man who had emigrated to Cape Colony in 1866, had been Rhodes' partner in financial speculations on the diamond fields, and had been instrumental with him in founding the " Goldfields

of South Africa Company "—the parent of the important
corporation afterwards known as the " Consolidated Goldfields." For the preceding five years he had sat in the Cape
Parliament as one of the members for Kimberley, and he was
now in thorough accord with Rhodes' schemes for northern
expansion. Mr. Maguire, who had been private secretary
to Sir George Bowen, the Colonial Governor, was also a
friend of Rhodes of many years' standing—their acquaintance dating from their undergraduate days at Oxford. Mr.
Thompson, who was a Cape Colonial by birth, and had been,
like Rhodes, a digger on the diamond fields, was selected
on account of his experience in handling natives and his
knowledge of Kaffir languages. While the British and Transvaal Governments were still exchanging despatches as to
the Moffat Treaty, these three gentlemen started on the long
wagon journey of nearly a thousand miles through a comparatively unknown country. Bulawayo was reached on the
20th of September, 1888, and no time was lost in approaching
the chief with proposals for a concession.

As the first party of any influence which had embarked
on such an enterprise, Rudd and his colleagues undoubtedly
possessed an advantage. Had their mission been delayed
another month they might possibly have been forestalled,
for others were already on the way, notably an expedition
composed of Messrs. Renny-Tailyour, Frank Boyle and
Riley, who were probably at that time, and certainly later,
supported by a wealthy German financier, Herr E. A.
Lippert.[1] The intrigues of this group subsequently proved
a most troublesome element in the negotiations with
Lobengula. There were also in Bulawayo a number of
minor concession-hunters, among them a trio of adventurous
young Britishers from the Transvaal—Messrs. Boggie,
Chadwick and Wilson—who had the good sense to see that
in the struggle between financial magnates they would
probably stand no chance, and at once threw in their lot
with Rhodes' men, to whom they afterwards gave their
staunch support. Finally, there arrived, about the middle

[1] Mr. Renny-Tailyour died near Bulawayo in 1895, and Herr Lippert
died at Hamburg in 1925.

of October, a Mr. E. A. Maund, whose errand deserves more careful reference. Mr. Maund had been one of Warren's officers during the Bechuanaland expedition, and, as already mentioned, had been despatched with two companions to Bulawayo in 1885, to acquaint Lobengula of the Protectorate which had been proclaimed over the country of his old enemy, Khama; for it was feared at the time that the Matabele chief was contemplating an attack on Khama, to settle by force the ownership of the disputed strip between the Macloutsie and Shashi Rivers. Maund was a man of debonair appearance and versatile accomplishments. He cultivated his opportunities with the chief to some effect, and gained considerable influence over him. Returning to England he got into touch with Mr. George Cawston, a City financier, to whom he exhibited samples of gold-bearing quartz which he had brought with him from Matabeleland, and made proposals for an expedition to secure a concession. Ten days after the ratification of the Moffat Treaty, Mr. Cawston, who had been keenly watching the course of events in South Africa, wrote to the Colonial Office announcing his intention, in conjunction with others, of sending a representative to Bulawayo to obtain from the chief a " treaty " for trading, mining and general purposes, and asking for the support of the Government through the High Commissioner. Lord Knutsford replied that no countenance could be given to such an agreement unless it were concluded with the knowledge and approval of Sir Hercules Robinson, and told Mr. Cawston that he and his friends would do well to be prepared to give satisfactory proof of their financial position. Although so guarded, this reply was quite sufficient encouragement for Cawston, who at once formed a small syndicate (the " Exploring Company ") and despatched Maund to try for a concession on the spot.

The arrival of Messrs. Rudd, Maguire and Thompson aroused no small stir in the little white community of Matabeleland. The fact that they represented a powerful group, which was prepared to offer liberal terms for a concession, was an open secret, and the private parties of Europeans, who, up to this time, had been playing their own hands, realised that they must now elect whether to support Rhodes' schemes, and rely on receiving consideration in any future settlement, or form themselves into a hostile camp, and use what influence they might possess with the chief to discredit the mission. The majority were content to play a waiting and watching game, hoping eventually to be bought over. Active opposition was confined to a small but determined clique who, in their anxiety for their own interests, wrought much mischief by imputing sinister motives to Rudd and his colleagues, disregarding the risk to which all white residents would be exposed, once suspicions as to any of their number entered the heads of the credulous natives.[1]

Rhodes' three envoys set to work immediately on arrival, and had numerous palavers with the chief and his Indunas. It is difficult to appreciate what a trial to their patience these meetings involved. The chief was no stranger to the methods of concession-hunters, and was alive to the value of the interests for which they were suing. His self-importance had been inflated by the obsequious attitude of those who had sought favours from him on previous occasions, and Rhodes' agents, like others, had to wait on his pleasure, to conduct their interviews in the unpleasant surroundings of the goat-kraal, and to participate in the tedious preliminaries of beer-drinking and beef-eating which Matabele etiquette demanded at an audience with " His Majesty."

The occasion was a trying one for Lobengula also. He was astute enough to realise that a crisis in the history of his people was approaching, and that not only individuals, but nations, were casting jealous eyes on his rich demesne : he endeavoured to temporise, playing one party off against the other, but gradually became alive to the conviction that unless he made terms with some one of the rival Europeans,

---

[1] Sir Sidney Shippard, in reporting to the High Commissioner on his visit to Bulawayo at this time, wrote :

" From all I can gather, a great deal of mischief has been made by two or three Europeans who have lived long in Matabeleland, and are anxious to prevent the granting of mineral concessions to others; and I have also been assured that certain men from the Transvaal, whose names have been mentioned to me, are doing their utmost to poison the minds of the Matabele against the English. These men are said to make no secret of their wish to see our throats cut."—*Blue Book* C. 5918, p. 123.

he might be overwhelmed by the wave of white occupation, as other African chiefs had been in the past. A few of his principal Indunas grasped this also—notably Lotje, an old general of great influence, whose counsels were always on the side of conciliation, and who remained a stalwart supporter of the Rhodes party until his death a little later by assassination. The bulk of the nation, however, only saw that the intruders were becoming more and more numerous and persistent, and they clamoured to have all white men put out of the country or destroyed, in the fatuous belief that the despatch of a handful of Europeans would arrest the tide of encroachment. Consequently, Lobengula, who had no such illusions, had a hard task to convince his people that the white men could not be kept back, and that the hour had come when their wisest policy would be to make the best terms possible with the party which appeared the most powerful and the least likely to abuse any concessions granted to them.

In the middle of October the tension became very acute. The uneasiness of the natives at this juncture was increased by the news that Sir Sidney Shippard was advancing with an escort of soldiers, which rumour magnified into an *impi* (army). The Imbezu regiment (the " King's Own "), nearly 1000 strong, had recently arrived in Bulawayo, and waited on the chief with a point-blank request that they should be allowed to settle the matter by killing all the *ama-Kiwa* (white men) in Matabeleland. They spent a whole day in arguing their case, and urged that the two or three dozen now in the country would be a mere breakfast to them, and that their deaths would frighten away others ; but if these were spared others would arrive, and gradually thousands of whites would find their way in. To these arguments Lobengula listened for a long while in silence. At the close of the day he replied, " The *ama-Kiwa* here are my guests, and you shall not touch them ; but if you want to fight white men you may go to Kimberley. Remain there and try to fight the white men, and you will see what they will do to you ! "

The mission of Sir Sidney Shippard, who was at this time

Deputy Commissioner of the Bechuanaland Protectorate, had no ostensible connection with Rhodes' schemes for a concession, but followed naturally on his expedition into the Northern Protectorate to inquire into the circumstances of Grobler's death. Besides the necessity for reassuring Lobengula over this incident, there were several important matters to be discussed. The question of the " disputed territory " was still unsettled, and was a source of irritation both to the Matabele chief and to Khama : it was desirable also that the treaty should be clinched by an embassy of a more distinctly formal character than Moffat's had been, while the growing interest which Matabeleland was exciting in the south, and the questions which might arise out of any influx of Europeans, demanded attention and discussion on the spot.

Sir S. Shippard was accompanied by Major Hamilton Goold-Adams and a detachment of sixteen men of the Bechuanaland Border Police, but although his object, and the meaning of this insignificant escort, had been fully explained to the chief by Moffat himself, the pacific nature of the visit was not accepted without apprehension by the natives, who at this time were so obsessed by the " invasion scare " that they suspected some underlying design in any unusual movement on the part of Europeans. Their instinctive uneasiness was increased by reports spread about that the Deputy Commissioner, though travelling with a few soldiers only, had behind him an army for the conquest of Matabeleland, which would be joined on arrival by another army from the north-east. Messengers were sent down to intercept the party, who were exposed to a great deal of insulting behaviour—only stopping short of actual violence —during their progress through the kraals to the south of Bulawayo. At two points they encountered regiments of Matabele, whose demeanour was ugly and threatening. At one village Sir Sidney was compelled to tarry for several days, while a message was sent on to Lobengula asking leave to proceed. Shortly afterwards the *Impandine*, a well-known *ama-Tjaha* regiment, arrived, and subjected him and his little escort to great annoyance. They performed a war-dance in front of the British camp, some of the *ama-Tjaha* running right up to the *scherm*, stabbing and poising assegais in the direction of the occupants, and yelling their intention of " wiping out " the whole party. It is probable that they had received injunctions to refrain from any molestation of the white men, but wished to provoke some act of violence which would have justified them in disregarding these orders and massacring them on the spot. Great forbearance, however, was maintained by Shippard's troopers in the face of this aggressive demonstration, and even when a few of the most daring of the natives leapt over the *scherm* and brandished their spears in the faces of the Deputy Commissioner and some of his companions, not a man flinched.

A few days later the necessary permission was received from Lobengula, and Shippard was suffered to proceed. He arrived at Bulawayo on the 15th of October, and his visit extended over a week, during which he held several *indabas*, or interviews, with the chief. At the first meeting the Deputy Commissioner was accompanied by Major Goold-Adams, Dr. Knight-Bruce (then Bishop of Bloemfontein), who was engaged on a missionary tour through the country, Mr. J. S. Moffat, the British Resident, and two clergymen of the London Missionary Society—Messrs. C. D. Helm and D. Carnegie. Both of these last were residents of long standing in the country, and were held in high esteem by Lobengula— Mr. Helm, indeed, being his most trusted adviser on all matters affecting European interests. Shippard, having been duly warned, took the precaution of having chairs brought for himself and his party, and was thus spared the humiliation of having to squat, native fashion, on the ground. Very few Indunas were present—the principal ones being old Lotje and Sekombo, the latter destined eight years later to be one of the chief leaders in the Matabele rebellion. Besides the discussion on the skirmish between Khama's people and the Transvaal Boers, and the other subjects referred to above, Shippard, at this and subsequent interviews, went very fully into the new relationship between the British and the Matabele as defined in the Moffat agreement, and reassured the chief as to the Government's

SIR SIDNEY SHIPPARD AT BULAWAYO, 1888

Left to right: Rev. D. Carnegie, L.M.S., Rev. C. D. Helm, L.M.S., J. S. Moffat, C.M.G., British Resident, Sir Sidney Shippard, K.C.M.G., Major H. Goold-Adams, B.B. Police.

[*To face p.* 72.

intentions. Lobengula had always hitherto regarded the British with friendly feelings, but the false reports so sedulously spread by Kruger's emissaries had undermined his confidence and engendered a fear of treachery, which it was Shippard's object to remove. He was able also to assure the chief as to the stability and influence of the financial group headed by Rhodes and represented at the kraal by Rudd, Maguire and Thompson, and to convince him that they were not of the same class as the ordinary " concession-hunters " and other adventurers who had been plaguing him for some time with their importunities, and that he could treat with these three with security and faith.

In the official report of his visit Sir Sidney stated that Moffat took a most gloomy view of the future, and regarded as inevitable, sooner or later, a general massacre of Europeans, more especially if, as he anticipated, any attempt were made by Transvaal filibusters to gain a foothold north of the Crocodile River. In this forecast Moffat seems to have misjudged both Lobengula's intentions and his authority over the unruly Indunas, but it must be admitted that it was Shippard's tactful diplomacy which restored calm at a moment when the atmosphere was charged with threatening indications, and when the lives of the Europeans hung in the balance. Lobengula himself could now feel that he was in touch with the officials of the " Great White Queen," and knew that he could count on her protection against the designs of the hated Boers. The Indunas saw that the reports of Shippard's sinister intentions had been false, and that they had been befooled by the authors of them. The Deputy Commissioner's return journey was a triumphant progress, and the natives who had flouted him on his way north were as oppressively civil as they had before been obnoxious.

Taking advantage of the improved situation, Rudd and his colleagues resumed their addresses, to which the chief now gave a favourable ear. A few days after Shippard's departure he agreed to grant them a concession for minerals over the whole of his territory and dependencies, in return for an annual subsidy, a gunboat on the Zambesi, and a thousand rifles. These terms were carefully drawn up by Maguire and brought before the chief on the 27th of October. Two days were spent in discussing and explaining the mutual undertakings before the Council of the Indunas, Mr. Helm, as interpreter, patiently going through the agreement, clause by clause, and translating the answers to the innumerable questions which the Indunas put to the delegates. Finally, on the 30th of October, the chief affixed his sign-manual to the document and handed it to Mr. Rudd.

A facsimile of a portion of the concession faces this page. The body of the document is in the handwriting of Rudd himself, while the deed, as well as the interpreter's certificate,[1] is signed by Mr. Helm. It will be noted that Mr. Moffat's signature is absent, and in fact this gentleman had left Bulawayo a day or two previous to the event. It was, of course, undesirable that the name of the officer representing the British Government should appear in a private commercial agreement.

The terms of the concession are straightforward. It may be noted in passing that the rights which were granted were in the first place complete and exclusive " charge " over all metals and minerals in Lobengula's " kingdoms, principalities and dominions "; the right to do all things necessary to win and procure the same, and to enjoy the profits and revenues derivable therefrom; and, secondly, an authority to exclude all other people seeking *land*, metals, minerals, or mining rights within these dominions. No rights over land were expressly granted to the concessionaires, but Lobengula undertook to grant no future concessions of land or mining rights without their concurrence. This provision became important later on in connection with the " Lippert Concession," which will be dealt with in its proper place. It may further be noted that no right to make laws or to try cases is referred to.

[1] The certificate is not shown in the illustration, but its terms were as follows :

" I hereby certify that the accompanying document has been fully interpreted and explained by me to the Chief Lobengula and his full Council of Indunas, and that all the constitutional usages of the Matabele nation had been complied with prior to his executing the same.

" Dated at Umguza River this thirtieth day of October, 1888.

CHAS. D. HELM."

charge over all metal and minerals situated and contained in my Kingdoms Principalities and dominions together with full power to do all things that they may deem necessary to win and procure the same and to hold collect and enjoy the profits and revenues if any derivable from the said metals and minerals subject to the aforesaid payment and Whereas I have been much molested of late by divers persons seeking and desiring to obtain grants and Concessions of land and Mining rights in my territories I do hereby authorise the said grantees their heirs representatives and assigns to take all necessary and lawful steps to exclude from my Kingdoms Principalities and dominions all persons seeking land metals minerals or Mining rights therein and I do hereby undertake to render them such needful assistance as they may from time to time require for the exclusion of such persons and to grant no concessions of land or mining rights from and after this date without their Consent and Concurrence provided that if at any time the said monthly payment of one hundred pounds shall be in arrear for a period of three months then this grant shall cease and determine from the date of the last made payment and further provided that nothing contained in these presents shall extend to or affect a grant made by me of certain mining rights in a portion of my territory south of the Ramokwebane river which grant is commonly known as the Tati Concession

This given under my hand this thirtieth day of October in the year of our Lord eighteen hundred and eighty eight at my Royal Kraal

Lobengula X
mark

Witnesses
Charles D Helm
J F Dreyer

C D Rudd
Rochfort Maguire
F R Thompson

FACSIMILE OF PORTION OF MATABELE CONCESSION

It is almost inconceivable that there can have been any mistake in Lobengula's mind as to the fact that he was giving away the whole mineral rights of his country, and not merely a permission to mine in one locality. That there should have been any uncertainty on this point is sufficiently disproved by the attestation of the Rev. C. D. Helm, who states that the document was not only interpreted, but explained to the chief. But as the suggestion was made later, and eagerly seized by the chief himself (who in this and other instances evinced a tendency to tergiversation), that all he had given was " a hole to dig in," it may be pointed out that in the two previous authenticated concessions—those granted respectively to Baines in 1871, and to Swinburne in 1878—the locality assigned for mining is most clearly defined, and that it is in the last degree improbable that Lobengula should have deliberately omitted a similar definition in the present case if he had intended to restrict the concessionaires to a special area. Moreover, the magnitude of the consideration precludes the " one hole " idea. Whatever Lobengula's desire may have been later, and however much it may have been politic to humour him, it is quite certain that at the time he gave—and gave knowingly—the whole mineral rights of his country, and received, in return, not only a valuable income, but a much-needed armament for defensive purposes.[1]

For the historical data in this chapter the following authorities have been consulted :

Blue Books C. 5524 and C. 5918.
From Ox-wagon to Railway, by A. Boggie.
Three Years with Lobengula, by J. Cooper Chadwick.
John Smith Moffat, by his son, R. U. Moffat.

In this and the succeeding chapters many details have been supplied by the late Mr. R. Maguire and other personal friends of the author who were resident in Matabeleland during the period dealt with, and from original letters in the possession of the British South Africa Company.

---

[1] The right to exclude rival concessionaires was exercised in December 1898 against a party headed by Mr. Alfred Haggard and the Hon. John Wallop, who were turned back from Tati by Maguire acting under the authority of Lobengula, and supported by an Induna and some Matabele sent by the chief.

CHAPTER VII

THE MATABELE ENVOYS

IMMEDIATELY after obtaining the chief's signature to the concession, Rudd, with the original document in his possession, but leaving a copy in charge of Mr. Helm, started down country. On his way to Capetown he nearly lost his life and the precious paper as well. His only companion was a Dutch transport-rider, H. J. Dreyer, one of the witnesses of the concession, and they had a trying journey through the Protectorate, which at this season—just before the rains—is parched and waterless in many parts. In endeavouring to find a good camping ground with water, Rudd, on one occasion, lost his bearings, and, after many hours of fruitless wandering, sank, exhausted and despairing, under a tree, in a fork of which he placed the document for which he had gone through so much. He would have perished of thirst, as many others more experienced in veld-craft have done, but for the providential appearance of some Bechuana natives, who happened to pass with their dogs. The latter scented the white man, and drew the attention of their masters, who were able to give Rudd water, and restore him to the track, where he found his cart. Near Palachwe—Khama's principal town—Rudd overtook Sir S. Shippard, to whom he showed his concession, and who subsequently wrote an important memorandum on it. At the end of November he reached Capetown without further adventure. Rudd doubtless thought that his task was completed, but there can be little doubt that his departure from Bulawayo was a tactical blunder, and probably, if he could have foreseen the trouble that lay ahead, he would have remained at the chief's side, and despatched the concession by other hands. It is true that he left his two colleagues Maguire and Thompson to watch Rhodes' interests, but he also left two formidable rivals, whose activity had been stimulated rather than restrained by the signing of the concession. These were Maund, representing the Cawston group of financiers, and Renny-Tailyour, the agent of the German speculator, Herr Lippert. We shall see what use they made of the opportunity created by the absence of Rudd, and, later on, of his partner Maguire.

A copy of the Matabele concession was sent by the High Commissioner to the Colonial Office, but before the arrival of the official despatch the Imperial Government heard rumours from unofficial sources of the terms of the agreement (which were known in the City by the middle of December), and though tardy in taking the initiative, they were not slow in criticising. Lord Knutsford at once made inquiries about the rifles which formed part of the consideration by Rhodes. " Do you think," he telegraphed to Sir H. Robinson, " that there is any danger of complications arising from these rifles? "

This was an awkward question, for the introduction of rifles into native territories was contrary to principles which had already received the blessing of the European Powers, though they did not take concrete form until the passing of the General Act of the Brussels Conference on the Slave Trade.[1] Fortunately Sir S. Shippard was able to supply a reassuring—if somewhat casuistical—answer to the inquiry. He pointed out that the substitution of long-range rifles for the stabbing assegai would tend to diminish the loss of life in the Matabele raids, and thus prove a distinct gain to the cause of humanity. A Matabele warrior, unaccustomed to the use of fire-arms, would, he thought, be far less formidable with only a rifle than when, assegai in hand, he stalked his victims as at present.

Sir Sidney added that from a political point of view it would be inexpedient to place any restriction on the supply of firearms and ammunition to Lobengula, while allowing an unlimited supply to be furnished to the Bechuana and other chiefs in and beyond the Protectorate. Lobengula was well aware of this supply, and if debarred from obtaining

---

[1] Art. VIII of the Act of the Conference of July 1890 prohibits the introduction of rifles into territories between lat. 20° N. and 22° S.

fire-arms through British sources would get all he wanted
through the Transvaal, so that a refusal by England to
countenance the introduction of guns would merely have the
effect of throwing him into the arms of the Transvaal Boers.

These rifles formed a most important element in the later
negotiations, for the chief felt that a formal acceptance of
them would clinch the contract, and it was some time before
he committed himself to this step. It may be interesting
to note that they were not actually used in Lobengula's
own time—not, in fact, until the rebellion of 1896—and
Shippard's argument, that the Matabele soldiers would be
less dangerous armed with rifles than with their familiar
assegais was a perfectly sound one.

We may now revert to the position, after Rudd's departure,
at Bulawayo, where Maguire and Thompson were left to
safeguard Rhodes' interests against the insidious attacks of
rivals. Unfortunately for Maund and Tailyour, their arrival
had only taken place when the negotiations for the concession were far advanced—Maund, indeed, having reached
Bulawayo but two days in front of Sir Sidney Shippard.
His disappointment was keen when he saw that he had been
forestalled, but his resources were by no means exhausted.
As a preliminary step he wrote to his principals assuring them
that a concession of trading rights was within his grasp, and
this communication reached England almost at the same
time as the news of Rudd's concession became known un-
officially in London. Without any idea of fusing their
respective interests, he and Renny-Tailyour then put their
heads together, to devise some counter-move which would
upset Rudd's *coup*. Neither of them had relinquished hope
of a personal concession, but both knew that Rudd's must
be got out of the way before any independent step could be
taken. With this common object they sought an opportunity for action, which at once presented itself in Moffat's
absence from Bulawayo. Reports had been circulated
by ill-disposed Boers and others that Queen Victoria (whose
personality had always inspired an immense respect in the
minds of African tribes) had no real existence. Renny-
Tailyour, who wanted Maund out of the way to enable him

to push his own designs, suggested that he should try to induce Lobengula to send home some envoys, to clear up the doubt about the Queen, and that if Maund himself could arrange to accompany them, his influence with the chief would be materially enhanced. The idea appealed forcibly to Maund, who realised that such a mission would give him an advantage over Rudd, and that, even if it did not result in his supplanting the Matabele concession with a new one of his own, it would enable him to claim favourable terms for his own backers. Lobengula also fell in readily with the proposal. He had been harassed and perplexed by the different stories told him by the various adventurers who had infested his kraal. Moffat was not there to advise him, and, even had he been on the spot, his position was a semi-official one only, for he had never been formally accredited as British Representative. Moreover, the chief had conceived a great liking for Maund, who was a man of good presence and persuasive speech—two attributes which are always effective in dealing with natives.

Once having grasped the suggestion, Lobengula was in a hurry to carry it out, and agreed without demur to bear all the expenses of the mission. To Maund also rapidity of action was all important, and he lost no time in drafting the letter which was to be taken from Lobengula to Her Majesty the Queen.

It ran as follows :

" Lo Bengula desires to know that there is a Queen. Some of the people who come into this land tell him that there is a Queen, some of them tell him there is not.

" Lo Bengula can only find out the truth by sending eyes to see whether there is a Queen.

" The Indunas are his eyes.

" Lo Bengula desires, if there is a Queen, to ask her to advise and help him, as he is much troubled by white men who come into his country and ask to dig gold.

" There is no one with him upon whom he can trust, and he asks that the Queen will send some one from Herself."

The letter was an exceedingly clever one. It will be observed that the granting of Rudd's concession was completely ignored, although the ink on the document was barely dry. The necessary amount of doubt is insinuated by the statement that the chief is much troubled by white men " who ask to dig gold," which is tantamount to a suggestion that the question of who was to be allowed to dig was still open. It is difficult to understand how this could have emanated directly from the man who, three weeks previously, had been haggling with Rudd as to the price which he was to pay for the right to dig. The last sentence was possibly intended to convey a hint that Maund himself should be sent out as British Agent accredited to Lobengula's court. It may be doubted whether the request for such a representative was ever expressed by the chief, for at a later date, as we shall see, he rejected the offer of one.[1] The letter was not attested, as most documents bearing Lobengula's signature were, by Mr. Helm the missionary, but was simply stamped with the " Elephant seal," which was usually kept by a local storekeeper in whom the chief reposed an undeserved confidence. In spite, however, of these suspicious circumstances the letter was subsequently accepted as a genuine expression of Lobengula's feelings and wishes. At the time it served Maund's purpose, and armed with it he set off in high feather. Two so-called Indunas were detailed for the mission—Babyana and Mshete, both well advanced in years, and Mr. Johann Colenbrander, a Natal colonist who had a thorough know-ledge of the Zulu language, and had originally been a member of the Renny-Tailyour party—a circumstance not without significance—went with them as interpreter.

Maund's embassy received its first check on its arrival, early in February, in Capetown, where the High Commissioner, Sir Hercules Robinson, questioned the *bona fides* of the mission, but having interviewed the Indunas, and having been assured that their sole object was to ascertain whether or not the " Great White Queen " had a real existence, he allowed the party to proceed. They reached

[1] Cf. Lobengula's letter of the 16th August, 1889 : " With regard to Her Majesty's offer to send me an envoy or Resident, I thank Her Majesty, but I do not need an officer to be sent. I will ask for one when I am pressed for want of one " (p. 111).

England on the 27th of February, 1889, and after a preliminary interview with Lord Knutsford, were actually
accorded the privilege of a personal audience with Her
Majesty. An amusing account of the difficulties which
had to be overcome in arranging their reception was given
to the Press by Lady Frederick Cavendish, who was a fellow-
passenger with the Indunas on board the Union steamship
Moor, and who appears to have been largely instrumental in
smoothing over the obstacles to their reception by the
Queen.

The two Matabele " chiefs " were a curiosity in England,
and, as is usual in such cases, a totally unnecessary amount
of attention was paid to them. It was, of course, quite
right that advantage should be taken of their visit to give
them some object lessons in the wealth and military strength
of the nation, and nothing could have been more appropriate than the arrangement that they should witness a field
day at Aldershot, and be taken over the bullion-vaults at
the Bank of England. There were other entertainments,
however, organised for their benefit, which were calculated
to inflate them with an undue sense of their own importance,
and to give them an erroneous impression of the relations
between a people in the van of civilisation and a barbarous
and savage race. A breakfast party was given in their
honour by that well-meaning but injudicious body, the
Aborigines Protection Society, and was attended by a number
of influential City men and politicians. The invitation card
stated that the envoys " had visited England to ask the
' Great White Queen ' to protect Matabeleland from being
' eaten up ' by intruders." The Chairman in his speech
expressed a hope that at no distant date " Englishmen and
Matabeles would meet together in the valleys of the Limpopo
as happily as they did that day in Westminster," and the
newspaper reports said that the breakfast would " quicken
the good feeling of the Matabele towards Englishmen ! "

These three quotations aptly illustrate the blend of con-
descension and complaisance which Englishmen unfamiliar
with natives employ towards those who visit their country.
No one in England saw anything ridiculous in such senti-

ments, but they were not without a moral to South Africans.

The envoys took back with them two letters, whose contents were so far-reaching that they are worth quoting in full.

The first is that in which the Colonial Secretary replied to Lobengula's letter, and reads as follows : [1]

" *Lord Knutsford to Lo Bengula.*
    " (Entrusted to Umsheti and Babaan.)

" I, Lord Knutsford, one of Her Majesty's Principal Secretaries of State, am commanded by the Queen to give the following reply to the message delivered by Umsheti and Babaan.

" The Queen has heard the words of Lo Bengula. She was glad to receive these messengers and to learn the message which they have brought.

" They say that Lo Bengula is much troubled by white men, who come into his country and ask to dig gold, and that he begs for advice and help.

" Lo Bengula is the ruler of his country, and the Queen does not interfere in the government of that country, but as Lo Bengula desires her advice, Her Majesty is ready to give it, and having, therefore, consulted Her Principal Secretary of State holding the Seals of the Colonial Department, now replies as follows :

" In the first place, the Queen wishes Lo Bengula to understand distinctly that Englishmen who have gone out to Matabeleland to ask leave to dig for stones have not gone with the Queen's authority, and that he should not believe any statements made by them or any of them to that effect.

" The Queen advises Lo Bengula not to grant hastily concessions of land, or leave to dig, but to consider all applications very carefully.

" It is not wise to put too much power into the hands of the men who come first, and to exclude other deserving men. A King gives a stranger an ox, not his whole herd of cattle, otherwise what would other strangers arriving have to eat ?

" Umsheti and Babaan say that Lo Bengula asks that the Queen will send him someone from herself. To this request the Queen is advised that Her Majesty may be

---

[1] The incorrect spelling of native names in this and other documents reprinted from Blue Books has been retained.

pleased to accede.   But they cannot say whether Lo Bengula
wishes to have an Imperial officer to reside with him permanently, or only to have an officer sent out on a temporary
mission, nor do Umsheti and Babaan state what provision
Lo Bengula would be prepared to make for the expenses and
maintenance of such an officer.

"Upon this and any other matters Lo Bengula should
write, and should send his letters to the High Commissioner
at the Cape, who will send them direct to the Queen.   The
High Commissioner is the Queen's officer, and she places full
trust in him, and Lo Bengula should also trust him.   Those
who advise Lo Bengula otherwise deceive him.

"The Queen sends Lo Bengula a picture of herself to
remind him of this message, and that he may be assured that
the Queen wishes him peace and order in his country.

"The Queen thanks Lo Bengula for the kindness which,
following the example of his father, he has shown to many
Englishmen visiting and living in Matabeleland.

"This message has been interpreted to Umsheti and
Babaan in my presence, and I have signed it in their presence
and affixed the seal of the Colonial Office.

(Signed) KNUTSFORD.

Colonial Office,
   26th March, 1889."

(SEAL)

The intentions of this letter were beyond reproach, but
it is impossible to conceive anything more unsettling in the
circumstances than the advice to the chief not to put too
much trust in the hands of the men who come first.   Three
months before this was written Lord Knutsford had received
the Rudd Concession from Sir H. Robinson, who, in his
covering despatch, had given the following advice :—" I
trust that the effect of this concession to a gentleman of
character and financial standing will be to check the inroad
of adventurers as well as to secure the cautious development
of the country with a proper consideration for the feelings
and prejudices of the natives."   Had Lord Knutsford, who
was fully aware of Mr. Rhodes' plans for developing Matabeleland, and should have realised their bearing upon
Imperial expansion, taken this advice, he could never have
been guilty of such a *bêtise* as this about the one ox and the
whole herd.   The only conceivable explanation of the phrase

is that it was inspired by the ingenious Maund.   As may be imagined, Lobengula was not slow in using it in the subsequent negotiations with Rhodes' representatives.

An equally maladroit letter was sent by the Aborigines Protection Society, who should never have been suffered to meddle in the matter at all.   The following is the text :

" *To the Chief Lo Bengula.*

" DEAR FRIEND,

" We send you a greeting by your messengers, whom we have invited to meet us during their stay in London.   The Society to which we belong has, for many years, striven to help distant races of men—races not well known in England, and not knowing England well—*to obtain justice at the hands of our fellow-countrymen.*[1]   We wish you to known that there is such a Society, and that its great aim is *to help the weak to live,* as well as the strong, and to require that the strong shall also be just.   *We have to oppose the actions of our own fellow-countrymen when they do wrong,* although those they are wronging may be strangers to us, and men of another race.

.   .   .   .   .   .

" We think you acted very wisely as a great chief when you despatched messengers to our Queen on the present occasion.   The digging of gold is a new industry among your people.   It is not new among white men.   Hence your wisdom in sending to our Queen and her advisers on this matter.   You already know the value of gold, and are aware that it buys cattle, and everything else that is for sale, and that some men set their hearts on it, and dispute about it as other tribes fight for cattle.   As you are now being asked by many for permission to seek for gold, and to dig it up in your country, *we would have you be wary and firm in resisting proposals that will not bring good to you and your people.*

" We trust your messengers will return to you accompanied by a messenger from our Queen who will tell you all her words, and who will help you to understand matters on which you may need his assistance.

" Wishing you and your people peace and prosperity, we sign ourselves on behalf of the Aborigines Protection Society

" YOUR FRIENDS."

[1] The italics are the author's.

The whole underlying suggestion in this letter is that Lobengula was being hoodwinked, whereas the Aborigines Protection Society was in just as good a position as Lord Knutsford for knowing Rhodes' intentions and the scope of his enterprise, and their failure to discriminate between the ordinary concession-hunter and the empire-builder is nothing less than remarkable.

Maund with his native companions left England early in April 1889, but did not reach Bulawayo until the following August, and in the intervening period important events happened, both in England and in Matabeleland, which entirely upset any ideas which he may have entertained for exploiting his interests in the latter country.

It will be remembered that when he found that his plans for obtaining mineral rights were foiled, he wrote to his London principals that he was certain of a trading concession, and that it would be granted to him upon his return to Matabeleland with the Indunas. Looking at inherent possibilities, it seems unlikely that Lobengula had given him any encouragement to count on this. It was with the utmost difficulty that he had been persuaded to grant a concession for minerals. Was it likely that he would immediately cap this by a monopoly of trading rights? On the other hand, Maund had undoubtedly acquired a personal influence over the chief, which, though perhaps not so great as he pretended, was strong enough to make him a dangerous rival, and one with whom the Rhodes party would have seriously to reckon.

Acting on Maund's advice, and spurred by the rumours, which reached England simultaneously, of the valuable rights gained by Rudd, Lord Gifford, the Managing Director of the Bechuanaland Exploration Company, and associated also with Mr. Cawston in the Exploring Company, wrote the following letter to the Colonial Office :

" London, January 3rd, 1889.

" I have the honour to inform you, for the information of the Right Honourable the Secretary of State for the Colonies, that Chief Khama is negotiating with the Bechuanaland Exploring Company, Limited, as to granting to it large trading rights, and generally as to securing the protection and welfare of his country to himself and people by opening it up to British enterprise.

"From information received from Mr. Maund, which I have had the honour to submit to the Colonial Office, it would appear that there is reason to believe that the Exploring Company, Limited, which I represent, will probably obtain somewhat similar rights in Matabeleland.

"The Exploring Company, Limited, will possibly be also largely interested in British Bechuanaland in view of the proposals that have been submitted to the authorities for the construction of a railway through that country.

"It has been suggested that if these schemes could be merged into one large undertaking supported by adequate financial resources, under Government recognition and with Government representatives resident in the countries, these territories might be rapidly settled and developed.

"I shall be pleased to learn whether, in the event of a scheme of the nature foreshadowed above being matured and formulated, it would be entertained favourably by the Government, and whether the Government would permit of a proposal being submitted with a view to obtaining a charter for settling, developing and trading over British Bechuanaland.

(Signed) GIFFORD."

To this letter an evasive answer was returned, but it was clear to the Rudd–Rhodes group that Maund's connection with Lobengula's embassy might put him in an advantageous position in approaching the Colonial Office, and it was imperative that Rhodes himself should be on the spot, to press his own claims, and to oust, or, if that were no longer possible, to absorb, conflicting interests. Accordingly, in March 1889, Rhodes proceeded to England, and for the first time began to show his hand. He was supported by Rudd and Beit, with the Goldfields Company and de Beers behind them, and the Matabele Concession as their trump card. On the other side were Cawston and Lord Gifford, representing the Exploring Company and the Bechuanaland Company, strengthened by Maund's mission to the Queen, and the shadowy prospect of a trading concession. A third factor was Mackenzie, the missionary and erstwhile Deputy Commissioner of Bechuanaland, who was now in London urging the Imperial Government, with all the eloquence that he possessed, to assume the direct administration of Lobengula's country, and on no account to allow it to be developed by any private commerical group.

Before describing the negotiations which followed, it will be desirable to state, as briefly as possible, the ambitious projects which Rhodes had now in his mind—projects which amounted to no less than the idea of acquiring for the British flag every bit of South and Central Africa which had not been definitely occupied by another Power.

For the events described in this chapter the main authority is :
Blue Book, No. C. 5918.

CHAPTER VIII

At the time when Mr. Rhodes embarked on the negotiations for a Royal Charter, namely, in the spring of 1889, his only tangible asset was the concession granted to Messrs. Rudd and Maguire by the Matabele chief. His ambitions, however, soared far beyond the limits of this document. He aimed, as has been said, at the acquisition of all native territories in South Central Africa not already parcelled out among other European Powers. If he could secure recognition of these as being within the British sphere of influence, he had hopes, by active occupation, coupled with concessions from their native rulers, of creating an indefeasible title to them, and of securing them as integral portions of the Empire, and as the territorial boundaries of the other Powers now gradually closing in on Central Africa were in many cases undefined or doubtful, it was most necessary that the sphere of the Charter should also be left undefined, so as to give him the chance of pushing occupation to the extremest possible limits.

He knew from experience that it was hopeless to ask the Government abruptly to assert a claim over further defined areas of Africa, and he feared lest, while the Government were hesitating and shilly-shallying, other Powers, without the fine scruples of England, would seize the spoil under our nose. A Chartered Company, on the other hand, would be less fettered : an act which would be a breach of international etiquette if committed by a government, would be attributed to commerical enterprise or business acumen if done by a Company.

Let us see what remained of Central Africa for Rhodes to scheme for.

1. *The Territory south of the Congo State (including Katanga).*—The southern boundary of the Congo Free State depended, in April 1889, upon a definition in the General Act of the Conference of Berlin. This marked one of the last rounds in the struggle between the Powers for the possession of Central Africa, and the final result was embodied in a document signed by their different representatives on the 24th February, 1885. Among other agreements recorded in the " General Act " was a clause declaring the " Conventional Basin of the Congo River " to be a neutral territory free to the trade of all nations, and the southern boundary of this huge area was defined as " the watersheds of the basins of the Rivers Zambesi and Logé." Livingstone's map gives Loké as one of the names by which the Kasai (an important tributary of the Congo rising in the Balunda country) is known. Doubtless this is the river which is meant, as it has a common watershed with the Zambesi, but this watershed can hardly be considered to affect the Katanga district, which lies to the east of it.

Side by side with the negotiations which led to this declaration, the International Congo Association—a lineal descendant of the original association formed by King Leopold after the Brussels Conference of 1876—had been quietly assuming sovereign rights over the conventional basin of the Congo—rights which were recognised by each European Power in turn, and were crystallised into the " Congo Free State " in April of the same year. The provisional boundary did not explicitly indicate the frontier on the south-east side between Lakes Mweru and Bangweolo and the head-waters of the Kafue River, and although there is little doubt that it was intended to include Katanga (at that time known as Garenganze, or Msiri's country, and believed to contain rich deposits of copper and gold), this intention was far from being clearly expressed.

With the vague knowledge then possessed by European diplomats of the geography of these remote and comparatively unexplored regions, it appeared quite possible that effective occupation, backed up by concessions from the local chiefs, might secure this territory for a neighbouring

Power. Rhodes was not blind to this, and inspired by the reports of its great mineral wealth he resolved to attempt it himself. But first he had to make sure that no precise limit should be placed on the " sphere of British influence " (a blessed phrase which Rhodes meant to translate as the sphere of the Chartered Company) in this direction.

2. *German East Africa.*—Another locality in which an opening presented itself for pushing British occupation was the gap of country between Lakes Tanganyika and Nyasa. On the strength of a number of concessions obtained by the redoubtable Carl Peters, Germany had in 1885 annexed in East Africa a huge tract of territory which was claimed by the Sultan of Zanzibar—another instance in which Bismarck stole a march upon Great Britain.

On the east or ocean side of Lake Nyasa German influence extended southward to the borders of Portuguese territory, and the boundary was fixed along the course of the Rovuma River by an agreement between the two Powers in 1886. Incidentally it may be mentioned that the 1886 agreement laid it down that Germany would not dispute Portuguese sovereignty over the region between Angola and Mozambique ! It was obvious that no time must be lost in inserting a British wedge between these two.

An agreement made in the same year between Germany and England as to their respective spheres in East Africa, while settling both the northern and the coastal boundaries of the respective parties, was silent as to the limit of the German sphere on the south-west, *i.e.* between Tanganyika and Nyasa, which consequently presented an open door for either to pass through. Here again Rhodes perceived an opportunity. The main object was to secure something which would satisfy the shibboleth of " effective occupation " laid down in the Berlin Conference of 1885. In the area of the Southern Lakes a first step had been taken by the establishment of British missions of various denominations on Lake Nyasa, the formation of trading stations by the African Lakes Company, and the construction of the " Stevenson road " between Nyasa and the south end of Tanganyika. These, however, were private enterprises,

and it was most desirable that they should be protected by
an Imperial ægis if a limit was to be set upon the encroachment of energetic and unscrupulous colonists of the Peters
type.

3. *Portuguese East Africa.*—The settlement of the African
Lakes Company and the English and Scotch missions in the
Nyasa area extended down to the Shiré River.   Here they
were of the utmost value in establishing a British title by
effective occupation against prescriptive rights claimed over
the same area by Portugal, which only awoke to the importance of asserting them when Germany began to squeeze her
on the northern side.   Besides her old-established ports on
the coast which gave her title from Cape Delgado to Lourenço
Marques, Portugal had for centuries maintained a sleepy
hold upon the River Zambesi by means of a number of
stations, the most westerly of which was Zumbo.   Inland
from the coast, and north and south of the river, her claims
to effective occupation were of the slenderest character, and,
alike on the Nyasaland, Mashonaland and Gazaland sides,
have given rise to diplomatic and even armed encounters.   It
will be sufficient here to remark that in 1889 Portugal was
making a belated effort to gain dominion over the Shiré
River and the western shore of Lake Nyasa, towards which
the missionaries and settlers, who had been established in the
Nyasa region since 1878, were also pushing their way.

On the Mashonaland side the boundary was also undeter-
mined.   On the south-east the Portuguese at this time
possessed no more than the littoral.   The interior, known as
Gazaland, was governed by a powerful native chief—
Gungunyana—who claimed all territory behind the coast
from Beira to Delagoa Bay, and collected tribute from natives
as far as Manica, and what is now Eastern Mashonaland.   It
is true that the Portuguese alleged that the whole of this
country had been granted to them by an act of vassalage,
made by certain natives at Lisbon on Gungunyana's behalf
in 1885, and confirmed by a Royal decree, but the genuineness of this document could hardly be accepted in the absence
of any attempt to take advantage of it, and it had been
repeatedly repudiated by the chief himself, who, moreover,

on more than one occasion before 1889, had expressed a desire
to come under the protection of Great Britain.

4. *The Transvaal.*—There is no necessity to dwell on the
position *vis-à-vis* the Transvaal. Its northern border had
been fixed as the Crocodile River by the Convention of 1884,
and although the Boers at various times put forward claims
to territory beyond this, and indeed actually attempted
later to enter with an armed force, the British Government
could be relied on to uphold the Moffat Treaty. In other
directions Rhodes might fear from bitter experience that he
could not depend upon any active assistance from the
Imperial authorities, and would have to play his game single-
handed, but in protecting a boundary which had been
definitely fixed by treaties he felt justified in counting upon
their support.

5. *The Western Boundary.*—The Portuguese boundary
between Khama's country and the Congo was as vague as in
East Africa. In theory, as has been said, Portugal claimed
a wide strip from west to east, linking the provinces of Angola
and Mozambique, and making a belt across the continent,
but effective occupation was non-existent beyond the
western tributaries of the Zambesi, and Rhodes could
reasonably hope to secure territory as far as the watershed
of that river, which roughly corresponded to the 20th degree
of East longitude.

It is apparent from the above that no absolute limit to
British enterprise had been imposed in any direction,
except the Transvaal borders, and those of the Congo and
German East Africa so far as they were defined, and with
this predominant fact in his head, Rhodes approached the
Colonial and Foreign Offices, his fixed determination being
to get some sort of a hold over all that was not yet in the
clutch of some other Power. He did not shut his eyes to the
fact that the Cawston–Gifford combination had to a certain
extent forestalled him in Matabeleland, but he saw that while
their pretensions could be employed as formidable obstacles
to his own plans, they were also capable of being converted
into useful adjuncts if he could only secure them. With
characteristic promptitude, therefore, he opened negotia-

tions for an amalgamation of interests. It may seem obvious now that the two groups could not develop their concessions side by side, and that combination was the inevitable solution, but at the time this result was not achieved without much delicate wire-pulling, chiefly on account of the difficulty of adjusting the relative financial shares of the parties concerned. This task was one in which Rhodes excelled, and by the end of April all had agreed on a union, under his leadership, with the object of securing a Charter. A Company—the " Central Search Association "—was formed, nominally to explore and mine, but really in order to apportion the respective shares of the promoters whose interests were pooled in it. The names of the Directors are worthy of record, though the Company had an ephemeral existence, and was liquidated as soon as it had fulfilled its *ad hoc* purpose. Lord Gifford represented the Bechuanaland Exploration Company and the Exploring Company, Rhodes the de Beers Consolidated Mines, the Goldfields of South Africa and the Matabele Concession, George Cawston and J. Oakley Maund the Exploring Company, Alfred Beit the de Beers Company, and Charles and Thomas Rudd the Goldfields. The Central Search Association was re-constructed into the United Concessions Company, which had the same Directors and carried the financial adjustment a stage further, in anticipation of the granting of a Charter.

It was Rhodes' lot on more than one occasion to put forward proposals which, at first regarded as extravagant, were seen as time went on to be within the range of practical politics. The Trans-Continental telegraph line, which was first mentioned in 1895, may be cited as a case in point. The idea of a charter, which had first openly been broached by Lord Gifford, had long been in Rhodes' mind, but whereas Lord Gifford's proposal had reference to Bechuanaland and Matabeleland only, the other had far wider ideas. These were communicated to his colleagues of the Central Search Association during that eventful April, and at first fairly took their breath away. While Gifford was talking about trading concessions, and Cawston was concentrating attention upon Matabeleland gold reefs, Rhodes suddenly sprung upon them his idea of uniting under one scheme the development of all South Central Africa from the Congo to the Transvaal and from Angola to Mozambique, and of connecting it with the territories of the British East Africa Company so as to form one vast belt of British territory from the Mediterranean to the Cape. Even King Leopold's ambitions had not gone so far as this, and one can picture the effect which his proposals had upon official minds, accustomed to move with extreme deliberation, when, a little later, Rhodes began soberly to discuss them at the Foreign and Colonial Offices.

The peg from which all his projects depended was the Matabele Concession, and it is not unlikely that, in the contemplation of such stupendous undertakings, the attention of Lord Salisbury and Lord Knutsford may have been distracted from a minute inquiry into the validity of such a slender support. At any rate the discussions between Rhodes and the Government resolved themselves into a tussle as to the scope of the Charter, and it was not without considerable opposition, and many interviews, that he convinced the Secretaries of State, as he had already convinced his own colleagues, of the necessity of imposing no boundaries to the sphere within which he was to be allowed to extend British influence. This was what he was striving for. " Give me a free hand," he said, " and leave it to me to secure all that can be secured."

Two minor difficulties had to be removed before the road was clear. Rhodes had to absorb or take into partnership the one remaining corporation holding interests within the sphere of the proposed Charter—the African Lakes Company —and he had to out-manœuvre a small but influential group of men who, inspired by that irrepressible enthusiast Mackenzie, were urging the Government to declare Imperial control over Matabeleland and adjacent territories, and to refuse to entertain any suggestions for relegating that control to a commercial Company.

The history of the African Lakes Company will be given in more detail in the chapters devoted to Nyasaland. It will suffice for the present to say that the Company was formed in 1878, as an adjunct to the Missions—especially those of the

Scottish Churches—which had opened up work in the countries first explored by Livingstone. Owing to a long and harassing war with the Arab slave-traders who infested the Lake districts, the Company's resources were at this time (1889) practically exhausted, and the work of the Missions, dependent as they were upon voluntary subscriptions, was seriously crippled. As a colonising agent it was of the utmost importance that the existence of the Lakes Company should not be jeopardised, and Rhodes offered to come to its assistance financially, on condition that the shareholders should amalgamate their interests with the Chartered Company. An exchange of shares was negotiated on the understanding that the new Company should support the missionaries in the region of Lake Nyasa, and use its best endeavours to suppress the slave and liquor traffic. In return for such assistance the Charter was to have the right at a future date to take over the land and administrative powers of the Lakes Company on indemnifying the latter's shareholders. A sum of £20,000 was eventually guaranteed by Rhodes towards the exchequer of the Lakes Company, and an annual subsidy of £9000 was promised for administrative purposes. At this stage there was no immediate intention on his part of developing the country, but his object was to secure the necessary foothold in Nyasaland for utilisation when the opportunity arrived.

It was of vital importance, however, that in the meantime no westward extension of German or Portuguese influence should be permitted, and Rhodes spared no effort to move the Government to prevent this by taking definite action. Very little encouragement could be extracted from the Foreign Office. Together with Mr. Albert Grey he had an interview on July 24th with Lord Salisbury, who, while professing willingness to abstain from coming to any agreement with Germany which would exclude British enterprise from the north-western shore of Lake Nyasa, or from the country west of the Stevenson road,[1] would not pledge himself to secure recognition of the right of Englishmen to occupy that

[1] Connecting the north end of Lake Nyasa with the south end of Lake Tanganyika, constructed by the African Lakes Company in the early 'eighties with the aid of a liberal contribution by Mr. James Stevenson, F.R.G.S., their chairman.

territory, nor would he undertake to give any Imperial support to an expedition to protect the interests of the Lakes Company on that side of Lake Nyasa. On one point only was he definite—that the Government would maintain their declaration that the navigation of and entry into the Zambesi must be free to all nations. He cautioned Rhodes that as British settlers in that region might have difficulties with the Portuguese, it would be wise for him to avoid any action which might induce the Germans to side with them, and on that account hinted that it might be more to Rhodes' interest to allow Germany to extend her influence westward, taking whatever securities might be necessary for freedom of trade and transit. The obvious conclusion from this was that Rhodes could not count on any diplomatic backing and must rely on effective occupation to secure the country west of Lake Nyasa.

The opposition of the Mackenzie group, though it did not seriously retard the fruition of Rhodes' plans, was sufficiently active to cause him some anxiety at the time. Mackenzie's policy, which he had been assiduously pushing during 1888 and the early part of 1889, may be summarised as follows :—Bechuanaland, and still more Matabeleland, should be freed from the influence of Cape Colony. These great tracts could never be satisfactorily administered from Capetown, where the Afrikander influence was predominant. The office of High Commissioner of South Africa ought to be separated from that of Governor of Cape Colony, as no man in the latter capacity could escape being biased by his immediate environment. In dealing with new native territories the employment of Boer methods would be deplorable, and any administration connected with Cape Colony must inevitably be tainted by Boer ideas.

Mackenzie was a sincere fanatic. He had conjured up this bogey of Cape influence and had allowed himself to become fascinated by it. He succeeded at different times in interesting—but only in interesting—such influential persons as Lord Rosebery, Mr. Joseph Chamberlain and Mr. Arnold Foster. He was never able to make public men generally see more than an academical difference between his policy and that of Rhodes. Both advocated the development of Matabeleland. It was known that this could be undertaken by private funds under the British flag. What did it matter whether those responsible were Cape politicians or not, so long as the Imperial Government reserved the ultimate control, and was not called on to provide expenses out of the national coffers? Bechuanaland had long been regarded as an expensive luxury : if the people of Cape Colony had a fancy for annexing it, why should they be thwarted?

Mackenzie deserved to fail because he completely missed the trend of Rhodes' diplomacy. Rhodes, with the union of all the South African States in his mind, meant to employ the Cape as a stepping-stone merely, or as a base. He knew that public support at the Cape was indispensable to his objects, and he won over Cape Colonists by painting in glowing colours the commercial advantages which would be theirs if they took part in his northward expansion. These advantages would have been practically the same had the Imperial Government assumed the responsibility for the northern territories, but direct Imperial control was the last thing which he desired. He knew how slow and inelastic administration from Downing Street would be. He wanted territory, and felt that he could get it more easily if the British Government was kept in the background as a support, and not thrown forward as a direct agent.

If anything, Mackenzie unconsciously promoted Rhodes' cause by drawing public attention to the importance of securing the northern territories. It began to be felt that it would never do to lose them, and when someone came forward and said, " I will acquire them for you, and you will not be asked to pay a penny towards the cost," it was regarded as puerile for Mackenzie to maintain his opposition to such methods on fanciful grounds. In fine, Mackenzie's agitation languished, and whatever toleration his views had received disappeared altogether when their champion himself was removed. In November 1889 he was seized with a sudden illness—largely brought on by his severe labours in the cause which he had so deeply at heart. Before he could resume his campaign the Charter was already some months old, and Rhodes' plans had matured too far to be arrested.

Of Mackenzie's sincerity and single-mindedness there can be no doubt, and as his policy was at one time regarded by many as an alternative to the Chartered Company, his views have been given at some length.

It must not be supposed that the adjustment of his relations with the African Lakes Company, or the settlement of other claims for recognition, such as that of the Tati Concessions (which though occupying much of his attention on his visit to England were really side issues), caused Rhodes to hesitate in bringing his main proposals to a climax. The formal application for a Charter was sent to the Colonial Office as soon as he had arrived at an understanding with the more important groups represented by Lord Gifford and Mr. Cawston. The actual letter of application emanated from the former on April the 30th, and was supported by one from Messrs. Rhodes, Beit and Thomas Rudd of the same date.

These are of sufficient importance to merit reproduction *in extenso* :

> " *The Exploring Company Limited,*
> *14, George Street,*
> *Mansion House, E.C.*
> *London, April* 30, 1889.

" MY LORD,

" With reference to our conversation at the interview kindly accorded by you to the Directors of the Exploring Company on the 17th instant, I beg herewith to submit the outlines of the scheme for the formation of a Company having for its object the development of the Bechuanaland Protectorate and the countries lying to the north. The objects of this Company will be fourfold :

" 1. To extend northwards the railway and telegraph systems in the direction of the Zambesi.

" 2. To encourage emigration and colonisation.

" 3. To promote trade and commerce.

" 4. To develop and work mineral and other concessions under the management of one powerful organisation, thereby obviating conflicts and complications between the various interests that have been acquired within those regions, and securing to the native chiefs and their subjects the rights reserved to them under the several concessions.

" I am authorised by the gentlemen who are willing to form this association to state that they are prepared to proceed at once with the construction of the first section of the railway and the extension of the telegraph system from Mafeking, its present terminus, to Shoshong, and that for this purpose a sum of £700,000 has already been privately subscribed.

" Having regard to the heavy responsibilities which are proposed to be undertaken by the association, and which cannot be considered as likely to be remunerative for some time; and whereas a proper recognition by Her Majesty's Government is necessary to the due fulfilment of the objects above-mentioned, we propose to petition for a Charter on the above lines, and we ask for an assurance that such rights and interests as have been legally acquired in these territories by those who have joined in this association shall be recognised by and receive the sanction and moral support of Her Majesty's Government.

" By this amalgamation of all interests under one common control, this association as a chartered company with a representative Board of Directors of the highest possible standing in London, with a local Board in South Africa of the most influential character, having the support of Her Majesty's Government and of public opinion at home, and the confidence and sympathy of the inhabitants of South Africa, will be able peacefully and with the consent of the native races to open up, develop and colonise the territories to the north of British Bechuanaland with the best results both for British trade and commerce and for the interests of the native races.

" I have etc.,
" GIFFORD,
" Chairman.

" The Right Hon. Lord Knutsford, G.C.M.G.,
   H.M. Principal Secretary of State for the Colonies,
     Downing Street, Whitehall, S.W."

" *The Gold Fields of South Africa, Ltd.,*
2, Gresham Buildings,
Basinghall Street,
London, E.C.
April 30th, 1889.

" MY LORD,
      " Having perused the letter of this date addressed to your Lordship by the Chairman of the Exploring Company,

Limited, with regard to the development of the territories
to the north of the Cape Colony, we beg to state that we are
prepared, as representing the Matabele Concession, and
having a very important stake in South Africa, to co-operate
cordially, with the approval of Her Majesty's Government,
in carrying out the scheme proposed. Arrangements have
already been made to that effect between the Exploring
Company and ourselves.

> " We have, etc.,
>   "C. J. RHODES,
>   A. BEIT,
>   THOMAS RUDD,
>   Chairman of the Gold Fields
>   of South Africa, Ltd.

" The Right Hon. the Lord Knutsford,
     Colonial Office, S.W."

Lord Knutsford now requested that a draft Charter might
be submitted, and in transmitting these letters for the consideration of the Prime Minister, stated that his consent to
hear the scheme in more detail had been prompted by the
following considerations :

> " If such a Company is incorporated by Royal
> Charter, its constitution, objects and operations will
> become more directly subject to control by Her Majesty's
> Government than if it were left to these gentlemen to
> incorporate themselves under the Joint Stock Com-
> panies Acts, as they are entitled to do. In the latter
> case, Her Majesty's Government would not be able
> effectually to prevent the Company from taking its
> own line of policy, which might possibly result in com-
> plications with native chiefs and others, necessitating
> military expenditure and perhaps even military opera-
> tions. The example of the Imperial East African
> Company shows that such a body may to some con-
> siderable extent relieve Her Majesty's Government
> from diplomatic difficulties and heavy expenditure. In
> Lord Knutsford's judgment such a Company as that
> proposed for the Bechuanaland Protectorate, if well

conducted, would render still more valuable assistance to Her Majesty's Government in South Africa.

" At present nothing could be more unsatisfactory than the condition of things existing in that quarter. Every year large grants have to be obtained from Parliament nominally in aid of civil expenditure, but almost altogether swallowed up in the maintenance of a semi-military police force, whilst the peace of the country is by no means as well assured as it ought to be, and fresh demands are being made on Her Majesty's Government for further expenditure on an increase of the police and telegraph construction, pronounced to be absolutely necessary for the safety of the country."

While the larger scheme was under consideration, Rhodes made a proposal for the immediate opening up of Matabeleland by virtue of the Rudd Concession. He asked that a British Resident should be appointed, and expressed his willingness to bear the cost of his maintenance. This Resident should be instructed to advise Lobengula, and to give the proposed Company moral support, so far as this could be done without entailing on Her Majesty's Government any responsibility or expense. If the request were complied with he offered to construct forthwith a telegraph line from Mafeking to Tati, and to bear the cost of its supervision. This also elicited a cautious but encouraging reply from the Colonial Secretary, who had taken the advice of Sir Hercules Robinson as to the expediency of the proposal.

Both in respect of the granting of a Charter and of the ancillary proposals for the appointment of a Resident and the construction of a telegraph line to Matabeleland, the Government had now gone too far to recede. This was fortunate for Rhodes' plans, as at this juncture a most unpleasant little bombshell dropped into the Colonial Office, in the shape of a letter—ostensibly from Lobengula—addressed to the Queen, and couched in terms which suggested that he intended to repudiate the Concession. To explain this document it will be necessary to take up the thread of events in Matabeleland, and this will be pursued in the next chapter. For the time being it is only necessary to say that, on its being communicated to Rhodes, on the eve of his return to South Africa, he obtained from Maguire an explanation which allayed the apprehensions of the Government and enabled the preparations for the Charter to proceed.

Two incidents, on the other hand, helped to further their progress. One was a letter written by the Rev. François Coillard, a French missionary who for some years had laboured in Barotseland in the western bend of the Zambesi River, praying, on behalf of the chief of that country, for a British Protectorate, and asking particularly for aid against a threatened raid from Matabeleland. The second was the receipt of an important memorandum from Mr. Moffat, pointing out fallacies in the policy advocated by Mr. Mackenzie, and showing that the granting of a Charter would not only relieve the Imperial Government of great expense and responsibility in opening up the interior regions, but would have the effect of terminating once and for all the disturbing efforts of concession-hunters who for years had been pestering Lobengula with their importunities.

Still a variety of petty obstacles had to be surmounted. Even when the draft of the Charter was before the Privy Council, objectors appeared, who threatened at the last moment to cause vexatious delays. The owners of the Tati Concession, not satisfied with the clause in the Matabeleland Concession specially reserving their interests from its provisions, demanded the insertion of similar clauses in the Charter. Sir John Swinburne, the original concessionaire, also claimed consideration for certain private interests of his own in Matabeleland which he contended were prejudiced by the Matabele Concession, and he asked the Privy Council to delay their approval to the Charter until he could be heard. Then the long-forgotten Baines Concession was dragged to light. It had passed into the hands of Messrs. Ochs, a well-known firm of diamond merchants, who now desired consideration for it. These and a number of other claims had to be carefully examined, the genuine ones winnowed from the sham, and a settlement effected with their holders, before the petitioners could show an unencumbered title to the Privy Council.

Eventually the Royal Charter was sealed under Letters Patent on the 29th of October, 1889. To the Directors representing the various financial groups which had been instrumental in obtaining it—*i.e.* Lord Gifford and Messrs. Cawston, Beit and Rhodes—three names were added at the instance of the Government, viz. the Dukes of Abercorn and Fife, and Mr. Albert Grey, all of whom became Life Directors. The text of the Charter is accessible in many books of reference and need not here be reproduced.[1]

[1] The enable Messrs. Rhodes and Cawston to come to the Imperial Government with their proposals for the Charter, amalgamations of the following interests were effected :

1. The owners of the Rudd Concession (Messrs. Rhodes, Alfred Beit and Thomas Rudd) ;
2. The Exploring Company, Limited (represented by Lord Gifford and Mr. Cawston) ;
3. The Austral Africa Company (represented by Mr. A. Haggard) ;
4. The owners of the " Wood, Francis and Chapman " Concession, which related to the " Disputed Territory " (Baron d'Erlanger's Syndicate) ;
5. The Bechuanaland Exploration Company (Lord Gifford) ;
6. The African Lakes Corporation ;
7. The Goldfields of South Africa, Limited ;
8. Lord Rothschild, Mr. Rhodes, Mr. Beit (Messrs. Jules Porges & Co.), and a certain number of private gentlemen having subsidiary interests in Matabeleland.

Authorities for the events narrated in this chapter :
Blue Book C. 5918.
General Act of Conference of Berlin.
The Partition of Africa, by J. Scott Keltie.

CHAPTER IX

DIFFICULTIES WITH LOBENGULA

ALTHOUGH it has been necessary for the continuity of this narrative to give some account of the various obstacles encountered by Rhodes and his friends during their negotiations in London for a Royal Charter, the arenas on which the real battles were fought lay in Matabeleland and the adjacent territories. Here occurred incidents which are not recounted in Blue Books and here the true romance of the Chartered Company was woven.

The story of events in Bulawayo will accordingly be resumed from the moment when Maund set forth on his diplomatic errand to the British Government, ostensibly as the disinterested guide of the Matabele envoys, but with the *arrière pensée* of utilising the mission for his own purpose.

After his departure Maguire and Thompson continued on guard at Bulawayo, their duty being to keep hostile influences from disturbing the chief's mind during such time as Rhodes was engaged in forming his Company and completing his arrangements for giving effect to the concession. Apart from the strain which this state of vigilance involved their daily life was dreary beyond measure. Now that active negotiations were at an end the frequent attendances on the chief and the tedious palavers which generally ensued were the only events which broke its monotony. Lobengula himself, whatever his real feelings may have been, maintained an outward show of friendliness, but this only partially compensated for the sullen hostility and even open insults which they had to endure without retaliation from the rank and file of the Matabele. The society of the few white men around them—hardy colonial adventurers for the most part, though with a strong leaven of frontier riff-raff—was uncongenial. The existence—the " ghastly exile," as Moffat called it—in the squalid surroundings of a Kaffir kraal became almost unbearable. Still they felt that it would be highly unsafe for either of them to leave the chief exposed to the influence of disappointed and intriguing rivals until he had given unmistakable proof of his intention of abiding by the concession and until their own principals had had time to act upon it. Lobengula had regularly accepted the monthly subsidy of £100 payable under the concession, but the rifles which formed an important part of the consideration had not arrived, and pending their delivery the bargain could hardly be regarded as clinched.

Early in April, however, the wagons containing the first consignment of these reached Bulawayo, and although the chief did not at once formally take them over, he placed a guard of his own soldiers in charge—an action which Maguire and Thompson construed as acceptance and, for what it was worth, a ratification of the concession. Even more welcome than the rifles was the simultaneous arrival from the south of two gentlemen who afterwards had much to do with shaping the destinies of the Chartered Company—Messrs. Leander Starr Jameson and Frederick Rutherfoord Harris. Both were medical men practising their profession at Kimberley, and the former had for several years been the close confidant and intimate personal friend of Rhodes. They were not at this time directly interested in the Matabele Concession, but the experience gained upon this visit enabled both of them to render valuable assistance to Rhodes immediately after their return.

Jameson found the chief suffering from gout and sore eyes, and having a small supply of drugs with him was able to afford relief where the noxious messes of the witch-doctors had failed. By this and by his breezy straightforwardness he completely won Lobengula's friendship; in fact the charm of his character exercised the same magnetic attraction on the savage ruler as it did on all Europeans who were brought into contact with him, and the confidence thus engendered was maintained through many trials.

Before Jameson's arrival Maguire had already gathered from correspondence that Rhodes and his friends were being subjected to a species of blackmail. The news of the Matabele concession, with reports, often exaggerated, of the money behind it,[1] had been the signal for the appearance of a multitude of plausible upstarts who scented plunder, and claimed—in some cases to have given valuable assistance which had helped Rudd and his colleagues to come to terms with the chief, in others to be themselves the owners of prior interests in the region which those terms affected. It might have been thought that every individual who had ever been north of Mafeking had acquired some " concession " either from Lobengula himself or from some petty chief pretending to be independent of him, or even from the Portuguese. These claims ranged from the Kalahari Desert to Manicaland and from the days of Thomas Baines to 1888. The more flimsy their foundations the more importunate were the demands, and Rhodes could not escape them either in South Africa or England. In conversation with Jameson during the latter's short visit to Bulawayo it was made clear to Maguire that his local knowledge would materially assist in winnowing the few claims that were entitled to consideration from the mass of bogus and unworthy ones, and he determined to join Rhodes forthwith. On the 11th April he obtained permission from Lobengula to leave Matabeleland,[2] and on the following day started in company with Jameson for Cape Colony, arriving in England early in June.

Maguire's departure, however, not only rendered Thompson's position, as the sole representative in Bulawayo of the concessionaires, more difficult and trying, but gave further opportunities of mischief to their antagonists, who had not abandoned their hopes of being able to wreck the agreement and now redoubled their efforts to that end. As a first step they set to work to poison the chief's mind. It was hinted that he had given away his whole country. He was urged

---

[1] The wildest ideas prevailed as to the financial resources of the owners of the Matabele concession. Even so well-informed a person as Mr. Rutherfoord Harris, in a letter a few weeks later to a friend in Bulawayo, wrote, " Rhodes has £70,000,000 underwritten for interior development " !

[2] The formal leave-taking and its date are important as evidence against the genuineness of the letter, referred to below, in which Lobengula was made, within a few days of Maguire's departure, to say that it had taken place without his knowledge or permission (see p. 108).

NOTICE.

I hear it is published in the newspapers that I have granted a Concession of the Minerals in *all* my Country to CHARLES DUNELL RUDD, ROCHFORD MAGUIRE, AND FRANCIS ROBERT THOMPSON.

As there is a great misunderstanding about this, all action in respect of said Concession is hereby suspended pending an investigation to be made by me in my country.

(Signed) LOBENGULA.

Royal Kraal,
    Matabeleland,
        18th January, 1889.

REDUCED FACSIMILE OF NOTICE IN *BECHUANALAND NEWS*

REDUCED FACSIMILE OF ORIGINAL NOTICE

[To face p. 107.

to repudiate the concession altogether.   James Fairbairn,
a trader who had resided many years at Bulawayo and had
acquired such influence with Lobengula that he was given
charge of the official " Elephant Seal," had been won over
by the rival group and become their tool.   Already before
Maguire's departure the anti-Rhodes party had secured the
publication in a down-country news-sheet—*The Bechuanaland News and Malmani Chronicle*—of the following :

" NOTICE

" I hear it is published in the newspapers that I have
granted a concession in *all* my Country to CHARLES
DUNELL RUDD, ROCHFORD MAGUIRE, and FRANCIS ROBERT
THOMPSON.

" As there is a great misunderstanding about this, all
action in respect of said concession is hereby suspended
pending an investigation to be made by me in my country.

(Signed) LOBENGULA.

Royal Kraal,
  Matabeleland,
    18*th January,* 1889."

The origin of this notice becomes clear when it is compared
with the MS. of the original which came into the possession
of the present writer at a later date, and a facsimile of
which faces this page.[1]   It will be observed that it was
undated and unsigned by the chief (who of course was unable
to write).   But it bears the impression of the " Elephant
Seal " and the signatures of three witnesses, none of whom
had any official standing with the chief, while all were
regarded at that time as unfriendly to the concession.

Immediately after Maguire's departure the plot to throw
doubt on the concession was carried a stage further—again
with the aid of the Elephant Seal.   The letter to which
reference was made in the last chapter was prepared,
enclosed in one addressed by Fairbairn to the Colonial
Secretary and conveyed to Capetown by the hand of Boyle,

---

[1] A photographic reproduction of the notice in the *Bechuanaland News*
is also given for purposes of comparison.   The text of the two documents
is identical and the mis-spelling of Mr. Rochfort Maguire's Christian name
appears in both.

a member of the Renny-Tailyour expedition. Its terms were as follows :

> " *To Her Majesty Queen Victoria from Lo Bengula, King of the Amandebele.*
>
> " King's Kraal, Umgusa River,
> April 23rd, 1889.
>
> " GREETING :
>   " Some time ago a party of men came into my country, the principal one appearing to be a man named Rudd.   They asked me for a place to dig for gold, and said they would give me certain things for the right to do so.   I told them to bring what they would give and I would then show them what I would give.
>
> " A document was written and presented to me for signature.   I asked what it contained and was told that in it were my words and the words of these men.
>
> " I put my hand to it.
>
> " About three months after, I heard, from other sources, that I had given by that document the right to all the minerals in my country.
>
> " I called a meeting of my Indunas and also of the white men, and demanded a copy of the document.   It was proved to me that I *had* signed away the mineral rights of my whole country to Rudd and his friends.
>
> " I have since had a meeting of my Indunas, and they will not recognise the paper, as it contains neither my words nor the words of those who got it.
>
> " After the meeting I demanded that the original document be returned to me.   It has not come yet, although it is two months since, and they promised to bring it back soon.
>
> " The men of the party who were in my country at the time were told to remain until the document was brought back.   One of them, Maguire, has now left without my knowledge and against my orders.
>
> " I write to you that you may know the truth about this thing, and may not be deceived.   With renewed and cordial greetings;
>
> " I am your friend,
> " LO BENGULA, his X mark.
>
> As Witnesses :
>   G. A. PHILLIPS,
>   MOSS COHEN,
>   JAMES FAIRBAIRN
>
>   W. F. USHER,
>   Interpreter."

Elephant Seal.

Even apart from the admission of Fairbairn (mentioned below), the letter carries internal evidence leading to a strong presumption that it was not a genuine expression of Lobengula's ideas. In the first place, had the interested persons desired to send the *ipsissima verba* of the chief they would unquestionably have obtained the assistance of the Rev. C. D. Helm to interpret them and to attest the letter. But Mr. Helm knew nothing about it. The Elephant Seal is no hall-mark—rather the reverse, for Fairbairn, to whom the die had been entrusted, was at this time completely under the influence of the anti-Rhodes clique. The remaining witnesses, as well as Usher, who signed as interpreter, were traders in Bulawayo of no particular standing. It was significant also that the letter was not sent as it should have been through Mr. Moffat, whom the white men, at least, recognised as the British representative, but was forwarded direct to Lord Knutsford. It appears probable that the disappointed concession-seekers in Bulawayo, having gathered from articles in the Press and from private sources that the Government were being approached by financiers and others interested in Matabeleland with proposals for a Charter, realised that unless they could throw doubt on the validity of Rudd's concession their own chances of making money would vanish. By misrepresentation to the chief they induced him to give instructions to Fairbairn for the preparation of a letter of inquiry, and the document in question was a version framed to suit their purpose. But its genuineness, suspected at the time, was afterwards completely disproved by Fairbairn admitting that he had concocted it himself from some notes given to him by Lobengula, and by a still later statement on his part denying all knowledge of the letter !

It reached its destination on June 18th—too late, happily, to interrupt the progress of the preparations for the Charter, the draft of which was actually in the post, and, damaging as such a communication might have been a few weeks earlier, the concessionaries felt that they could now regard it as a misfire. At the same time it created the uncomfortable sensation that the course of events in Matabeleland, which they had not been watching as closely as they should, was not altogether smooth, and it revealed the fact that the opposition to Rhodes' plans was by no means dead.

Maund, who had now reached Capetown, and was just about to start up-country for Lobengula's kraal, was apprised by telegraph towards the end of April of the amalgamation of interests which had taken place in London since his departure, and was instructed to throw whatever influence he possessed with the chief on to the side of the Matabele concession. He did not, however, reach Bulawayo until August, the journey through Bechuanaland in the middle of the dry season proving more than usually arduous.[1] By this time Moffat had returned, and had taken up the position—to use his own words—of " an official kept on the spot as a medium of communication between the Government and the chief." It was not until a later date that he was definitely commissioned as British Resident. Upon their arrival Maund and the Indunas at once had an audience with the chief, at which Moffat was, of course, present, and to which Lobengula also summoned all white men then resident in Bulawayo.

Upon hearing the Queen's letter [2] read, Lobengula at once denied that he had asked Her Majesty to send him " someone from herself," and in this he was supported by the two envoys, Babyana and Mshete, the latter of whom had signalised his return by a carousal among his friends, and attended the *indaba* in a fuddled and aggressive mood. It is probable that the passage in Lobengula's letter to the Queen of November 1888, in which the request for a British representative is made, went further than the chief actually intended. Mshete also vehemently asserted at the meeting that he had been told (by Lord Knutsford, presumably) to advise the chief not to allow any white men to dig for gold in Matabeleland *except as his servants*. In this he was not corroborated by Babyana, who throughout comported himself in a far less hostile manner than his drunken colleague.

Whether this was Mshete's own idea or one inspired by the

---

[1] It must be remembered that the railway at that time extended no further north than Kimberley, and three months was not at all an unusual duration for the journey by bullock-wagon over the 1000 miles of rough and often waterless road through Bechuanaland.   [2] See p. 82.

opponents of the Rudd Concession can only be surmised, but Lobengula eagerly seized upon it. He was getting confused by all the conflicting suggestions which had been put before him during Maund's absence by the Renny-Tailyour party, one or more of whom had been in almost daily association with him during the past eight months. While it is unlikely that he contemplated a complete breach of faith with Rudd, it is certain that he had become nervous of the consequences of the document to which he had put his signature. The idea of the white men working as his servants not only tickled his vanity, but seemed to provide an escape from the difficulties which haunted him, and he dictated to Moffat the following remarkable letter in which he refers to a suggestion that he had given away to Rudd not merely the minerals but his whole country.

" *Matabeleland, August* 10*th*, 1889.

" I wish to tell you that Umshete and Babyaan have arrived with Maund. I am thankful for the Queen's word. I have heard Her Majesty's message. The messengers have spoken as my mouth. They have been very well treated.

" The white people are troubling me much about gold. If the Queen hears that I have given away the whole country it is not so. I have no one in my country who knows how to write. I do not understand where the dispute is, because I have no knowledge of writing.

" The Portuguese say that Mashonaland is theirs, but it is not so. It is all Mziligazi's country. I hear now that it belongs to the Portuguese.

" With regard to Her Majesty's offer to send me an envoy of resident, I thank Her Majesty, but I do not need an officer to be sent. I will ask for one when I am pressed for want of one.

" I thank the Queen for the word which my messengers give me by mouth, that the Queen says I am not to let anyone dig for gold in my country except to dig for me as my servants.

" I greet Her Majesty cordially,

his

Lo Bengula X

mark."

This letter was addressed to Sir Sidney Shippard for transmission to the Queen. Like the spurious one of April the 23rd, it was too late to alter the course of events, and as a matter of fact it did not reach England until November the 18th, by which time the Charter had been irrevocably granted, and the Rudd Concession thereby tacitly accepted; moreover, two or three days before its receipt—viz. on November the 15th—Lord Knutsford had despatched a further message to Lobengula in circumstances which will be explained later.

Lobengula's letter was dictated at an *indaba* held on August the 10th. Moffat, who took it down from the chief's lips, speaks pathetically of the conditions under which it was committed to paper. " I wrote it," he says, " with an empty champagne case for a table, in a kraal full of goats and sheep." The surroundings in which these interviews took place were certainly disgusting. The goat-kraal was the invariable meeting-place, and here beneath the burning sun, in an atmosphere reeking with the pungent smell of the goats, and of the meat roasting for the chief's consumption, pestered by the myriads of flies attracted by the blood, Europeans had to sit through long palavers lasting sometimes for three or four hours.

After the despatch of this letter the opposition redoubled its campaign of calumny and misrepresentation. Mshete, puffed up by the fuss that had been made about him in England, played into their hands. The unfortunate passage in the " Queen's letter " (written, of course, before the granting of a Charter had been put forward as a definite project, but none the less ill-advised), in which the chief was urged not to part with his whole herd of cattle to one stranger, but to give one ox, so that other strangers might have something to eat, was seized upon by Renny-Tailyour and his allies with avidity. They reiterated their assertions that Rudd was claiming the whole country, and urged the chief to abide by his determination to allow him only " a hole to dig in." The letter from the Aborigines Protection Society was also a useful tool in skilful hands. " Be wary and firm in resisting proposals that will not bring good to you and your people." This, of course, referred to Rudd, Maguire, and Thompson, who had beguiled the King into surrendering his country to them !

These repeated pin-pricks dismayed and incensed the unhappy chief. Moffat came under the general ban of mistrust. He might represent the Queen, but had he not always espoused the cause of Rudd, Maguire and Thompson ? The last-named was powerless to stem the tide of suspicion. He had never been a *persona grata*, and was now under the stigma of having cheated Lobengula into signing away his country. The old Induna Lotje, who, more far-seeing than the others, had been the principal supporter of the proposals put forward by Rudd, and was now a loyal adherent of Thompson, was the first victim of the general reactionary policy. On the 10th of September the machinations and intrigues of its promoters culminated in the execution of this Induna, who was strangled on the nominal charge of witch-craft. Once let loose, the fury of Lobengula knew no bounds, and Lotje's assassination was followed during the next few days by the barbarous " wiping out " of his family, his slaves, and his adherents, to the number of over sixty.

Lotje's crime was sympathy with the white people, and his death was one of the indirect results of Lord Knutsford's letter of March the 26th (the " Queen's letter "). The anti-Charter schemers were in the ascendant. They had appealed to barbarism and baffled Moffat, and for a time the prospects of a peaceful opening up of Matabeleland looked black indeed ! The murder of Lotje struck terror into the heart of Thompson, whose nerves, unstrung by a year of ceaseless anxiety amid the depressing and humiliating surroundings of the chief's kraal, now completely gave way. On the day of the murder he had been visiting Mr. Helm at Hope Fountain, the station of the London Missionary Society, a few miles south of Bulawayo. Returning in the evening with a cart and four horses he met, just outside the kraal, a native acquaintance who informed him of the news. His alarm was increased by seeing armed natives whose demeanour, to his excited mind, appeared suspicious. He

at once jumped to the conclusion—a not unnatural one—
that his own life was in serious jeopardy, and, hastily un-
harnessing one of the horses, he rode it bareback to Fair-
bain's store, where he borrowed a saddle. Then dashing
off to the main road he hardly dared to rest until he had
reached the mining camp at Tati, a hundred miles distant.[1]

It is unlikely that Lobengula's anger would have carried
him to the extreme length of doing away with an Englishman, as he was cunning enough to know that this would have
been a false move, and would have stirred up a hornet's
nest. Nevertheless Thompson's flight, following so closely
upon Maguire's departure "without notice," was a most
unfortunate step at this juncture. All the three concessionaires had now disappeared, and the chief was exposed, more
than ever, to the intrigues of the opposition gang. These
could only partially be counterbalanced by the influence of
Moffat, whose hands, as the representative of the Imperial
Government, were tied, and who had not yet been informed
of the real position in England. It is true that Maund was
on the spot, but Maund had never been of the Rudd party,
and, however strongly he might now throw his weight on to
their side, the chief would remember that he had formerly
been in the other camp, and would mistrust him. The
other white men directly employed by Rhodes in Matabeleland were Thompson's brother, a man called Stevens, Wilson
and Chadwick, who had originally belonged to Boggie's
expedition, and Colenbrander, who had accompanied the
Matabele envoys as interpreter, but to none of these would
the chief look for help or guidance in a tight place. The
situation was fraught with dangerous possibilities, not the
least of which was that Lobengula might formally and
solemnly repudiate the concession.

Luckily Rhodes was quick to grasp the critical position.
As soon as he learnt what had occurred, without the loss of
a moment of time he arranged to despatch Dr. Jameson to

---

[1] The horse which bore Thompson in this remarkable ride was for some
time in the possession of the writer. It was a notorious bolter, and its last
achievement was to carry the ill-starred Captain Gwynydd Williams into
the midst of a Matabele *impi* during the war of 1893. Neither Captain
Williams nor the horse (" Bulawayo ") were ever again seen alive.

Bulawayo, to exhibit to the chief the original concession
(which had been sent up in anticipation of any such trouble
as had arisen, and was now in Moffat's custody) and by tact
and diplomacy to endeavour to counteract the suspicions
which the insinuations of the opposition clique and Thompson's precipitate flight had provoked.

Prior to his departure Thompson had repeatedly urged
Rhodes to visit Bulawayo in person.   Moffat also considered
that it would be sound policy for him to meet Lobengula face
to face, and he continued in his belief after Thompson had
gone.   The Matabele ruler had heard a good deal about
Rhodes, and knew that he was the moving spirit behind the
concession.   He knew too that a big Company was being
formed to develop the rights which he had granted, and he
fully expected that Rhodes, as the head of the Company,
would shortly make his appearance.   In fact when old
Sam Edwards, a few weeks previously, had started for the
Cape Colony, Lobengula had said to him, " If you meet
Rhodes, turn back with him."   All Europeans in the
country believed that he was the only man who could reduce
the chaos to order, and the one party hoped for his arrival
as intently as the other dreaded it.   Nevertheless, it is
quite inconceivable that Rhodes could have exercised the
patience and tact which Jameson afterwards displayed, and
by which, without a doubt, he saved the concession.
Unrivalled in dealing with Europeans, Rhodes had at this
time little experience of natives other than those on mines,
and would have been impatient of the restrictions to which
the life in Bulawayo would have daily exposed him.   To
regain Lobengula's confidence was an object not to be
attained by one or two skilful encounters, but by long and
judicious handling, and for such a task Jameson was
unquestionably better fitted.   Before the end of September
—less, in fact, than three weeks after the assassination of
Lotje—Jameson had started from Kimberley.   He took
with him Mr. Denis Doyle, a clever interpreter thoroughly
used to dealing with natives, and Major Maxwell, who afterwards for some time represented the Charter at Bulawayo.
At Mafeking they found Thompson, who was with some

difficulty persuaded that it was Rhodes' express desire, as well as in his own interests, that he should return to Mata-beleland. At Tati Jameson met Sam Edwards and took him back also to assist in reassuring the chief, and the party thus augmented arrived at Bulawayo on the 17th of October, little more than a month having elapsed since Thompson's precipitate departure.

In the letter of April the 23rd, to which reference was made above, the chief was made to say that he desired the original of the Rudd Concession to be returned to him. The clear inference was that he intended to repudiate the transaction and to tear the document up. Jameson, however, took the bold course of ignoring the possibility of such an action on Lobengula's part, and, immediately on arrival, presented himself at the royal quarters accompanied by Doyle and Thompson, and with the concession in his pocket.

They found Lobengula with Moffat in the buck-kraal and at once got to business. The chief poked some sarcastic jibes at Thompson, twitting him with having " crept away under the sand," but he was unaffectedly pleased at seeing the doctor, who explained that he now came as representing Rhodes. The original concession was produced, and first translated into si-Ndebele by Doyle, afterwards being handed to the chief, who requested " Joni " (as he called Moffat) also to read it. Then followed an anxious moment. There was nothing to prevent the chief from destroying the paper there and then, but possibly the singular respect which all uneducated natives entertain for a written document may have deterred him. After hearing Moffat's translation he admitted that the terms were identical with those of the copy which Helm had shown him, but still maintained that his intention had been to give Rudd only " one hole to dig in " and not all the gold in his country, and stated that he must again refer the whole matter to the Council of his Indunas. For the time being Moffat was to keep the paper until the discussion took place. As may be imagined, Jameson was greatly relieved when he saw the concession back in safe hands. To gain time he was prepared to accept " one hole to dig in " as a commencement, and to start a few prospectors at Ramaquabana, whence they could work southwards towards Tati, where good gold reefs were reported, allowing the larger question to stand over for a while. What he wanted to avoid was the acceptance of a new document with less favourable terms. After the ill-advised phrase in the Queen's letter about the ox and the herd of cattle, he knew that it was hopeless to expect Lobengula to ratify all at once the mineral concession over his whole country.

Satisfied then, on the whole, with the results of this preliminary *indaba*, Jameson devoted the next few days to diplomatic conversations with the European intriguers, who were all united in a conspiracy of greed, and were daily becoming more importunate. Renny-Tailyour, the ring-leader of this section, being powerfully supported in Europe, was the most difficult to deal with. His demands were enormous : nothing would satisfy him short of one quarter of Mashonaland, including the favoured district of Mazoe— reputed rich in gold—to develop which Lippert could easily raise several millions in Hamburg. Jameson devoted considerable time and all his powers of persuasion to induce him to trust to Rhodes making a favourable settlement with his principal, but his efforts met with no conspicuous success. An opportune diversion was created by the arrival of some native messengers with a report that two Portuguese officers, with 300 armed native soldiers, had entered Mashonaland immediately south of Zumbo, and that they were engaged in building forts and distributing Portuguese flags to the local chiefs—news which so disturbed Lobengula that he made Moffat write a protest [1] and talked of despatching an *impi* to the spot if no satisfactory reply were forthcoming.

Many wearisome days were occupied in discussions

---

[1] The Portuguese expedition was reported to be building a fort on the Umniati River about 200 miles N.E. of Bulawayo. The information was brought by native spies. The text of Moffat's " ultimatum " was as follows :

" My people have informed me that a party of Portuguese are hoisting the Portuguese flag and building a fort at the junction of the Umniati and Nyabosa Rivers. I send these messengers with this letter to ask you by what authority you are doing this in country which belongs to me. I am your friend Lobengula " (*Blue Book* C. 5904, p. 187).

between the chief and his Indunas, as to what had actually been granted to Rudd. Some of the older ones—notably Mhlaba (the regent) and Machau (Induna of the Imbezu regiment)—favoured the Rhodes party, and pointed out the value of the guns in view of the possibility of a Portuguese invasion, which was now acting as a counter-irritant, but the younger men were unanimously against them. One or two regiments indulged in war-dances and loudly demanded the dismissal or slaughter of all white men in the country. But Lobengula always temporised and repeated the sardonic advice which he had used before : " They are my friends. If you want to do some killing, go to Kimberley, where there are plenty of white men who have no claim on me." His object was to gain time, and to find out more about the movements of the Portuguese in the north and the Boers in the south. Jameson, on the other hand, while prepared to play a waiting game within reasonable limits, was hopeful that the Portuguese threat would force a decision and induce Lobengula to accept the guns, and so clinch the concession. If in the meantime he accepted the " hole to dig in," and started prospecting in Matabeleland proper, there would be justification for having armed police to protect the workers, and this he was anxious to arrange before the coming winter of 1890.[1]

During this anxious period the news of the granting of the Charter reached Bulawayo, and enabled Moffat to inform Lobengula that the Charter was Rhodes, that it was represented by Jameson and his friends, that they were the only people in Matabeleland whom the Queen recognised, and therefore the only ones in whom he could repose confidence.

---

[1] The rumours of Portuguese incursions to a certain extent played into Jameson's hands and were made the most of by him, but they had the further effect of increasing the suspicion against Europeans in general. Both Portuguese and British were *ama-Kiwa* (white men), and both were trying to gain a foothold in the country. It was bruited abroad in November that F. C. Selous, the hunter, was helping the Portuguese, and that they had a chain of four camps extending from Zumbo as far as the Umniati River. As a matter of fact Selous did visit the Portuguese settlements on the Zambesi in September and October of 1889, but so far from helping them, he was doing his best to undermine their pretensions to occupation in North-eastern Mashonaland, and actually obtained signed statements from some of the chiefs in the neighbourhood of Mazoe that they were independent of Portuguese authority.

Moffat pointed out that the Charter gave Rhodes the right
to raise troops who could fight for Lobengula against intruders and repel invasion.   The chief, who was now wavering,
replied that he never wanted help and could fight for himself,
but the Portuguese threat was nevertheless having its effect.

In the meanwhile Rhodes in the south began to take steps
to raise a force of police, who, in the first instance, were to
form a reinforcement of the mounted Bechuanaland Police
and were to remain in the Protectorate until required either
to tackle filibusters in Matabeleland or to escort a body of
settlers to work under the concession.   All this was known
to Moffat, whose position hitherto had been an extremely
delicate one.   He was not, even now, formally accredited as
British Representative at Bulawayo,[1] but he had spent
nearly two years in Matabeleland in his quasi-official
capacity, and he was thoroughly convinced that Rhodes'
policy was the only one that could save the native and
European communities from internecine struggles.   Up to
the time of the granting of the Charter any assistance
rendered by him to Rhodes' party had to be of a very
guarded nature.   The news of the Charter eased his position
in some degree, as it made his policy clearer and gave him a
freer hand.   For example, it came to his ears that Renny-
Tailyour had pretended that he had been sent out by the
Queen, and he took an early opportunity of confronting this
worthy with the chief, and forcing him to admit publicly
that he held no sort of official status.

It would be wearisome to give a detailed account of the
interviews which Jameson held, almost daily, with the
Matabele chief, in the unpleasant surroundings of the buck-
kraal, or to dwell further on the plots and devices by which
the different opposition parties sought to embarrass him.
His policy throughout was to win Lobengula's confidence and
to secure by diplomacy a peaceful occupation of the country.
All others concerned believed that that occupation would be
impossible without fighting, and with this view military
preparations were being made for the expedition which, it

[1] For Moffat's formal appointment see Lord Knutsford's despatch of
November 15th announcing the Charter.   This did not reach Moffat till
the end of December.

was now decided, should be despatched into Mashonaland during the dry season of 1890. But Jameson, though he never discouraged these preparations, maintained that, if he could once persuade the chief to authorise the entry of the expedition, hostilities during its actual progress could be avoided. The Martini-Henry rifles which formed part of the consideration of the Rudd Concession had reached Bulawayo, but Lobengula had not yet decided to take them over. On the other hand, he regularly received the monthly instalment of his subsidy, and this inspired Jameson with a feeling of confidence that he would ultimately grant the required consent.

Early in December Jameson's patience was rewarded by something a little more definite. The following conversation took place :

JAMESON. " King, we want to know where we are to commence digging."

LOBENGULA. " Where do you want to dig ? "

J. " Wherever the King likes. He knows where the gold is : we know nothing. . . . You have given away Tati : well, let us begin from above Tati, where we shan't interfere with your people."

L. " Yes, that is nice ! Go and dig there " (pointing to the south).

J. " If we don't find gold there, what then ? "

L. " Then come to me, and I will tell you to dig there " (pointing to Mashonaland).

J. " Well, I will go to-morrow with Sam (Edwards) and start some men to work, and in ten days I will come again and tell the King what I have done."

L. " Yes, that is nice ! Go nicely, my white men, and come back soon."

This, of course, is a condensed report of a talk which occupied an hour or more. It was the first definite permission that Jameson had received to make a move, and he lost no time in starting a prospector named Maddox and three other white men at work on some reefs on the west side of the Tati road—the earliest mining work attempted by the Chartered Company in Rhodesia. But when Renny-

Tailyour and his ally Boyle tried, a few days later, to get Lobengula to give them also a " hole to dig in," the chief referred them to Jameson as head of the white men in the country, from which it will be seen that the Kimberley doctor had materially changed the complexion of affairs during the last three months of 1889.

While Jameson was engaged at Bulawayo in repairing the mischief wrought by the Matabele embassy to England, and the evil counsels of hostile white men, and in winning back by degrees the confidence of the chief, Rhodes had not been idle in the south, for, in addition to preparations for pushing his enterprise into the remoter areas included in the Chartered Company's sphere, he was using his best endeavours to procure the despatch of another letter to Lobengula which should counteract the bad effects of the parable about the single ox and the herd of cattle, contained in the one brought out by Maund.

The final execution of the Charter presented a favourable opportunity for such a communication, and Lord Knutsford was moved to indite the following despatch, which was sent to the High Commissioner (now Sir Henry Loch, who had recently replaced Sir Hercules Robinson) on the 15th November, with a request that it should be transmitted to Lobengula through Moffat.

" *Message to Lo Bengula.*

" 1. I, Lord Knutsford, one of the Queen's Principal Secretaries of State, am commanded by Her Majesty to send this further message to Lo Bengula. The Queen has kept in her mind the letter sent by Lo Bengula, and the message brought by Umshete and Babaan in the beginning of this year, and she has now desired Mr. Moffat, whom she trusts, and whom Lo Bengula knows to be his true friend, to tell him what she has done for him and what she advises him to do.

" 2. Since the visit of Lo Bengula's envoys, the Queen has made the fullest inquiries into the particular circumstances of Matabeleland, and understands the trouble caused to Lo Bengula by different parties of white men coming to his country to look for gold; but wherever gold is, or wherever it is reported to be, there it is impossible for him to exclude white men, and, therefore, the wisest and safest course for him to adopt, and that which will give least trouble to himself and his tribe, is to agree, not with one or two white men separately, but with one approved body of white men, who will consult Lo Bengula's wishes and arrange where white people are to dig, and who will be responsible to the chief for any annoyance or trouble caused to himself or his people. If he does not agree with one set of people there will be endless disputes among the white men, and he will have all his time taken up in deciding their quarrels.

" 3. The Queen, therefore, approves of the concession made by Lo Bengula to some white men, who were represented in his country by Messrs. Rudd, Maguire, and Thompson. The Queen has caused inquiry to be made respecting these persons, and is satisfied that they are men who will fulfil their undertakings, and who may be trusted to carry out the working for gold in the chief's country without molesting his people, or in any way interfering with their kraals, gardens or cattle. And, as some of the Queen's highest and most trusted subjects have joined themselves with those to whom Lo Bengula gave his concessions, the Queen now thinks Lo Bengula is acting wisely in carrying out his agreement with these persons, and hopes that he will allow them to conduct their mining operations without interference or molestation from his subjects.

" 4. The Queen understands that Lo Bengula does not like deciding disputes among white men or assuming jurisdiction over them. This is very wise, as these disputes would take up much time, and Lo Bengula cannot understand the laws and customs of white people; but it is not well to have people in his country who are subject to no law, therefore the Queen thinks Lo Bengula would be wise to entrust to that body of white men, of whom Mr. Jameson is now the principal representative in Matabeleland, the duty of deciding disputes and keeping the peace among white persons in his country.

" 5. In order to enable them to act lawfully and with full authority, the Queen has, by her Royal Charter, given to that body of men leave to undertake this duty, and will hold them responsible for their proper performance of such duty. Of course this must be as Lo Bengula likes, as he is King of the country, and no one can exercise jurisdiction in it without his permission; but it is believed that this will be very convenient for the chief, and the Queen is informed that he has already made such an arrangement in the Tati district, by which he is there saved all trouble.

" 6. The Queen understands that Lo Bengula wishes to have someone from her residing with him. The Queen, therefore, has directed her trusted servant, Mr. Moffat, to stay with the chief as long as he wishes. Mr. Moffat is, as Lo Bengula knows, a true friend to himself and the Matabele tribe, while he is also in the confidence of the Queen and will from time to time convey the Queen's words to the chief, and the chief should always listen to and believe Mr. Moffat's words.

> (Signed) " KNUTSFORD,
> Her Majesty's Secretary of
> State for the Colonies.

Downing Street,
  November 15, 1889."

At the instance of the Company, and with the object of emphasising the weighty character of this despatch, it was decided that it should be presented by special envoys, and two officers of the Royal Horse Guards—Captain Victor Ferguson and Surgeon-Major Melladew—who were accompanied by the senior non-commissioned officer of the regiment—Corporal-Major White—were selected for this novel duty.

Although an improvement on its predecessor, the despatch is a curiously weak one in some respects. Jameson had been constantly impressing upon the chief that Rhodes was the principal and prime mover in the concession, and in these representations he had been backed up by Moffat. Rudd and Maguire were now mere memories at Bulawayo, and Thompson, owing to the unfortunate mistake of his flight, was still regarded with some mistrust and disfavour. The chief was satisfied that Rhodes was the man he had to deal with, and that Jameson, who had replaced Thompson and was a favourite at Court, was there as Rhodes' representative. Yet in the whole letter the name of Rhodes is not once mentioned !

" The Queen understands that Lobengula wishes to have someone from her residing with him." This sentence is a continuation of the suggestion in Lord Knutsford's previous letter of the 26th of March, but it makes curious reading by the side of Lobengula's reply of the 10th of August, which had crossed the later one in the post : " With regard to

Her Majesty's offer to send me an envoy or resident, I thank Her Majesty, but I do not need an officer to be sent.   I will ask for one when I am pressed for want of one."

The whole letter is a blend of conciliation and dictation. It " talks down " to Lobengula (who was by no means a novice at diplomacy), but at the same time practically orders him to leave disputes among white men to be " decided " by the white men themselves—a demand quite likely to elicit another snub from the chief, who might reply, " Who made you the Induna over my country? " besides being rendered abortive by the succeeding sentence—" No man can exercise jurisdiction in the country without the King's permission."

Again, the counsel to agree with one approved body of white men is a remarkable recantation of the previous advice to give the stranger an ox and not the whole herd.   It was meant to cancel this previous advice, but the intention is so crudely expressed as to carry nothing but confusion to the native mind.

However, such as it was, Jameson and Moffat had to make the best of this despatch, and considering that it was drafted by men who were very imperfectly acquainted with the intimate essentials of the situation, it served its purpose—a letter of introduction for the Chartered Company—fairly well.

The envoys arrived in Bulawayo on Monday the 27th of January, and, in accordance with their instructions, went straight to Moffat's house.   On the 29th they were received in audience by the chief at Umganin, the only other white men present being Moffat, Jameson and Doyle the inter-preter.   Chairs were provided for all—a rare compliment— and Lobengula not only received the letter graciously, but manifested the greatest interest in the Guardsmen who had brought it.   Their accoutrements and uniform excited his wonder; he took off and handled one of the cuirasses, asked them to go through the sword exercise, and, in inviting them to attend the " Great Dance," which was to take place during the following week, made a point of their appearing in full panoply.   The usual entertainment of

beef and beer enlivened the interview, which—if nothing
else—was undoubtedly a pictorial success.

Jameson followed up the Queen's letter at another *indaba*
a few days later. He opened by informing Lobengula that
his prospector Maddox had found no payable gold at Rama-
quebana, and did not wish to push northwards towards
Bulawayo for fear of disturbing the native villages. " Well,"
said the chief, " you had better look for another place."
" Might he go east ? " said the doctor, pointing towards
Mashonaland. " Yes," was the reply. A map was produced showing a route which had been projected by Selous
and which, skirting all Matabele kraals, took first a north-
easterly course from Matabeleland and then headed due
north towards Mazoe. A request was also made that Selous
should be allowed some of Lobengula's own men to help
him cut a road for wagons. To this also the chief assented,
and Jameson retired in high feather.

Having achieved as much as was possible he now made
preparations to leave Bulawayo for a while, for Rhodes was
anxious for his advice in connection with the preparations
which were being made for the expedition in the winter.
Before his departure, however, he attended the " Great
Dance," which passed without the slightest *contretemps*, no
rudeness or insulting behaviour being levelled, as had too
often been the case, at the European onlookers. Jameson
" got the road " from the chief on February the 13th, 1890,
after a sojourn of four months of ceaseless anxiety and
vigilance at the kraal. He had gained his object ; had lifted
the chief out of his former attitude of black suspicion, and
had secured the promise of a peaceful entry for Rhodes' men
into Mashonaland. The value of this work to the British
South Africa Company, and incidentally of course to Great
Britain, was incalculable, and it is hardly too much to say
that no other man could have carried it through. Had an
attempt been made to occupy Mashonaland without
Lobengula's acquiescence, the Matabele war of 1893 must
have been anticipated by three years, with the difference
that the European forces would have been fighting for a
foothold instead of defending a possession. Moreover,

Lobengula would have considered himself betrayed by England, and the Company's title to Mashonaland would have been marred from the outset by an ineffaceable blot.

A day after Jameson's departure the chief summoned the envoys to hear his reply to the Queen's letter, and a long *indaba* took place at which several of the leading Indunas, as well as Moffat, Colenbrander and Doyle, were present. Lobengula grumbled a good deal at the intrusion of Rhodes into the correspondence. He had not sent Babyana and Mshete to England to talk about Rhodes, but about Thompson and Maguire, who were said to have persuaded him to sign away his country. Why had Rhodes now put words into the Queen's mouth? He (the chief) had been told that he could choose the men who should be allowed to dig in his country, but now Rhodes had persuaded the Queen to say that the right to dig was to be given to him only.

To these and similar complaints Moffat and Doyle did their best to reply, and eventually the chief sent an answer saying that he was still thinking over the words brought by Babyana and Mshete, without committing himself to a definite yea or nay on the matters broached in Lord Knutsford's despatch. He did, however, commit himself a week later by taking over the rifles which had all this time been lying at Mvutjwa, and which he now placed in charge of Chadwick. By this important step he demonstrated his final ratification of the Matabele Concession.

The main authority used in compiling this chapter is :

Blue Book C. 5918.

Use has also freely been made of notes made by the author in 1889 and 1890 of the progress of events in Matabeleland, and of information given to him by the late Sir Starr Jameson, Denis Doyle, J. Colenbrander and F. R. Harris.

CHAPTER X

THE PIONEERS

THE best known and most picturesque episode of the early history of Rhodesia is, without doubt, the march of the Pioneer column from their camp at Macloutsie to Mount Hampden. In fact the occupation of Mashonaland was conducted in so public and conspicuous a manner that the achievements of the Chartered Company's pioneers in other fields were to a certain extent overshadowed and eclipsed by it. But Mashonaland was only part of a much greater whole, and it must not be imagined that Rhodes was allowing his immediate measures for the possession of this part to divert him from his designs for acquiring the remainder. The progress of these will be recounted in due course, but it may be useful, at this point, to interrupt the story of Matabeleland and Mashonaland in order briefly to mention the less public steps taken by Rhodes to compass the end which he had in view—the seizure of all unappropriated territories in South Central Africa.

When he returned from England to South Africa in September 1889 the granting of the Charter was assured, and he at once faced the numerous responsibilities which he had imposed upon himself and his co-Directors.

Besides the occupation of Mashonaland under the Rudd Concession these responsibilities were as follows :

(a) The extension of the Cape Railway system northwards from Kimberley towards the Zambesi;

(b) A corresponding extension of the Cape telegraph line; and

(c) Preliminary expeditions to break the ground for the occupation of the more remote territories covered by the Charter.

(a) *Railway Extension*

One of the two objects for which the original Exploring Company was formed was to obtain a concession or subsidy from the Imperial Government for the construction of a railway into Bechuanaland. The negotiations with the Government had made considerable progress by the time that the question of a Charter was first broached. The Exploring Company had secured a promise of being allowed the first right of building the railway, and of receiving in return certain land grants, mining rights and fiscal privileges. Part of the understanding arrived at in 1889 between the Directors and Rhodes was that the Chartered Company should, when constituted, take over the undertaking as to the railway and the corresponding rights, and it was also arranged with the Government that the proposed Company should receive, in substitution for some of the fiscal and mining privileges, a grant of 6000 square miles of vacant Crown land in Bechuanaland in consideration of the section from Kimberley to Vryburg, and a similar grant for an extension to Mafeking, together with a fair proportion of any revenue which might result from the discovery of gold within these areas. Soon after the granting of the Charter Rhodes entered into a provisional agreement with Sir Gordon Sprigg's Ministry by which the Cape Government undertook to give facilities for the construction of the line to the borders of the Colony, and, after its completion to Vryburg, to work the line at Colonial rates, with the right to purchase it outright on certain specified terms. Early in 1890 the Cape agreed to avail itself of this right of purchase during the following year, and, a large amount of capital being thereby set free, Rhodes was enabled to make an offer to proceed with the Mafeking section, to which Lord Knutsford on behalf of the Bechuanaland Government gave his consent.

(b) *The Telegraph Line*

Simultaneously with the extension of the railway, but starting from a point considerably in advance of the existing terminus, the Company embarked on the construction of a telegraph line towards the promised land. The first objective was Palapye—Khama's principal town—and the section between Mafeking and this point—a distance of some 240 miles—was completed in October 1890. It was next carried on a further 225 miles to Macloutsie, and thenceforward was continued without any serious intermission, and closely in the wake of the Pioneers, towards Mashonaland.

(c) *Occupation of Further Territories*

Beyond the confines of Lobengula's territory were certain objective points to which Rhodes desired to carry the Charter, and in the majority of cases they corresponded with the seats of great African chiefs, from whom his first business would be to obtain concessions.

South of the Congo State lay the realm of Lewanika, Paramount Chief of the Barotse country, and overlord of a number of neighbouring tribes whose characteristics were known vaguely from the explorations of Livingstone in the 'fifties, and from the reports of successive travellers, one of the last of whom was F. C. Selous. A concession had already been given by Lewanika to a Mr. H. Ware, and Rhodes determined to acquire this and to amplify it by further treaties with the chief. Lewanika had shown a disposition to consider a British Protectorate, and it was important to be beforehand with the Portuguese of West Africa, in whose interests several exploring expeditions had already been hovering on the frontiers of Barotseland.

In November 1889 Rhodes commissioned Mr. Frank Elliott Lochner, an officer of the Bechuanaland Police, to conduct an expedition to Lewanika's kraal, and negotiate for a comprehensive concession. This will be described in detail in a later chapter.

Still further north was the Chief Msiri's country, then called Garenganze, and now known as Katanga. Whether this district lay within the conventional boundaries of the Congo State was doubtful, but Rhodes determined to put the matter to the test. Early in 1890 he entered into an arrangement with Mr. Joseph Thomson, the famous Central

African explorer, to proceed from the east coast to this distant spot, and endeavour to come to terms with the chief on behalf of the Chartered Company. Accounts of Mr. Thomson's expedition, and that of Mr. Alfred Sharpe, which had the same object in view, will also be given hereafter.

Towards Lake Nyasa the ground had been broken by missionaries. Further spade-work was rapidly being accomplished by Mr. Harry Hamilton Johnston, who came to South Africa in 1890 to discuss with Rhodes plans for carrying the British " Raj " into the regions lying between the Lake and the Congo State. He had already displayed so much activity in East Africa that Rhodes could comfortably leave the organisation of future development in his hands.

Finally, there remained East Africa south of the Zambesi River. Two important chiefs were here to be tackled— Gungunyana of Gazaland, and Umtasa of Manica—but the former was known to claim the Manica chief as a dependent, while the Portuguese asserted dominion over both. Rhodes decided to approach Umtasa from the Mashonaland side, through Colquhoun or other suitable agent, and to send a separate emissary to Gungunyana, so as to secure a double hold on Manica and its gold reefs. For the Gazaland expedition he selected Mr. Aurel Schulz, a Colonial medical practitioner of herculean frame, who had a thorough knowledge of natives and had already gained the reputation of being a daring explorer.

In May 1890 most of these lieutenants met Rhodes at Kimberley for a final discussion of plans. It was a notable occasion—the assembling of these quiet eager men, all with a record of empire-work behind them, all straining at Rhodes' leash to be off to fresh adventures, and all inspired by the zeal of the master-spirit for the new-born undertaking.

There was Joseph Thomson, whose brilliant fame as an explorer had been won by successive expeditions in Masailand, Nigeria and the Sudan, and with him a young Grant, son of that Grant who shared with Speke the honour of discovering the sources of the White Nile and the Kingdom

RHODES WITH CONSUL JOHNSTON AND OTHER PIONEERS AT KIMBERLEY, MAY 1890

Standing, from left to right: J. Grant, J. W. Moir, Joseph Thomson.

Seated, from left to right: J. Rochfort Maguire, H. H. Johnston, C. J. Rhodes, A. R. Colquhoun.

of Uganda. There too was John Moir, known from Tanganyika to the Zambesi by his native nickname of " Mandala," the founder of the African Lakes Corporation which
was henceforward to work hand in hand with the Charter
in the country which Livingstone bequeathed to Scotland.
There was Harry Hamilton Johnston, who had already
earned laurels both in West and East Africa, but whose
greatest opportunities were yet to come. There was also
Archibald Ross Colquhoun, the explorer of Yunnan, and
Jameson fresh from the conference with the Matabele chief
and ready for new fields to conquer.

All looked to Rhodes, and when he gave the word " Go ! "
they passed away quietly each to his allotted work. The
group broke up—as it had assembled—unnoticed. How
the busy share-brokers who thronged the Kimberley Club
would have stared could they have guessed the instructions
which each of these men carried in his pocket-book !

Having shot out his tentacles to these distant regions,
Rhodes was now able to concentrate attention on the work
nearest at hand—the expedition to Mashonaland. As a
matter of fact the recruiting of a force for this object had
been started less than a fortnight after the signing of the
Charter. Rhodes' original idea had been to take advantage
of the existing organisation of the Bechuanaland Border
Police and to provide the cost of extra squadrons to serve
as escort to a number of picked men who should constitute
the first settlers in the new territory, and with that intention
a small detachment of young colonials was enrolled in
Kimberley and despatched on November the 9th, 1889, to
Mafeking to join the Bechuanaland Border Police.[1]

Subsequently it was thought better that the Company
should raise its own military forces, and the Government
authorised the enrolment of a special police corps to escort
the working party to Mashonaland, and afterwards to assist
in preserving law and order. The selection of the
" Pioneers "—the men who were to cut a road into the
country and form the nucleus of the future settlement—was

[1] These young men—about a dozen in number—were afterwards
known as " Rhodes' Apostles."

a different matter. It was not necessary that these should be chosen with a view to purely military duties, but at the same time it was imperative that they should be kept in a body, and under control, until a pacific occupation was accomplished, and they could safely proceed to mining and other occupations. Although there was an abundance of the right material in Cape Colony and other parts of the sub-continent, it was felt that the number of the original settlers should be limited. In the end it was arranged that these Pioneers should be engaged under contract. Three enterprising young colonists, who had themselves been members of the Bechuanaland Border Police, and had thus acquired practical experience of the rough life of the interior, and especially of the exigencies of African transport, offered to select, organise and equip a body of men to cut the road to Mashonaland, and to provide all the necessary transport, for a fixed sum. These were Messrs. Frank Johnson, Maurice Heany, and Henry Borrow,[1] and their names will ever be honourably associated with the British occupation of Mashonaland.

The two hundred " Pioneers " were mainly recruited in South Africa, and were of many trades and professions. Each man was guaranteed certain land and mineral rights upon completion of the contract ; until then they were to form a corps under military discipline. The " British South Africa Company's Police " were enrolled with practically the same object, but, inasmuch as they were to be employed in the first instance on strictly military duties, they were attested for a fixed period of service, and were placed under officers seconded from the Imperial and Colonial forces. The command of the combined force of Pioneers and Police was entrusted to Lieut.-Colonel E. G. Pennefather (of the 6th Dragoons), who had served with distinction in the Zulu and Boer campaigns. During the early months of 1890 recruiting for the two forces proceeded apace. Great eagerness was manifested to join the expedition, and the

---

[1] Mr. Heany was an American citizen who had gained considerable experience of Indian warfare ; the other two partners were British colonists.

applications far exceeded the limited number required.
Recruits were therefore only admitted after careful selection,
and it is safe to say that no finer *corps d'élite* than the British
South Africa Company's Police and the Mashonaland
Pioneers has ever been raised. Batches of recruits were
forwarded from time to time to the northernmost station of
the Bechuanaland Police on the Macloutsie River, which
bounded the "Disputed Territory," and this spot became
the Company's base camp.

In describing the personnel of the expedition there has
been a slight anticipation of events. When Jameson left
Bulawayo the enrolment had just commenced. His own
idea had been to send forward a few wagons at a time,
which would have been a cheap plan and would have prevented any alarm or excitement among the Matabele, but
he found that different counsels had prevailed while he
had been in Bulawayo. For one thing, authoritative
information had reached Rhodes that preparations were
being made for a "trek" of Zoutpansberg Boers into
Mashonaland during the coming winter, in defiance of conventions and treaties. Again, in spite of Jameson's reassuring despatches as to Lobengula's attitude, the reputation
for treachery and ferocity enjoyed by the Matabele regiments
had convinced these below that the entry of small parties
would be attended by grave risks, and that it would be
better that the reality of the movement should be shown at
once by the despatch of a substantial and well-equipped
force. They did not delude themselves with the idea that
an organised inroad of Europeans was likely to be welcomed
by the Matabele, and they argued that a compact expedition
would be less likely to provoke active interference than one
composed of little detachments dribbling in at intervals.

As the Pioneer force grew the plan of campaign was
elaborated. Difficulties disappeared before the enthusiasm
of the moment. The fact that Lobengula had granted no
land rights, no powers to make laws, nor authority to settle
disputes—deficiencies which had sorely exercised Jameson
a few weeks previously—was tacitly disregarded. Preparations were made for allotting farms to those of the Pioneers

who would undertake to occupy them, and for a small establishment of civil officials who could form the embryo of an administrative service. Suitable officers for all the varied posts in the new country came ready to Rhodes' hand as if by magic. He had the happy faculty of attracting the men he wanted, and never was it displayed more conspicuously than when he was preparing to occupy Mashonaland. As guide and intelligence officer for the expedition he secured Frederick Courtenay Selous, an English public-school man, who had already spent eighteen years in elephant-hunting in the interior, and who now undertook to find a route by which the healthy plateau of Mashonaland could be reached without interfering with Matabele kraals. No one was better adapted for such a task. For the responsible post of Chief Magistrate and for the initial work of administration another capable officer was most opportunely available. This was Colquhoun, who, besides possessing a thorough knowledge of governmental work, gained during many years' service in India, was an explorer of considerable note, and had gained the gold medal of the Royal Geographical Society in recognition of an intrepid journey to Western China and the Burmese frontier. Jameson was to accompany the column in the capacity of Rhodes' representative, which, though nominally an unofficial post, meant that the guidance of the Company's policy would be largely in his hands. In the innumerable details incidental to these preparations Rhodes was assisted at Kimberley by Dr. Frederick Rutherfoord Harris, who was appointed South African Secretary of the Chartered Company, and to whose extraordinary energy and *flair* for organisation the success of the occupation was largely due.

It must not be supposed that this military activity had escaped the notice of Lobengula. He was kept fully advised of all that was going on by the Matabele who were working for white employers at Tati and Macloutsie. Up to the middle of February, when Jameson left Bulawayo for the south, these preparations had not assumed very noteworthy proportions, but immediately after the doctor's arrival in Kimberley with the news that Lobengula had sanctioned the entry into Mashonaland, every possible effort was made to get ready for a start in June. It was important that the Pioneers should reach their destination in time to get settled before the commencement of the heavy rains in November, and it was calculated that at least three months would be occupied in conveying the force to a suitable spot on the high veld. The Company's representative at Bulawayo in Jameson's absence was Denis Doyle, and early in March he took steps to reassure the chief by again explaining the route which the Pioneers would take as mapped out by Selous. The actual objective was Mount Hampden, an isolated and conspicuous hill lying a few miles south of the Mazoe range and well known to Matabele raiders. Lobengula raised no opposition. He even evinced some anxiety for the mining party to start, for rumours of the projected Boer trek from Zoutpansberg had reached his ears, but he once more repeated his desire to see Rhodes personally. " The Queen says Rhodes is the man I must trust : therefore I want to see him." It may seem unfortunate that this very natural wish could not be gratified. That Rhodes did not come remained a grievance, and was made the pretext for objections raised by the chief later on to the advance of the column. At the same time it is difficult to believe that an actual meeting between the two would have led to any good results. The chief knew that Jameson was " Rhodes' mouth," and it is unlikely that Rhodes himself could have achieved a better understanding than had already been attained. If Jameson had remained at the kraal, in all probability no protests would ever have been raised against the Company's movements, but in Jameson's absence the chief became suspicious, and it was feared that at the eleventh hour he might upset the contemplated expedition by sending objections to the High Commissioner. Once more, therefore, Jameson undertook the journey to Bulawayo, which he reached on April the 27th. Knowing thoroughly the character of the man he had to deal with, and feeling that any concealment was likely to cause trouble later on, he unfolded in some detail the whole plan of campaign, viz. that Selous was to find a route, and with an advance party to cut a road; that 100 wagons of provisions and mining tools were to follow, and that if necessary a detachment of the police now at Macloutsie was to accompany the Pioneers for their protection. Lobengula was somewhat taken aback and at first looked away and hummed a tune to conceal his embarrassment. It was the police, or " soldiers," as he regarded them, that he was afraid of, and at last he turned to Jameson and asked why they were wanted, for white men had worked at Tati for a long time without police. " Mashonaland," replied the doctor, " is much further away than Tati, and the Queen's Government would not allow men to be taken so far unless they are protected." He reminded Lobengula that they were the Queen's subjects, and that Rhodes had her authority in the Charter to raise soldiers. " Against whom," asked the chief, " are the workers to be protected?" " Against Boers," was the reply, " or Portuguese, or anybody else who might molest them." It was explained that Rhodes had held a meeting with Kruger, and that the latter now knew that he would not be allowed by the Government to enter Mashonaland, but nevertheless stray Boers and filibusters might make the attempt, and it was necessary to guard against it.

Point after point was raised by the chief, only to be met by ready answers from Jameson. There were objections to Selous, who, long before, had incurred Lobengula's anger by shooting a hippopotamus without permission, but he was reminded that Selous was the only man who could be depended on to find a good route. " Why choose that route? Why not come through Matabeleland?" " Because the Queen's letter said that the Matabele people were not to be interfered with, and therefore they must go outside them."

In the end Lobengula realised that events had proved too strong for him. He had, in a sense, burnt his boats by accepting regularly the subsidy stipulated by the Matabele concession; he had even taken over the guns, and had put his own nominee—Chadwick—in charge of them. " I do not refuse," he said at length, " but let Rhodes come."

With this qualified assent Jameson had to content himself, and a few days later he left Bulawayo for the last time to make final preparations for Selous to start. The two protagonists in the long diplomatic encounter were not destined to set eyes on each other again, for Jameson's next arrival in Bulawayo was after the chief's flight in 1893.

The safety of the missionaries had caused Jameson some uneasiness. They were themselves apprehensive of trouble, and this feeling was increased when, soon after the interview which has just been described, Lobengula called the *Imbezu* and *Induba* regiments into Bulawayo. Jameson's personal feeling was that the chief would not use force to prevent the expedition advancing, but in this opinion he was almost alone, and it was clear that if fighting once commenced the position of these defenceless men and women with their families would be perilous in the extreme. On the other hand, he saw that any warning from him would probably cause a general exodus of Europeans, which might fan the smouldering irritation among the blacks and precipitate the very crisis he was anxious to stave off. But this risk had to be faced, and he promised to give the missionaries timely notice of the movement of the column, so as to enable them to leave Bulawayo if they desired.

For the moment there seemed to be no grounds for apprehension in Bulawayo. Renny-Tailyour had left some weeks before with fervent assurances that, as far as he was concerned, the game was up, and that his opposition to the Charter was over. At the end of May the chief accepted his subsidy without any objection, though he indulged in a good deal of abuse levelled at Jameson, Doyle and all others connected with the Company. There were still irreconcilables among his fighting men, and to calm their importunities he consented to send a letter to the High Commissioner formally protesting against the military preparations on his borders. He entrusted it to Doyle, who paid a flying visit to Capetown, where he obtained auto-graphed despatches from Sir H. Loch and Rhodes reassuring the chief as to the meaning of the troops and the intentions of the Company. Loch also wrote to Moffat, who was at

Khama's town, asking him to return with Doyle to Bulawayo, where his presence would be useful in keeping the chief's mind free from anxiety during the advance of the expedition. In Doyle's absence Major Maxwell was left in Bulawayo to represent the Charter, and unfortunately he took upon himself to issue a formal warning to all residents in Matabeleland against remaining in the country, and even arranged for a general midnight flight.   It was the very contingency against which Jameson had hoped to guard.   The movement leaked out, and, as he had anticipated, it incensed the chief and revived, both in him and the natives at large, all the old suspicions which Jameson had been at such pains to allay.   The fighting men, whose anxiety at the military preparations on the border had so far been expressed in murmurs, broke into angry reproaches when they learnt that the missionaries were preparing to escape, and loudly clamoured to be let loose against the whites.   Enraged as he was, the chief kept his head.   To appease the *amaTjaha* he made a scapegoat of Doyle, the last person whom he had interviewed as to the expedition.   " It is all Doyle ! " he exclaimed.   " He has given my words falsely to Rhodes ! " He consulted Sam Edwards, who soothed his fears, and consented to write a letter in the chief's name to the officer in command at Macloutsie, and for the time being no further step was taken, though the bitter feeling against Doyle remained.

Meanwhile the preparations on the border went on.   By the middle of June 1890 all was ready for a start, and Rhodes received the following telegram from Sir Henry Loch, the High Commissioner :

" Having carefully considered the political position, the Governor and High Commissioner considers the time has arrived to give his consent to the entry of the Company's forces into Mashonaland by the route already agreed upon —that is to say, by a route which will skirt Matabeleland proper and leave all Matabele kraals to the north and west of the expeditionary force.

" You are therefore at liberty to instruct Colonel Pennefather that as soon as he receives from Major-General

Methuen a certificate in writing that he is satisfied with
the general efficiency of the Company's forces, the Pioneer
force may advance on the authorised route, supported by
such portion of the Company's Police as may be deemed
necessary by Colonel Pennefather.

" Should the preparations of the Company's Police force
be in advance of the Pioneer force, and should circumstances
render the earliest possible advance expedient, Colonel
Pennefather may then use his discretion as to crossing the
Macloutsie in advance of the Pioneer force, but he should
not proceed far ahead; the object to be attained is the
peaceful occupation of Mashonaland, and it is desirable
that all officers should be instructed to be most careful and
prudent in the treatment of the natives with whom they
may be brought in contact, and to respect their prejudices
and susceptibilities."

By these words the Imperial Government stood committed to a definite sanction of the occupation of Mashonaland. There could now be no drawing back.

The Police had their main camp on the Macloutsie River,
which separated Khama's country from the " Disputed
Territory," and on the 15th of June the Pioneers, who had
been encamped by the Matlaputla, a small tributary stream,
were moved to Grobler's Drift. Before entering upon the
initial stage of their march—the advance to the Shashi
River—both forces underwent inspection by General the
Honourable Paul Methuen (afterwards Lord Methuen), who
remained with them until they crossed into Matabeleland.
Formal permission for a forward movement was received on
June the 24th, and the Pioneers forded the Macloutsie on
the 27th, followed by the main body of the Police, three
hundred strong, the remainder, under Sir John Willoughby,
second in command, being left at Macloutsie to follow the
column in due course as a rear-guard. Selous, with a gang
of natives lent by the Chief Khama, had cut a road as far
as the junction of the Tuli and Shashi rivers—on the
boundary of Lobengula's territory—at which point it was
proposed to establish a new base camp and to erect a fort.

At Semalali spruit, half-way between the Macloutsie and
Shashi, the column was met, on the 30th June, by Mr.

Boyle, who was accompanied by the Induna Mshete and a party of Matabele, bearing the letter written for Lobengula by Sam Edwards, which read as follows :

" Has the King killed any white men that an *impi* is collecting on his border? Or have the white men lost anything that they are looking for? "

To this letter, which appeared a moderate one, Jameson, in his capacity as Rhodes' *alter ego*, replied :

" Rhodes has no complaint against the King. These men are a working party, protected by some soldiers, and are going to Mashonaland along the road already arranged with the King, and as authorised by him at Umganin. The road passes at least a hundred miles from any of his kraals. No offence will be given to the Matabele."

Some of the natives returned with Jameson's reply, but Boyle with Mshete and a few attendants proceeded to Capetown to interview the High Commissioner, and Mr. Helm, the missionary, went with them to act as interpreter.

Just then Doyle overtook the Pioneers, on his way back to Matabeleland, having no suspicion of the odium which had accumulated against him during his absence. He passed on to Tati, and there he met one of the Indunas, who, possibly inspired by the chief, warned him that his life would be in danger if he proceeded to Bulawayo, and that he would be foolish to go on. He realised that his presence at the capital could do no good and might even provoke trouble. Colenbrander, who had acted as interpreter to Maund's Indunas, was now at Bulawayo in the Company's employ, and could be depended on to use his best influence with the chief. Accordingly, with Jameson's consent, Doyle turned his back on Matabeleland and joined the column.[1]

At the Shashi, where a fort was erected (Fort Tuli), the

---

[1] The following is a list of Europeans who were at the chief's kraal at this time : Mr. Moffat, Major Maxwell, Messrs. Colenbrander, Wilson, Chadwick and Vavasseur (a nephew of Moffat's), all of whom were supporters of the Company; Messrs. Dawson, Fairbairn and Tainton, traders; and Mr. Riley, the sole survivor of the Renny-Tailyour *junta*.

column was delayed for some little time for the arrival
of certain necessary stores. This made Jameson very
impatient, for the locality was not a healthy one, and horse-
sickness made its appearance, with fatal results in several
cases. Moreover, disquieting reports reached him from
Bulawayo about Lobengula's letter to the High Commissioner. It was stated that either Boyle or Riley had
been in possession of the Elephant seal for some hours before
its despatch. Possibly it might contain a repudiation of
the concession—the engagement of Boyle gave colour to
such an idea—and in any case it was advisable to get the
column well under weigh before the mission could reach
Capetown.

But all was at last ready, and on the 11th of July the
advance column, consisting of the Pioneers, the escort of
200 Police, and a few specially selected parties of prospectors,
forded the Shashi and began the long march towards
Mashonaland.

The story of the expedition has been graphically told by
several of those who took part in it, and nothing more
than a sketch in outline of its principal features need be
given here. There were few striking incidents. The force
had been so well provided that everything worked smoothly.
The health and morale of the men were excellent. All were
fired with the spirit of adventure. The natives they encountered were shy and scared but not unfriendly. Never did
an expedition proceed with fewer impediments. Still no
precautions were omitted. " Laager " was formed at every
halt, to guard against surprise; a search-light apparatus
was brought into use at night, and scouts and patrols were
incessantly hovering round the flanks and rear of the column.

On three occasions there were visits from bodies of
Matabele. On July the 21st and 26th small independent
parties appeared, and were interviewed and reassured.
From the second of these the Pioneers learnt that preparations were being made to overtake and stop the expedition
—intelligence which had the effect of increasing the vigilance
and bracing the resolution of the whole force. On August
the 6th occurred the solitary incident of the march. The

column had just crossed the Lundi River—an important tributary of the Sabi—when, to the astonishment of all, a mounted European was seen cantering towards the laager. It was Colenbrander, who had ridden hard with relays of horses to overtake the column and was the bearer of a letter from Lobengula containing, as he said, peremptory orders for the expedition to stop. He explained that he had been despatched eleven days before from Bulawayo together with Chadwick and a party of Matabele headmen with instructions to take the letter to Tuli camp, where it was thought that they would intercept the column.[1] On reaching the fort and finding that they were too late, the Indunas ordered Colenbrander to follow the column and deliver the letter to its Commander, but Chadwick, who was, nominally at any rate, the " King's man," they detained at Tuli. When the letter was opened by Pennefather it was found to be couched in the usual indeterminate language. It ran as follows :

" I gave permission for gold digging in the country near Samu's kraal.[2]

" From whom did the Dakatéla (Dr. Jameson) hear that the King has given leave for digging in the Mashona country ?

" Did not the Dakatéla agree at Bulawayo to dig only in such places as the King might appoint ?

" Now he wants to dig in a place, and the King will not allow it.

" Does he want to raid the King's country and dig by force ?

" The Dakatéla says the King showed the road at Umganin, but did he understand the King's words on that day ? "

It is, of course, quite possible that the news of the column having crossed the Shashi River on the 11th of July should

[1] Mr. Chadwick afterwards informed the writer that Lobengula himself knew beforehand that his messengers would miss the column at Tuli, and resorted to this artifice partly as a means of satisfying the demands of his restless young warriors, who were enraged at the presence on the border of Pennefather's force, and partly to give a chance of escape to Colenbrander and Chadwick, whose position in Bulawayo as paid servants of Rhodes was daily becoming more jeopardous. It was an instance— one of several—where Lobengula employed his natural astuteness to help his white friends out of danger.

[2] The reference is to the Ramaquabana River near Tati, where " Samu," i.e. Sam Edwards, resided.

have reached Bulawayo by the 13th, for news travels very rapidly among natives. Still there is nothing in the above sentences which appears to bear special reference to this event, although this was the construction placed on the letter at the time. Rather it seems to have been written in answer to Jameson's message from Semalali (quoted on p. 140), and therefore to have been a continuation of the correspondence commenced before the column had left Macloutsie camp. It will be noted that Lobengula carefully abstains from a direct repudiation of his promise to Jameson, and takes refuge in involved questions. Colenbrander's explanation was that he was becoming more and more embarrassed by the turbulent *ama-Tjaha*, and wrote the letter to temporise with them. This accords with his general conduct at the time. Between his anxiety to avoid an open breach with Rhodes and Jameson and the necessity of keeping in hand his excited regiments he was in an awkward dilemma. He met the difficulty by talking in a bellicose manner and doing nothing. Nearly every regiment in the country was ordered to Bulawayo for review, and paraded in full war-dress of ostrich and crested crane feathers, but to their entreaties to be allowed to attack the " white *impi* " he always responded, " Wait for my word." Towards Moffat,[1] while really friendly, he simulated hostility. On the 15th of July for the first time he refused to accept his monthly subsidy. By these and other outward acts he feigned militant intentions which he was far from entertaining in reality. That he was thus able to hold his *ama-Tjaha* in restraint must be recorded to his credit, for, with the exception of a few of the older councillors who advocated peace, he had the whole nation against him.

Jameson construed the chief's letter as an order to the column to retire, and handed it to Colonel Pennefather, who wrote back as follows :

[1] Although Moffat knew that he had nothing to fear from the chief himself, his position during this critical period was perilous in the extreme. On one occasion he was in imminent danger. Crossing the Umguza with Vavasseur and Tainton, he and his companions encountered a number of natives of the *Isiziba* regiment, who closed in on them in a threatening manner. They only got through by sheer coolness, and the slightest exhibition of fear would have cost them their lives.

" In obedience to the Queen's orders I must go on, but I will remain on the high veld, and then, if the Queen orders me back, I will go."

This reply, which appears a singularly weak one, holding out as it does the possibility of a future retirement, was taken back to Tuli and handed to the Indunas by Colenbrander, who then proceeded to Cape Colony to explain the situation to Rhodes. Before Pennefather's message could reach Bulawayo the Pioneer force had reached the high veld, and the Matabele must have realised that for that season at any rate the " white *impi* " was out of reach.

Owing to the necessity for keeping clear of Matabele kraals, the column was unable to take the more convenient and better-known route along the hunters' road which followed the watershed between the tributaries of the Zambesi, Limpopo and Sabi, and is approximately the line over which the existing railway has been constructed, but was forced to bear well away to the east through the low veld, where the streams had grown into formidable obstacles. The villages of the indigenous Mashonas passed on this part of the road were invariably perched in the most inaccessible rocks, and their inhabitants were as timid as wild animals —the natural effect of fifty years' experience of Matabele raids. Although every effort was made to assure them that no violence was intended, it was not without much persuasion that they could be induced to come nearer than shouting distance, and bring their grain, pumpkins and fowls for barter with the troops. The low veld consists largely of broken and thickly wooded country in which an attack by natives familiar with the ground would have been difficult to repel and might even have spelt disaster. Every nerve, therefore, was strained to reach the plateau of Mashonaland before the Matabele could collect their forces for a trial of strength. Actually no large body of Matabele ever came within striking distance of the column, but the scouts, upon whom fell the arduous duty of constant patrols on its left up to a distance of thirty miles, had abundant proof that *impis* were on the move during the

advance of the expedition through the low country, keeping
in touch with its every movement by means of spies, and
ready, without a doubt, to pounce upon it at the slightest
sign from Lobengula. To Selous, the guide of the Pioneers,
this part of the country was unfamiliar, but his unrivalled
veld-craft enabled him, about a month after the start, to
discover, amid the steep and apparently impenetrable hills,
a passage leading directly to the plateau a thousand feet
above, having gained which the expedition was practically
secure from molestation. The relief to all was indescribable. For weeks they had been toiling in a tropical atmosphere—sometimes cutting their way through heavily tim-
bered valleys, at others hauling their wagons by drag-ropes
across rivers infested with crocodiles and impassable for the
oxen unaided—never able to see more than a hundred
yards or so to right or left of the track, and constantly on
the *qui vive* against surprise. The last two days of laborious
ascent through the steep pass had been the most anxious
of all, for the rugged nature of the surrounding country
rendered scouting and patrol work nearly impossible and
there was no room to form an effective laager in the narrow
defile. Suddenly, on the morning of August the 13th, they
emerged on to the edge of a park-like grassy savannah,
nearly 4000 feet above sea-level, and extending in an unbroken stretch as far as the eye could reach. The strain
was at once relaxed and they felt that they were indeed on
the threshold of the promised land. To the gorge which
opened the way to Mashonaland they gave the name—long
since forgotten—" Providential Pass." At the edge of the
plain a second fort—" Victoria "—was built and a small
garrison left in charge. Here the column was overtaken
by the rear-guard, under Sir John Willoughby, consisting
of one troop of the Police (the remaining troop having been
left to garrison Fort Tuli), with a number of slaughter stock,
horses and wagons carrying supplies. These had started
from Tuli nearly three weeks after the advance column, but
as they had a cleared track to march on were able to make
more rapid progress, and covered the 200 miles through the
low veld in eighteen days. After a brief rest the column

set out again with new vigour on the 19th August on a course almost due north in the direction of Mount Hampden and Mazoe.

On September the 3rd they arrived at the head-waters of the Sabi River, and found themselves in a district which was beyond the ordinary range of Matabele raids and where the influence of the old dynastic Mashona chiefs to some extent survived. One of these—Mtigeza—had his villages close to the line of march, and it was considered wise to establish a third fort—named Charter—in this locality. Here too was a convenient starting-point for the mission to Umtasa and other chiefs who were said to rule the eastern districts of Mashonaland, and Jameson and Colquhoun, according to a pre-arranged plan, struck eastward with a small escort, leaving the main body to proceed to its objective.

On the 11th the Pioneers forded the Hanyani River and shortly afterwards arrived within sight of Mount Hampden.[1] A favourable spot having been chosen, near to a stream of running water, and on the slope of a neighbouring hill, known to the natives as Harari, a halt was called and the column formed laager for the last time. On the 12th of September, before a general parade of the little force, and to the accompaniment of a salute of guns, the Union Jack was hoisted. Prayer was offered by the Chaplain (Canon F. Balfour) and possession was formally taken of Mashonaland in the name of the Queen.[2] Then a final fort was

---

[1] We owe this curious name to Selous, who explains in his well-known work, *Travel and Adventure in South-East Africa*, that, finding that the Kaffirs knew no name for the hill, he called it " after that good Englishman, John Hampden, who struggled so manfully for, and eventually gave his life in defence of, the liberties of his countrymen in those days when the second prince of the House of Stuart reigned in England." Mr. Theodore Bent, though a fellow of the R.G.S., and usually well informed, missed the allusion. In his *Ruined Cities of Mashonaland* he says of the hill, " It has an historic interest as a landmark, *named after one of the first explorers of Mashonaland* " !

[2] Whatever the effect of this proceeding was, it certainly did not constitute " annexation," as some thought at the time, nor did it *per se* create a British Protectorate over the occupied region. The whole field of operations of the Company was, however, declared to be within the sphere of British influence and to be " under Her Majesty's Protection," by a proclamation of the High Commissioner in April of the following year, and the Protectorate was re-affirmed in several later Orders in Council.

[Photo by W. E. Fry

[To face p. 146.

A MASHONA VILLAGE IN 1890

erected and, in accordance with time-honoured custom, labelled after the Prime Minister of the day—" Salisbury." It is perhaps a matter for regret that no distinctive native name was available, as in the case of Bulawayo.

Nominally, at any rate, the occupation was now an accomplished fact. The achievement, though unaccompanied by any sensational incident, was a notable one, and formed a fitting prelude to the more stirring episodes which were shortly to follow. Carried out without the loss of a single life—without even a serious casualty—the expedition reflected the greatest credit upon all ranks of the Chartered Company's force and upon every person connected with its organisation.

The members of the column proved worthy of their choice. With hardly an exception they settled in the new territory, and though their numbers have been sadly reduced by later wars and the inevitable misfortunes of frontier life, the survivors still cherish the title of " Pioneer " with just pride, while the Occupation remains an outstanding epoch from which, like the Hegira in the Moslem calendar, all events in Rhodesia have since been reckoned.

According to the finding of the Judicial Committee of the Privy Council twenty-eight years later, the administration of the Chartered Company, prior to the conquest of the Matabele, rested on the assumption of jurisdiction by the Crown within the territorial sovereignty of a native ruler who remained the source from which it was ultimately derived. Even after the destruction of Lobengula's power by the Company's forces, and his death as a fugitive in 1894, the fiction of a Protectorate was maintained and no portion of Rhodesia was ever annexed or became an integral part of the British sovereign's Dominions during the Company's administration. It consequently became necessary, before granting self-government to Southern Rhodesia, formally to annex the territory by Order in Council. The anomalous status of the territory during the Chartered régime appears the more remarkable when it is remembered that the Judicial Committee held that in spite of its failure to annex, the Crown must be presumed to have taken to itself, after the conquest of the Matabele, the ownership and the right to dispose of the land.

In connection with the events described in this chapter the following authorities have been consulted :

Blue Book C. 5918.
Published reports of the British South Africa Company.
Travel and Adventure in South-East Africa, by F. C. Selous.

Use has also been made of Journals kept by the author at Kimberley in 1890, and information supplied to him by various members of the Pioneer expedition.

CHAPTER XI

THE OCCUPATION OF MANICA

No fixed boundaries having been assigned by the Charter to the Company's sphere of operations, it was inevitable that its agents should, sooner or later, find themselves in conflict with the Portuguese at those points where the latter's claims to sovereignty were not supported by *bona fide* occupation. For more than three centuries the Portuguese had enjoyed facilities for establishing real colonies in East Africa, and had failed to utilise them. The history of their arrival on the coast, of their intercourse with the peoples they found there, and of their efforts—vigorous at the outset, weakening as time went on—to gain a foothold in the regions further inland have been described by a long series of writers, commencing with João de Barros and ending with Livingstone, but one may be permitted here to recall a few salient facts to assist in explaining the relations which now arose between them and their new neighbours.

Portugal is indisputably entitled to the credit of being the first European Power to effect a settlement on the African shores of the Mozambique Channel. Prior to the sixteenth century a brisk trade in native produce was carried on there by Arabs from Aden, Muscat and the Persian Gulf, who not only built depots on the coast as far south as Sofala, but instituted caravan routes into the interior.

The Arab coast trade was gradually attacked during the early part of that century by successive expeditions under Francisco d'Almeida, Pedro d'Anhaya and Tristan da Cunha, until, by 1520, the control of the littoral from Guardafui to Lourenzo Marques had passed into the hands of the Portuguese. There is no evidence that the new-comers attempted at this time to push their influence inland, and although contemporary maps show lakes and a river, corresponding

roughly with Lakes Nyasa and Tanganyika and the River
Zambesi, it is probable that these features were inserted on
the hearsay reports of Arabs or native traders, and not from
actual observation.   For forty years they remained content
with their trade on the coast, but in 1560 Gonzalvo da
Silveira, a Christian missionary, made a journey to Monomotapa,[1] where he was assassinated, and during the next few
years two expeditions were directed towards Tete and
Manica, where reports of rich silver and gold mines had
attracted the cupidity of the settlers.   The first, under
Francisco Barreto, ascended the Zambesi as far as Sena,
from whence it pushed in the direction of the Mazoe River
with the object of seizing the mines in the Kalanga country
(Monomotapa), and the second, led by Vasco Fernandes
Homem, actually reached the gold diggings of Manica and
beheld the natives at work with their primitive processes for
extracting the precious metal.   Both enterprises, however,
had to be abandoned owing to the treachery of the natives,
and no real hold was gained over the interior.   Towards the
end of the sixteenth century, the troubles with Spain arose,
and no leaders could be spared for further adventures in
Africa.   Thenceforth the Portuguese, although they claimed
sovereignty over Monomotapa, contented themselves with
their seaports and the navigation of the Zambesi, from which
they could carry on their trade for gold with the indigenous
natives from inland.   They built forts and established farms
at Sena and Tete; a few of the bolder traders may have set
up stations even within the kingdom of Monomotapa, but
no effort at government was made and no official occupation
ever again attempted.   Upon the abolition of the slave-trade
the commerce of East Africa dwindled to insignificance.
Politicians in Lisbon would take no interest in distant
settlements producing no revenue; the settlers themselves
had lost their energy through long association with the
natives, and none seemed able to discern the possibility of
wealth behind the barren coast-line.   Exceptions there were,
of course—men such as Paiva d'Andrade and Serpa Pinto,
whose pulses still throbbed with the old fire, and who strove

[1] See footnote to p. 55.

to infuse some enthusiasm into the Government at home and into their fellow-colonists in Africa, but the nation which had produced Henry the Navigator, Vasco da Gama and Barto-lemeo Diaz was sick; the Treasury was empty; the colonists of the fever-stricken coast towns were not of the *sang pur*, but a debased brood, tainted too often with negro blood, and lethargic from long inactivity.

On their maps the region claimed in 1890 as Portuguese stretched from about the eleventh to the twenty-seventh parallel of South Latitude, and covered the little-known districts east and west of Lake Nyasa, the whole of the Zambesi basin, and the country to the south as far as Lobengula's kingdom. Originally Mashonaland and even Matabeleland were also included, while to the north of the Zambesi it was boldly asserted that from Mozambique to Angola all belonged to Portugal, but latterly her most sanguine champions had realised—not without some plain speaking on the part of Lord Salisbury—the futility of pretending to a dominion over territories where no vestige of occupation was visible, and so the claim to Lobengula's country was abandoned, and all efforts concentrated on saving the remainder.

Seen from the Indian Ocean the coast of this part of Africa presents an unattractive prospect. For hundreds of miles the monotonous banks of sand are only relieved from utter barrenness by mangrove swamps reaching, with gnarled root-coils, to the water's edge. Here and there one may see a clump of sad palms, many of them lopped of foliage—mere poles, surmounted by calabashes to catch the juice exuding from their gaunt and decapitated trunks. Inland, the sand-dunes and swamps gradually give place to scorched plains of grass, broken by dense jungle in the neighbourhood of the rivers, and by mimosas and palm-groves in the drier parts. In these expanses lions and antelopes to this day roam unmolested. The rivers are tenanted by hippopotami; their slimy banks are the haunt of crocodiles and myriads of tropical wild-fowl. During the annual rains they over-flow the adjacent country for many miles, and leave a deposit of rich alluvial mud. The Rovuma, the Pungwe, the Sabi and the Limpopo rivers, but chief of all the Zambesi, are ceaselessly washing down quantities of fine silt, forming sand-banks, which shift and alter the course of the stream, and at their estuaries grow into formidable bars—a great hindrance to navigation.

At a distance of from two to three hundred miles from the sea the character of the landscape again changes. Forest trees become frequent; the grassy plains give place to more broken country with brisk streams; and there is a rise— sometimes gradual, oftener abrupt—until eventually a plateau is reached, varying from 3000 feet above sea-level in Manica, to 7000 feet or more at the south end of Lake Nyasa. The marginal ridge is a continuation of the Drakens-berg or Quathlamba range of South Africa : it may be traced along the borders of the great lakes Nyasa and Tanganyika to Mounts Kilimanjaro and Kenia in the north, and is pierced only by the Zambesi, the Sabi and the Limpopo rivers. Beyond the ridge, north and south of the Zambesi, lie the open champaigns of Nyasaland and Mashonaland—well-watered, well-timbered and temperate. So admirably adapted are these tracts for European settlement that one fails to understand why, during three centuries, no deter-mined effort was made to wrest them from their aboriginal occupants. But Portugal, prolific as she was in navigators, could not produce a Cortez or a Pizarro.

The character of the black population varies with the land. On the plateau we find hardy, vigorous tribes; in the low country, towards the sea-board, the enervating heat and luxuriant vegetation have bred a sluggish race. Here, where cereals grow almost without cultivation, and game of all kinds is abundant, there is little incentive to work. At the time of which I am writing the native tribes were steeped in indolent langour, and the sparse Portuguese settlers were fast sinking to the same level. Degeneration was aided by inter-breeding. Few European women could withstand the debilitating climate, and a bastard race had been evolved, combining the worst qualities of both parents. Two prin-cipal ports—Mozambique and Lourenzo Marques—and four lesser ones—Ibo, Quilimane, Sofala and Inhambane—were all that betrayed the vaunted colonisation, and at these a sleepy trade was carried on in quill-gold, ivory, and other interior produce by Bunniahs and Goanese half-castes, listlessly supervised by a few underpaid and half-hearted officials and soldiers from Lisbon. Had no pressure from outside forces been applied the process of deterioration would have continued, but the time was approaching when the torpor of centuries was to be rudely disturbed.

Reduced to its actual merits, the issue between the Chartered Company and the Portuguese resolved itself into the question whether it was preferable for East Africa to be seized by live settlers, with the capacity and intention of developing its commercial resources, or to remain the unimproved property of an exhausted nation, lacking both the means and the inclination to raise it out of its primeval barbarism. But international questions cannot always be decided on their merits. Portugal did undoubtedly possess claims in East Africa, and, however desirable it might be, in the general interests, for those claims to be brushed aside, the comity of nations demanded that they should be respected so far as they could be substantiated by facts. Had the local Portuguese been the only obstacles in his path, Rhodes would have speedily possessed the whole coast from the Zambesi to Lourenzo Marques. At two points—in Manica and in Gazaland—he made determined efforts to drive British civilisation seawards; and that he partially failed was due, not to lack of enterprise, but to the exigencies of European diplomacy, which cannot be disregarded nowadays, as they might perhaps have been in the sixteenth century.

The province known for centuries as Manica, including the district which, in 1890, belonged to the Chief Umtasa, was originally a portion of the great empire of Monomotapa. From earliest times it was famous for its gold mines, and allusion has already been made to the attempts made by Portuguese adventurers in the sixteenth century to wrest it from the dominion of the so-called " Emperor " of Monomotapa. Notwithstanding the ill-success of these expeditions, the Portuguese continued to lay claim, not only to Manica, but to the whole of the ancient empire, which, according to their accounts, extended westwards as far as the Umniati River and included all Mashonaland. In support of this contention they produced a " deed of cession " which had been executed, so it was said, by the ruler of Monomotapa in 1630, when one Dom Nuno Alvarez Pereira was Governor of Mozambique. They also pointed to evidence of their occupation in the shape of ruined forts, plantations of lemon-trees, and other *vestigia* of civilisation in various parts of the country.

Where this legendary title was overlapped by Lobengula's concession it was treated with very scant respect by the British Foreign Office. It would be tedious to recapitulate the correspondence exchanged between the two Governments on this point. Suffice it to say that, in spite of the impassioned protests of the Portuguese, Lord Salisbury refused to recognise their claims. So far, therefore, as Lobengula's authority extended the Chartered Company had nothing to fear. Two questions however remained to be dealt with : (1) What was the eastern limit of Lobengula's dominion, and (2) was there a reasonable prospect of securing any rights beyond this limit ? As regards the first, careful inquiries made by Colquhoun, from native chiefs and others, convinced him that no Matabele raiding parties had ever crossed the Sabi River, the course of which ran close to the intersection of Longitude 32° East with Latitude 18° South. West of that river might be considered to belong to Lobengula. East of it certainly did not, and, unfortunately, the whole of Manica lay to the east of the Sabi, Umtasa's kraal, the new focus of interest, being distant from it about forty or fifty miles.

Now besides pointing to their ancient rights of discovery the Portuguese, for the last few years, had been making hasty efforts to substantiate their title by effecting some semblance of occupation of the various territories of East Africa to comply with the principles of the Berlin Conference. The prime mover in these attempts was that gallant and indefatigable officer, Colonel Paiva d'Andrade, who, as far back as 1878, had obtained from his Government a concession to develop the gold mines of Manica, and more recently had been engaged in endeavouring to establish Portuguese influence along the Mazoe River and other southern tributaries of the Zambesi. We have already seen the anxiety which these movements on his north-eastern borders had occasioned to Lobengula, and it has been shown how they were instrumental in precipitating the granting of the Rudd Concession.

d'Andrade also succeeded in floating two companies for gold-mining in Manica, and eventually their interests were absorbed by a larger corporation—the Mozambique Company—which undertook the commercial exploitation, under Government, of a large extent of country, including the tract ruled by Umtasa. Areas were granted to individual speculators—generally Goanese and other half-castes—who, in return for a fixed contribution to the Treasury, were authorised to squeeze what revenue they could from the unhappy natives. It may be really understood that the leasing of the *Prazos de Coroa* (Crown estates)—as these were called—to persons of such a character opened the way for flagrant oppression and extortion. One of the most powerful, and, it must be admitted, capable, of the Prazo-holders was a Goanese named Manuel Antonio de Souza, whose head-quarters were at Gouveia in the Gorongoza province immediately north-east of Manica, and whose name was held in detestation and fear from Tete to the Sabi. By sheer strength of character this man had attracted to himself a force of several thousands of desperadoes—some pure negroes, others of mixed blood—with whose assistance he terrorised the natives over a wide extent of country. He possessed a harem recruited from the young girls of the native kraals; he monopolised the trade of the Gorongoza and Barue districts; he raided and plundered all chiefs who showed the least sign of resistance to him, and carried on every species of villainy—not excepting slavery—without interference from the Government or from the Mozambique Company. The former indeed found him a valuable "colonising agent," and, in return for his services in coercing various native chiefs into accepting the Portuguese flag, had appointed him *Capitão-Mór* (Commandant-General, or

Military Governor) of Barue, with the rank of Colonel in the national army.

The *Prazo* system had not, in 1890, actually touched Umtasa. In point of fact the Portuguese, looking on him as a feudatory chief under Gungunyana, chief of Gazaland (whom they regarded as a vassal of the Crown), had never troubled to go through the formality of conquering or annexing his territory.[1] Their assumption of dominion over Gungunyana was, however, based on very flimsy foundations, as will be seen from what follows.

Whatever title to Gazaland the Portuguese may have originally obtained from its discovery by Vasco da Gama was cancelled in the early part of the nineteenth century by the incursion of natives from Zululand. The nucleus of the tribe which now occupies Gazaland was a small party of Zulus, the adherents of one So-shangane,[2] who, like Mziligazi, and about the same time, broke away from the parent tribe and formed a new nation. So-shangane migrated in a north-easterly direction, and after pursuing the usual Zulu programme of devastation against the weaker natives along his line of march, eventually settled near the Sabi River, and between the mouths of the Limpopo and Zambesi. For a time he was accompanied by u-Zwangendaba, another Zulu freebooter, but the two leaders soon quarrelled, and the latter was forced to go still further north, and crossed the Zambesi into Nyasaland, where he founded the aba-Nguni (Angoni) tribe. So-shangane settled down and took the name of Manukuza, while his people became known as the aba-Gaza or ama-Shangana. They fared better than the Matabele, for instead of having to face a hardy and virile race like the Boers, they only found a few weak Portuguese in drowsy occupation of the coast settlements. These could

---

[1] This is the only inference that can be drawn from their neglect to exercise any direct supervision over Umtasa. On the other hand, it was afterwards averred by the Marquis de Soveral that Umtasa had in 1876 made a " renewal " of voluntary submission to Manuel Antonio de Souza, and offered his forces for assisting in a war against another local chief, and that in return for this submission he was made " Sergeant-Major of Manica." The Portuguese claims to Manica depend on so many conflicting statements that it is difficult to ascertain the exact truth. Their main contention was that Umtasa was the vassal of the Gaza chief."

[1] Also known as Manukuza. See p. 32, footnote.

make no stand against the Zulu *impis*. Massacres took place in rapid succession at Spirito Santo (near Lourenzo Marques), Inhambane and Sofala, and the Portuguese were glad to come to terms with the savage blacks, and to leave them in undisturbed possession of the whole of the interior.

Upon So-shangane's death in 1858 his son Maweva succeeded, and continued to harass the Portuguese, but another son, Umzila, who had been banished for some act of insubordination, offered to crush Maweva if the Europeans at Spirito Santo would help him with fire-arms, and, the offer being accepted, he usurped the sovereignty in 1861. At this time, in order to secure their help, he professed great friendship for the Portuguese, but neither over him, nor over his son Gungunyana, did they try to assert any dominion. They had been too severely handled in their encounters with the first invader, So-shangane.

The weaker Bantu tribes—ama-Tonga, for the most part —were one by one exterminated by the Gaza chief, their cattle confiscated, and their women and young boys incorporated into the Zulu stock, which rapidly became rich and prosperous. The Portuguese they suffered to remain at their coast towns, not because they were afraid of them, for Gungunyana could muster a considerable body of warriors, with which the Portuguese colonial troops were wholly inadequate to cope, but because they had acquired a taste for strong drink. The white men could gratify this craving, and found it easier and more profitable to retain their influence by trading rum than by resorting to any show of force.

It was constantly maintained, however, by the Lisbon Government that the Gaza chiefs had surrendered their rights, and two documents [1] were ultimately produced upon which this contention was based :

1. A treaty with Umzila, dated the 2nd of December, 1861, whereby the chief agreed to remain a " tributary chieftain and subject of the Portuguese Crown," obeying all orders from the Government of Lourenzo Marques.

2. An act of vassalage executed at Lisbon by two delegates from Gungunyana, on the 12th of October, 1885, in

[1] For the text of these see *Blue Book* C. 6495, pp. 64—66.

which the chief swore obedience to the King of Portugal, and undertook to exclude the dominion of every other nation.

The first of these may be dismissed at once. It was signed by four Portuguese gentlemen in the Government quarters of Lourenzo Marques, and contains no mark or signature by Umzila or any other native. Moreover, it was tacitly admitted as of no effect by the subsequent action of the authorities in endeavouring in 1885 to come to terms with Umzila's son and successor.

The second document is a lengthy affair of sixteen clauses, one of which provides for the establishment of a Portuguese Resident at the royal kraal, and of subordinate officials in different parts of the country, while another promotes Gungunyana to be a Colonel of the 2nd Line ! But the authority of this deed, like the other, is impugned by the fact that it does not even profess to have been seen by Gungunyana. It was executed in the Naval and Ultramarine office at Lisbon by several Portuguese officers—one of whom is described as Special Envoy of the chief—and by two natives —stated to be subjects of Gungunyana—but there is nothing to substantiate the authority of the envoy, nor to show that the chief himself ratified or indeed had any cognisance of the document.[1] We cannot, of course, exclude the possibility of some act of vassalage having been extorted by the Portuguese during one of the chief's periods of intoxication, but it is significant that he afterwards expressly denied knowledge of any such submission.

This was the situation when an attempt was made by the representatives of Great Britain and Portugal to settle their respective boundaries in East Africa by means of a Convention. The negotiations were not directly induced by any disturbing incident in Manica or Gazaland, for none had then taken place. They were due to a series of differences which had arisen further north—in Nyasaland—where a number of small collisions had occurred between explorers

---

[1] All these points were fully set out by Lord Salisbury when the two documents were flourished at his head in support of the Portuguese claims, and it is rather surprising to reflect that shortly afterwards he retreated from his first position, and surrendered Gazaland to Portugal in face of urgent protestations from the chief himself.

and traders of the two races, and a somewhat acute crisis had supervened. The necessity of laying down a hard-and-fast line in Nyasaland suggested a general settlement of the boundary throughout East Africa, all the more so because the British South Africa Company was engaged in occupying territories adjacent to those of the Portuguese.

The negotiations between the two Foreign Offices progressed more rapidly than Rhodes had bargained for. He had arranged that Colquhoun should leave the Pioneer column as soon as it reached the Mashonaland plateau, and proceed with all despatch to Manica, with the object of securing treaties or concessions from Umtasa and any other independent chiefs he might find outside Lobengula's borders, and he had also sent Dr. Aurel Schulz to Gungunyana's kraal on a similar errand, in the hope of obtaining a concession over Gazaland. But Colquhoun could hardly reach Umtasa's before the end of August, while Schulz only arrived in Gazaland in July, and had barely had time to make his position secure with the chief. It was a serious blow, therefore, to Rhodes to find at this moment that both Manica and Gazaland were in imminent danger of being handed over to Portugal before he could strike a blow to save them.

A Convention was actually signed by Lord Salisbury and Senhor Barjona de Freitas (the Portuguese Minister in London) on the 20th of August, 1890,[1] and only required ratification by the two Governments to become final. Under it the whole of Manica and Gazaland fell within Portuguese East Africa, the Sabi River being fixed as the easternmost limit of the British sphere. It appeared as if nothing could prevent the future of these two provinces being irrevocably settled, when, to Rhodes' immense relief, an unexpected respite occurred. The terms of the Convention were published in the Lisbon papers of the 21st of August, and were at once violently assailed by the whole of the Republican and Progressist Press as an act of spoliation. The opposition was renewed in the Cortes and culminated in the resignation of the Ministry. The final ratifications were never exchanged, and the British Government refused to remain

[1] For the text of the Convention see *Blue Book* C. 6212.

bound by the agreement.[1] The door which had so nearly closed was once more opened a little way for Colquhoun and Schulz.

The information which Colquhoun himself had received up to the middle of August led him to believe that the Convention had been signed, and that the boundary line between British and Portuguese territory had been fixed at the 33rd degree of longitude.[1] The immediate necessity, therefore, which presented itself to him was to fill in the hiatus between the Sabi River—the assumed limit of Lobengula's dominion—and the 33rd degree of longitude, by securing concessions from any chiefs who asserted their independence, and so clinching the British title.

The position taken up by Rhodes was characteristically different. In the first place he dismissed the idea that Umtasa was a subject chief, and held that he was a Paramount, independent of Portugal and independent of Gungunyana. He knew that everything possible had been done by the Directors of the Company and by himself to attain a more easterly boundary line by means of the Convention, but now he saw a possibility of the Convention being rejected by the very people to whom it was so favourable, and he opined that if rejection came about the Charter would be supported by the British Government in retaining whatever rights and concessions it had in the meantime obtained east

[1] It was afterwards arranged between the contracting Powers to adopt a *modus vivendi* regarding their respective spheres, which, while giving free transit over the Zambesi and Pungwe Rivers, should debar either Power from making treaties, accepting protectorates, or exercising any acts of sovereignty within the limits laid down in the abortive Convention, but this understanding was not arrived at till the 14th November, 1890. The months between August and November meant everything to Rhodes, and were destined to be pregnant with events in Manica and Gazaland. The text of the *modus vivendi* is given in *Blue Book* C. 6212.

[1] Rhodes seems to have fallen into the same error. Article 2 of the Convention described the line as starting from a point opposite the western extremity of the ten-mile radius of Zumbo; thence running due south to latitude 16°; thence following the 16th degree to its intersection with longitude 31° E.; thence eastward to the point where the Mazoe River crosses longitude 33° E.; thence due south along that line *to its intersection with latitude 18° 30'; thence westward to the River Masheke; thence down the Masheke and afterwards down the channel of the Sabi River to its confluence with the Lunti River;* and thence to the north-east point of the frontier of the Transvaal. This would have given the Portuguese the whole of the Rhodesian districts of Melsetter and Umtali and the southern half of the district of Makoni.

of Mashonaland, *even if they extended down to the coast.* He therefore urged Colquhoun to pursue a firm and bold policy in Manica, and as soon as he knew definitely that the Convention had been abandoned he instructed him to recognise no boundary-line whatever. At the same time he begged Jameson to make his way to the coast and find out by personal investigation what the Portuguese occupation amounted to.

On September the 3rd, the Pioneers having reached the head-waters of the Sabi River, where their third fort was to be built, Colquhoun left the column and started for Manica. He was accompanied at the outset by Jameson, Selous and a slender escort of seven mounted men. The little party took a south-easterly course through an undulating and well-wooded country with occasional open glades of grass, and numerous clear streams of running water. Fields of rice, millet and ground-nuts gave evidence of a dense population, and indeed the natives themselves flocked in large numbers to stare at the unusual spectacle of a body of white men picking their way across the veld. Some of them were bewildered at the horses. Never having seen mounted men before, they regarded steed and rider as one strange animal until the illusion was broken by a trooper dismounting. Native products—pumpkins, maize, fowls and sweet potatoes—were brought in for barter in abundance, and exchanged for strips of calico—coined money being also unknown to them. At two or three of the principal kraals on the line of march Colquhoun palavered with the chiefs, informed them of the occupation of Mashonaland, and reassured them as to its object. On all these occasions he was greeted in a friendly and even enthusiastic manner. An unfortunate accident on the third day prevented Jameson from accompanying the party into Manica. His horse stumbled and threw him heavily, breaking three of his ribs, and he was obliged to make a painful journey back to the Pioneer column.

Crossing the Sabi, and later its tributaries the Macheke and Odzi, the travellers halted on the tenth day close to Umtasa's main village. The kraal itself they found at the

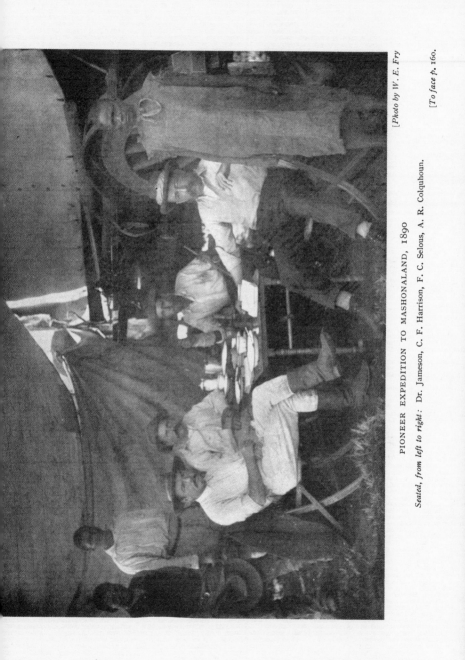

PIONEER EXPEDITION TO MASHONALAND, 1890

Seated, from left to right: Dr. Jameson, C. F. Harrison, F. C. Selous, A. R. Colquhoun.

[To face p. 160.

head of a pass in the mountains, concealed from below in inaccessible fastnesses, and overshadowed by a sheer and massive wall of granite, towering five hundred feet or more above it—an admirably chosen position, and impregnable, at any rate to native enemies. After a while the chief, who had been apprised of their arrival, came to visit them in state.

Colquhoun, in his autobiography,[1] gives an amusing description of this interview. " It must be confessed," he writes, " that the appearance and presence of the hereditary and reigning monarch of the ancient kingdom of Manica were not quite what one would desire to see in so great a ruler. No doubt the utmost resources of his wardrobe had been taxed and brought into requisition. . . . He appeared attired in a naval cocked hat, a tunic (evidently of Portuguese origin but of ancient date, and forming perhaps some of the ancient remains, to which the attention of the world had been so pathetically drawn), a leopard skin slung over his back, the whole toilet being completed by a pair of trousers that had passed through many hands, or, rather, covered many legs, before assisting to complete the court uniform of the ' Roitelet Matassa,' as the Portuguese termed him. He was preceded by his court jester, who danced round him, uttering strange cries and ejaculations, and singing his praises (in which Umtasa cordially joined) as ' the lion or leopard who walks by night and before whose name the Portuguese tremble.' The retinue was completed by a few girls carrying calabashes of Kaffir beer, and by a crowd of Indunas (or councillors) and other loyal subjects."

Umtasa was in no sense a great despot like Lobengula, and was held in very low esteem by the Portuguese, who gave him only the honorary rank of Sergeant-Major, whereas Gungunyana, as we know, had been made a Colonel of the line. In his own estimation, nevertheless, he was a Paramount Chief, and owned allegiance to no man. He assumed the grandiose style of *Mufamba Bosuko*—" the one who walks at night-time "—but for all that he was ready to grovel by daylight before anyone who made a show of strength. He would doubtless have granted a concession to the Portu-

[1] *Dan to Beersheba*, by A. R. Colquhoun, 1908.

guese had he been threatened by them, but they regarded him as a vassal of the Gaza king and would have weakened their own case by recognising his right to take such an independent step. There is ground for believing that he did make some sort of grant (which had, however, been allowed to lapse) to a Mr. Reuben Beningfield, of Natal, and it is probable that he could have been cajoled or bullied into signing any paper that was put before him. At the time of Colquhoun's visit he had learnt of the advance of the Pioneers, whose numbers were, of course, magnified by native rumour, and he knew that they were within a few days' march of his town. The Portuguese of the coast had not caused him serious anxiety. There was one who was of far greater influence—Manuel, the great " Capitão-Mór " of Gouveia, though at the moment he was not near enough to occasion Umtasa any apprehension. But the British expedition was a real and imminent threat, and Umtasa thought it judicious to hasten to pay homage to the " White Chief," and, with a cordiality which was probably assumed, agreed to discuss a treaty at his own kraal on the following day.

On the 14th of September, therefore, Colquhoun, accompanied by Selous and an interpreter, with two other members of his staff, proceeded to the kraal and engaged in a long interview. The occupation of Mashonaland and its objects were fully explained to the chief and his Council of Indunas, who had been greatly impressed by what they had heard of the magnitude and importance of the expedition. Interrogated as to whether he had come to terms with any other party, Umtasa vowed that he had signed no treaty, that he had granted no concession to the Portuguese, nor, with one exception (a verbal permission to Beningfield to dig for gold), to any private individual, and that he was wholly independent of Gungunyana. Without any of the hesitation which had been evinced by Lobengula on a similar occasion, with an alacrity, indeed, which was almost suspicious, he agreed to a concession in the form which Colquhoun, with some forethought, had already drawn up, and signed it there and then with two of his councillors as witnesses. The document was more carefully worded and comprehensive than the Rudd Concession, and, besides giving the fullest mining and commercial rights to the Company, bound the chief explicitly to grant no concession of land to other parties. The Company undertook to assist in the propagation of Christianity and in the education of the natives. There was also a clause stating that the covenant was to be considered " in the light of a treaty or alliance made between the Manica nation and the Government of Queen Victoria."

Colquhoun at once set to work to ascertain the amount of territory covered by his concession. He was disappointed to find that, owing to the defection of certain chiefs formerly owning Umtasa as their overlord, Manica proper had shrunk to somewhat jejune proportions; in fact he was unable to prove Umtasa's sovereignty beyond Maçequeçe—thirty miles to the east—while between that point and the sea were a number of petty chiefs, with each of whom it would be necessary to deal if British claims were to be pushed to the coast. Some officials of the Mozambique Company were known to be established at Maçequeçe itself, and several English, French and American prospectors were said to be at work in the vicinity, under rights purporting to be granted by them. After visiting the Umtali valley, where he found three or four of these,[1] he despatched Selous with a small party to Maçequeçe, where for the first time the agents of the British and Portuguese Companies met face to face.

The Baron João de Rezende, " Intendente of Native Affairs," and representative of the Mozambique Company, received Selous and his companions with chilly politeness, and at once informed them that they were trespassers. He had heard of the doings at Umtasa's kraal. He had, in fact, just despatched a letter to Colquhoun, protesting against his intrusion, with an armed force, into a district which had long been the cherished possession of the Crown of Portugal. He alleged that the treaty had been wrung from the chief

---

[1] Mr. E. de Kergariou (a native of Jersey) and Mr. Moodie were mining on the Umtali river; Mr. Jeffrey was at work on the same river a little higher up, and on the ridge between the Umtali and Revue were MM. de Llamby and Mencan (French). Messrs. Crampton and Harrison (English) had an encampment at Maçequeçe and were prospecting in the neighbourhood.

by threats, and that the presence of " an enormous force of cavalry " at the source of the Sabi had overawed him into submission. Selous was not disposed to argue this question with him, and returned. The letter of protest reached Colquhoun on the same day, being handed to him by two Portuguese gentlemen and two natives who were described as envoys of the Chief Umtasa. He replied by denying the threats and stating that he had acted under instructions from the British South Africa Company.

The two natives had certainly been sent by Umtasa, who had apparently been overtaken by some qualms as to the wisdom of his action in coming so hastily to terms with the British expedition. In this, and in many subsequent events, he came out in his true character as a trimmer—anxious to conciliate every party of whom he had any cause to be afraid, and quite capable of breaking any promises if they seemed likely to get him into trouble. Now on being taxed with sending messengers to Maçequeçe and with the imminent prospect in front of him of a visit from Rezende, he implored Colquhoun not to desert him.

But important duties were calling Colquhoun back to Mashonaland. The column had reached its goal, Mount Hampden, and the presence of the Administrator was necessary at the new head-quarters. He left, however, one of his escort—Mr. Trevor, a good native linguist—at Umtasa's, and engaged that a Police detachment, as stipulated in the concession, should be sent down as soon as possible, with the balance of the subsidy promised on behalf of the Company. With this Umtasa, who was in reality horribly nervous of being left alone now that he had for once taken a decisive step, professed himself satisfied, and Colquhoun, after instructing Trevor to watch carefully the course of events, and to report at once should any attempt at intimidation be made by the Portuguese, left for Mount Hampden to rejoin the column of occupation. He intended on his way back to visit and establish friendly relations with a number of petty chiefs between the Sabi and Odzi Rivers, who had never been raided by Lobengula and regarded themselves as independent. He had at first thought that to make formal treaties with these would have been a confession of weakness, but on learning that they had already been visited with similar intentions by Portuguese emissaries, who had even gone west of the Sabi to Mashona chiefs, such as Mtigeza and Gutu, he saw that it was imperative to checkmate them, and accordingly he concluded treaties with all chiefs whose status in regard to Lobengula was at all uncertain.

The next step was to press home his success in Manica by effective occupation. Police had been promised to Umtasa, but a peaceful occupation by prospectors might be more convincing and satisfactory than the mere presence of a military force. Colquhoun made arrangements for both. Lieut. M. D. Graham,[1] with four men of the B.S.A. Company's Police, was sent to Umtasa's kraal at once as an advance party, and finding, on his arrival at Fort Salisbury, that Lieut.-Colonel Pennefather had left for the south, Colquhoun decided to send a small detachment under the next senior officer—Captain Patrick W. Forbes—who was instructed to occupy as much territory as possible under the concession, and to endeavour to secure further concessions eastward towards Pungwe Bay. If Paiva d'Andrade threatened Umtasa with an armed force, Forbes was to request him to withdraw from Manica : if force was actually employed, he was authorised to effect a military occupation of Maçequeçe. The Police detachment was to be followed by a body of prospectors, who would be the pioneers of a permanent settlement.

Forbes reached Umtasa's on the 5th of November, 1890. He learnt that d'Andrade was at Maçequeçe with an armed force of two or three hundred men, and, deeming that his presence there with such a following betokened an intention to take reprisals on Umtasa for his action in granting the concession, sent Lieut. Graham with a letter requesting him to withdraw. Failing immediate compliance with this request, Forbes stated (in the vague phraseology customary in such cases) his intention of taking whatever steps he considered necessary for the protection of the chiefs and their territory from Portuguese interference. He was

[1] Now Col. M. D. Graham, C.B., C.M.G., etc.

scarcely in a position to carry out this threat. He could not count on any support from Umtasa, who was in a state of abject terror now that the Portuguese were showing their teeth, and, including Graham's detachment, the forces at his disposal amounted to eleven men all told; but he had sent an urgent message to Fort Salisbury for assistance, and hoped that reinforcements would arrive before any decisive action was forced upon him. At Maçequeçe Graham found not only d'Andrade, but also the black general, Manuel Antonio de Souza, with an escort of over two hundred natives, described by the Portuguese as *machileiros* (litter-carriers), but armed for the most part with rifles and sword-bayonets. The Baron de Rezende, and two or three clerks of the Mozambique Company, completed the sum total of the Portuguese population, but Manuel was accompanied by a Goanese woman and several native girls—a convincing proof, as was afterwards urged, of the pacific nature of his movements.

d'Andrade treated Forbes' letter with contempt, and refused to write a reply. He appeared to regard the proceedings of the British South Africa Company in Manica as a piece of mad folly. He repeated the old argument about Umtasa being a vassal of Gungunyana, and added that ten years back the chief had personally sent an elephant's tusk full of earth to Manuel in token of submission. All the officers spoke very impressively to Graham regarding the Portuguese colonisation. Rezende stated that preparations were being made to construct a railway from the coast, and Graham gathered that every effort was being made to create a vraisemblance of occupation. d'Andrade warned him that if the Chartered Company persisted in remaining he would summon Lobengula from the west and Gungunyana from the south, while Manuel—to whose standard 20,000 men would rally in a week—would come down from the north, to hem the Pioneers in and cut off their retreat, at all of which Graham merely bowed, and, having taken careful note of all that could be seen, returned to Forbes' camp two or three miles from Umtasa's.

On the following day Manuel with about seventy of his

black soldiers entered Umtasa's village, and hoisted the Portuguese flag in front of the chief's hut. Trevor, the Police trooper left by Colquhoun, reported this to Forbes, who at once sent Graham to repeat to Manuel the warning which he had already sent to d'Andrade. The Goanese evinced great indignation. He had come to see Umtasa, who was his friend, and when he had finished his business he was proceeding to Mangwendi's kraal further west, and he would like to see the Englishman who was going to stop him !

On November the 11th Denis Doyle, who had been sent by Colquhoun to represent the Civil Administration in Manica, and to assist Forbes as adviser on native affairs, reached the camp, and brought the welcome news that twenty-five men of the Police under Lieut. the Hon. E. Fiennes [1] were on the road, and might be expected in three or four days. It was agreed that nothing could be done until their arrival, but Doyle visited the kraal, interviewed the unhappy chief, who was now between Scylla and Charybdis, and infused a little courage into him. Umtasa even undertook to hold a meeting, at which the English should attend, when he would announce to Manuel definitely that he wished the Company's men to remain in his country. On the 13th Forbes sent messengers to meet the approaching reinforcements and order their commander to push on with the mounted men, leaving the wagons to follow, and, pending their arrival, he issued a notification to the effect that Manica having been occupied under the treaty of the 14th of September, all residents would in future be under the Company's regulations. The next day d'Andrade reached the kraal and, as a counterblast to Forbes' notice, sent out an invitation to the European residents to meet him there on the 15th November, in order to hear the chief formally declare that he and his country belonged to Portugal.

Umtasa admitted to Doyle that a meeting was to be held on the 15th, and that Manuel had been pressing him to declare himself for the Portuguese. He was now being pestered to sign a document stating that he had ceded his

[1] Afterwards Sir Eustace Fiennes, Bart., Governor of the Leeward Islands.

country to Manuel *twenty* years before, when he was a young man, and that this cession had escaped his memory when he had made the treaty with Colquhoun. d'Andrade had boasted that he meant to drive the English out of the country, and that if Umtasa refused to sign the document, Manuel would " eat him up " as he had Mtoko.[1] Umtasa stoutly maintained that these threats would never induce him to break faith with his new allies, but Forbes had no implicit confidence in his protestations, and, as the conspirators were all in one spot, he made up his mind to try to catch them together at dinner-time on the day appointed for the meeting.

Most opportunely, at two o'clock on the afternoon of the 15th, just as Forbes was on the point of starting, the reinforcements so anxiously looked for arrived from Fort Salisbury, and with them came two of the officers of the disbanded Pioneer Corps—Captain H. F. Hoste and Lieutenant E. C. Tyndale-Biscoe. Messengers came in to report that the meeting had opened, so Forbes, with Doyle, Hoste and eight men, clambered up the steep ascent to the kraal, while Fiennes and Biscoe, with the remainder of the Police, were sent to disarm d'Andrade's natives, who were outside the stockade, between the kraal and the Englishmen's camp. The latter was out of sight of the kraal and the approach of the Police was not observed. d'Andrade and Manuel, relying on their superior force, had never dreamt of any active interference, and had posted no guards, while the natives were absorbed in the proceedings of the *indaba*. Not until they were actually inside was the presence of the Police detected. At that moment the meeting was just breaking up. The half-dozen European prospectors who had attended, on d'Andrade's invitation, were strolling away to their camp a little distance off. Rezende and de Llamby, the French engineer of the Mozambique Company, were still there. The Portuguese flag was flying from a pole erected in the *aringa*, or small open space in the centre of the kraal,

---

[1] This was a chief on the borders of Gorongoza who had offered a very strong resistance to Portuguese incursions. For some months Manuel had been engaged in a campaign against him—the *Guerra da Matoko*—but the result had not been so favourable to the Capitão-Mór as d'Andrade's boast would imply.

and round it was a crowd of gaping natives. d'Andrade and Manuel had withdrawn with the chief into a large hut facing the square.

Suddenly from the outskirts of the crowd came the cry " Inglezes ! " and as the little group of men in brown corduroy appeared the natives scuttled into their dwellings. The slight commotion was heard by d'Andrade, who hastily emerged from the hut and found himself confronted by two or three of the troopers. " What are you doing here? " he demanded angrily. " I am Colonel d'Andrade ! " whereupon Forbes, who had caught the name, walked up and told him to consider himself a prisoner. Manuel, who followed immediately, was also arrested, as were Rezende and Llamby.

d'Andrade, though enraged at the indignity, maintained his composure well under the trying circumstances. He protested that he was at the kraal in a civil and private capacity, as Director of his Company, but Forbes declined to discuss the point, and told him he could make his explanations to Colquhoun. The redoubtable Manuel, who had not enjoyed many opportunities of meeting British officers, lost all his braggadocio and implored his captors to spare his life ! Umtasa's people were at first somewhat excited, but on being assured by Doyle that the quarrel was with the Portuguese only, they relapsed into their ordinary indifference. Upon the appearance of Fiennes and his supporters Manuel's black soldiers—the so-called *machileiros*—had fled precipitately into the rocks, some of them leaving in such haste that they abandoned their rifles, which were promptly impounded by the Police.[1]

---

[1] The dates of the various stages in the episode at Umtasa's kraal are important in their relation to the negotiations in Europe, of which, however, the principal actors—Forbes and d'Andrade—were, obviously, ignorant. It was urged on behalf of the Portuguese case that the arrest of d'Andrade and Manuel on the 15th November was a violation of the *modus vivendi* signed on the 14th. But the Company's forces were in occupation of Umtasa's kraal by virtue of a concession granted two months previously. The Convention with Portugal, which would have given Umtasa's district to the Portuguese, had been rejected by themselves, and on the 8th November, when Manuel replaced the Union Jack by his own flag, the *modus vivendi* had not been signed. Forbes' subsequent action, though taken one day after the signing, was, as Sir Henry Loch pointed out, a part of and consequent on the occurrences of the 8th November; moreover, it was not then possible for him to be aware of the existence or contents of the temporary agreement.

Forbes' next step was to notify all the English and Colonial prospectors of his action, and to call upon them to assist him if the necessity arose. His appeal was promptly responded to, the only dissentient being de Llamby, who had been released immediately after his arrest, and now refused to recognise the Chartered Company's authority. Rezende, whose presence was necessary at Maçequeçe to protect the stores belonging to the Mozambique Company, was also released at once, and he and de Llamby returned to their quarters. d'Andrade and Manuel were despatched the following day, as comfortably as circumstances would permit, to Fort Salisbury, having given their *parole d'honneur* to make no attempt at escape or at communicating with the natives on the way. After interviewing Colquhoun they were sent viâ Tuli to Capetown in charge of a Police officer, every possible step being taken to ensure their comfort on the journey. After passing Fort Tuli they were met by Jameson, who, seeing that they could not possibly do any further mischief, gave them their freedom on the understanding that they were to complete their journey to Capetown.

From Capetown d'Andrade penned an able and voluminous despatch giving his version of the circumstances He adhered to his contention that his presence in Manica had no political or military significance, that he was there simply as a Director of his Company, attending to business matters, and that he visited Umtasa to hear some statements with reference to certain concessions granted by his Government to the Companha da Moçambique—Manuel and Rezende being his guests. Their escort consisted solely of palanquin and equipment carriers, whose arms were intended for shooting game. Had it been his intention to make a military demonstration he could have requisitioned for 10,000 men from the Capitão-Mór and obtained them at once, without mentioning the assistance which would have been forthcoming from Gungunyana and other chiefs. On arrival at the kraal he found that Umtasa had raised the flag which d'Andrade himself, " dressed in full uniform," had hoisted there with his own hands nearly two years before, when, in the presence

of all the assembled representatives of various mining syndicates, the chief had affirmed his allegiance to that flag.
Finally, he and his colleagues were victims of the duplicity
and treachery of Umtasa, who had planned this trap in conjunction with the British South Africa Company.

But these arguments, and many more which he urged in
similar vein, had very little bearing on the real issue—the
question of Portugal's title to Manica. Into the rights and
wrongs of the arrest it is unnecessary to enter. What is
certain is that Forbes' *coup de main* had the most salutary
effect on the natives. For years past the name of Gouveia
(as they called Manuel) had carried terror far and wide.
Taking the place of a native chief in his own district of
Gorongoza he had conducted raiding expeditions, like Lobengula, against all the adjacent tribes. His mode of travelling,
with his " wives " in their *machilas*, and his numerous
retainers, more resembled the progress of some powerful
Arab slave-dealer such as Tippoo Tib. His followers had
carried on a system of *dacoity*, against which their unhappy
neighbours dare not raise a hand. This dreaded brigand
they had now seen grovelling before a handful of the
" Inglezes " who had no palanquins, no slaves, no wives, and
were commanded by a short square man armed only with a
sjambok. Nothing better could have been designed to
raise the prestige of the Company, and the recollection of
this incident sufficed to keep Umtasa out of mischief on
several subsequent occasions when his neighbour Makoni and
other native chiefs were rebellious and troublesome.

One of the immediate results of the arrest was the desertion of the half-caste employees of the Mozambique Company
at Maçequeçe. Rezende, who was naturally much upset
by the whole circumstances, asked leave to return to
Portugal, which was readily agreed to by Forbes on behalf
of the Chartered Company. Rezende's conduct, like
d'Andrade's, throughout this affair was dignified and
honourable. Had there been more of such men in Portuguese
East Africa the history of the Colony would have been
different. To-day the leading officials are men of the highest
character, education and social standing, but up to the time

of the Umtasa affair, with a few exceptions such as d'Andrade and Rezende, there were only half-castes and the lower kind of adventurer in authority. If any *ex post facto* justification is required for Rhodes' forceful policy in Manica, it may be seen in the fact that, from this moment, the Portuguese began to accord rational treatment to their East African possessions. The improvement has been maintained, as no one will deny who, remembering what Sofala and Delagoa Bay were like in the early 'nineties, visits Beira, Lourenzo Marques and other settlements of the Portuguese in East Africa to-day. The original impetus came from Rhodes, who, by stimulating their colonising instincts, which were only dormant, was really their greatest benefactor.

Shortly after d'Andrade's return to Europe the Lisbon papers published the most grotesque and garbled versions of the " outrage " to which he had been subjected. The *Jornal do Commercio*, a prominent organ, had some quaint comments—not altogether uncomplimentary to the English —on the incident, portions of which are worthy of reproduction :

" When Paiva d'Andrada went to Maçequeçe, so little did he think that he was going to be attacked by the English, and so little did he know that they were in league with Umtasa, that he only took with him the porters and carriers who were absolutely necessary. Manuel Antonio de Souza was only accompanied by a few persons. He took his wife with him and her black maids, and this clearly shows that the object of his journey was not bellicose. . . . Shortly after their arrival . . . an English officer made his appearance and delivered to d'Andrade a letter in which Captain Forbes intimated that as they were threatening Umtasa he called upon them to withdraw at once. . . . Naturally our people did not pay any attention to the statement made by the Englishman, the more so as they knew that he had not a sufficient force to injure them. It was, however, decided that Manuel Antonio should go and speak to Umtasa, because the latter was an old friend of his, and because it was with his assistance that the chief had obtained possession of his territory. Manuel Antonio proceeded to the *aringa*, but merely on a visit, taking his wife, her black maids, and also the necessary number of carriers. On his arrival there he was received by Umtasa, who, however, did not quite succeed in concealing the mistrust caused by the visit; but a few hours after, when the negro had ascertained the intentions of his friend, his sense of mistrust entirely vanished, so much so that he declared that he had always been a Portuguese, that he had never signed any treaty with the English, and that he was anxious to come to an understanding on this matter with d'Andrada.

" Manuel Antonio at once acceded to this just wish on the part of Umtasa, and sent to call d'Andrada, who was then at Umtali, to which place he had proceeded very quietly, and whence he returned accompanied by some of the miners there, a good many of whom are Englishmen in the employment of the Mozambique Company, and among them was also a Boer.   On his arrival at Umtasa's he found Manuel encamped at his *aringa*, at some distance from the straw hut of the chief, and on the best terms with him.   He installed himself at the same place, and shortly after he, as well as those who had accompanied him, were received by Umtasa.

" The reader who has perused this simple narrative has surely not discovered the slightest ground for any apprehension on the part of our fellow-countrymen; no more did they; and d'Andrada felt even more confident when he saw the Portuguese flag flying at the terrace of the *aringa*—the very flag which he had hoisted two years ago, on that very flagstaff, which he recognised, as it was very crooked.

" Little did he know that the negro was still more crooked.

" There was not a single Englishman in the *aringa*, and those under Forbes were encamped at a distance of nearly two kilometres.   Umtasa said in the presence of all, including the English miners and the Boer, that there were only two persons there (and on saying so he raised up two fingers), namely, he and the King, in proof of which let them look at the flag which was flying at the *aringa*.   He positively declared that he had not signed any paper with the English, and that if he lied, let them cut off his hands !

" We think that that ought to be done to him, but the amputation ought to be made higher up.

" The conference having been brought to a termination, and after the exchange of mutual courtesies, everyone withdrew, and d'Andrada entered the straw hut of the chief with him, and commenced a friendly conversation. [*Here follows an accurate account of the arrest.*]   On all sides the negroes of our friend the Chief Umtasa were to be seen armed with assegais, spears and rifles.   The treachery had

been admirably prepared and even the kiss of Judas was not
wanting. . . .

" On the following day d'Andrada and Manuel were conveyed in a cart which proceeded in the direction of the Cape,
under a strong escort.   During this journey our countrymen
were able to observe that there is only a small number of
Englishmen in that Territory, and that they appeared to be
ill-provided with the necessaries of life; and this was noticed
from the fact that although they did their best to treat them
in the best manner they could, even so far as to force them to
accept a case with bottles of excellent champagne, for many
days they had nothing else to eat but Oxford sausages.
d'Andrada also noticed that the English were badly lodged
in canvas tents, and had to lay their heads on their horses'
saddles."

For the historical data in this chapter the following authorities have
been consulted :

The Beginning of South African History, by G. M. Theal.
The Zambesi and its Tributaries, by David and Charles Livingstone.
Travel and Adventure in South-East Africa, by F. C. Selous.
Blue Books C. 5904, C. 6212, C. 6370, C. 6495.
Dan to Beersheba, by A. R. Colquhoun.

CHAPTER XII

THE SETTLEMENT OF MASHONALAND

WITH the erection of " Fort Salisbury " the contract entered into by Messrs. Johnson, Heany and Borrow was discharged, and the 180 Pioneers, together with the few prospectors who had been permitted to follow on the heels of the expedition, were free to mark out mining claims and farms. The majority had one thought uppermost in their minds—the gold depicted in such dazzling language by Mauch, Hartley and other early explorers. One of the Pioneers had brought with him a copy of Baines' book containing fantastic accounts (from which quotations have already been made in Chapter I) of quartz reefs, miles in extent, bearing visible gold. These became familiar by repetition and aroused the wildest expectations.[1] Hartley Hill and Mazoe were the localities indicated by Baines as the richest, and thither many of the Pioneers hurried with picks, drills and shovels supplied by Johnson and his partners, never doubting that a few months of simple quarrying would make them rich beyond the dreams of avarice. A few of the more wary ones anticipating that the diggers would soon come to the end of their resources, and apprehensive of the approaching rainy season, remained near the fort, where they set about the construction of rough thatched huts built, native fashion, of poles daubed with mud and cow-dung, and gave out that they were prepared to do business in claims, undertake legal work and act as agents for the flotation of syndicates and companies. Others, with an eye to the future, exercised their right to mark out farms (to which, however, no title could be given), while half a dozen of the most promising were

[1] The identical copy is in the author's possession, and the passages in question are heavily scored.

selected by Colquhoun to act as his administrative staff. To every party of six or seven that went out prospecting a wagon and span of oxen were supplied on loan by Johnson, Heany and Borrow, who also let it be known that they were willing to go into partnership with the discoverers of payable reefs. In the background of all this mining activity was the Chartered Company, which, in allowing private individuals to benefit by its rights under Lobengula's concession, stipulated for the retention of a fifty per cent. interest in all claims pegged or for half the vendor's scrip in any mining Company formed, while reserving to itself the first right of flotation ! But these remarkable conditions were not at the outset regarded as a matter of great concern, so confident were all of the vast wealth ready to be seized. The experience gained in the recent gold rush at Witwatersrand led to the idea that there must be, somewhere in Mashonaland, a main reef, or, as the Americans in the expedition termed it, a " mother lode," and all efforts were concentrated on the search for this. Ere long, however, the gold fever gave place to disillusionment. Quartz reefs were found in abundance, often indeed showing visible specks of the precious metal, but it speedily became clear that rapid wealth was not to be attained by the laborious process of beating it out with pestle and mortar, and that costly and elaborate crushing machinery must be dragged up from below before any real recovery of gold could be made. The fact also that the most promising districts were honeycombed with ancient workings created an uneasy suspicion that the unknown diggers of former days had already picked out the eyes of the country.

In anticipation of the success of the Pioneer expedition, several parties representing syndicates formed for gold prospecting left Cape Colony for Mashonaland in the latter part of 1890, and the moment it was known that the column had reached its objective, further expeditions were organised with all despatch. Arguing from what had happened in the Transvaal, those taking part were obsessed by the idea that there was a danger of the rich things being snapped up by the first arrivals, and in spite of the distance and the certainty that the journey would be an extremely arduous, possibly even a dangerous one, there was keen competition to be early on the scene.   This was particularly noticeable at Kimberley—then the advanced base of the speculator class in South Africa.   The prospectors were not blind to the necessity of starting well equipped.   They realised that with the uncertainty of obtaining forage or food supplies on the way it would be folly to embark on a *trek* of more than 1000 miles in light vehicles drawn by horses or mules, and impatient as they were to reach the new goldfields, they were constrained to rely on ox-wagons for the conveyance of their mining tools, stores and camp outfit. But in too many cases they made insufficient provision for supplies after reaching their destination, for few foresaw that there would be any difficulty in keeping open the line of communication or in getting regular consignments of food-stuffs by wagon from the south, and no one grasped the possibility of having to spend six months, or even more, on the road.

And so from September onwards the cry was " Northward ! " and before long there was a steady line of wagons and Scotch carts moving through Bechuanaland and Southern Matabeleland, and a growing stream of traders and transport riders from the older colonies, miners from Australia or California, speculators from Kimberley and " new chums " from the mother country, all with their faces turned towards the same goal.   A delightful journey it seemed in the dry invigorating atmosphere of Bechuanaland, with an abundance of game-birds and small buck to be shot at and no serious difficulties of transport, until, towards the end of November, with little or no warning, the rains began in earnest.

That wet season was, throughout South Africa, the heaviest in the memory of man.   It caught the Pioneers and the Chartered Company's officials unprepared, and it had disastrous results for those who were on the road. The worst hardships were encountered by the parties who had managed to get beyond Fort Tuli.   There for some months any forward movement was practically impossible.

Wagons were hopelessly stuck in the black *vleys* or on the banks of the Umzingwani, Lundi and other flooded rivers. The enforced delays in the low veld and the exposure to the torrential rains were a severe trial to inexperienced travellers. They were ignorant of the elementary precautions against malaria—in those days thought to be due to the exhalations from swamps. Hardly a single one escaped fever, and in the absence of drugs, proper food and medical aid many succumbed. For years afterwards the outspans at these rivers bore melancholy records, in the shape of little heaps of stones or crosses and initials rudely carved on tree trunks, of the last resting-place of many a young adventurer who had set out a few months before from Cape Colony, full of hope, to seek his fortune.

The Europeans already established in the new settlements in Mashonaland were in hardly better plight. A contract made by the Company with a firm in Port Elizabeth for continuous supplies of rations broke down hopelessly and wagons which started from Kimberley in October 1890 did not reach Fort Salisbury in some cases until the following April. The reserve stores which Johnson had with forethought provided for his own Pioneers had to be shared with the Police and prospectors and were soon exhausted, and the isolated communities at Forts Victoria, Charter and Salisbury, at Hartley Hill and other mining camps, were reduced to such wretched and scanty food— pumpkins and millet meal for the most part—as they could induce the natives to barter for beads and calico. Their clothes and boots were worn out; their ill-constructed huts gave little protection against the weather. To add to the general misery the conveyance of mails, which for the first few weeks after the occupation had been carried between Tuli and Salisbury by mounted despatch riders, had perforce to be suspended owing to the swollen rivers, and no communication was possible between Mashonaland and the outer world from the end of December until the middle of February 1891.

As soon as the possibility of an interruption in communications was realised, the Company's officials in Cape

Colony despatched boats with wire and hempen ropes for the purpose of maintaining a postal service across the largest rivers, but they did not reach Tuli in time to be effective. It was not until the end of March that the floods subsided sufficiently to permit the advance of the lông train of wagons which had been held up at various points along the road, but as soon as movement recommenced, the immense stores which had accumulated at Tuli were rapidly pushed forward. By the middle of 1891 communication with Mashonaland was more or less normal, and the procession of gold-seekers and speculators from the south once more commenced.

Let us turn for a moment to Dr. Jameson, who had been compelled by an accident to leave Colquhoun's original expedition before it reached Manica and to rejoin the Pioneer column. Shortly after the final halt at Fort Salisbury a difference of opinion arose between the two leaders owing to the ambiguity of Jameson's position in relation to the administration of the new territory. Accustomed to the traditions of the Indian Civil Service, Colquhoun, who had assumed the post of Administrator, did not recognise " the Doctor " [1] as holding any official status whatever, and was disinclined to allow him the freedom of action which he claimed. Jameson, on the other hand, was regarded by Rhodes as his personal representative, and carried on a direct correspondence with his principal on all matters of policy, sometimes passing on Rhodes' instructions to Colquhoun. In these circumstances some friction was inevitable, and although an open breach was avoided by the tact of both parties, the divided responsibility was a clog on rapid action. Realising this, Jameson, as soon as his injuries permitted, determined to leave Mashonaland for the time being to Colquhoun, and to explore the country between Manica and the coast. The Administrator, considering that it would be unsafe and inexpedient for any member of the column to go eastward at the moment, was

---

[1] In the early days this was Dr. Jameson's invariable sobriquet among both white men and natives. The more familiar " Dr. Jim " was a nickname bestowed on him after the Raid by admirers outside Rhodesia.

strongly opposed to this move, but was over-ruled by
Jameson, who started early in October, taking as companion Major Frank Johnson, the leader of the Pioneers.
On their way to the coast they met the Baron Rezende,
who was then awaiting the arrival of Colonel Paiva
d'Andrade, and who offered them hospitality and assisted
them with information as to the route, and later on they
encountered d'Andrade himself with a few native carriers.
Between Umtasa's kraal and the sea-board they passed
only four points which could by any stretch of imagination
be regarded as Portuguese stations, viz. Chua, which consisted of a collection of grass huts occupied by half a dozen
Portuguese and Frenchmen—mostly engineers connected
with the survey of a route for the railway which was then
being talked about; Maçequeçe, also called Fort d'Andrade,
the head-quarters of the Mozambique Company, and Sarmento and Neves Ferreira on the Pungwe River—small
stations of a few grass huts, each in charge of a Portuguese.
Finally they reached Beira, which was a somewhat more
pretentious settlement at the mouth of the river. Here a
flimsy stockade, with mud towers at each corner, called
by courtesy a "fort," was garrisoned by thirty native
soldiers under a European commandant. A corrugated
iron building used as a Custom-house, a bungalow for the
officers, and a few sheds and tents were dotted over a sand-
bank, which at high water became an island, while another
bungalow occupied by Colonel Sarmento, the agent of the
Mozambique Company, was situated on the mainland
opposite.

But Jameson saw enough of the estuary (then known
as Massanzani Bay) to realise that it was capable of forming
one of the finest ports on the east coast of Africa. The
mouths of the Pungwe and Busi rivers combined to form
a wide harbour, several miles across, unhampered by any
bar, and sufficiently deep to afford anchorage for large
vessels up to within a few hundred yards of the sandy
beach. He thought too that the Pungwe would prove
navigable for shallow-draught steamers for at least a hundred
miles inland, and that it could be connected by a wagon

road with Maçequeçe and the Company's fort at Umtasa's. True, the prevalence of tsetse fly over a wide section of the intervening country was a formidable obstacle to ox-transport, but this pest might be expected to disappear when the large herds of antelope and buffalo, which swarmed over the Pungwe flats, had been driven away, as it had already disappeared in Natal and other parts of South Africa. The pre-eminent fact was that here, less than two hundred miles from the Company's nearest post, was an excellent natural harbour, and it would be strange indeed if such a comparatively short distance could not be bridged by a road, and later a railway, for bringing supplies into Mashonaland. Jameson had long appreciated the immense drawback of being dependent for supplies on bullock-transport over the terrible stretch of a thousand miles which separated Fort Salisbury from the Cape railway system, and, compared to this, the physical difficulties of the Pungwe route seemed trifling.

Johnson, exuberant at his success with the Pioneer expedition, began at once to form plans for a coach-service from the new port into Mashonaland, ignoring, or at anyrate underrating, the obstacle of the tsetse fly, which afterwards wrecked his scheme. On arrival in Cape Colony he spoke so enthusiastically of the East Coast route that the sickliness of the low country, the difficulty of conveying provisions, and the other disadvantages seemed insignificant, and a number of enterprising colonists began to make preparations for entering Mashonaland viâ Beira during the ensuing winter.

A steamer had been chartered to meet Jameson and Johnson at Beira, and they arrived at Kimberley on the 15th of November. Here Jameson spent two or three weeks discussing plans with Rhodes, during which the suggestion was made that an expedition should be sent from Fort Salisbury to assist Dr. Schulz in Gazaland, and early in December he was off again viâ Vryburg and Tuli, arriving at the fort on Christmas Day.

At the close of the year 1890 some attention in Europe was focused upon East Africa and the struggles between the British and Portuguese Companies. In Lisbon popular feeling was influenced by the reports of d'Andrade as to his " betrayal " and arrest, supplemented by the fantastic and garbled versions of the incident sent to the Press by less responsible writers. Indignation meetings were held ; bands of students paraded the streets crying out for reprisals, and such pressure was brought to bear upon the Government that preparations were made for the despatch of a military expedition to East Africa to put a stop to the encroachment on Portugal's traditional rights.[1] Similar scenes took place in Lourenzo Marques, where the Governor held a public meeting to call for volunteers, and the streets were placarded with the notice, " Against England, who wants to rob us of our African Colonies. Courage ! " In London there was an equally strong, if less demonstrative, resolve that the British advance in East Africa should not be checked by the bogey of Portugal's historical claims. This was quickened on receipt of the news of aggressions against natives in British territory north of the Zambesi by a force under Major Serpa Pinto, further reference to which will be reserved for a later chapter. At the same time it was recognised in influential City circles that these skirmishes on the border were delaying the opening up of the new territories to commercial development. Many of those who had subscribed to the capital of the Chartered Company held that the wiser course would be to avoid further efforts to expand the Company's sphere by force, to make the best of what had been secured, and to await an opportunity of arriving at a settlement with the Mozambique Company, which would be equivalent to an arrangement between the two Governments.[2] In some quarters it was suggested that Portugal might be willing to dispose

[1] The first detachments of a force were actually despatched on January 15th under command of Colonel Azevedo Coutinho.

[2] Such a settlement was favoured by the fact that a considerable amount of English money was invested in the Mozambique Company. One of its founders and Directors—Count Penhalonga—although Portuguese by birth, was actually the head of a London firm of shippers, and subsidiary syndicates had been formed with English capital to work concessions in Manica and Sofala under licence from the Mozambique Company.

of her African possessions south of the Zambesi for a cash consideration. She was bound by treaty to give England the first refusal, and she was known to be in want of funds, and to have heavy claims to meet in regard to Delagoa Bay. If England shirked a purchase, Germany would not be slow to step in. In fact it was widely rumoured that a powerful German syndicate had been formed to purchase further territory in East Africa, and was already angling for it.

In the meanwhile Forbes had followed up his successful stroke at Umtasa's by a demonstration first towards Gorongoza, the district hitherto dominated by Manuel, and later in an easterly direction, in the hope of acquiring further territory from the independent chiefs towards the coast. d'Andrade's repeated protestations that the various Europeans in the neighbourhood were merely engaged on the business of the Mozambique Company led Forbes to believe that the so-called " occupation " was the Company's affair, and had no direct authority from Portugal, and he felt justified in securing by treaty all he could while the door lay open. In these manœuvres he encountered no opposition from the Portuguese, but he did not delude himself by thinking that they had yielded at the first round, and felt sure that their withdrawal was only temporary—*pour mieux sauter*. The coast land round the port of Beira lay within the tribal limits of the native chief Senkombe, who had recently paid tribute to Gungunyana—proof positive of the slenderness of the Portuguese authority—and Forbes, with a soldier's rough-and-ready logic, saw no reason why a treaty with this chief, followed by effective occupation of his kraal, should not lead eventually to the eviction of the few Portuguese who kept a feeble hold on the port itself.

Full of these ambitious ideas he pushed steadily eastward, making treaties with the petty chiefs—all tributaries of Gungunyana—in the Pungwe valley, and, though much hampered by sickness in his little troop, and by the dearth of provisions, was actually within two days' march of the sea, when he was overtaken by peremptory orders from

Colquhoun to fall back on Maçequeçe.   A provisional agreement had been arrived at between Britain and Portugal on the 14th of November,[1] whereby the *status quo ante* was re-established for six months.   Rhodes had given orders that the new arrangement must be strictly respected, and all hope of securing further concessions had to be abandoned, for the time being at all events.

But although Forbes was ordered to retire from the Pungwe district, Manica proper was not vacated.   A small detachment of Police under Captain Heyman was left for the protection of Umtasa at a point seventeen miles from Maçequeçe on the western side of the Umtali Valley.   The Company were determined that they should not be dragooned out of their rights under the treaty with Umtasa, and therefore continued to maintain their occupation of his country.   Their view was that under the *modus vivendi* of November the 14th, each party agreed to abstain from the acquisition of *new* rights within what would have been the sphere of the other if the August Convention had been accepted by both.   But the treaty with Umtasa was made two months before the *modus vivendi* came into being, and consequently ranked as one of the accomplished facts which would have to be recognised whenever the Convention came up again for discussion.[2]

Although the extension of its territory eastward was

---

[1] The so-called *modus vivendi*.   See p. 159, footnote.

[2] It should be noted that the English Foreign Office would not admit this construction of the position, but held that the non-ratification of the August Convention by the Portuguese Cortes did not become a settled fact until the 15th of October, when the session of the Cortes closed without its accomplishment.   On the 14th of September, therefore (the date of the Umtasa Concession), it was, so far as the Company's Agents knew, a treaty on the point of ratification.   The agreement with Umtasa was inconsistent with the terms of the Convention, and the subsequent refusal of the Cortes to ratify the latter gave no force or validity to an agreement which British subjects were not justified in concluding.   The eventual inclusion of Manica in the British sphere was a matter of arrangement, the Foreign Office, as a set-off, conceding to Portugal a large tract of country north of the Zambesi between Zumbo and Tete.

Apart from any other considerations, the removal of the Police from Manica would have been disastrous.   The prospectors in the district would have probably set up a sort of government of their own, and would have found willing allies among the Boers of the Zoutpansberg, who were always ready to repeat the tactics which had so nearly succeeded in Stellaland.

checked, a good deal of progress was made in consolidating
the Company's position in other parts of Mashonaland.
North of Umtasa's and on the British side of the Convention
line, Selous concluded a "treaty" with Mtoko, an independent chief who had successfully beaten off Manuel in
1889.[1] Further west some trouble arose with Lomagunda,
a chief who in past years had been regularly raided by Lobengula's *impis*. All danger on that account having apparently
been removed, and strong pressure having been brought
to bear on him by Manuel's agents, Lomagunda was foolish
enough to express contempt for the Company's troops,
and hoisted the Portuguese flag. As his district was seventy
or eighty miles inside the provisional boundary line, a
detachment of Police was promptly sent to bring him to a
proper understanding of his new position.

Since the despatch of his message by Colenbrander in
July, Lobengula had manifested no overt opposition to the
movements of the Chartered Company's forces. As a
matter of fact very little of what was going on in Mashonaland was known at Bulawayo. The excitement which had
been so tense at the time of the first advance gradually
relaxed as the column proceeded eastward and it became
apparent that no interference was contemplated in Matabeleland proper, and, though some of the *matjaha* regiments
retained their bitter feeling, the peaceful counsels of the
older men prevailed. The chief had, as we know, despatched
a mission, composed of Boyle and the old Induna Mshete,
to Capetown, to protest against the proceedings of the
Company, but, so far from evincing any sympathy with
them, the High Commissioner had administered a sharp
rebuke to the white man for his conduct in abetting the
hostile element in Matabeleland, and the envoys had returned
discomfited. The uncompromising attitude of Sir Henry
Loch on this occasion made a profound impression on
Lobengula, who now clearly realised that the Charter had
the British Government behind it. On October the 17th—

---

[1] Treaties were also made with Makoni and Manguendi, chiefs living
on the western side of Manica, who had no arrangements with the Portuguese, and for many years had been free from Matabele raids.

a few days after the return of Mshete—he sent for James Dawson—one of the better class of traders in Bulawayo— and desired him to go to Mashonaland, and apply to the Company for the reservation of a piece of land in the chief's name, so that he could work it for his own benefit. Whatever the chief's intentions may have been, this step was construed by the Company into a tacit acceptance of their own occupation, and the request was at once acceded to.

The calmer aspect of affairs did not lull Moffat into thinking that all fear of further trouble was over, and he constantly urged the necessity of a watchful policy. No raids were likely to be undertaken so late in the year, but it was not at all improbable that in the winter of 1891 an attempt might be made to raid the Banyai, or even some of the more eastern tribes of Mashonas, in revenge for their acknowledgment of the Company's authority. Moffat was the reverse of sanguine, and warned Rhodes that trouble might come from Mashonas, and men of other tribes once subject to Lobengula, engaging themselves to work for European masters, and, having thus been drawn into the Company's operations, claiming their protection against their quondam sovereign.[1]

Immediately after the disbandment of the Pioneers, Colquhoun, authorised by Rhodes, issued a notice provisionally introducing a simple scheme of civil and criminal jurisdiction based on a draft prepared by Sir Sidney Shippard, but the Colonial Office refused to give its imprimatur to this act, on the ground that no authority had been granted by Lobengula! Negotiations were thereupon set on foot to obtain from the chief the power of making laws for the white men in his country. Another defect in the Matabele Concession—the absence of a land title—was for the time being disregarded, and, in anticipation of a land settlement being effected, leave was granted to the Pioneers to peg out and occupy farms of 3000 acres in Mashonaland.

---

[1] If the Matabele had any thought of raiding the Banyai in 1891 it was probably checked by the attempt made in that year by Transvaal Boers to occupy Southern Mashonaland. Moffat's forebodings were, however, justified by the outbreak of July 1893, which arose from the very causes which he had anticipated.

To save returning to this point it may be as well here to recall how the difficulty was afterwards overcome. The terms of the Rudd Concession were as follows : " I do hereby undertake . . . to grant no concession of land . . . from and after this date without their [Rudd and his colleagues] consent and concurrence." This, of course, while precluding further land concessions, conferred no rights upon Rudd.[1] In defiance of this clause Renny-Tailyour persuaded Lobengula in 1891 to grant to his principal, Herr Edward Amandus Lippert, the German financier, the exclusive right for one hundred years to deal with all land in Mashonaland and Matabeleland, the chief agreeing all the more readily as he thought by this means to avenge himself on Rhodes' Company for gaining a stronger position than he had expected. But he over-reached himself completely. Rhodes, for a large consideration in cash and land, purchased the Lippert Concession outright and considered that by so doing he had established the Chartered Company in a firmer position than ever. It would, of course, have been open to the Company, as assignees of the Rudd Concession, to have disputed the validity of the Lippert agreement on the ground of its contravening the above-quoted clause. But even if they could have successfully upheld their legal rights (which would have been practically impossible in dealing with a native chief) they would not have strengthened themselves, for Lobengula would have been most unlikely to grant the Company anything more than he had given Rudd. It appeared far more politic to take advantage of the chief's infringement of his former undertaking and to buy the concession for cash.

The Secretary of State for the Colonies (Lord Knutsford) having satisfied himself as to the genuineness of the con-

---

[1] *The Times*, in commenting on the absence of a land clause in the Rudd Concession, said (December 27th, 1890) : " It is a question whether Lobengula *had* any equitable title to transfer. Had he attacked the expedition on the way up to Mashonaland and thus provoked the defeat so carefully prepared for him, the question of title would have been settled by *force majeure*." This is a reasonable assumption, but it by no means follows that the title so lost would have vested in the Company by right of conquest.

cession and as to its actual transfer to the Company, formally expressed his approval of both transactions, with the sole stipulation that the concession should not be assigned with out the previous sanction of Her Majesty's Government, and endorsed the deed of transfer to this effect.[1] It was not unreasonable to suppose that this clinched the matter for good and all, and indeed for close on a quarter of a century the Crown allowed the Company to sell the land, and to deal with it as owner, without a hint or suggestion that there was any flaw. The disappearance of Lobengula in 1894 evoked no official statement that the Company's position in regard to the land had in any way been impaired, and the Company (though it did not rely exclusively on the Lippert Concession) proceeded with its policy of land settlement without a qualm as to the security of its title. It had, however, reckoned without the lawyers, and it remained for the Judicial Committee of the Privy Council to upset this fool's paradise; to discover that the Lippert Concession was merely a personal contract; that if it bound Lobengula's successors, they were such successors only as came to his throne under his title, and not successors to his sovereignty who came to it by right of the sword, and that as a title deed to the unalienated lands of Matabeleland and Mashonaland it was valueless!

[1] *Blue Book* C. 7171, pp. 9, 10.

The following authorities have been consulted :

Blue Books, C. 6212, C. 6495, C. 7171.

Journals and notes written by the author in 1890 and 1891 have also been utilised.

CHAPTER XIII

THE GAZALAND CONCESSION

FROM the year 1890 onwards the operations of the British South Africa Company were extended simultaneously in so many directions that it is impossible to narrate them in one unbroken story, and although Mashonaland continued for some time to be the principal focus of activity, some digression is desirable at this point in order to take a rapid glance at what was happening in the other regions which had been thrown open by the Charter to Rhodes' enterprise.

After the check in Manica described in Chapter XII, the Company's agents resolved to spare no effort to secure Gazaland, and Jameson decided personally to carry out the suggestion which Rhodes had made, that an expedition should be sent there from Fort Salisbury. With this object he made preparations at the end of December 1890 for marching across country to Manhlagazi, the chief's kraal.

For fifteen months he had been almost incessantly on the move. He had just completed an arduous journey from Fort Salisbury, via Beira, to Kimberley and thence back over the Pioneer road. The torrential rains of summer had now begun in earnest, and the route to Manhlagazi lay through an unknown country and must involve the fording of several large rivers. Natives might be hostile, food would inevitably be scarce—the difficulties were sufficiently patent to have deterred the most resolute traveller. In all his career Jameson had never undertaken a more dangerous and disagreeable task than this, yet it never occurred to him to rest on his oars and await a more favourable opportunity, for he knew that time was of the most vital consequence. It was essential, however, that he should be accompanied by a competent native linguist, and for this purpose no one was better qualified than Denis Doyle, who volunteered for the duty, while at the last moment they were joined by Mr. G. B. Dunbar Moodie, one of the Manica prospectors, who had thrown in his lot with the Company after Forbes' occupation. A week was spent at Umtali (as the new camp near Umtasa's was now called) to get together a few native carriers and some trade goods and provisions, and, on the 10th of January 1891, the three pioneers cheerfully set out on their journey into the unknown.

Space will not permit a description of their adventures, and it is more important that some account should be given of the progress made by Dr. Schulz, who, it will be recalled, had already been sent to Gazaland to open preliminary negotiations with Gungunyana. The two essentials of his mission were secrecy and despatch. For the Portuguese were now on the alert. By the middle of the year 1890 they were thoroughly awakened to the dangers which threatened their decaying colonies, and, at the very moment when Schulz started, a force of five hundred native troops under Senhor Jose Joaquim d'Almeida [1] was being equipped at Lourenzo Marques for service in Gungunyana's country, where it was proposed to station a resident official. To conceal his real purpose, therefore, Schulz arranged to join, as a private speculator, a prospecting syndicate which was being fitted out by a Mr. Shepstone of Natal, and in this disguise, after a trying journey, he reached Manhlagazi on September 11th. He found that the chief was already beset by Europeans engaged in the usual game of " concession-hunting." The one in greatest favour was a German trader named Fels, who had resided at the kraal for a considerable time, had dubbed himself " Adviser to the King Undungazwi (Gungunyana)," and had twice acted as the chief's delegate to the Natal Government, to beg for British intervention against the Portuguese. With him was his wife—a proficient Zulu linguist—and they had already obtained from the chief the promise of two concessions—one to work minerals, and the other to fish for pearls at the mouth of the Limpopo

[1] Senhor d'Almeida, like many of the Portuguese officers at that time in East Africa, was a Goanese, of so swarthy a complexion as to be practically a black man. The dark hue of these officials partly explains why they were held in such low estimation by the natives.

River.   Further concessions [1] were supposed to be held by
a Mr. F. J. Colquhoun and two gentlemen from Natal—
Messrs. McKillican and Fryer.   These had acquired so
powerful an ascendancy with the chief that Schulz deemed it
politic to conciliate them before proceeding with his own plans
and accordingly he severed his connection with the Natal
syndicate, and enlisted the support of the concessionaires
by guaranteeing that the Chartered Company would respect
their rights in the event of coming to terms with Gungunyana.
There was some little delay before he could talk business
with the chief.   A rebellion had broken out among the Cho-
pies, a subject tribe, and the chief was engaged in the usual
ceremonies preparatory to the despatch of an army of 12,000
men to crush the insurgents.   It was not until the 20th of
September that Schulz could obtain a personal interview.

Gungunyana was *un roi fainéant*, lacking both the strength
of mind of his father Umzila, and the shrewdness of his
kinsman Lobengula.[2]   He had fuddled away his wits with the
trade rum and inferior wine with which he was kept liberally
supplied by the Portuguese.   At the time of Schulz' visit
he was a confirmed drunkard,[3] and it was difficult to catch
him in a sober interval.   Moreover, although he had
inherited a vast kingdom, extending from Amatongaland
to the Zambesi, he had failed to consolidate the influence
won by his father.   The intrigues of disreputable Portuguese
had undermined his authority.   Fearful of tackling him
with a military force of their own, they sought to weaken his

---

[1] Claims to mineral and other rights under concessions, real or imaginary,
sprang up like mushrooms when it was found that the Chartered Company
were gaining a foothold in Gazaland.   It was a repetition of what had
occurred in Matabeleland.   Mention may be made of one, more important
than the rest.   Gungunyana's father Umzila had, in 1874, granted to one
John Agnew of Natal a mining concession (with the usual accompanying
rights) over a large area in the angle formed by the Zambesi and Ruenya
rivers, including the country adjacent to Tete.   The concession was confirmed by Gungunyana in 1889, and attempts were made to substantiate
it in 1891, but the bulk of the district affected became Portuguese by the
treaty of June in that year, and in any case the right of the Gaza chiefs
to such a distant tract could not possibly be recognised.

[2] One of Lobengula's wives was a sister of Gungunyana.

[3] The natives generally of the Gazaland coast were demoralised by drink.
Rum, 75 per cent. over-proof, was imported from Delagoa Bay by Arab
traders along the Komatie River, and a large stock was kept by half-
caste Portuguese traders at Manhlagazi.

power by sowing discontent among the subordinate tribes.[1]
The result was that, though anxious to throw over the
Portuguese, and constantly protesting that they only existed
by his tolerance, he lacked the will-power to eject them by
force and secure a real freedom. He longed for the protection of a British alliance, and readily gave ear to Colquhoun
and others who urged him to rid himself of the hated
intruders, but his courage failed him when any Portuguese
were actually present.

At the preliminary interview, after Schulz, supported
by Mr. and Mrs. Fels, McKillican and Fryer, had explained
his errand, and pictured the advantages of a treaty with the
Chartered Company, the chief stoutly maintained his
independence of the Portuguese and complained of the
annoyance they had caused him. He was particularly
bitter against Almeida, whom he charged with having played
him false over some land which had been occupied without
his sanction. Then he went on to describe his efforts to
secure protection by England. Time after time he had
sent messengers to Natal to seek advice and help, but in
vain. His prayer was that the Queen " should take him by
the hand and not let him go," and Umzila, his father, had
had the same desire.

Other *indabas* to the same effect followed, Schulz always
assuring the chief that an agreement with the Company
would be tantamount to an alliance with the British Government, which was responsible for the Charter. Finally, on
the 4th of October, 1890, in the presence of his principal
Indunas and of the whole English party, Gungunyana
stated his willingness to grant full mineral and commercial
rights over his whole territory, on condition that the British
South Africa Company supplied him with a thousand rifles
and twenty thousand rounds of ammunition, and undertook
to pay him a subsidy of £500 per annum. He engaged to
ratify this bargain in writing, upon delivery at his kraal
of the guns and cartridges, and the first instalment of the
subsidy.

[1] There is ground for suspecting that the Chopieland rebellion was
engineered by Portuguese emissaries.

So far Schulz' mission had progressed satisfactorily, and he lost no time in sending the news of his success to Rhodes in a letter which McKillican and Fryer undertook to convey to him at Kimberley.   But how to get the rifles and ammunition to the chief's kraal was quite another matter.   True, the chief had said, with a magnificent gesture, " The whole coast is mine.   Bring the guns and the money by sea through my port at the mouth of the Limpopo," but Schulz and Rhodes both knew that the Portuguese would hesitate at nothing to prevent delivery by this means.   Manhlagazi was situated in latitude 24° 40' S., and longitude 33° 30' E., at a point some forty or fifty miles from the left bank of the Limpopo River and about one hundred miles from its mouth.   The river was believed to be impassable for any vessels but those of light draught, owing to the existence at its mouth of the bar common to nearly all East African rivers. The nearest station of the Chartered Company was Umtali, four hundred miles distant across country, and this in turn was some five or six hundred miles from the Company's main depot, Fort Tuli.   To drag guns and ammunition over this immense stretch on bullock-wagons was an almost impossible task, as no road had been cut beyond Umtali, and parts of the intervening country were low-lying and swampy.   On the other hand, a short and expeditious route was presented by the river, if the bar could be navigated, and if interference by the Portuguese could be avoided.   The latter had some sort of Custom-house, or, as they called it, a " fiscal station," near the mouth, and were most unlikely to allow free passage to rifles if the slightest suspicion of their destination and purpose were aroused.   Gazaland fell within the Portuguese sphere under the Convention of August, and consequently too under the *modus vivendi* of November the 14th, but as the concession had been obtained on October the 4th—in the interval, that is, between the miscarriage of the former and the inception of the latter— the Chartered Company's agents considered themselves justified in the assumption that it was granted at a time when they had a free hand between Mashonaland and the sea-coast.   They thought that a written concession, sup-

ported by a mission from the chief begging for British
protection, would give them an indefeasible claim over the
Gaza country, and from this standpoint deemed it of vital
importance that the verbal concession should be ratified in
writing before the expiration of the *modus vivendi* on May
14th, 1891. The immediate problem was how to get the
guns, cartridges and money to Manhlagazi before that date.
Obviously by the Tuli route this was a sheer impossibility.

McKillican and Fryer reached Kimberley on the 3rd of
December, 1890, and as a preliminary step Rhodes decided
to send McKillican back with Mr. J. A. Stevens, one of the
Company's officers, to take the first instalment of the
subsidy, while he suggested to Jameson, who was just
starting back for Mashonaland, that he should endeavour
to open negotiations with Gungunyana through Manica,
and we have seen what steps Jameson took to carry out this
behest. On arrival at Manhlagazi on December the 26th,
Stevens and McKillican found the kraal in a state of great
excitement at the advent of Almeida (who now styled himself
" Superintendent-in-Chief of Native Affairs ") with several
Portuguese officers, forty white marines, and the contingent
of black soldiers from Delagoa Bay. Up to this point Schulz
and Fels had succeeded in keeping the chief in good humour,
by assuring him that the guns and money would soon arrive,
and that all trouble from the Portuguese was at an end. The
return of the expedition from Chopieland—victorious, with
seven thousand warriors wearing the death-plume [1]—had
helped to fortify his determination to shake off the Portuguese, and before the whole army he had proclaimed that
henceforth he belonged to the English. " That man," he
had said, pointing to Schulz, " is now my friend, but if his
people treat me as the Portuguese have, I will kill him ! "
He had followed up this declaration by a further message
sent to Rhodes by the hand of Frank Colquhoun. Up to
this point, I say, all had gone well. But the appearance
on the scene of Almeida with a military force somewhat
shook the chief's resolution, and, as no guns or money had
arrived, it was with some difficulty that Schulz induced him

[1] A sign that each had killed his man.

to summon the Portuguese Commander and his staff and confront them with his new policy. Eventually a meeting took place on the 29th of December, when, with Schulz at his side, the chief, in a blustering manner, said that he allowed the Portuguese flag (which was still flying at his kraal) to remain there merely out of courtesy, and claimed the right to pull it down whenever he pleased, and to hoist the Union Jack in its place. He then denounced Almeida and accused him of lying, afterwards calling on Schulz to explain his mission. Almeida protested that the questions at issue must be settled between the Governments of England and Portugal, whereupon the chief cried out, " Not without consulting me shall you settle this question ! " The meeting then degenerated into a verbal encounter between Schulz and Almeida, and ultimately broke up in anger and disorder.[1]

Schulz' anxiety may well be imagined. Although for the time being he had contrived to hold Almeida at arm's length, he foresaw that the chief's confidence in the British Company would evaporate unless some tangible proof of its good faith were immediately forthcoming. No reliance could be placed on the word of a savage who passed from one fit of drunkenness into another. Long contact with low Portuguese adventurers, who promised much and performed nothing, had destroyed his respect for white men, and Schulz had hitherto been unable to satisfy the besotted chief that he was on a different footing from the other white men who had visited the kraal. Moreover, he suspected Gungunyana of playing a double game, and, in his greed for better terms, of coquetting with both sides—on the one hand assuring Almeida of his undying loyalty and friendship for Portugal (though he always refused to sign a paper to this effect), and on the other plying Schulz himself with irritating demands for additional presents. He was in constant communication with Lobengula, and learnt that

---

[1] Two accounts of this meeting have been published—one by Schulz, the other by Almeida—which are so hopelessly irreconcilable that any attempt to extract the truth from them would be fruitless. It appears, however, that the chief, finding himself between two fires, played one side against the other and finally, without making any definite pledges, dissolved the assembly.

the Matabele chief had received from the Chartered Company a gift of two valuable bulls. Well, he also must have two bulls. He wanted a horse as well, and a pair of mastiffs, and so on.

Schulz represented all this in a letter to Dr. Rutherfoord Harris (the South African Secretary of the Company), which he smuggled out by the hand of Stevens at the end of the year, and warned him that unless the rifles and other goods were sent at once, he could not hold his own against the machinations of Almeida. Harris was fully alive to the risk of despatching the rifles and ammunition by the coast route, but any hesitation vanished as he read Schulz' letter, and realised that without prompt action the Gazaland Concession was lost. Accordingly he decided on the somewhat hazardous plan, suggested by Gungunyana himself, of running a cargo up the Limpopo River.[1] Rhodes had sailed for England about the middle of January, and all responsibility devolved on Harris. But the latter, besides having a passion for a plot, was not the man to allow the grass to grow under his feet. Within a few days of the receipt of Schulz' letter, he purchased at Port Elizabeth a small screw-steamer of about one hundred tons—the *Countess of Carnarvon*—and discovered a skipper (Captain Buckingham) who was familiar with the navigation of East African rivers. On February the 10th the cargo of rifles and cartridges, together with some calico, umbrellas and other trade-stuff popular with natives, was quietly shipped by Stevens, who had agreed to return to Manhlagazi, and was now accompanied by another of the Company's officers—Captain Augustus Pawley—with a small detachment of British South Africa Company's Police specially enrolled for the purpose. A start was made on the following day, and at the outset all went well. At Durban, where a short stay was made for coaling, there was a Portuguese Government

---

[1] As a measure of precaution, in case of the failure of the east coast attempt, Harris gave orders for a party of twenty-five men with wagons, and a number of rifles and rounds of ammunition to proceed from Fort Tuli to Gazaland, but the undertaking was a hopeless one, owing to the impassable condition of the roads, and subsequent events caused its abandonment.

steamer, whose presence caused some little anxiety to the passengers on the *Countess*. She proved to be the *Maréchal MacMahon*, a Customs boat, and apparently had no guns, but they were relieved when they saw her go up on the slips for repairs. On February the 17th the little British steamer safely crossed the bar of the Limpopo in three and a half fathoms of water, and steamed up the river, while those on board kept a sharp look-out for natives who could carry a message to the chief's kraal. At sunset they drew into the bank and anchored for the night, and shortly afterwards observed a canoe, with some Europeans and native paddlers, approaching them from up stream. The white men, three in number, having boarded the steamer, announced that they were Portuguese officers, that their place was three or four miles further on, and that they came to pay a friendly call, but that if the Englishmen wished to go further they would be subjected to an official visit on the following morning. Captain Buckingham, who spoke Portuguese, entertained them with refreshment, and later they departed for the night. When morning came, however, they failed to appear, and after waiting some little time Buckingham hove anchor and proceeded up the river, flying the British ensign over the stern of his vessel. A few miles up they passed two or three shanties on the bank and saw their friends of the previous evening, who shouted at them and ran up the Portuguese flag. Not knowing that this was the Custom house, nor desiring any further interviews, Buckingham disregarded their signals and went on, and, after steaming ahead for two or three hours, dropped anchor near a native village called Chaichai, where there was a small landing-stage. The local chief, Umswabi (or Schwabe), came on board and stated that this was the spot where the goods for Gungunyana should be landed, and Buckingham began at once to discharge his cargo. Messengers were sent to Manhlagazi asking for carriers for the rifles and other goods, and in the meanwhile they were stored in one of Umswabi's huts. On the evening of the 21st the messengers returned with letters from Schulz and a riding mule for Stevens, who started early on the 22nd for his forty-five-mile march to the kraal, taking the money, but leaving the rifles in charge of Pawley. Barely had he left Chaichai when some Portuguese officers, with about 150 native soldiers, arrived on the scene, and, after reconnoitring the position, took possession of the landing-stage, thus cutting off communication between Buckingham on the steamer and Pawley and his men at the village. The former, therefore, having ascertained by signals that the shore party were all right, hove anchor, and, as previously arranged, made for the river mouth, proceeding without further adventure to Durban. His orders were, after effecting certain necessary repairs and shipping coal and stores, to return to Chaichai in a week's time to fetch Schulz and Stevens.

The force of black troops which had suddenly descended on Umswabi's kraal was commanded by Senhor Ignacio de Paiva Rapozo, who described himself as Intendente (Civil Officer) of Bilene—a district of Gazaland; and he at once took possession of the guns and ammunition, and notified Pawley that a sum of £2000 Customs duty must be paid before they could be released. Pawley protested in an amusing and bombastic letter, in which he cited history and international law, and derided the necessity for collecting Customs by means of a large body of troops accompanied by " a machine-gun of murderous propensity," but he eventually arranged with Rapozo to give a personal bond in £2000 for the payment to the Portuguese Government of whatever dues might prove to be legally claimable, in return for which the guns and ammunition were surrendered. They were at once conveyed to Manhlagazi by the carriers sent down for the purpose.

Rapozo was evidently uncertain of his ground and allowed himself to be bounced into giving up the arms. A refusal would have put the Chartered Company's agents into a very awkward predicament, but the course he followed gave cause for suspecting that the Custom-house and duties were invented for the occasion, and condoned *pro tanto* any offence which might be alleged against the Company in bringing the guns up the river.

On the 2nd of March, while the delivery of the guns and cash at Gungunyana's kraal was proceeding, Jameson,

Doyle and Moodie arrived, travel-stained and weary after their long journey from Umtali, suffering badly from fever, and with knocked-up horses. They had followed native paths, and passed through mountains, forest and swamps alternately, subsisting for the most part on pumpkins and Kaffir porridge, with an occasional goat or fowl traded from the villagers, for they had started with a meagre commissariat. For the last fifty miles they were practically wading in country inundated by the unusually heavy rains. But their arrival, coinciding with the delivery of the guns, was most opportune, for the chief well knew that they represented a British force in the background—the same force which had occupied the territory of Lobengula and Umtasa. His vacillation came to an end. With such powerful allies at his side he could ride the high horse with Almeida (who was still at the kraal), and he lost no time in calling a full meeting of his councillors, and in formally signing the document which confirmed the concession of the 4th of October. Jameson, Schulz, Doyle and Stevens also subscribed as representing the Company, and the whole of the interpretation was carried on and vouched for by Fels.[1]

At this meeting Gungunyana repeated his appeal to be taken under the direct protection of the British Crown, and announced his intention of immediately sending Huluhulu and Umfeti, two of his Indunas, to England to plead his cause. Turning to Doyle—whose fluency in the Zulu language especially appealed to him—he said before the whole assemblage, " Here are my men ! Take them to the Queen, and let them tell her my words. I want the Queen to hold me up and be my shield." Later in the day he selected a large elephant's tusk—the usual native symbol of submission—as a present for the Queen. As it was impossible for the Indunas to leave at once, arrangements were made for them to follow later with Schulz. There was nothing now to detain Jameson, and with the concession in his custody, and accompanied by Doyle, Moodie and Stevens,

---

[1] A clause in the concession stated that it was to be considered in the light of a treaty of alliance between Gungunyana and the Government of Her Majesty Queen Victoria. For this free use of Her Majesty's name in connection with a commercial bargain a mild rebuke was afterwards administered to Rhodes by the High Commissioner.

he left for the river, where he hoped to find Buckingham and the steamer.

On his arrival at Durban Buckingham had noticed that the Portuguese Customs steamer, the *Maréchal MacMahon*, which had been undergoing repairs on his previous call, was afloat again. He ascertained, moreover, that she was usually engaged in cruising up and down the coast, on the look-out for smugglers. and he deemed it prudent to give her a wide berth. Accordingly, as soon as his cargo was on board, he cleared for " Guam," [1] and early on the morning of the 27th of February he slipped out of port. The *Maréchal MacMahon* had, as he surmised, been observing the movements of the *Countess*, and followed her up the coast a few hours later. Buckingham reached the old anchorage on the Limpopo on the 1st of March and waited there several days for the passengers from Manhlagazi. On the 7th the *MacMahon*, which had been waiting at the river mouth, steamed up and dropped anchor about twenty yards astern. One of her officers was at once sent to the British steamer, with inquiries as to her name and business, and orders that she should lower her flag. This Buckingham at first refused to do, but on threats being used he complied under protest. The next day the party from Manhlagazi reached the river and went on board. The sequel may be given in Dr. Jameson's own words :

" Within five minutes an order came to the captain ordering him not to leave his anchorage, and requiring his signature of consent. This he refused to give. The next evening the captain was ordered to send all his crew and passengers on board the gunboat. This was complied with, with the exception of myself and Mr. Doyle, the latter being too ill to be moved.

" Fourteen armed sailors and soldiers were then placed on board the *Countess*, and next morning the two vessels proceeded down the river, Captain Buckingham not being permitted to have anything to do with the navigation.

" Three days were occupied in the journey to Delagoa Bay, a journey of eighty miles, the passengers of the *Countess* on board the gunboat being very harshly treated : on the

---

[1] " Guam "—a nautical phrase for " nowhere in particular."

first night placed in the hold, with all the filthy Portuguese and niggers, and afterwards, objecting to this, having to remain on deck through very stormy weather, resulting in a very bad attack of fever and ague to Mr. Moodie.

" On arrival at Delagoa Bay passengers and crew were declared free, but the vessel was detained for duties and fine under charge of alleged smuggling."[1]

It would be futile to embark on a discussion of the merits of the contention between the Portuguese and the Company as to the right of Gungunyana to grant a concession. The matter was finally settled, in favour of the former, by the treaty of the 11th of June, 1891. Opinions may differ as to the wisdom of the Company in sending a cargo of fire-arms into a territory whose ownership was under debate between higher authorities, but the seizure of the vessel was wholly without justification. The Portuguese authorities had put themselves out of court by allowing the cargo to be landed, and accepting a bond for payment of their unascertained dues, and Lord Salisbury very properly insisted on the release of the ship. It may be doubted whether the incident of the *Countess of Carnarvon* had any prejudicial effect on the final settlement of the boundaries. Even admitting that a breach of the *modus vivendi* took place, it was more than counterbalanced by acts of aggression on the part of the Portuguese in various parts of East Africa.

The fate of Gungunyana's embassy to the Queen must be mentioned. Of the natives selected as his representatives, the elder, Huluhulu, a pure-blooded Zulu, over sixty years of age, had represented the Gaza chiefs on several previous missions of a similar nature—in each case to the Government of Natal. He and his colleague, Umfeti, with Doyle as escort and interpreter, reached England towards the end of May, and, as in the case of the Matabele envoys, they were taken to see the sights of London and other large cities, besides being entertained by several of the Directors of the

---

[1] Captain Pawley and his men marched to Manhlagazi, but subsequently returned to Chaichai, where they suffered intensely from fever and privation, the seizure of the *Countess* having deprived them of the means of existence. One unfortunate trooper succumbed. It was not until the 23rd of April, and then only after repeated representations from the British Government, that the survivors were brought down to Delagoa Bay by the *Maréchal MacMahon*.

Chartered Company. At various meetings they gave a lamentable account of the demoralising effect on the natives of Gazaland of their intercourse with the Portuguese, who ruined their men with drink and debauched their women, and they vehemently repudiated the suggestion that their country was under the protection of men who always paid tribute to their chief. On June the 2nd the two Indunas were accorded an interview with the Prime Minister, to whom they delivered Gungunyana's message in these words :

" Tell the Queen to deliver me from the Portuguese. I do not want to shed white men's blood, but if the Queen hands me over to these people I shall fight to the death against their interference."

It seems hard that, in the general settling up of the Anglo-Portuguese question, this once splendid tribe of Zulus should have been sacrificed, but the Prime Minister had many interests to consider, and to have maintained a claim on Gazaland would undoubtedly have delayed a settlement, and prejudiced British interests in other parts of East Africa. He refused recognition to the concession which had cost the Company such strenuous efforts, partly because it had been based on the erroneous assumption that the Government had given its tacit consent, and partly because it purported to include portions of the East African littoral which on several occasions had been admitted by Great Britain to lie within the Portuguese sphere. Although the British gains in Manica and Nyasaland scarcely compensated for the loss of Gazaland, with its immense native population, the Chartered Company had some cause for satisfaction with the boundaries laid down in June 1891, while the Portuguese had to submit to less favourable terms than those proposed by the original Convention. But Gungunyana, to his bitter disappointment, was handed over to the latter, who a few years afterwards wreaked stern vengeance on him for having endeavoured to assert his independence.

The following authorities, amongst others, have been consulted :
Blue Books C. 6370, C. 6495.
Notes written by the author in 1890 and 1891 have also been used.

CHAPTER XIV

BAROTSELAND

So far we have been dealing exclusively with the progress of occupation south of the Zambesi, and we may now turn to the expeditions which, as mentioned in Chapter X, had been organised with the object of obtaining a foothold in the vast *terra incognita* which lay beyond that river.

The publication of David Livingstone's journals in 1874 created an immense wave of missionary enthusiasm in Great Britain, and a determination to open up to Christianity the dark places of Mid-Africa. For some reason, however, which is not very clear, this impulse took practical shape in Nyasaland only, and notwithstanding the graphic accounts published in Livingstone's lifetime of his explorations along the Upper Zambesi and of the many remarkable tribes he found there—some, like the Makololo, distinguished by a high degree of social advancement, others a prey to the cancerous inroads of the slave-trade, but all alike steeped in black heathenism—no serious effort was made to carry the civilising influence of the Gospel to Barotseland, which, in 1889, remained as unknown to the world as when Livingstone left it in the 'fifties. A few intrepid explorers such as Serpa Pinto from the Portuguese colonies on the west, and Selous and Dr. Holub from the south, had brought back tales of the barbarism of the natives, the glories of the Victoria Falls and the abundance of game and ivory in the regions north and east of the Zambesi; one or two traders even, more daring than most of their kind, had made occasional expeditions to the Barotse and Batoka tribes. But these men could be counted on one's fingers, and although what was gleaned from their accounts was stirring enough to have acted as a magnet to British missionaries— always most eager to push where the dangers and difficulties are greatest, and ever ready to risk their lives in the endeavour to bring light to benighted humanity—Livingstone's work found few successors in those regions. A small body of Jesuits had endeavoured in 1880 to establish themselves in Lewanika's dominions, but had retired, disheartened by the truculence of the natives, and reduced by the ravages of malaria; a branch of the Basutoland French Protestant Mission, under a devoted leader, François Coillard, was carrying on a precarious and unfruitful work at one or two stations along the Zambesi, but, with the solitary exception of Frederick Arnot (1882), no English missionary had succeeded in establishing a permanent foothold.[1]

When Livingstone crossed the Zambesi in 1851, and struck up his remarkable friendship with the Makololo and their intelligent Chief Sebitoani, the river tribes were just entering upon a period of war and revolution which did not finally terminate until the country came into the hands of the Chartered Company. Originally the banks of the river were populated by a number of detached tribes, whose fortunes were constantly fluctuating as one or the other gained an ascendancy. Among these were the Batoka, who dwelt on the high plateau north of the Victoria Falls; the Basubia, who were essentially river men, and inhabited the marshy lands adjoining the Zambesi and Chobe, and the Barotse,[2] who lived further north along the fertile valleys of the Upper Zambesi.

Early in the nineteenth century one of the characteristic Bantu invasions swept over these weak tribes. An army of the Makololo, who were an offshoot of the Basuto family, fought its way from the south through Bechuanaland and across the Zambesi, under the noted general Sebitoani, a man of great strength of mind and purpose, who easily became master of the Batoka and Basubia, and settled down as lord of a large tract of country along both banks of the

---

[1] In 1859 Messrs. Helmore and Price of the London Missionary Society started with their families for the far interior, and actually reached the Zambesi, but most of the party perished (some think were poisoned by natives, though Livingstone denies this), and only Price and one of the Helmore children escaped to return to the coast.

[2] These names should properly be Matoka, Masubia and Marotse, but I have adhered to the customary spelling.

Zambesi in the neighbourhood of Sesheke. Marambwa, the Paramount Chief of the Barotse, had not long died, and a dispute was in progress between his brother Selunalumi and his son Sepopo, both striving for the succession. The tribe was split into two factions, and the supporters of the rival claimants had entered upon a feud which, like the Guelphs and Ghibellines in Italy, they prolonged till long after its original cause was forgotten. Upon Sebitoani's arrival the partisans of Selunalumi besought him to annex their country, whereupon the legitimists, who espoused Sepopo's claims, fled northwards to the upper reaches of the river. Having accepted the invitation, the Makololo conqueror ruthlessly slew all prominent leaders who might cause trouble later on, and imposed his own language upon his new subjects, whom he ruled for many years with severity, but on the whole with wisdom. His aim was to weld the disintegrated tribes into a nation powerful enough to repel the Matabele and other enemies on his frontiers, and, had he been followed by a man as capable as himself, the distinctions of language and customs might gradually have disappeared and the river tribes might have endured as one people. But during the weaker rule of his successor, Sekeletu (1850–1864), the individuality of the different sections began to reassert itself. One after another the tribes rebelled, until finally in 1865 the exiled branch of the Barotse under Sepopo descended upon the survivors of the original Makololo stock, and assegaied them without quarter, sparing only the women and girls.[1]

Sepopo completed his victory by conquering and enslaving the Batoka and other tribes near the river, and, by 1866 he reigned supreme over the whole of the country that had paid tribute to Sebitoani.

The Barotse régime was at first stained dark with blood, for intestinal troubles continued to rend the race for some years, one chief succeeding another in rapid succession. About the year 1870 the position was held by Nguana-wina,

[1] The massacre was so complete that only one solitary Makololo man escaped, but to this day traces of their occupation are seen in the lighter hue of some of the people, and in their language, which is still largely spoken among the tribes near the Zambesi.

a grandson of Marambwa, but his cousin Robosi (the late paramount Lewanika) headed a rebellion, and succeeded in ousting him and getting the reins into his own hands. The usurper afterwards strengthened and extended his power by conquering the Mambunda, and conducting raids against the Mashukulumbwe and other surrounding tribes. Having gained his position by bloodshed and murder he allowed no possible enemy or rival to survive. No white man was suffered to pass the frontiers of his kingdom, and Serpa Pinto, Holub, and other travellers have borne melancholy testimony to the bloodthirsty and treacherous character of the Upper Zambesi tribes at this period. In 1884 the tyranny of the chief brought its own reward. A plot was formed to overthrow him, and the revolutionary party, after murdering his whole family,[1] drove Lewanika himself to take refuge in the country south of the Zambesi, and placed its own nominee, a boy named Akufuna, in the position of chief. Lewanika, however, was not a man to be easily got rid of. With the assistance of the chief who had harboured him, he succeeded in gathering a number of his partisans, and within a year of his banishment returned to Barotseland, where, after several engagements, he deposed the boy-chief and re-established himself in the seat of his forefathers.

The Barotse now began to emerge from the welter of bloodshed and anarchy in which they had so long been struggling, and Lewanika's government, though still marked by extreme harshness, became directed to strengthening his own tribe against outside assaults. In this object he was encouraged by M. Coillard and his colleagues of the French Mission, who arrived on the scene in 1886. Their advent certainly marks the opening of a new era of peace, though the change took some years to accomplish. Lewanika, who had been nurtured in an atmosphere of plots and intrigue, could not wean himself at once from the suspicion which he entertained towards all who surrounded him, and in which for some years the white men were included. The perils

---

[1] His son, the present Chief Yeta, then a mere lad known as Litia, was the only one who escaped.

XIV   BAROTSELAND   207

and threats, not to speak of privations and hardships,
suffered by Coillard, his brave Scottish wife, and his slender
band of colleagues, would fill a volume. In all the history
of missionary endurance there is no more inspiring story
than that of this heroic and devoted Frenchman, who,
surrounded by savages, a daily eye-witness of their fierce
brutalities, and exposed to incessant assaults and depredations, maintained throughout an attitude of calm and
unswerving determination. If he did not succeed in con-
verting many to Christianity, he was at least rewarded
before his death by the spectacle of the old conditions of
barbarism and bloody strife being superseded by the blessings
of British government. This result he was largely instrumental in bringing about, for it was Coillard who, after
securing the chief's confidence by his single-mindedness,
ultimately persuaded him to put himself under the protection of the Queen of Great Britain.

Before the upheaval which started with the Makololo
invasion, the river tribes, and especially the Barotse, had
attained a fairly high level of social development. During
the successive civil wars their tribal institutions, together
with their arts and crafts, naturally suffered, but their
habits were sufficiently ingrained to be able to survive the
period of stress, and by 1889 we find the Barotse once more
enjoying a remarkably complex constitutional and social
system. The chief's sovereignty, though paramount, was
not absolute and despotic like that of Lobengula or Tshaka.
In all affairs of State he was assisted by a Prime Minister
(*Ngambela*) and a body of councillors nominated from
among the high-born Barotse—by himself, it is true, but
representative of different sections of the country, and
possessed of well-defined powers. The position of the royal
family was distinctive. In obedience to an ancient custom
a considerable influence in public affairs was exercised by
the *Mokwaes*, or sisters and female relatives of the supreme
chief. Several of these were governors of districts, where
they possessed all the attributes of male chiefs, being, in
fact, addressed and referred to by masculine titles. In a
country where polygamy among the males was general, the

husbands of the *Mokwaes* alone were allowed no other wives. Indeed, these ladies were to all intents polyandrous, as although etiquette forbade their having more than one consort at a time, they enjoyed the right of divorce (otherwise restricted to men) and frequently changed their husbands. The most powerful of the *Mokwaes* was the chief's eldest sister, whose head-quarters were at Nalolo, a town on the west side of the Barotse valley, not far from the capital, Lialui. Besides having control over her own district she exercised a strong influence over the affairs of the nation, and maintained a style which closely approached that of the Paramount Chief, having her own Prime Minister and Council, her own State barge and band, and being greeted like her brother by an elaborate royal salute. The King's sons and relatives—male and female—although they occupied an important position in the country, were not entitled *per se* to seats in the Council. Rather did they constitute a Second Chamber or Privy Council, not sitting as a body, but consulted independently by the King himself.

The pure-blooded Barotse were the only ones in the kingdom accounted free. The members of the other tribes which composed the nation, having been brought under Lewanika's rule by conquest, were regarded and treated as slaves,[1] and were obliged to pay an annual tribute to the Paramount, and to render service from time to time to their lords and masters. Their very wives and children were not their own, but were liable to be seized and given to the aristocracy. With each of these subject tribes a provincial governor of Barotse blood was placed, to ensure the payment of tribute, and to report all matters of interest to head-quarters. Many of these subject tribes were skilled in handicrafts—the Basubia, for instance, being net-makers and fishermen, the Matotela blacksmiths, the Mampukushu cattle-breeders, and so on. The Barotse proper were skilled in basket-work, wood-work and ivory-carving—even the members of the " royal family " being expert in these arts.

[1] The one exception was the Mambunda tribe, which enjoyed an immunity from slavery in return for providing all the sorcerers and physicians of the country.

Their buildings were of elaborate construction, and far superior to those of any African tribe to the south of them.

Although the sale of his people to alien slave-dealers was never countenanced by Lewanika himself, the traffic in slaves was carried on quite openly by the half-civilised natives of the Portuguese district Angola. These traders, who were known as Mambari, lived by pillage on the borders of the Barotse kingdom, and paid annual visits to the country, and even to Lialui itself, under the pretext of buying ivory and rubber, but seldom returned without a long stream of unhappy captives, for whom there was a ready market at Bihé and among the northern tribes. So long as they refrained from violence in the Barotse valley their visits were tolerated by the chief, who did not forget that a party of Mambari which happened to be at Lialui when he was struggling to regain his kingdom had taken up arms on his behalf, and by timely assistance had turned the tide in his favour.

A distinction must be drawn between the recognised slave status of the conquered tribes of Lewanika's dominions (whose existence on the whole was not marked by severe oppression) and the condition of those who were bought or captured by the Mambari for export. The horrors of the latter traffic have been laid bare in the writings of Livingstone, Arnot and other explorers, but although at the time of the British occupation it still lingered in the more remote parts of the country, it speedily disappeared under the forcible measures which our officials used to repress it. The domestic serfdom which played an important part in the social system of the Barotse was eventually brought to an end by an edict of Lewanika, who, under pressure from the Chartered Company, agreed to the emancipation of the slave tribes in 1906.

A few words must be said of the physical characteristics of the country, and of the natives comprised under Lewanika's rule. Roughly his authority extended over the whole of the upper basin of the Zambesi and the western portion of that of its important affluent, the Kafue River. The extreme northern part, near the watershed between these two rivers and the Congo system, is a well-watered plateau richly mineralised, and famous from distant times for its deposits of copper ore.   The great artery of the territory is the River Zambesi.   For nearly a thousand miles of its course it sweeps round country owning allegiance, in 1889, to the Barotse chief.   In so long a passage, as may well be imagined, it presents varied aspects—now meandering with sluggish current through the low and fertile marshes of the Barotse valley, now dashing riotously over rocky barriers, and at last pouring its entire volume into the rift of the Victoria Falls, emerging through a narrow, precipitous and inaccessible gorge, and rushing on towards the Portuguese colonies on the east.   The Zambesi is the resort of innumerable varieties of game, feathered and four-footed.   In the open sandy reaches between the rapids the multitude of wild-fowl is bewildering, and must be seen to be appreciated. Besides many kinds common to all the great rivers of South Africa, pelicans, flamingoes, ibises, and other striking species peculiar to the tropics are to be seen in great numbers; the banks clothed with papyrus and bamboo give sanctuary to herons, egrets, and morose-visaged marabu storks; the brakes and undergrowth are tenanted by myriads of finches and small fowl; in some parts the general effect of so much bird life is as though one were enclosed in a gigantic aviary. Hippopotami disport themselves in the pools, and constitute a terror to the traveller by canoe; crocodiles are equally numerous, and in some parts, as, for instance, at Sesheke, are so audacious that they have been known to snatch human victims from the bank or from a boat, which gives colour to the idea that they retain a memory of the days when offenders were flung wholesale to them as a cheap and expeditious method of execution.   Buffaloes and many kinds of antelope are found on the banks in most parts. Elephants, too, are to be seen here and there, and have always been specially preserved by the chief for his own gain.

The value of the Zambesi as a waterway is impaired by the frequent rapids which bar progress between the Kafue confluence and the Barotse valley.   At present, and probably for many years to come, the upper river must

DUG-OUT CANOE DESCENDING THE MAMBOVE RAPIDS,
ZAMBESI RIVER

MASHUKULUMBWE NATIVES: N.W. RHODESIA

remain unnavigable except by clumsy native " dug-outs,"
whose thick solid keels allow them to be manœuvred with
impunity over places where no European craft could live.
Both the Kafue and Zambesi run, for portions of their course,
through low flat country bordered by sand-hills, and these
districts are subject, in consequence, to annual inundations.
Round Lialui, the native capital, a vast tract is thus flooded
in the rainy season, and acquires a fertility which resembles
that of the Nile valley. The denizens of this part, which is
the exclusive reserve of the real Barotse, are compelled
every year by the floods to migrate *en bloc* with their cattle
to the neighbouring hills, returning when the waters recede.
The swampy nature of the Barotse valley renders it anything but a health-resort for Europeans, but the natives
seem to thrive uncommonly, and their physique and intelligence are above the general level of Bantu races.

Lewanika's sovereignty in 1889 embraced some twenty
tribes [1] with many subdivisions. These varied immensely

[1] A list of the more important tribes may be interesting, and the
following table shows the industries of some of them with the form in which
their annual tribute was paid to the Paramount Chief :

1. *Central Tribes :*
   Marotse, workers in wood and ivory.
   Matotela, iron-workers. Tribute in hoes, spears and axes.
   Mamboe.
   Mankoya, canoe-builders and net-makers.
   Matoka, shepherds and hunters. Tribute in hides.
   Bamakoma.
   Mambunda, skilled in making mats, baskets and wooden utensils.
   Masubia, fishermen and canoe-builders.

2. *Southern Tribes :*
   Mampukushu.
   Makwengari.

3. *Western Tribes :*
   Baluchasi.

4. *Northern Tribes :*
   Bachibokwe.
   Balovale, hunters, rubber traders. Tribute in skins.
   Balunda, rubber and ivory traders. Tribute in tusks.
      (Only the southern section of this large tribe paid tribute to
      Lewanika.)

5. *Eastern Tribes :*
   Bakaundi, ivory traders.
   Bakwakwa.
   Mashukulumbwe.

in character and pursuits. Between the cultured, if some-what indolent, Barotse aristocracy on the west, and the wild, naked Mashukulumbwe east of the Kafue River—the latter hardly a tribe at all, being split up into innumerable septs, with no tie but a common language and a common enmity against strangers—there was a wide gulf. These extremes were linked up by a miscellaneous collection of peoples differing in speech and in degrees of advancement, the hardiest and the most tractable being the Batoka, who may have gained some superiority of character by closer intercourse with the Makololo, and by their proximity to the Matabele and other southern tribes, against whom they were constantly on the defensive. The Makololo influence survived in their language, which was a *lingua franca* along the river, and was in use even among the Barotse proper, only a few of the chiefs and members of the royal family retaining their ancestral speech (Sirozi or Serotse) for private intercourse. The difficulties of governing so heterogeneous a group of peoples must have been enormous, and it is a surprising proof of Lewanika's king-craft that he had succeeded in consolidating them sufficiently to be able to hand them over as one nation to the British Protectorate.

In 1886 the northern tribes of Bechuanaland were brought under the Queen's protection. Lewanika was deeply interested in this. He was in constant and friendly com-munication with Khama, and quickly grasped the advantage of the British alliance, which would safeguard the Bechuanas for ever against Matabele aggressions. To Lewanika also the fierce hordes of Lobengula were a cause of incessant anxiety, and he began to cogitate on the possibility of a similar arrangement for himself and his people. In 1887 he received a definite warning that the Matabele were con-templating a raid across the Zambesi and that they were being encouraged by some of the Batoka, who were pre-paring canoes and inviting them to come to their assistance against the Barotse. In face of this threat he turned to Khama for advice. " I understand," he wrote, " that you are now under the protection of the great English Queen. I do not know what it means. But they say there are soldiers living at your place, and some headmen sent by the

Queen to take care of you and protect you against the
Matabele. Tell me all as a friend. Are you happy and
quite satisfied? Tell me all. I am anxious that you should
tell me very plainly, your friend, because I have a great
desire to be received like you under the protection of so
great a ruler as the Queen of England." He also took
counsel of M. Coillard, who, although not an Englishman,
was in touch with the English, and would know how to
advise him; and in January 1889 Coillard, at Lewanika's
request, wrote the following letter to Sir Sidney Shippard,
the Administrator of Bechuanaland :

" The King Lewanika is most anxious to solicit that the
Protectorate of the British Government should soon be
extended to him and to his people. For reasons of prudence
suggested by our local circumstances, I thought it advisable
not to yield too easily to his desire, in order as well to test
his sincerity as to make sure of the disposition of his headmen. But the King's persistence removes all motives for
further delay. I therefore lay before you his urgent
request. . . .

" Many a Zambesian has found his way to the Diamond
Fields, and come back deeply impressed with the prestige
of the British Government. The tale of what they have
seen and heard, and of its dealings with the native races,
naturally leads their chiefs and their countrymen to yearn
after the protection of Her Majesty the Queen's Government.

" A second request which I have to lay before your Excel-
lency from the King Lewanika is concerning a threatening
invasion of the Matabele. The Matabele have some months
ago made a raid among the Matoka and the Mashukulumbwe,
and they have boastfully declared that their next war-path
would be this year, 1889, to invade Barotseland.

" Such rumours in a country so recently agitated with
civil wars are calculated greatly to disturb the peace of
the land, and cause much mischief.

" The King Lewanika has heard that Lobengula, King of
the Matabele, is under Her Majesty's Government. He
therefore respectfully asks whether such a raid could be
made without the sanction of the Queen's Government.
He trusts you may give these grave matters your serious
consideration, and do your utmost to prevent the Matabele
invading his country, and spreading terror and desolation
among the tribes north of the Zambesi."

This letter, when it eventually reached the Colonial Office, which was not till the following August, elicited a friendly, but guarded, and consequently disappointing, reply from Lord Knutsford. However, a month later, Shippard informed Coillard that Rhodes was making ready to step in where the Government was hesitating. In the meantime several enterprising traders had pushed their way into Barotseland, and, as was the invariable practice with such gentry, began to worry the chief for concessions. One of them, Mr. Harry Ware of Kimberley, more persuasive than the rest, succeeded in June 1889 in getting Lewanika's signature to an important document granting to him and his assigns the sole right of mining for precious stones, gold, or other minerals in the Batoka country. In return for this privilege Ware agreed to pay the chief £200 a year, with a royalty of four per cent. on mineral discoveries, and pledged himself to respect the fields and villages of the Barotse, to refrain from killing elephants, and to keep out all intoxicating liquors.

Lewanika's hankerings after a British Protectorate reached the ears of Rhodes just about the time of the granting of the Charter. His hands were then full of the multitudinous details of the expedition to Mashonaland, but he decided at once to send a mission to the Barotse chief. The Ware Concession had been purchased by a group of Kimberley speculators, of whom Messrs. H. J. King and C. E. Nind were the chief, and Rhodes, feeling that it was likely to be an embarrassing obstacle to his own plans, resolved, with characteristic directness, to acquire it. Negotiations were opened, and, in spite of considerable opposition, the concession became his property, in exchange for £9000 in cash and ten thousand shares in the British South Africa Company. The next step was to induce the British Government to accede to Lewanika's prayer for protection. But here he was at once confronted with European complications. Difficulties with foreign Powers were imminent. The territory north of the Zambesi had been recognised by both France and Germany as subject to the influence of Portugal, and the Government were unlikely to be influenced to declare a Protectorate on the strength of a mere mining concession.[1]

Meanwhile Rhodes selected a Mr. Frank Elliot Lochner, a former officer of the Bechuanaland Police, for the task of carrying out a mission to Lewanika. He was a man thoroughly used to up-country travelling and was, more-over, *persona grata* with Khama—an important advantage, for Rhodes relied on Khama to further his plans for coming to terms with the Barotse chief.

Lochner with three companions—Captain Armstrong and Messrs. Bagley and Fraser—left Kimberley for the arduous journey of over a thousand miles early in October 1889. His route lay through Khama's country and from Palapye, the principal kraal, along an old hunters' road, which kept to the westward of Matabeleland, and crossed the Zambesi near Sesheke, the former seat of the Makololo chiefs. To that point he was to travel by ox-wagon and from there onwards by native canoes to Lialui. It was originally designed that after effecting an understanding with Lewanika Lochner should proceed to visit the chief or " king " of Garenganze, whose territory had not up till now been recognised by the British Government as falling within the Congo Free State, and was consequently regarded by Rhodes as fair game. It was of vital consequence to secure these distant regions even though no immediate settlement could be undertaken, for the Matabele treaty had given a lead to all sorts of adventurers and concession-hunters, and foreign Powers also were on the alert and might forestall the Chartered Company. But Lochner's progress was obstructed by the unprecedentedly heavy rains, and he did not reach the river till the end of December, by which time it had become apparent that more active steps must be taken if Garenganze was to be saved from the Belgians, who were known to have designs on it. Rhodes therefore

[1] Rhodes did not want the western boundary of Barotseland defined. There was a possibility that later on it might be possible to exchange some of this territory for Portuguese possessions on the east coast. He believed —wrongly as it turned out—that Lewanika's influence extended as far west as the Cunene River, or approximately to 16° East Longitude, and in any case he wanted to have a free hand as long as possible.

decided to send another mission from the east coast to Msiri, the Garenganze chief, and to restrict Lochner to the negotiations with Lewanika.[1]

In March 1890, after a journey of incredible hardship, Lochner, greatly enfeebled by attacks of fever contracted on the river, arrived at Lialui. His two companions (Captain Armstrong having turned back at the Zambesi) and himself were welcomed by M. Coillard, who took Lochner to his comfortable house at Sefula and patiently nursed him back to health. The provisions of the expedition were exhausted, and had it not been for the hospitality of the good missionaries, the three Europeans would have been reduced to native fare.

Mischievous influences had been at work since Ware's departure, and the chief, under the constant insinuations of a reactionary party, and in the continued absence of Ware himself or anybody representing him, was beginning to believe that he had been duped. At their first meeting Lochner was informed that as so many of the principal councillors, whose presence was necessary in any political discussion, were absent on a war expedition against the distant Mashukulumbwe no decisions could be arrived at, but, despite the arguments of opponents, who were apprehensive that he might be inveigled into parting with the country, the chief showed himself as eager as ever for a British Protectorate, and was quite prepared to treat with the mission, if satisfied that it represented the Queen. Coillard was also a very strong supporter of the Protectorate policy, but his isolated position as a missionary made him anxious to stand well with all parties, and being fully aware of the unpopularity which clung round him in connection with the Ware Concession, which he had supported, he was reluctant to pose too conspicuously as the champion of the new arrivals.

In these circumstances Lochner saw that to leave any doubt in the chief's mind as to the royal authority from

---

[1] It is interesting to note that Rhodes at this time was considering a suggestion that H. M. Stanley should be engaged to secure the territories north of the Zambesi.

which the Charter emanated, or to dwell on the fact that it was granted to a commercial company, would spell failure. The native mind would be incapable of grasping the distinction between the direct Protectorate of the Crown and the same thing exercised through the medium of the Charter, and the only way to gain the confidence of the chief and his ministers was boldly to assure them that a treaty with the Company was tantamount to an alliance with the Queen. Had he not adopted this course Lewanika would have refused to deal with him, and Barotseland might never have been added to the Empire—might even have become the prey of a foreign syndicate with no nice scruples as to how it acquired territory. But Rhodes and Lochner were afterwards fiercely assailed in the Press for tricking the chief into giving his country away, by fraudulently pretending that the Barotse mission was sent direct from the Queen— an unfair accusation which will be referred to again on a later page.

During April and early May Lochner was debarred by his own ill-health, and by the absence of the war party, from resuming active negotiations, but on the Queen's birthday (May 24th) he was well enough to organise a *fête* or demonstration which the chief and most of his headmen attended. Four oxen were killed to provide a feast, athletic sports were held in good English fashion, and the revels wound up with a display of fireworks, by which the assembled multitude, never having witnessed anything of the sort, were greatly impressed.

Lochner had already lived down some of the suspicion which had at first surrounded him, and which had been sedulously fostered for his own ends by an English trader then resident at Lialui. The birthday celebrations carried him at once into popular favour. The war party had returned victorious, bringing with them the submission of the turbulent Mashukulumbwe, who had been a perpetual source of trouble on the eastern frontiers. Everything was propitious for the full proposals to be laid before the chief and his parliament, and a *pitso* (council) was summoned for the 26th June, at which he was invited to state them.

Full notice had been given of this meeting and representatives of many of the subject tribes came into Lialui,
some of them having travelled long distances to be present.
Coillard grasped the opportunity of taking evidence as to
the dimensions of the kingdom, which, to Lochner's satisfaction, proved to be far wider than either of them had
imagined. From the Ganguella country on the west to
the confines of the Mashukulumbwe country on the east,
and from the watershed of the Zambesi on the north to the
Chobe and Lomba Rivers and the Zambesi main stream on
the south, all the tribes paid tribute to Lewanika and acknowledged him as their paramount. The Barotse chief was
over-lord of Shinti's country, formerly part of the great
kingdom of Muata Yamvo beyond the Zambesi, shown on
old maps, but long since broken up. Shinti had been much
harassed by Mambari slave-traders, and had recently
applied to Lewanika for help, which was granted in exchange
for submission. Lochner also learnt that iron mines were
worked by the natives in several districts, though he could
get no information as to the existence of gold.

The *pitso* was at first divided and distrustful. For a
long time it seemed as if the reactionary party would
prevail and a decision adverse to Rhodes' hopes be given.
Trouble was sown by three European traders, Sell, an
English Colonial, Webers, a Boer, and Middleton, the agent
of a Mafeking firm, who told the natives that Lochner was
merely an adventurer like Ware, that his mission was a
bogus one, and that if the Barotse gave him what he wanted
they would soon not have enough ground to sit upon.
These statements were stoutly denied by M. Coillard and
his colleague, M. Jalla, but the suspicions of the councillors
were aroused; they feared a snare and refused to be convinced that all was above-board.

At the critical moment the scale was turned by the
official arrival of Makoatsa, a headman of the Ba-Mangwato,
who had been expressly sent by Khama as his ambassador,
to urge acceptance of Lochner's proposals. This man now
entered the *kothla*, and, after doing obeisance to the King,
obtained permission to deliver his master's message to the

assembled chiefs. He compared British protection to a savoury dish which Khama had tasted and wished to share with his friends. He reminded them of the sanguinary revolutions which, in the near past, had rent their country, and which would inevitably recur unless they put themselves in the hands of the great White Queen, and wound up by repeating that the Company represented by Lochner was composed of the " Queen's men," who were charged by Her Majesty with the duty of carrying civilisation to the native tribes of the interior. This impressive appeal won the day, and, by a unanimous vote, the *pitso* decided for the treaty.

The chief now descended to the more sordid discussion of pounds, shillings and pence, and astonished Lochner by his business-like comprehension of these details. He argued for some time as to the amount of subsidy which was to be paid to him in return for a concession, and could not be induced to abate his demands for £2000 a year. After an ordeal of cross-questioning and haggling, which seemed to Lochner interminable, the terms of the covenant were at length settled, and Lewanika himself, his son and heir Litia,[1] his Prime Minister and thirty-nine councillors and district chiefs, affixed their marks to the document which brought within the civilising influence of Great Britain a territory well-nigh as large as Germany.

The date of this concession—27th June, 1890—is noteworthy, for it anticipated by four days only the signing of the Anglo-German agreement, which purported to give Germany access to the Zambesi from the west coast of Africa, by means of a narrow strip of territory (the so-called " Caprivi Zipfel "), extending from the north of Namaqualand to the junction of the Linyanti River with the main stream.[2] It was also executed prior to the Anglo-Portuguese

[1] The present Paramount Chief, who assumed the name Yeta on his accession.

[2] The German boundary was described as from the intersection of 22° South Latitude with 21° East Longitude, northward *along the line of* 21° *to the point where it crosses the* 18th *parallel*, eastward along that parallel to the River Chobe (Linyanti), thence down the main channel of that river to its junction with the Zambesi. Then came the following proviso : " It is understood that under this arrangement Germany shall have free access from her Protectorate to the Zambesi by a strip of

agreement which assigned to Portugal everything west of the Zambesi down to the Katima-Molilo rapids, but this, as we know, was rejected by the Cortes, which thereby gave Rhodes the chance of re-asserting Lewanika's rights up to 20° East Longitude.

The Barotse Concession gave the Chartered Company full mining and commercial rights over the whole of Lewanika's dominion. The chief bound himself to enter into no similar covenant with any other individual, Company or State. He recognised the Protectorate of Queen Victoria, but expressly retained his constitutional authority as chief of the nation, and safeguarded the freedom of his people, and their towns, lands and cattle from interference. He further undertook to use his best endeavours to suppress those two scourges of Central Africa, witchcraft and slavery. In return for this the Company undertook to protect the King and nation from all outside interference and attack; to further the education and civilisation of the native tribes; to appoint and maintain a British Resident in the country; to recognise elephants as royal game; to respect the rights of the natives to certain named iron mines; to refrain from mining oper-ations between Sesheke and Lialui, which was the part inhabited by the Barotse people proper, and not to throw the country open to general immigration without the consent of the King and his council. The payment of the four per cent. royalty under the Ware Concession was ratified pending a further agreement, and a yearly subsidy of £2000 was also agreed to.

The ceremony of signing concluded, the chief presented Lochner with two immense tusks of ivory—the universal native token of submission, now employed to signify his acceptance of a British Protectorate. Shortly afterwards he sent a special envoy to Garenganze to announce the step which he had taken to Msiri, the chief of that country, and to find out what were his views towards a British alliance.

---

territory which shall at no point be less than twenty English miles in width.'' But with the boundaries thus defined (which were based on imperfect information) Germany could not obtain access to the Zambesi, because the point of intersection of 21° East Longitude with 18° South Latitude happened to be on the north side of the Okavango River, and consequently in Portuguese territory !

Lochner's health had been seriously undermined during the trying march to Barotseland in the rainy season, and a four months' residence in the reeking swamps round Lialui had not improved matters. It was out of the question that he should embark on a further expedition, and he accordingly obtained leave to return to Cape Colony. Hardly had he turned his back when the campaign of intrigue reopened. The traders who had at first opposed the concession began to envenom Lewanika, and to stir up mischief between him and the Chartered Company. The Company's agents have only themselves to thank for the trouble which ensued. They should never have suffered the chief to be left without a trustworthy representative. It is true that Rhodes had intended to send Mr. H. H. Johnston to watch the Company's interests, to explore the resources of the country and to develop the concession, but circumstances prevented Johnston from taking up the post. He was wanted elsewhere, and no steps were taken to provide a substitute. From the first Coillard had urged that a Resident should be stationed in the country to retain the King's confidence and shield him from the machinations of unscrupulous white men. But the mistake made in Matabeleland was repeated, and with similar results. It was hardly surprising that the chief should resent the disappearance of the Company's representative immediately after he had got his signature to the concession. With no one to refer to just when he had taken this momentous step, his nervous doubts returned, and when the suggestion was made that he had been betrayed he readily swallowed it. Suspicion gave place to rage, which was vented upon the unfortunate Coillard and his brother missionaries, who were accused of having conspired with Lochner to trick him out of his country, and for some time they stood in a position of grave peril. In October 1890, Mr. Middleton, at the request, so he stated (and there is no reason to doubt it), of Lewanika, wrote to Lord Salisbury to say that the chief repudiated the concession as having granted far more than was intended; that his only wish at the time was to be taken under British protection, and that he had imagined Lochner to be the direct envoy of Her Majesty the Queen.

For once the Government acted firmly and unhesitatingly. A reply was sent through Sir H. Loch assuring the chief that he was really under the protection of the British sovereign, that no other Power would be allowed to molest him, and that the Chartered Company was fully recognised by the Queen. Sir H. Loch added that Consul Johnston would ere long visit Barotseland as Queen's Commissioner. Somewhat relieved at this, the chief waited patiently for the appearance of the Commissioner, whose appointment had been expressly guaranteed by Lochner, and was now again assured by the Government, but when month after month had passed by without fulfilment of the promise, he relapsed into his old mood of doubt and distrust. He was beset, too, by domestic troubles. The Court was enmeshed in intrigue. The British alliance had had many opponents, whose policy now appeared to be justified, and at any moment a spark might set ablaze the inflammable elements, and his sovereignty might collapse in a revolution. Writing in September 1892, M. Coillard says : " The King at present professes to be very friendly with us (the missionaries), but his feelings for the British South Africa Company are still as suspicious as ever. He does not trust in the Protectorate of the British Government through the Company, and he firmly believes that such a Protectorate is a blind and a falsehood. . . . A large village has been formed at Kazangula in order to watch the ford and to control the crossing of any stranger. He is suspicious of all white men and can only be restored to confidence by the presence of a *bona fide* Resident."

Shortly after this was written Lewanika received a visit from a certain Dr. Johnston, a medical missionary from Jamaica, who had made his way across Angola from the west coast. This gentleman rather injudiciously allowed himself to be made the repository of the chief's grievances, and subsequently published them in a book.[1] The value of his statements is considerably impaired by the rabid prejudice which he manifests throughout this work against the Chartered Company, but his story was eagerly seized

[1] *Reality versus Romance in South Africa*, by Dr. J. Johnston.

upon by the anti-Charter Press in London, and particularly that part of it which related to deceptions which, it was alleged, Lochner had perpetrated on the Barotse chief. According to Dr. Johnston, Lochner had falsely represented himself as a messenger direct from Queen Victoria, and the elephants' tusks given to Lochner by Lewanika were really intended as a present to Her Majesty, but had been nefariously seized by the Company to decorate their Board-room in St. Swithin's Lane. In its anxiety to publish the misdeeds of the Chartered Company the *Daily Chronicle* did not question the authenticity of Dr. Johnston's tale, but accused the Company of " the meanest form of embezzlement—not from the nation or Empire, but from the Queen herself." Fortunately Lochner was in England at the time this statement was published, and was able to refute it by pointing to MM. Coillard and Jalla, who were parties to the whole transaction, and would have been the last to countenance any false representations in a matter which so nearly concerned them. Lochner had assured the chief of British protection, and this assurance was endorsed later by Sir H. Loch on instructions from Downing Street. Nevertheless the failure of the Government, or the Charter, or both, to carry out the terms of the agreement by appointing a Resident was a natural cause of indignation in the King's eyes, and might have seriously jeopardised, or even shipwrecked, the plans for the future settlement of the country.

The downfall of Lobengula in 1893 to a great extent restored the confidence of the Barotse, but for two years no active steps were taken by the Company towards the development of the vast territory comprised in the Lochner Concession. The French Protestant missionaries, and a few hunters and traders, constituted the entire European population. In 1895, however, the Foreign Office appointed Mr. Hubert Hervey, of the Company's Southern Administration, as Resident Commissioner in Barotseland, and early in 1896 he was to have proceeded to his post, when the outbreak of the Matabele rebellion put a stop to all travelling south of the Zambesi. During the hostilities which followed Mr. Hervey unfortunately lost his life, having been mortally wounded in the Matoppo Hills. On the termination of the native rebellion, the Foreign Office, at the request of the Company, appointed Mr. R. T. Coryndon,[1] a former member of the Mashonaland Pioneer Force, and, like Mr. Hervey, an officer of the Southern Administration, to the post of Resident Commissioner. This gentleman proceeded to Barotseland in June 1897, with a small staff of Englishmen, and at once commenced the difficult task of organising an Administrative Service. He secured the co-operation of Lewanika and his principal chiefs, and the country entered upon an era of peaceful progress which has happily remained unbroken until the present time.

[1] Afterwards Sir Robert Coryndon, K.C.M.G., Governor of Kenya, and High Commissioner of Zanzibar. He died in 1925.

CHAPTER XV

THE LAKE COUNTRY

ALTHOUGH that part of South Central Africa formerly distinguished as *North-Eastern* Rhodesia was brought at an early stage under the control of the Charter, and although its rescue from barbarism was marked by stirring episodes of personal heroism and self-sacrifice, it has remained to this day the least known of the territories which Rhodes was instrumental in adding to the Empire.

As the scene of David Livingstone's final and most arduous journeys—where, remote from his fellow-countrymen, he succumbed at length to hardship and exposure—the British Protectorate in this region may be regarded as an imperishable monument to one of the greatest explorers of our own or any other age. The basin of the four great lakes—Nyasa, Tanganyika, Mweru and Bangweolo—has a history and a romance peculiarly its own. Unlike other parts of the Chartered Company's possessions, its development was from the east coast. With comparatively few exceptions it has not afforded a settling ground for colonists from the south, and, though its physical appearance differs very little from that of Mashonaland and Matabeleland the essential characteristics of South African colonies are wholly absent.

At the outset the wide prevalence of an insignificant insect, the tsetse fly, had much to do in creating this difference. Had South Africa, thirty years ago, been stripped of its ox-wagons, its Cape carts and its saddle horses it would at once have lost half its character. These features were entirely absent in many parts of Nyasaland and North-Eastern Rhodesia. It was long ago known that no domestic animals could survive in districts infested by the tsetse, though the danger of its bite to human beings has only been demonstrated within recent years. Before the introduction of motor vehicles, therefore, travellers had either to march on foot or to have recourse to the *machila*, a sort of rough palanquin or litter borne by natives, while all goods were transported from place to place on the shoulders of human porters. Many forms of sport also, in which horses and dogs play a part, have always been denied in these districts. The employment of natives as beasts of burden has had a marked influence in moulding their character, and in enlarging the barrier between them and their white neighbours, who still hold here, much more than in Africa south of the Zambesi, the prestige which at one time surrounded the *sahib-log* in India. Another cause of difference was the Arab influence, which has left a distinctly Oriental impression upon the natives, with a corresponding effect on Europeans, who in their mode of life have fallen into many habits characteristic of Anglo-Indians.

In former days a great interior kingdom extended from Lake Mweru to the confines of Barotseland and included the whole of the country drained by the Upper Congo and its tributaries. Its inhabitants, although of mixed origin, were known collectively as Ba-Lunda, and the dynastic title of the Paramount Chief was Muati Yamvo, a name encrusted, like Monomotapa, with many half-legendary associations, but few historical facts. Under the paramount were a number of satraps or governors of substantial provinces, and when, early in the nineteenth century, the Lunda kingdom began, after three hundred years of supremacy, to crumble, two of these, namely Garenganze and Kazembe, east and west respectively of Lake Mweru, became detached under an independent ruler.[1] At a later date Msiri, an alien who had seized the chieftaincy of Garenganze, quarrelled with Kazembe and founded a separate kingdom.[2]

[1] A third of the Lunda feudatories, Shinti, whose country lay more to the west, as already mentioned, became subject later to the Barotse king (see p. 218).
[2] Kazembe could not have completely shaken himself free at the time of Livingstone's visit in 1867, for the explorer mentions that he was collecting slaves to send to Muati Yamvo as tribute.

Before Livingstone's expeditions this part of Africa had been traversed, without geographical results of any value, by two or three Europeans, and probably by several half-caste, *i.e.* Goanese, traders, from Angola, Zumbo, and Tete.[1] The most notable of the Europeans was Dr. Lacerda, a Portuguese professor, of remarkable prescience and ability, who, apprehensive lest the recent occupation by the English of Capetown (1795) might be the first initial step of a great northward expansion which might eventually drive a wedge of British territory between the Portuguese settlements in West and East Africa, induced his Government to send him on an exploring expedition from Tete into the interior. The vision of an overland route (*viagem à contracosta*) from Mozambique to Angola dominated him in the same way as, a hundred years later, the idea of an all-British route from the Cape to Cairo inspired Rhodes. Its realisation was frustrated, however, by his death at Kazembe's town, south of Lake Mweru, in 1798. This was the only serious attempt made by the Portuguese to open up Central Africa prior to our own times. All their other claims to pro-prietorship were based on native reports of the existence of lakes and rivers, or on the journeys of half-caste slave and ivory traders from the Zambesi.

East of Lakes Mweru and Bangweolo and towards Nyasa the original inhabitants of the country were divided into several large and scattered tribes. On the north were the Awemba, who dwelt in the high table-land known as the Nyasa-Tanganyika plateau; on the south a group of people, with a common language, generically named Anyanja (dwellers by the water), whose branches extended from the Luangwa River to Nyasa and the Shiré highlands. West

[1] The *pombeiros* (travelling traders) Baptista and José wandered, between 1802 and 1811, from Angola, through Muati Yamvo's country, to Kazembe's, and thence to Tete; Monteiro and Gamitto conducted an expedition from Tete to Kazembe's in 1831 and 1832; Silva Porto travelled extensively in South Central Africa from 1849 onwards, but although in more recent times Serpa Pinto, Capello and Ivens figure honourably among the explorers of the regions between the Zambesi and the Congo, the Portuguese, in the latter part of the nineteenth century, enjoyed no monopoly of this part of the continent, for our knowledge of which, in fact, we were, until 1890, mainly indebted to Livingstone, Cameron, Selous and Arnot.

of the Luangwa were tribes of Batoka origin resembling in appearance and speech the inhabitants of Northern Mashonaland, and between these and the Barotse confederacy were the Wa-Lenji and I-Ramba. For the most part these races were weak and peaceful, and in consequence they became the victims of a series of invasions by stronger tribes from adjacent territories. Thus the Awemba were over-run and more or less dominated by Arabs from Zanzibar, Kilwa and other ports on the coast, who early in the last century sent caravans into the interior, and gradually extended their influence, until in the 'eighties they had established stations as far west as Mweru and as far south as the Anyanja country. The objects of their expeditions were ivory and slaves; they found willing coadjutors in many of the chiefs, especially at the north end of Nyasa, and their religion presented attractive features to the natives, who readily adopted Mahometan customs, dress and even language.

The Anyanja tribes in turn became subject to two bodies of invaders, the Angoni in the north and the Wa-Yao in the south. The former were a branch of the early Zulu raiders who fled with Zwang-endaba from the oppressive tyranny of Tshaka.[1] Two of Zwang-endaba's principal successors were his sons Mpeseni and Mombera, the former of whom settled in the neighbourhood of what is now Fort Jameson, while the latter occupied the country of the Ba-Tumbukwe tribe on the shores of Lake Nyasa. The Wa-Yao (generally known as "Yao") came from the eastern side of the lake and swept down on the other flank of the luckless Anyanja, eventually occupying the Shiré highlands. They were a robust and warlike people, who gave endless trouble to the early missionary settlements.

Still further south, in the lower Shiré district, a curious condition arose. The indigenous tribes were subjects of yet another group of aliens. When Livingstone made his first expedition down the Zambesi from Barotseland he brought with him as porters and camp assistants a number of Makololo—the olive-skinned southerners who had accompanied Sebitoani.[2] At the close of the expedition these

---

[1] See p. 32, footnote.   [2] See p. 204.

men elected to remain in the Shiré district, where, by
their energy and superior intelligence, they speedily assumed
a position of authority over the local natives, and though
not more than a score or so in number, constituted themselves, like the Mamelukes in Egypt, a ruling caste. On
the banks of the Zambesi the natives (Chikunda) came
under the corrupt government of the Portuguese, whose
head-quarters were at Tete.

The dominant bands of invaders, Arabs, Angoni, Yao,
and Makololo, were constantly at loggerheads with one or
other of their neighbours, and a more unsettled and dis-
organised condition it would be difficult to imagine. It
may well be understood that the life of a pioneer missionary
was an uphill one.

Livingstone, after exploring the Shiré and discovering
Nyasa, Tanganyika, Mweru and Bangweolo, died at
Tshitambo, at the south end of the last-named lake, on
May 1st, 1873. Some years before this event, while investigating the Shiré with Dr. (the late Sir John) Kirk,
he had been joined by Bishop Mackenzie and his colleagues
of the "Universities' Mission." They were the forerunners
of the great missionary movement which afterwards played
an important part in colonising Nyasaland, but they encountered so much opposition from the aggressive Yao that five
years later the enterprise was for the time being abandoned.
The long disappearance of Livingstone in 1869 and 1870,
his sensational discovery by H. M. Stanley, and the story
of the hardships which he had endured fascinated the public
at home and drew the eyes of the world to Central Africa.
When the news reached England a little later that his life
had closed, the pathetic circumstances of his last moments,
as revealed by his journals and the reports of his native
attendants, sent a thrill of emotion through Great Britain
and an intense desire to carry on the work which he had
initiated. His advice to the Cambridge undergraduates—
" I have opened the door, I leave it to you to see that no
one closes it "—became the watchword of the Central
African pioneers, just as missionary effort throughout the
world was inspired by Christ's final injunction to his apostles,

" Go ye and teach all nations." In 1875 a body of Scotch missionaries set out for Lake Nyasa, and further contingents followed in quick succession. A small steamer was placed on the lake, Blantyre and other stations were founded, gardens laid out, and industrial schools established for natives. Traders, artisans and planters came in the wake of the missionaries, and effective occupation was thus inaugurated. The existence of the settlement was officially recognised in 1883 by the appointment of a British Consul to reside at Blantyre, but no further steps were taken for its protection against the predatory native tribes surrounding it. The Government was not yet alive to the value of African colonies.[1]

The only means of access to the Nyasa districts was the Portuguese port of Quilimane, on the northernmost side of the huge delta of the Zambesi, whence by a tortuous channel native " dug-outs " and lighters could ascend, not without difficulty, to the river beyond. Merchandise for the missionary stations had to be trans-shipped at the mouth of the Shiré River, which tapped Lake Nyasa, and connected the Highlands with the Zambesi. But the Shiré was only navigable as far as Katunga, which lay south of the British settlement, and from that point all goods were conveyed by native porters to Blantyre and the shores of the lake.

In order to secure the regular transport of supplies from the coast and to organise the trade in native produce, which was absolutely essential for the maintenance of the missions, steps were taken to raise capital, and, in 1878, a limited liability concern—the famous African Lakes Company—was formed, under the management of the brothers John and Frederick Moir, for carrying on a trading and transport business in conjunction with the missions. An attempt was also made to connect the north end of Lake Nyasa with Lake Tanganyika, where some of the missionaries had established themselves, and the Company undertook the construction of a road—afterwards well

[1] An exhaustive survey of the early history of exploration in the Lake districts and of the foundation of the Christian missions in Nyasaland may be found in Sir Harry Johnston's *British Central Africa*, published in 1898.

known as the " Stevenson road," [1] which, though never completed, became at a later date the boundary between German and British territory.

It must not be supposed that the life of the early settlers was free from anxiety. From the outset they had to contend with unusual obstacles. The sickliness of many of their original stations led to a heavy death-roll. They often suffered from want of provisions, and the difficulty of transporting goods from Quilimane added enormously to the trials of the work. Moreover, they had to encounter strenuous opposition at different times from the mixed tribes of natives by whom they were surrounded, and especially from the Mahometan Arabs of the north, who saw that their ancient freedom and facility for slave-raids would be doomed if the Christians gained a permanent foot-hold. In 1888 this opposition burst into open hostility, and a state of war commenced at the north end of the lake, which continued until the Arabs were finally crushed under the vigorous measures taken by H. H. Johnston.

Lastly, the Nyasa settlers were hampered and harassed by the Portuguese on the Zambesi. Up to the early 'eighties the Portuguese in this, as in other parts of the continent, had been asleep. Their stagnant occupation of the coast-lands had not been disturbed by the advent of a few parties of missionaries, and nothing had occurred to create any anxiety as to their trade with the interior. North and south of the Zambesi mouth, and for a certain distance along the banks of the river, a semi-effective occupation was maintained through the agency of *prazos da Corôa* (Crown estates), the holders of which paid an annual sum to the Mozambique Treasury in exchange for the right to collect taxes and to trade, and were directly under the administration of *Capitaes Môres* (Commandants) appointed by the King. Almost invariably these Commandants, and the prazo-holders as well, were Goanese half-castes, whose authority was endured by the natives only on account of the facilities which they provided for the importation of

[1] After Mr. James Stevenson, a Director of the African Lakes Company who subscribed liberally to the cost of construction.

spirits and guns, and who winked at, or even participated in, the traffic in slaves, which lingered on like a festering ulcer throughout Central Africa. The *prazos* themselves were in many cases worked by slave labour—caravans of unfortunate natives being brought down from the Nyasa region by Arab and Swahili traders, and sold to the half-breed owners of the estates. The Portuguese were alive to the value of Quilimane and the Lower Zambesi as the key to the inland trade, and exacted heavy duties on goods destined for Nyasaland.[1] But in regard to the interior they were apathetic. It could not vanish, and, as long as no other Power evinced a desire to seize it, they were content to allow it to remain dark and unopened—a happy hunting-ground for slavers and other riff-raff.

In 1886 appeared the first signs of an awakening among the Powers of Europe, and Portugal, becoming anxious at the possibility of the harmless Nyasaland missionaries growing into a substantial colony, saw that she must make haste to avert such a development, and to check the incipient settlement before it spread further into the interior. She entered, in that year, into important Conventions with France and Germany, each of which contained a clause recognising her exclusive claims to the territories which separate the provinces of Angola and Mozambique, and admitting the right of His Most Faithful Majesty the King to extend to these regions "his sovereign and civilising influence." Thus it was sought by a stroke of the pen to lock up an area of hundreds of thousands of square miles as a reserve at the disposal of what was then the most feeble Government in Europe! This immense tract comprised the whole basin of the Zambesi, Matabeleland, and the district of Lake Nyasa up to the latitude of the Rovuma River, and, while in the entire area there was not a vestige or sign of Portuguese jurisdiction or authority, there were countries which included British settlements,

---

[1] Professor Drummond, in *Tropical Africa*, has an amusing story of how, having paid duties to the Portuguese to enable him to enter the country, he evaded a further demand—made as he was leaving Quilimane on his return to England—for payment of a tax for "residing in the interior."

and others in which Great Britain took an exceptional interest. Lord Salisbury, therefore, without delay, issued a dignified and peremptory challenge, and declined to recognise Portuguese sovereignty in these territories.

Before the diplomatic correspondence on this point terminated a new means of irritation was devised by the Portuguese. The handful of British settlers had, as has been said, become involved, during 1888, in a struggle with the Arab slave-traders at the north end of the lake, who were seeking to oppress the native tribes, gradually over-running the whole country, and spreading devastation in all directions. The settlers were faced with the alternative of exterminating this vermin or evacuating the country. They were absolutely dependent on supplies of ammunition from the coast. Yet the Portuguese authorities refused to allow any guns or ammunition to pass Quilimane. For a whole year they pursued these irritating tactics, each consignment being made the subject of representations from the Foreign Office. Their pretext was that the arms might be traded to natives, and when assured that they were only intended for the defence of the British settlements, they magnanimously offered to intervene themselves for the protection of the missionaries, alleging that the missions round Lake Nyasa were within the limits of Portuguese influence.

The British Government of the day had no desire or intention of asserting their own sovereignty over the Nyasa district. All that was sought was that the English and Scotch settlers should be allowed to import and export their merchandise, without hindrance, through Quilimane, on payment of a reasonable transit duty. They refused to recognise Portuguese claims beyond the confluence of the Shiré and Ruo Rivers, but had no thought of assuming an active control, unless forced to do so by circumstances. Unfortunately, or rather fortunately, these circumstances were not long in forthcoming. During the latter part of 1888 an imposing expedition was despatched from Lisbon, with the object (disclosed in the Press, though denied by the authorities) of extending, consolidating and securing

Portuguese occupation north and south of the Zambesi.[1] Among those who accompanied it was Paiva d'Andrade, who, as we have seen, subsequently confined his attention to the districts in the south. The destination of the main body was kept secret, but it soon transpired that it was intended to operate in the Shiré district, and although the Governor of Quilimane, with unconscious humour, assured our consular representative that it was a *Missão civilizadora*, sent out for the purpose of assisting the English missions, it speedily became apparent that the real and only object was to plant the Portuguese flag in the country of the Angoni and Makololo, and to intimidate the local chiefs into making so-called " treaties " admitting the sovereignty of Portugal.

On its departure from the coast all disguise as to the military character of the expedition was thrown off. Several thousand native troops, well armed with small artillery, and with a complete campaigning equipment, proceeded to the Shiré River under the command of Antonio Cardoso, a captain in the Navy. On arrival at the east side of the lake, owing to desertions, sickness, and the hostility of the native chiefs, Cardoso's force found itself in difficulties, and he appealed to Lisbon for relief. The home Government then despatched the indomitable Major Serpa Pinto, an officer whose energy and courage had been demonstrated on previous occasions in Africa, but whose zeal frequently outran his discretion, to convey reinforcements and to take command of the army. He arrived at Quilimane in June 1889, and soon afterwards started for the Shiré River. Had not England been able to produce a man who was a match for Serpa Pinto it is not unlikely that the southern portion of Nyasaland would have been irretrievably lost. As has often happened, however, the right man was there in the person of Mr. H. H. Johnston, who had been appointed H.B.M.'s Consul for Mozambique, and who, placing a liberal construction on his commission, determined to put an end once and for all to the system of pin-pricks which had for months been making the existence of the Nyasa settlers intolerable.

[1] *Blue Book* C. 5904, p. 48.

Just before his arrival in July 1889, a discovery had been made of immense importance in its relation to the opening up of the interior to commerce and civilisation. Mr. Daniel Rankin, a young Scotchman engaged in the Consular service, had for some years been studying closely the navigation of the Zambesi, and early in 1889 he announced that the Chinde stream, which opened near the southern extremity of the delta, offered a navigable entrance to the main channel, and that its mouth, besides affording good sheltered anchorage, was deep enough to admit coasting steamers during the greater part of the year. This meant a direct entrance from the sea to the Zambesi, which, as an international waterway, could not be closed to British commerce.

Johnston lost no time in putting Rankin's discovery to a practical test. On July 28th he ascended the Chinde mouth in H.M.S. *Stork*, and five days later reached, without serious difficulty, the Shiré River, thus demonstrating that it was possible for an ocean-going steamer to enter the Zambesi, and that, with one trans-shipment, goods could be conveyed to a point beyond the recognised limits of Portuguese territory.

Johnston proceeded up the Shiré, and found Serpa Pinto collecting his forces a short distance below the Ruo, with the object of marching upon the Makololo. A meeting took place between the two, at which Pinto courteously attempted to persuade the British Consul that he was conducting a scientific expedition into Nyasaland, that he was being obstructed by the Makololo, through whose territory he wished to pass, and that, unless Johnston could induce them to withdraw their opposition, bloodshed might ensue. But Johnston was not to be beguiled by Portuguese plausibility. He warned the gallant Major of the serious results which hostilities against the Makololo would have upon the safety of British subjects in the Shiré highlands, and hinted in unmistakable language that the action contemplated might jeopardise the friendly relations between England and Portugal. He did not stop short at this protest, but arranged with Mr. Buchanan, the Acting Consul for Nyasaland, to declare a British Protectorate over the

Makololo and Shiré districts north of the Ruo, and to send a formal notification of this to Serpa Pinto.[1] By this bold step he called checkmate to Pinto, and irrevocably committed the British Government to a responsibility which they should have undertaken a year or more before.

Unfortunately he was not in a position to make the Protectorate an effective one by a display of force. Mlauli, the Makololo leader, was growing impatient of the constant presence of the Portuguese troops on his frontier, and could with difficulty be restrained from attacking them. The Portuguese, on the other hand, gradually goaded Mlauli to resistance by sending out armed parties to raid and plunder defenceless villages, and by announcing their intention of advancing into the Makololo country. These provocations eventually had the natural result : Mlauli's men attacked the Portuguese on the Shiré, and sustained a crushing defeat, with heavy losses. Serpa Pinto now left for Mozambique to obtain further instructions, and his command on the Shiré was taken over by João Coutinho. This officer was more impetuous even than his predecessor, and having been appointed " Military Governor of the Shiré," and in the absence of Johnston, who was now far away on Lake Nyasa, he determined to force a crisis. In December 1889 he crossed the Ruo and occupied Chiromo in British territory; he then proceeded with his force along both banks of the Shiré, driving Mlauli and other Makololo chiefs before him, and reached Katunga, where he halted to make preparations for a further advance on Blantyre. He announced his intention of annexing the whole country up to the lake, and, to crown his audacity, called upon the British at Blantyre, Zomba and elsewhere to put themselves under the protection of Portugal or abide by the consequences.

Coutinho's escapade had the satisfactory result, which years of petty aggressions had failed to achieve, of forcing the Government at last to grapple with the situation. He had slaughtered a number of natives under British pro-

[1] The protectorate was officially announced in a public notice issued by Buchanan on the 21st of September.

tection and trespassed within the sacred precincts of British territory. Bitter indignation surged through England on this outrageous insult becoming known, and the entire Press, with the exception of one or two ultra-Radical journals, clamoured for reprisals on the Portuguese. It seemed intolerable that peaceful British colonists should be at the mercy of these blustering *conquistadores*. Lord Salisbury was constrained to take decisive action, and, on December the 31st, he sent an ultimatum to the Lisbon Government. The customary excuses from the Portuguese Foreign Office, accompanied by the usual patriotic rodomontade, followed, but the British Premier was implacable. The authorities at Lisbon recognised that England was in earnest, and on the 12th January, 1890, they sent a telegram to the Governor-General of Mozambique ordering the immediate evacuation of the Shiré and Makololo country.[1]

Thus when the new year opened the way lay once more clear for British expansion. Rhodes was not slow to take advantage of it. He knew that Nyasaland was safe in the hands of the indefatigable Johnston, but he had his eye upon the regions beyond, to which Johnston's commission did not extend, and which must be swept into the net of the Charter ere they were seized by rivals. Portuguese encroachments had been rudely checked both north and south of the Zambesi, but it would not be long before other nations—Belgians or Germans—would be creeping in where the Portuguese had failed, and Rhodes determined, if possible, to be the first in the field.

[1] Lord Salisbury's ultimatum also demanded the withdrawal of all Portuguese troops from Mashonaland.

CHAPTER XVI

HOW KATANGA WAS LOST

BEFORE Rhodes could move, Johnston, who, being on the spot, was better situated, began to take action. After his meeting with Serpa Pinto in August 1889, he proceeded to Blantyre, where he found Mr. Sharpe,[1] who had been assisting the Lakes Company in their struggles with the Arabs[2] of North Nyasa, preparing to start on a hunting and trading expedition towards the Luangwa River. Johnston asked him to undertake, on behalf of Great Britain, the task of negotiating treaties with the chiefs in the country he was about to traverse, a proposal to which Sharpe readily agreed. He first proceeded westward from the Shiré, keeping close to the Portuguese border, until he reached Undi's town in longitude 32°. He concluded treaties with all chiefs *en route*, and so brought under British influence the country north of the 15th degree of latitude, between 32° and 35° East Longitude. Some of this area, however, was subsequently included in the Portuguese sphere.

Returning to Blantyre, he found that Johnston had gone to Lake Tanganyika, and he therefore proceeded on a second journey in a direction to the north of his previous one. He left Lake Nyasa at Bandawe, and struck southeastwards towards Mpeseni (now Fort Jameson). There he

---

[1] Now Sir Alfred Sharpe, K.C.M.G., C.B., who originally came to Nyasaland from Fiji, where he held a Consular post, in order to obtain some big-game shooting. On his arrival he found the trouble between the Arabs and the British settlers coming to a head, and gladly volunteered his assistance. He afterwards joined the Administration and became Governor in 1897. Circumstances thus converted a chance visit into a permanent and distinguished career.

[2] No detailed account is given of the Arab war, because it principally concerned the settlement of Nyasaland proper. This settlement had an important bearing on the Chartered Company's operations in North-Eastern Rhodesia, and, in fact, paved the way for them, but although the Company gave liberal financial assistance towards its early administration, Nyasaland was at no time an integral part of the Chartered territories.

found a German named Karl Wiese, in Portuguese employ, and a Portuguese officer—Senhor de Solla—who had completely poisoned the mind of the Angoni chief against the British. Sharpe realised that there was no chance of success in this quarter, and at the beginning of 1890 returned to the lake, where he resumed preparations for his hunting excursion. While so occupied he again met Johnston, who informed him of the formation of the British South Africa Company, and of its relations with the exhausted Lakes Company, which Rhodes was preparing to absorb, and invited him to undertake further expeditions on behalf of the amalgamated concern. Sharpe consented to this, and was forthwith appointed Commissioner for the Chartered Company.

Three journeys were sketched out : the first to secure Chikusi and other doubtful chiefs at the south end of the lake; another to the Luangwa River, which was to be followed down to its junction with the Zambesi, and the third and most formidable to Lake Mweru and Garenganze (Katanga) beyond. From each independent chief he was to secure full mineral and commercial rights, and in return he was to pledge the Company to protect him and his people from all outside interference, to place a British Resident in the country, and to promote Christian missions and education; to stamp out slavery, and generally to advance the civilisation of the native tribes. The treaties were also to include a clause to the effect that they were equivalent to a covenant of alliance with the British Government, in token of which the Union Jack was to be formally bestowed upon each chief accepting them.

The first expedition presented no difficulties, and in March, after concluding a satisfactory agreement with Chikusi, Sharpe returned up Lake Nyasa to Domira Bay, from which point he proceeded due west towards Mpeseni, making a treaty *en route* with Chiwere, a chief whose territory bordered the lake. At Mpeseni, as on his previous visit, he met with opposition. The Angoni chief was evilly disposed towards the British, and refused point-blank to entertain the suggestion of a treaty. A large number of Sharpe's carriers were here induced to desert him, and his progress was much impeded.   Sickness broke out among the remaining members of the ulendo (expedition), and caused further vexatious delays.   In spite, however, of these drawbacks Sharpe reached the Luangwa, and followed it down to a spot near its junction with the Zambesi, at the new Portuguese settlement of Zumbo.   He avoided Zumbo itself by a short detour, intending to explore the Zambesi higher up, but his supplies were nearly exhausted and he was obliged to return.   During this journey he effected a number of further treaties on the same terms as before.   He also found evidence of gold at Missara (or Misale) south-east of Mpeseni's, and heard stories of mines (of which traces still remained) having been worked there, many years before, by Portuguese half-castes.

On his return to Blantyre, at the beginning of July 1890, Sharpe began preparations for the more ambitious expedition across country to Garenganze (Katanga).   In the meantime Rhodes, unaware that Johnston had arranged for this to be undertaken by Sharpe, had been making other plans. For the somewhat hazardous enterprise of tackling Msiri, the Paramount Chief of that little-known territory, he had selected Mr. Joseph Thomson, who, though unacquainted with Garenganze, had conducted several successful expeditions in other parts of the interior, including one in the year 1880 to the north end of Nyasa and the country between that lake and Tanganyika, and who was without question the most intrepid African explorer since Livingstone.

Accompanied by Mr. J. A. Grant, Thomson left Kimberley in May 1890, and proceeded to Delagoa Bay, where he began to equip his expedition.   He had resolved to enter East Africa by Quilimane (the Chinde mouth having not yet come into general use), but as it was of vital importance that his destination and connection with the Company should not leak out, he kept all his plans secret.   The granting of the Charter had quickened all sorts of adventurous young colonists, who, either on their own account, or on behalf of syndicates—British and foreign—were preparing to start for the unknown interior.   Both at Lourenzo Marques and

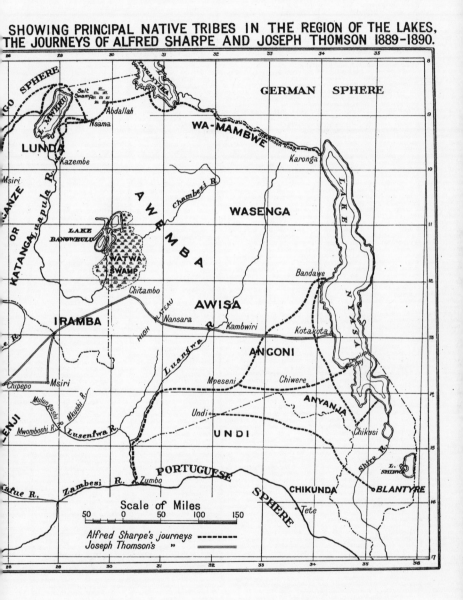

SHOWING PRINCIPAL NATIVE TRIBES IN THE REGION OF THE LAKES,
THE JOURNEYS OF ALFRED SHARPE AND JOSEPH THOMSON 1889-1890.

GERMAN SPHERE

CONGO SPHERE

LUNDA

WA-MAMBWE

WASENGA

AWEMBA

WATWA SWAMP

LAKE BANGWEULU

AWISA

ANGONI

IRAMBA

ANYANJA

UNDI

PORTUGUESE SPHERE

CHIKUNDA

BLANTYRE

Salt Swamp
Abdallah
Nsama
Kazembe
Msiri
Karonga
Chambezi R.
Bandawe
Chitambo
Nansara
Kambwiri
Kotakota
Mpeseni
Chiwere
Undi
Chikusi
Chipepo
Msiri
Mwomboshi R.
Mulungushi R.
Mkushi R.
Lusenfwa R.
Zumbo
Zambesi R.
Kafue R.
Tete
L. Shirwa
Shire R.

L. MWERU
Luapula R.
KATANGA OR MANGANZE
HIGH PLATEAU
Luangwa R.
LAKE NYASA
TANGANYIKA

Scale of Miles
50   0   50   100   150

Alfred Sharpe's journeys - - - - - -
Joseph Thomson's   "   ————————

at Quilimane Thomson encountered several of these. One
party of six, backed, it was said, by German capital, and
headed by a well-known concession-hunter, Mr. Louis
Patrick Bowler,[1] was on the point of departure for Nyasaland. Another party was being formed by a Mr. Austin,
who had recently visited Nyasaland for purposes of sport,
and was now returning on a more serious mission, as agent
for a Scottish exploring company, and there were others
whom it is unnecessary to mention. All were keeping the
strictest secrecy as to their intentions; but all were bent
on the same errand.

The arrival of so many " hunting parties " at Quilimane
was creating some uneasiness among the authorities, and
before Thomson was permitted to proceed inland, his
luggage was subjected to a rigorous search at the Customs,
while he himself was required to sign a document stating
that his object was purely sport and scientific research, and
that he had no intention of making treaties or doing anything prejudicial to Portuguese interests in " countries under
their influence," the last words enabling him to give the
pledge with an easy conscience. It was of supreme importance to be beforehand with the other land-grabbers and
concession-hunters, and these formalities were annoying,
but he learnt that Bowler was waiting to be joined by
Rankin (the discoverer of Chinde), and this gave him a start
which he was not slow in turning to advantage.

Having secured a large gang of porters from Mozambique,
he finally set off for the interior during the last week of June.
In spite of Thomson's assurances, and the secrecy of his
preparations, it is probable that the authorities at Quilimane
smelt a rat. He passed unmolested into the Zambesi and
up the Shiré, but on arrival at the mouth of the Ruo, which
was the recognised limit of Portuguese influence, the stern-

---

[1] Mr. Bowler was a Pretoria citizen who claimed to have obtained in
1888 a concession from chiefs in N.E. Mashonaland independent of Lobengula. On the strength of this he endeavoured, unsuccessfully, to obtain
funds from Rhodes. Towards the end of 1889 he posed as the representative of a concern bearing the extraordinary name of " The Upper and
Lower Zambesi Navigation, Exploration, Trading, Land-acquiring and
Colonisation Company, Limited," and his present expedition was the
outcome of this.

wheel steamer, in which he was travelling in company with several missionaries, was fired upon, and although her cargo and passengers were successfully landed in British territory, she was arrested by orders of the irrepressible Coutinho on the return journey. Thomson himself had a narrow escape a few days afterwards. Having unwarily ventured in an open boat across the Ruo, he was bombarded from the Portuguese fort, and had the greatest difficulty in escaping, under a regular fusillade, to the shelter of the bank. These incidents gave rise, of course, to stern remonstrances from the British Government, but before reparation was made they were lost sight of in the general excitement which followed Forbes' exploit in Manicaland.[1]

At Blantyre Thomson met Sharpe and learnt, much to his surprise, that this gentleman was preparing to undertake the identical errand for which he himself had been engaged. After discussion it was decided that each should proceed with his plans, but that Sharpe should start from the north end of Nyasa, and, skirting Lakes Tanganyika and Mweru, should enter Garenganze from the northern side, while Thomson was to work his way round the southern shores of Lake Bangweolo to meet him. Thus if one failed in reaching the goal there was still a chance of the other succeeding.

This satisfactory understanding was arrived at about the middle of July, and a few days later Sharpe started for the north end of the lake. Having engaged a number of Wa-Mambwe carriers at Karonga he struck inland on August 1st. On his way towards Tanganyika he met Mr. Fred Moir, Joint Manager of the African Lakes Company, who was returning from a visit to Ujiji, and who allowed one of his staff, Mr. Barton, to join the Garenganze expedition. From the very outset Sharpe experienced great difficulty in obtaining porters, the local natives refusing to proceed more than a short distance. He received, however, a good deal of help from the Arabs in the vicinity of Lake Tanganyika, notably from Bwana Teleka at Sumbo and Abdallah bin Suliman, an important and intelligent chief south-west of the lake. Finally, at the village of Nsama, the original

[1] See Chapter XI.

native chief of all this country, he obtained sufficient native porters to carry his goods to Garenganze, and after crossing the Kalungwisi River, and keeping down the eastern shores of Lake Mweru, he reached, on the 29th of September, the town of Kazembe. This name has been borne by a series of chiefs, the first of whom broke away from the Lunda supremacy early in the nineteenth century. Livingstone travelled through the country in 1867 and 1868 and experienced much kindness and hospitality from the Kazembe of that time, but prior to this the place had been visited by several Portuguese—notably Pereira, an ivory trader, who was through the country in 1796, Dr. Lacerda, who as already mentioned, died there in 1798, and Major Monteiro in the 'thirties. Previously to Sharpe's arrival the last European of any note to visit Kazembe was Lieut. Giraud, a French naval officer, who explored this part of Africa in 1883. For generations a feud had existed between Kazembe's people and those of Garenganze on the opposite side of the lake—two tribes which had originally been one. A few years after Livingstone's visit the Garenganze chieftaincy had been seized by Msiri (Msidi), a son of the ruler of the Unyamwesi country, east of Tanganyika, who originally came to trade copper, and then settled permanently in the land. This man successfully resisted Kazembe and threw off his yoke. The two tribes were thenceforward independent; but their hostility continued, and Sharpe found that he could expect no help from Kazembe towards his mission to Msiri.

The chief received him well, but refused to allow him to pass through his country to Garenganze. When Sharpe persisted, he found that his food supplies were cut off, and his porters intimidated, and eventually he could only persuade seventeen " boys " to accompany him on the next stage of his journey. Moreover, Kazembe sent messengers ahead of him, and warned all natives along the Luapula River to refuse him food and porters, and to prevent him from using their canoes for crossing the river. Three days after leaving Kazembe's his provisions were exhausted, and the few men who had remained with him threw down their loads. Sharpe then started with one native,[1] and one piece of trading-cloth, and on seeing this seven of his Atonga porters relented, and again shouldered their burdens. It was futile, of course, for him to hope to accomplish his purpose with so miserable a following, and one can only admire the dogged resolution which pushed him on. He first directed his steps eastward so as to get away from the native villages, with the intention of turning to the south and leaving Kazembe's country before approaching the Luapula. That day both he and his escort went without food. He rigged up a sort of canoe from strips of bark with the ends patched up, but after carrying this rough contrivance six miles to the river, he found it impossible to render it water-tight. Nearly in despair, he decided to return to Kazembe's and make another effort to come to an arrangement with the chief. In his satisfaction at having, as he thought, effectually stopped the mission to Garenganze, Kazembe received him with open arms, supplied him and his porters with food, and even agreed to accept the British flag and sign a concession and treaty.

Sharpe's next plan was to return to Abdallah's, and having obtained fresh porters to try to push round the north side of Mweru, crossing the Luapula where it emerges from the lake. In this he was successful; Abdallah, whose town he reached on the 17th October, gave him some men to carry his goods, and twenty-five *askaris* (soldiers) to conduct him to the river, which he crossed six days later. A fortnight's march in a south-west direction over a grassy mountainous plateau brought him at length to Msiri's head-quarters.

At this time the only Europeans in that country were two missionaries, Messrs. Swan (a Yorkshireman) and Faulkner (Canadian), who had first arrived in 1887. The founder of this enterprising mission, Mr. Arnot, was absent on a journey to Bihé, in Angola, 600 miles west of Garenganze. Msiri's was an important mart for traders from many distant parts—Arabs from Zanzibar and even Uganda, Portuguese half-castes from Benguella, Baluba from the Congo and

---

[1] It should be mentioned that Barton had been sent back to Nyasa on arrival at Kazembe's.

Chikonda from the Zambesi, all meeting there with their different wares. Copper, salt, ivory and slaves were what they sought, and muzzle-loading guns, powder and caps, with cloth, beads and European trade-goods of every description, were tendered in exchange. The chief had an immense store of ivory, which was the form in which his numerous vassals paid their annual tribute. He was a man of no mean ability, and from a small and dependent province he had built up a kingdom which extended from the Luapula and Lake Mweru to the Lualaba, and covered the whole of the south-east portion of the present Congo State. Like Mziligazi he retained his influence by relentless severity, sending raiding-parties periodically to the more distant parts of his State, and visiting with instant and merciless punishment any signs of disaffection. Human sacrifices were frequent. The death penalty was an almost daily occurrence at the capital, and the stockades of the royal residence were decorated with the rotting heads of decapitated victims.

When Sharpe arrived, the missionaries, though kowtowing to Msiri, and appearing to be at his beck and call, exercised in reality a good deal of weight in public affairs, and had become the chief's advisers on most matters of political import. Arnot had, not without just grounds, put him on his guard against concession-hunters, and had warned him to beware of people who asked him to sign papers, for they would rob him of his country. Unfortunately Arnot was away, and his colleagues did not possess sufficient discrimination to discern that Sharpe was no mere adventurer. On first meeting the chief he found him suspicious, though outwardly friendly; but when the subject of a concession was broached the fury of the old savage knew no bounds. This must be one of the robbers that Arnot had warned him against—the men that wished to filch away his country ! No talk about the Great Queen of England and the advantages of protection, no arguments as to the evils of the slave-trade could assuage his wrath. The missionaries, who might have smoothed matters down, avoided any participation in the business, and for some time Sharpe feared open violence. However, beyond ordering him to surrender the carriers who had accompanied him from Abdallah's and Nsama's, on the grounds that these chiefs were his ancient enemies, Msiri refrained from any extreme measures.

Finding it hopeless to pursue his original plan, Sharpe thought he would go south to Katanga, and satisfy himself as to the extent of the copper-belt, and as to whether the reports of gold-reefs were well founded. But in this also his desires were at once frustrated by the chief. He could get no news of Joseph Thomson, and saw that it would be courting disaster to try to reach Katanga except with a considerable armed force.

Msiri eventually compelled Sharpe to quit the country by the way he had entered it, and sent men with him to enforce compliance. The return journey occupied two and a half months, and was wretched in the extreme; heavy rains were falling, and, with clothes and boots worn out, and his store of provisions reduced to starvation point, the explorer was in a sorry plight. In spite of these trials, which were aggravated by the difficulty of engaging or retaining porters, he managed to reach the north shores of Lake Nyasa on January 24th, 1891, and after some weeks' delay in waiting for a steamer, finally arrived at Mandala (Blantyre) on February 17th. Since September 1889 he had been incessantly on the move, and although he failed in the principal object of his last journey, he had accomplished a great deal in these fifteen months. He had established satisfactory treaties over the whole of the districts between the three lakes, Nyasa, Tanganyika and Mweru, and had thus added to the British flag the major part of North-Eastern Rhodesia. The value of his expeditions can hardly be over-estimated. Before he started these parts were at the mercy of Germany on the north and Portugal on the south, and, although their boundaries were fixed by treaties with Great Britain, the intervening territory might easily have become the prey of one or more of the land-grabbing syndicates whose agents infested the country, and who would have subsequently sold them to the highest bidder, or blackmailed Rhodes by real or bogus concessions. It was a country with immense possibilities of trade. The African Lakes Company, which could have reaped a rich harvest, was neglecting its òpportunities. It had no supplies of trade goods, and consequently the abundant stores of ivory were finding their way to the coast through the hands of Arab merchants. Sharpe warned Rhodes that unless immmediate steps were taken to establish depots in the area which he had secured, the whole trade would sooner or later pass into the hands of the Germans of East Africa.

Turn we now to Joseph Thomson, whom we left at Blantyre preparing for the expedition to the south of Lake Bangweolo, with the object of meeting Sharpe, if possible, at Msiri's. Accompanied by J. A. Grant and by Charles Wilson, an employé of the African Lakes Corporation, whose services were lent by Mr. Frederick Moir at Mandala, Thomson left Kotakota on the western shore of Lake Nyasa at the end of August 1890. With a caravan of one hundred and forty native porters he travelled due west, without stopping to negotiate any concessions, until he reached the country of Kambwiri, a chief of Kiwende on the Luangwa River. This hasty progress was a mistake, for the country traversed, although within the British sphere, had not at that time been secured by the Chartered Company, and some trouble was afterwards caused by Messrs. Bowler and Rankin, who, following hard on Thomson's heels, joined Wiese (the German seen by Sharpe at Mpeseni's) and obtained concessions in the self-same area.

With Kambwiri, whose rule extended for forty miles on either side of the Luangwa River, Thomson had no difficulty in coming to terms, and he clinched the agreement by making an Arab trader, Salim-bin-Nasser, who had great influence with the chief, a party to it. After some trouble with his Atonga porters, who attempted to desert, Thomson headed for Tshitambo's, the scene of Livingstone's death in 1873, and found himself on a plateau, some 4000 feet above sea level, forming the watershed of the Luangwa River on the east and the Luapula and Lake Bangweolo on the west. At this point began a series of misfortunes which culminated

in the failure of the principal object of his enterprise.   From
the time of leaving Kotakota he had experienced trouble
with his porters, which had only been smoothed over by the
employment of great tact and firmness.   About the middle
of September, when he was traversing the district of Mbalala,
governed by a female chief, Nansara, smallpox broke out
among the carriers, and thenceforward the disease dogged
his footsteps.   Thomson himself also fell sick, his illness
being aggravated by the anxiety caused by the pestilence
among his men and the incessant fear of desertions.   He
paused a few days at Tshitambo's to put the sick in quaran-
tine and give the sound ones a chance to rest, but on resuming his march on the 6th October he found that the tidings
of the disease had preceded him, and the whole country-side
rose to prevent him from passing on.   Day by day one or
more of his men sickened or died, until his *ulendo* was
reduced by fully one-third of its original strength.   Occasionally he was able to leave a few of the sufferers at a friendly
village, but more often the inhabitants were aggressive,
and he was unceremoniously hustled on.   West of Tshitambo's he descended into a trackless, guideless wilderness
bounded by the Watwa swamps, and had no alternative but
to turn south towards the watershed of the Luapula and
Kafue Rivers, and into a country known as Iramba.   Here,
close to the site of the present Bwana Mkubwa mine, the
Atonga porters finally mutinied, and declared their intention
of walking back to Lake Nyasa, nine hundred miles to the
east.   To try to reach Garenganze in such circumstances
would have been insane, and Thomson resolved to abandon
the attempt; but he was loth to turn back, and made up his
mind to push on through Sitanda [1] towards the Mashukulumbwe country on the southern bend of the Kafue River,
taking only a small party and leaving Grant and Wilson
behind.   He came to terms with the mutineers, who remained
in Iramba with Grant, and succeeded in reaching Chipepo.
His ailment was now causing him excruciating pain, and to
add to his troubles the rainy season set in.   He was far too

---

[1] Sitanda's village lay between what are now known as the *Silver King*
and *Broken Hill* Mines.

ill to proceed, and was reluctantly compelled to turn his
column eastwards towards Lake Nyasa.   He rejoined Grant
and Wilson, and a dreary march ensued, through a country
sodden with the rains, and with smallpox still hanging on the
flanks of his discontented following.   He hoped to rest at
Mpeseni's, but the truculent Angoni chief proved so hostile
that Thomson and his party had to make a nocturnal flight
to escape a massacre.   Ultimately, in broken health and
spirits, and with but a remnant of his expedition, he reached
Kotakota at the beginning of the new year—a few days
before Sharpe's arrival at the north end of the lake.   The
native chief Jumbe received him hospitably, and he was able
to enjoy a long rest on the shores of the lake while waiting
for a steamer to take him south.

Thus failed the second of the two expeditions to Msiri's,
and their united effect was only to turn the attention of the
Belgians to the coveted country.   Katanga was probably
intended by the General Act of the Berlin Conference to be
included in the Congo Free State, but one of the principal
stipulations of this Act was that new occupations on the
coast (and inferentially in the interior also) of Africa, in
order to secure recognition by the Powers, must be effective.
At the time of the expeditions of Sharpe and Thomson any
rights claimed by the Congo Free State over Garenganze
existed merely on paper, and if Rhodes could have succeeded
in planting the British flag in these regions, he would not only
have been acting within his rights, but might have established a title which it would have been no easy matter for
another Power to upset.

Realising the danger of another and more successful
British attempt which would probably indeed have been
undertaken by Joseph Thomson, had his health been equal
to it, the Belgians made strenuous efforts to convert their
paper sovereignty into a real one.   Immediately after
Sharpe's departure a strong expedition was despatched to
Msiri's from the Upper Congo under Lieut. Paul de Marinel,
who failed, however, to persuade the chief to execute a
treaty.   A like result attended a second venture under the
command of M. Delcommune early in 1891.   This was

organised by the Katanga Company, which was an international syndicate with a Charter from the Congo Free State,
and a directorate composed of English, French and Belgian
financiers.[1]

But a third expedition—also sent out by the Katanga
Company—was more successful. It was led by an officer of
the British Army, Captain William Grant Stairs (a Nova
Scotian by birth, and a distinguished member of Stanley's
Emin Pasha Relief Expedition), who was accompanied by
several Englishmen and Belgians. It left Zanzibar in
July 1891, and, after crossing the Unyamwezi country and
Lake Tanganyika, arrived at Msiri's at the end of the year.
Garenganze was then in a state of ferment. The chief's
persistent cruelties had alienated most of his subjects, who
were on the verge of open rebellion. As on previous
occasions he spurned all inducements to execute a treaty
or to sign any act of submission, but he could no longer count
on the fidelity of his own people, and, on being threatened
by Stairs with forcible measures, he took refuge in flight.
In a skirmish which ensued the old chief was shot dead by
one of the Belgian officers, and Stairs promptly took
possession of the country in the name of the Congo Free State.

Msiri was a bloodthirsty tyrant—an anachronism, like
Lobengula, and the world was well rid of him. Nevertheless
one can imagine the howl of indignation which would have
been raised by the Aborigines Protection Society and other
well-meaning English busybodies had one of Rhodes' men
served Lobengula as Stairs served the chief of Garenganze.
Moreover, while not wishing to detract from the vigour and
resolution of Stairs' achievement, one cannot help regretting
that he should have placed these qualities at the service of a
foreign Power in a contest against a British Company—the
more so as one knows, from the published statement of one
of his officers,[2] that he was prepared to repel Joseph Thomson or any of Rhodes' lieutenants by force of arms if he found
them encroaching on Garenganze or Katanga. He did not

---

[1] Sir William Mackinnon, founder of the British East Africa Company,
Sir John Kirk, the upholder of British ascendancy at Zanzibar, and
Commander Cameron, the African explorer, were among the Directors.

[2] *With Captain Stairs to Katanga*, by Dr. J. A. Moloney, pp. 207, 208.

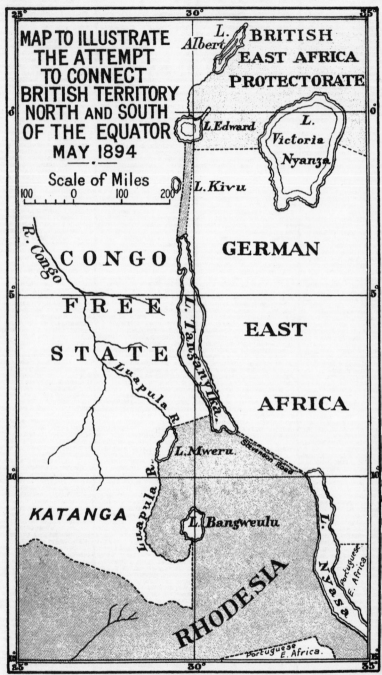

MAP TO ILLUSTRATE
THE ATTEMPT
TO CONNECT
BRITISH TERRITORY
NORTH AND SOUTH
OF THE EQUATOR
MAY 1894

Scale of Miles
100   0   100   200

L. Albert

BRITISH
EAST AFRICA
PROTECTORATE

L. Edward

L. Victoria Nyanza

L. Kivu

GERMAN

R. Congo

CONGO

FREE

STATE

Luapula R.

L. Tanganyika

EAST

AFRICA

Stevenson Road

L. Mweru

L. Bangweulu

KATANGA

Luapula R.

L. Nyasa

Portuguese E. Africa

RHODESIA

Portuguese E. Africa.

Projected lease by Congo Free State to Britain

long survive his success, for he succumbed to blackwater
fever at Chinde on the eve of embarkation for Europe.

Before leaving this part of Central Africa reference may
be made, briefly, to the efforts made to connect the spheres
of the two British Chartered Companies in the north and
south and to secure an uninterrupted line of communication
between Rhodesia and the waterway of the Nile.

The respective boundaries of the British and German
spheres in the regions of the Great Lakes were defined by an
agreement made between the two Powers in July 1890.
The Stevenson road between Lakes Nyasa and Tanganyika
fell, under this agreement, to England, but to the north of
Tanganyika, and between that lake and Lake Albert Edward,
the German sphere was brought up to the eastern boundary
of the Congo Free State. Consequently, although there was
an open route for British trade from the south as far as the
extreme northern part of Tanganyika, further progress was
barred by the German strip of some hundreds of miles intervening between the lake and British East Africa. To
circumvent this Lord Kimberley in 1894 entered into an
agreement with the Free State for a lease, for an undefined
period, of a port at the north end of Tanganyika, and of
a strip of territory, twenty-five kilometres in breadth,
connecting this port with Lake Albert Edward. It was a
clever stroke of diplomacy, and the Foreign Secretary richly
deserved the credit which he assumed to himself in the
self-satisfied despatch in which he announced it to the
Legation at Brussels.[1]

The advantage accruing to England did not, however,
escape the vigilant eyes of the German Foreign Office, and
a protest was instantly addressed to the British Government,
pointing out that this lease infringed the understanding
between Germany and the Congo Free State as to their
mutual boundary, and, whether the strip of territory were
contiguous to the German frontier or at some distance from
it, would have the effect of interrupting direct trade communication between the two States. Undoubtedly this was
the case, and with equal certainty it may be affirmed that

[1] *Parliamentary Paper*, C. 7360.

had the positions of Britain and Germany in the matter been reversed, the latter Power would have clung with the tenacity of a bulldog to the agreement. Not so, however, the British Foreign Office of 1894. Having carefully explained that no obstacles to Germany's trade relations with the Congo Free State were intended, and that arrangements could have easily been made to overcome such difficulties, if they existed, Lord Kimberley—capitulated! The proposed lease was abandoned. The connection which he had announced with such a flourish of trumpets in May 1894 was weakly surrendered in the following month, and the chance of an " all red " route from Capetown to Cairo was lost—as it then appeared—for ever ! [1]

Joseph Thomson's expedition was by no means fruitless. He had linked up the districts secured by Sharpe with the outskirts of Lewanika's possessions, which fell to the Chartered Company under the Lochner Concession, but which certainly never extended beyond Sitanda. The Iramba country was afterwards declared to be within the Congo Free State, but with this exception the whole of the area through which Sharpe and Thomson had so gallantly conducted their expeditions was included in the sphere of the Chartered Company.

A recapitulation of their principal concessions may be useful, and is given below.

I. *Mr. Alfred Sharpe's treaties and concessions.*

    (a) KAZEMBE, chief of the Lunda country S.E. of Lake Mweru. Kazembe formerly ruled over Katanga and Garenganze west of the lake, but had been ousted by Msiri, one of his tributaries, who had set up an independent kingdom.

    (b) NSAMA, chief of the Ilawa country, now the most northerly part of the British sphere. Nsama was formerly a powerful ruler whose territory extended far south and east, but had been greatly reduced by Arab incursions.

[1] See *Parliamentary Paper*, C. 7390. The connection between the British colonies south and north of the Equator was restored by Article 23, Part I, of the Treaty of Peace with Germany after the Great War, by which the greater portion of German East Africa was handed over under a mandate to the British Crown.

II. *Mr. Joseph Thomson's concessions.*

    (*a*) KAMBWIRI, chief of Kiwende, on the east side of
        the Luangwa River and north of Mpeseni's.

    (*b*) KATARA,

    (*c*) NANSARA (female chief).
        (West of the Luangwa and between that river
        and Tshitambo.)

    (*d*) TSHITAMBO, paramount of Kalinde, which included
        the Bisa plateau from Mbalala up to Lake
        Bangweolo.

    (*e*) MSIRI,[1] chief of the Ba-Usi country, East and West
        of the Luapula River, and South of Bangweolo.

    (*f*) KALANGA,

    (*g*) SIMESI,

    (*h*) MGUEMBA,

    (*i*) MSIRI,[1]
        " Sultans " of Eastern, Western, Central and
        Southern Iramba, respectively.   The last named
        was situated near the present station of Mkushi.

    (*j*) CHIPEPO, " Sultan " of the Wa-Lenji country in
        the middle basin of the Lukanga.   Included the
        district where the *Broken Hill Mine* is now
        situated.

    (*k*) KANYESHA, chief of S.W. Ilala.

    (*l*) CHAWIRA, chief of the Western a-Senga.

    (*m*) CHEVIA AND MIEMBWE, a-Senga chiefs.

On his return to Blantyre, in March 1891, Thomson
despatched his lieutenant, Wilson, in the direction of Tete,
with the object of ascertaining what Messrs. Bowler and
Rankin had been doing, and as far as possible to checkmate
their schemes.   The parts between Blantyre and Tete are
rugged and sparsely populated; the wet season of 1890–1891
was an exceptionally severe one in the whole of the Zambesi

[1] It will be noted that two of the chiefs from whom Thomson obtained
concessions were named Msiri.   Although neither was the Msiri of Garenganze, the fact caused some confusion at the time, it being at first thought
that Thomson had actually accomplished the principal object of his
expedition—a concession over Garenganze.   Even so well-informed a
writer as E. P. Mathers seems to have fallen into this error (*Zambesia*,
p. 438).

basin, and the trials of this journey, following so closely on the arduous expedition to Lake Bangweolo, were too severe a strain on Wilson's constitution. He succeeded in penetrating to the Revubwi River, and in gaining concessions from certain petty chiefs who lay to the south of those visited by Sharpe on his first expedition in 1890, but was unable to pursue his journey beyond this river, owing to a mutiny among his porters, and could gain no definite intelligence regarding the movements of Bowler and Rankin. On the return march he was subjected to constant attacks of malaria, and only managed with extreme difficulty to reach Blantyre, where he died a few days later. The tale of deaths in that wet season was a long one. Wilson was one of the first of the Chartered Company's employés to lay down his life in the performance of his duty. He was a man of exceptional promise, and the premature ending of his career was greatly regretted by whose who had come in contact with him. The strip over which Wilson gained his concessions was included in Portuguese territory by the agreement made by Lord Salisbury three months later, so that his life-sacrifice was made in vain !

In compiling this and the two preceding chapters, reference has been made to the following authorities :

The Zambesi and its Tributaries, by David Livingstone, 1865.
The Lands of Cazembe, by Captain R. F. Burton, 1873.
Livingstone's Last Journals, by H. Waller, 1874.
Garenganze, by F. S. Arnot, 1889.
Livingstone and the Exploration of Central Africa, by H. H. Johnston, 1898.
With Stairs to Katanga, by J. A. Moloney, 1893.
British Central Africa, by H. H. Johnston, 1898.
Travel and Adventure in South-East Africa, by F. C. Selous, 1893.
The Partition of Africa, by J. Scott Keltie, 1891.
Blue Books C. 5904, C. 6495, C. 7360, C. 7390.

The early history of Barotseland and adjacent countries is based largely on information supplied direct to the author by Lewanika and other native chiefs in 1903.

CHAPTER XVII

MORE TROUBLE WITH PORTUGUESE : THE LAST ACT

THE force which was mobilised at Lisbon during the popular indignation which succeeded Major Forbes' exploit at Umtasa's kraal arrived at Beira towards the end of February 1891, and during the next two months was slowly and with extreme difficulty, pushed towards Manica. The expedition was ill-equipped with medical stores and led by inexperienced officers. The raw students, of whom it was largely composed, could not battle against the malaria which they encountered in the pestilential swamps of the Pungwe valley. The result was an exact repetition of what had befallen Francisco Barreto's Zambesi expedition three hundred years earlier. The ancient spirit of the Portuguese, which had flashed up in the students for a moment under the supposed insult to their flag, died away before the physical obstacles of the enervating climate. It was lamentable to see the morale and discipline of the army perishing in spite of the strenuous efforts of the few leaders who maintained their determination.

An able officer, Colonel Joaquim Machado, had been appointed Governor of Sofala, and proceeded to Beira, where, on the 18th of March, immediately after the seizure of the *Countess of Carnarvon* on the Limpopo, he issued a decree proclaiming martial law throughout Sofala and Manica, and, in defiance of the *modus vivendi*, declaring the port of Beira and the Pungwe waterway closed to foreign traffic. Several thousand native levies were collected at Sena under the command of the Governor of Quilimane, and it was the manifest intention of the authorities to bring these down to join the white soldiers on the Pungwe, and, with the combined force, to make a desperate effort to regain possession of Manica.

At this time a small detachment of the Chartered Company's Police, under Captain H. M. Heyman,[1] was encamped on the west side of the Umtali valley, about seventeen miles from Maçequeçe, for the purpose of affording protection to the Chief Umtasa, and to supervise the construction of a road to the Odzi River.   Rhodes had given orders that the *modus vivendi* was to be strictly respected, and, although at the outset four troopers remained at Maçequeçe to guard the stores abandoned there by the Baron de Rezende, they were subsequently withdrawn.   Negotiations had been opened between London and Lisbon for a fresh treaty, and it was important that nothing should take place locally which might prejudice our position, or give colour to Portuguese allegations of a departure from the *status quo*.   Nevertheless, Lord Salisbury let it be known, from the commencement of these fresh negotiations, that his Government was not prepared to give such favourable terms to Portugal as had been offered by the treaty of 1890, which the Cortes had rejected.

Meanwhile Rhodes and his colleagues on the Board of the Chartered Company were resolved to take full advantage of the provisions of the *modus vivendi*, which was to run till May 14th, and although they were obliged to move their Police back to the west of Maçequeçe, they were determined to assert the right to make use of the Pungwe River, which, under the agreement, was open to British commerce.   As a result of the over-confident reports which Major Johnson had disseminated through South Africa after his trip with Dr. Jameson from Fort Salisbury to the coast, numbers of colonists were preparing to enter Mashonaland by the eastern route, and some had actually passed Beira, and were struggling along the native paths which led towards Mashonaland.   Johnson, with his partners Heany and Borrow, now undertook to construct a road to the border from the nearest navigable point on the river, and, in utter disregard or contempt for the tsetse fly with which the Pungwe flats teemed, to run a service of mule-coaches for the conveyance of mails and passengers.   In pursuance of this object a road-

[1] Now Sir Melville Heyman.

making party of Europeans and natives, a large quantity of stores and building material, and an American mail coach were despatched from Durban, and on April 13th arrived at Beira in the Union Company's steamship *Norseman*, which was accompanied by a river-tug, the *Agnes*, for transport purposes on the Pungwe. In view of the probability of opposition from the port authorities, Captain Sir John Willoughby, of the Company's Police, was put in charge of the whole party.

As might have been anticipated, the Governor, Senhor Machado, was equally determined not to allow the Company to get a footing on the river. He refused to allow the party to proceed and threatened to repel them by force, should they persist in attempting to pass beyond the roadstead. A Portuguese corvette, the *Liberal*, and two gunboats, the *Auxiliar* and *Tamega*, were there to give emphasis to his refusal. Sir John Willoughby made repeated efforts to induce him to alter his determination. He pointed to Article 2 of the *modus vivendi*, which ran as follows :—" The Government of His Most Faithful Majesty the King of Portugal and the Algarves engage to permit and facilitate transit over the waterways of the Zambesi, the Shiré and the Pungwe, and also over the landways which supply means of communication where these rivers are not navigable." And again :—" The King of Portugal further engages to facilitate communication between the Portuguese ports on the coast and the territories included in the sphere of action of Great Britain, especially as regards the establishment of postal and telegraphic communications and as regards the transport service." He also tendered the full transit duty on the goods which he proposed to take up with him. But all his appeals were unavailing. The Governor informed him that the interior was open to everyone except those connected with the British South Africa Company, with whom, on account of their having broken the *modus vivendi*, and of being still in illegal occupation of Portuguese territory, where they were inciting the natives to revolt, a state of war existed.

After giving due notice of his intention to proceed peace-ably up the river, Willoughby gave orders to the *Agnes* and another tug, the *Shark*, to pick up the lighters containing his goods and cast off, and himself took up a position on the bridge of the former, but he had scarcely proceeded a quarter of a mile when the Portuguese opened fire from the *Tamega*, while the other gunboat closed in upon his little flotilla. The *Agnes* and *Shark* were seized and the passengers ordered to return to the *Norseman*. Although the Governor himself was conciliatory and courteous, the subordinate officials made no attempt to conceal their hostility, and it was evident that the soldiers were in an undisciplined and mutinous condition, and would have fallen upon the British party on the smallest provocation. Indeed hostile demonstrations against the few British residents in Beira actually took place, and a serious outbreak might have occurred at any moment. Prompt steps were required to avenge this latest insult, and to secure the lives and property of Englishmen on the coast. On the news reaching the Foreign Office Lord Salisbury called upon the Portuguese Government to order the officials in Beira to throw open the port and river, and, as he had learnt by experience on previous occasions that orders from Lisbon were tardily carried out, or even disregarded, by the local officials in East Africa, he made it clear that he would brook no shilly-shallying, by despatching three warships from Simonstown—the cruiser *Magicienne*, and the gunboats *Brisk* and *Pigeon*—to the scene of the trouble. At the same time a naval officer—Captain Pipon—was sent to Beira as Consul. The British ships arrived at Beira on the 28th April, and the effect of their appearance was magical. The *Agnes* and her lighters were released (on pay-ment of a fine which was given under protest and refunded later), and the road-party with the goods suffered to pass into the river.

At this stage it appeared that Great Britain had gained her point, and that no further trouble would be experienced by persons entering Mashonaland from the east coast. The opening of access to the Chartered Company's territories was extensively advertised by Messrs. Johnson, Heany and Borrow, who, somewhat prematurely, offered to conduct passengers to Mashonaland by this " shortest, quickest, and cheapest route." Up-country, however, events were not proceeding so smoothly, and a spark might at any moment precipitate a conflagration. On the 3rd May Colonel Pennefather, who was in Manica, received reports from natives of a general advance by the Portuguese forces upon Maçequeçe. A party of eighteen of the Police, under Lieut. Bruce, were at Umlewan's kraal in the Kiteve country, and these were now ordered to fall back on Umtali, while Colonel Pennefather decided to reconnoitre the Revue valley to gain further information. On the 4th, however, he received a summons to the south of Mashonaland in connection with the threatened incursion by the Transvaal Boers (an account of which will be given later), and had to take his departure hastily, without effecting his design. On the 6th of May the Portuguese entered and occupied Maçequeçe, and Captain Heyman, who was now in command of the little British force, deeming that Umtasa was threatened, took up a position on Chua Hill, which overlooked the approaches to Umtali, Umtasa's kraal, and Umlewan's. He had with him thirty-three of the Company's Police, dismounted, fifteen volunteers (members of the disbanded Pioneer force) and a 7-pounder gun.

On the 9th of May Heyman, accompanied by one of his non-commissioned officers, who was a Portuguese linguist,[1] and exhibiting a flag of truce, went to Maçequeçe, where he found Colonel Ferreira,[2] " Governor of Manica," Captain Bettencourt and seven other officers, with 200 white troops and 300 black Angolese soldiers. In response to inquiries Colonel Ferreira stated that the *modus vivendi* had not been extended, and that no new convention had been agreed upon [3]

---

[1] By a coincidence this was the son of Sir Robert Morier, formerly British Minister at Lisbon.

[2] It is a further curious coincidence that the leaders of both the attempts which were made in 1891 to dispute the territorial claims of the Chartered Company—that by the Portuguese in Manica and that by the Boers in Southern Mashonaland—should have borne the same name—Ferreira.

[3] He was technically right on both points, but within a week the *modus vivendi*, which in the ordinary course would have expired on the 14th May, was extended in order to give time for the conclusion of a new treaty, and its acceptance by the Cortes. The articles of this Convention had been agreed upon early in May between Lord Salisbury and the Portuguese Minister in London, M. de Soveral.

that martial law had been proclaimed, and that he was there to drive the English out of Manica, but that if Heyman would withdraw with all the Company's forces to the west side of the river Sabi, he—Ferreira—would facilitate the opening of the coast route.   To this, of course, there was but one answer, and having delivered it Heyman returned to his camp.   Although he had left no doubt as to his intention of remaining where he was, he received a visit on the following day from one of the Portuguese officers, who appeared, ostensibly, to repeat the " order to quit," but in reality to gain information as to the position and numbers of the diminutive garrison.   His report must have been a satisfactory one, for, on the afternoon of the 11th, it was seen that the whole Portuguese force was advancing upon Heyman's position in two columns.   Having arrived within a range of six hundred yards, they deployed into line, and opened a heavy fire upon the garrison, the white troops with repeating rifles, and the Angolese with Sniders.   Heyman's picket was, of course, driven in, but he sent out ten men as skirmishers along the slopes of his position, and returned the fire with his 7-pounder and rifles.

The Portuguese officers behaved with coolness and pluck, but their men were spiritless and half-hearted, and, though rallied again and again, could not be induced to approach within four hundred yards of the British entrenchment. Their marksmanship was contemptible.   During two hours' fighting no single member of Heyman's force was hit.   He feared, however, that the enemy might work round to the rear of his position, and, with the object of preventing this, kept up a correspondence by signals with an imaginary force in the rear.   The ruse succeeded, for an Engineer officer in the Portuguese lines read the signals, and any intentions they may have had of making such a movement were thereby averted.   The British rifle-fire was well directed, and at length Ferreira's men, who were halted on the edge of a small ravine, retreated to take cover behind a ridge, whence, on being pressed, they fell back on the fort.   Heyman's 7-pounder ammunition consisted of sixty rounds only, and before it was exhausted the limber and trail of the gun were smashed by a shot from the Portuguese artillery, whereby his only piece was put out of action.   By some good fortune, however, the very last shell pitched right in the middle of the fort, and the Portuguese, thinking that he had found the range, immediately abandoned their position and fled helter-skelter.   Their losses were not ascertained at the time, but from reports brought in from natives it was estimated that twenty were killed, and it was also found that Captain Bettencourt was severely wounded.   One white and one native soldier were taken prisoners.

On the first shot being fired all the natives in Heyman's garrison decamped, but Umtasa's people climbed a precipitous rock and watched the engagement from a safe distance, scenting opportunities of loot when one or the other side was driven back.   On the following morning, as no signs of the enemy were visible, and it was seen that his flag was no longer flying over Maçequeçe, Heyman sent out a reconnoitring party, which found that the fort had been completely evacuated, and was already being looted by the natives.   Everything was in great confusion; nine machine-guns were in position with their carriages but minus the breech-blocks; many thousands of rounds of ammunition had also been abandoned, as well as most of the baggage, and the fort was strewed with a dense litter of provisions, wine and clothing, including even some feminine garments ! Heyman's men had some difficulty in driving off the looters and securing the guns and ammunition, which, with some of the provisions, were removed to his camp at Chua.   The fort at Maçequeçe was then blown up.

It was acertained from the white prisoner that the attacking force was part of an expedition which had left Lourenzo Marques in February, that they had taken three months to march up from Neves Ferreira on the Pungwe River, and had suffered greatly from malarial fever *en route*.   The main army, which had started from Portugal about the same time, was still at Neves Ferreira, incapacitated by fever, and unable to advance from lack of transport.   Owing to the desertions of his native camp followers Heyman was without carriers, and was therefore unable to follow up his success.   Many of his men had no boots, and the clothing of all was in rags. On the 15th of May he managed to get together a patrol to follow the Portuguese, but Ferreira had anticipated this and sent back a party under a flag of truce to parley, and so gain time for the escape of the remainder. Lieut. Fiennes, who commanded the patrol, refused their request to be put in possession of their stores at Maçequeçe, but he was compelled to wait for a couple of days on the Revue River to enable some mounted reinforcements, which had been ordered from Salisbury, to catch him up. During this delay Bishop Knight-Bruce arrived from Beira, and brought the news that Major Sapte, Military Secretary at Capetown, was just ·behind, with orders from the High Commissioner for the retirement of the Chartered forces to the west of Maçequeçe. Although he knew that these orders must have been despatched long before the recent attack by the Portuguese, Fiennes decided to wait, and in due course Major Sapte arrived with the orders as stated. Had he disregarded the Bishop's warning, there is very little doubt that his reinforced patrol would have swept the country down to Beira. The delay enabled the fugitives from Maçequeçe to make good their escape, the black troops flying to Gouveia, while the Europeans reached Chimoio, where they took refuge in a recently erected fort, situated in such difficult country that it would have been hopeless to have attempted to dislodge them.

After this gross breach of the *modus vivendi*, aggravated by the employment against the British of black troops, Rhodes pressed for authority to occupy Beira, and for the cession of a strip of country from the coast to Mashonaland. He pointed out the difficulty of developing the Chartered Company's territory with over 1600 miles of land-route, and urged definite occupation of the East Coast route, because he knew that the Portuguese soldiers and officials in East Africa were quite beyond the control of Lisbon, and would disregard European agreements. The coast authorities were so cowed by the reverse in Manica, and by the presence of the British warships in Pungwe Bay, that they were ready to agree to almost any terms, and a less magnanimous

Ministry might have given effect to Rhodes' demands without incurring any serious opposition.   But the negotiations for the fresh treaty were already far advanced.   Before full details of the Chua engagement arrived in Europe, a memorandum containing the basis of an agreement had been initialled by Lord Salisbury and the Portuguese Secretary for Foreign Affairs, Count Valbom, and the British Premier, in the absence of complete information as to this latest affray, was disinclined to delay the long-deferred understanding on the eve of its consummation, or to hold the Lisbon Government answerable for the errors of distant and irresponsible officials.   His complaisance was taken instant advantage of in Lisbon.   Twelve months before, the news of such a collision as had occurred in Manica would have been the signal for a passionate and violent demonstration against the British, and an outburst of fervid chauvinism, but the bitter experiences of the last few months and the deplorable condition of the country's finances had opened the eyes of all classes to the enormity of the blunder which had been made in rejecting the old treaty, and they were ready to accept peace at any price to save themselves from further disaster.   To get the Convention signed quickly—that was their one idea.   The preliminary steps were hurried through, and on June the 11th the House of Peers gave its formal assent by a majority of 83 votes to 6.

The same *volte-face* in public opinion was exhibited in East Africa.   The news of the repulse of Ferreira's attack reached Beira through fugitives from the scene of the engagement, who naturally exaggerated the disaster.   The effect was instantaneous, and as the first reports were confirmed by other refugees, the port officials began hastily to conform to all the suggestions made by Consul Pipon.   The fine extorted from Willoughby for the *Agnes* affair was refunded, on the ground that it was ascertained that there had been no intention of smuggling—which should have been sufficiently obvious at the time of the incident, seeing that Willoughby more than once tendered the Customs dues.   The " state of siege " proclaimed on the 18th March was raised on the plea that " the causes which led to it had ceased ! "

The port was thrown open freely to foreigners, and Colonel Machado, the Governor, displayed every willingness to promote friendly feelings, and to meet Captain Pipon's suggestions for facilitating intercourse with the interior.

On July 3rd, 1891, the new treaty was formally ratified by both Powers and the long-standing quarrel which had stirred up so much bad blood in Nyasaland, Manica, Gazaland and elsewhere was brought to a conclusion.

Though it finally shut off all hope of securing Gazaland, and ignored their aspirations to a portion of the coast-line, the new Convention was distinctly more favourable to the British South Africa Company than its ill-fated predecessor. The principal territorial change was an extension of the English sphere in Manica, the line being so drawn as to include the whole of the plateau, save what was necessary for the purpose of leaving Maçequeçe on the Portuguese side. As a set-off to this alteration it was agreed to make a large change in favour of Portugal in the territorial dominion upon the north side of the Zambesi above Tete. The whole of the north bank between Tete and Zumbo as far as the 15th degree of latitude was recognised in the Convention as Portuguese. Lord Salisbury defended this arrangement, which relinquished part of the territory acquired by Alfred Sharpe, as " having the advantage of recognising some historical claims which at one time did exist, though their present scope cannot be very clearly determined, as well as of providing an equivalent for the territory ceded in Manica." These being the lines upon which he dictated the settlement, it is obvious that the strip of land connecting Mashonaland with Pungwe Bay, so much desired by Rhodes, could only have been granted in return for large concessions in some other direction, which the Chartered Company could ill have afforded.

The stipulations in the *modus vivendi* which bound Portugal to facilitate and promote transit over the waterways of the Shiré and Pungwe, and also over the landways which supplied means of communication where these rivers were not navigable, were extended to the Limpopo, the Busi and the Sabi, and were made perpetual.

The boundary of the Barotse territory, which was recognised as British, was not defined by this Convention, as, with the limited knowledge of the locality possessed by both parties, accurate delimitation was impossible.   It was left to be settled by a joint International Commission.

The Anglo-Portuguese Convention of the 11th June, 1891, was the final fencing-off of the Chartered Company's sphere. True, the north-western border was not settled until many years afterwards, but the adjustment there was entirely a matter of evidence before an independent tribunal and gave rise to no picturesque incidents on the spot.

For the events described in this chapter the main authority is :
Blue Book C. 6495

CHAPTER XVIII

THE BANYAILAND TREK

IN the same year—1891—the Transvaal Boers made a last desperate effort to filch a portion of the rich province which they had always regarded as their *hinterland*.

The attempt was concentrated upon the low country on the north side of the Limpopo River, between its two tributaries the Sabi and the Lundi. This was the ancestral demesne of a Holi tribe known as the a-Banyai, which, in spite of its proximity to the Matabele raiders, had contrived, by planting its villages in rocky and inaccessible fastnesses, to escape extinction, and even, to a certain extent, to hold its own.

In October 1889 it was bruited about that the Boers of the Northern Transvaal were plotting to obtain by force the country which they had lost by diplomacy. The Transvaal Press contained open hints that the enrolment of volunteers was secretly proceeding, and that the command of an expedition to seize Southern Mashonaland was to be offered to a well-known Colonial officer. It may be conjectured that an invasion of this sort would have been essayed years before had not the gold fever kept adventurous spirits dallying round Witwatersrand, but it is indeed surprising that the Transvaalers, who were always ready for a raid, and whose mettle was just as keen as when their forefathers had fought Mziligazi, should have delayed for so long to snatch a land which was known to be rich in game and of great fertility, and was only separated from their own back-country by a river which at several points was easily fordable on horseback. Possibly they may have entertained a wholesome respect for Matabele assegais, or they may have failed to foresee that the British advance would be so rapid, and, as their own progress northward had been spread over

seventy years, may have considered that there was plenty
of time to occupy the trans-Limpopo districts at their leisure.
Be this as it may, the farmers of the Transvaal were in 1889
becoming discontented.   They were annoyed by heavy taxes
and alarmed at the increasing cost of living; they found
themselves jostled by an increasing swarm of *uitlanders*, daily
becoming more restless, and, now that there was a temporary
lull in the gold boom, daily permeating further and further
into the country; they saw their land in every direction being
bought up by foreigners, and, like their forefathers, who had
trekked away from the Cape to avoid the pressure of English
settlers, they longed to get farther north, where they could
live a free life, unhampered by the burdens of civilisation.
Mashonaland they had always marked for future occupation,
but now, to their chagrin, they perceived that British speculators were forestalling them, and that unless they bestirred
themselves, Mashonaland would be lost for ever.

In February 1890, Rhodes learnt from Selous, who had
just returned from Zoutpansberg, in the Northern Transvaal, that arrangements had been completed for a " trek "
which was to take place during the approaching winter
months.   Fifteen hundred or two thousand mounted Boers
were to cross the Limpopo River at Middle Drift, near the
inflow of the Umzingwani,[1] and then to trek northwards,
eventually crossing the Lundi River and seizing the southern
portion of Mashonaland.   The names of Jan Dupreez,
" Field-cornet " of Rhenosterpoort, Klein Barend Vorster,
son of the well-known Commandant, and other prominent
and experienced hunters were mentioned in connection with
the plan.   Delegates had been sent to the Free State, and to
Paarl, in the Cape Colony, to enrol further recruits.   The
Portuguese of East Africa were alleged to be privy to the
scheme; indeed, the Johannesburg *Star* asserted that the
leaders had received a sort of charter from the Portuguese
Government to open up Mashonaland.   After annexation

[1] There were five drifts or fords on this portion of the Limpopo—Baines'
Drift and Rhodes' Drift communicating with the Northern Protectorate,
and Massebi's Drift, Middle Drift and Main Drift leading to the Banyai
country.   The two first were guarded by detachments of the Bechuanaland Border Police as soon as rumours of the trek were heard, but the three
latter were, of course, at this time unprotected.

the trekkers were to form themselves into an independent Republic, and would hold a conference with delegates from Portuguese East Africa for the partition with them of the whole of Mashonaland.

Bold as this programme may appear to-day, it was by no means impracticable at a time when the extent of Lobengula's influence was not definitely known, and when not a single British soldier or official existed north of the Bechuanaland Protectorate.   Officially, of course, President Krüger knew that Boer pretensions to Matabeleland or Mashonaland would not be tolerated for one moment, but this trek was ostensibly to take place independently of the Transvaal Government.   At any rate Rhodes deemed the news so serious that he urged the Imperial authorities to retain Swaziland, as a guarantee of good faith on the part of the Pretoria Volksraad, pending a British occupation of Mashonaland.

It was rather troublesome for the British Government, so soon after the granting of the Charter—an act which had been freely criticised—to be involved in diplomatic difficulties with two different nations—Portugal first and now the Transvaal—as to questions arising out of the Chartered Company's sphere of operations, but the Foreign Secretary rose to the occasion, drew " Oom Paul's " attention somewhat sharply to the persistent rumours, and asked him what steps he proposed to take to repress an unauthorised movement by his burghers.   The old President saw that the Government was not in a mood for trifling, and, at his own suggestion, a meeting was held on the 12th March at Blignaut's Pont on the Vaal River, at which the matter was thrashed out between himself, the President of the Orange Free State, the High Commissioner (Sir Henry Loch) and Rhodes.   The result of this conference was that Krüger undertook that he would at once stop any attempt at the invasion of Mashonaland from the Transvaal side.   He was as good as his word, for when, in June, a number of Boers began to muster on the south bank of the Limpopo, in spite of the fact that they were backed up by influential burghers of the Republic (among others by General Piet Joubert), he threatened severe penalties if they attempted an entry, and so scared the would-be trekkers that no movement took place. The assembled Boers dispersed, and for that season the trek was scotched.

For a time no further threats were heard, and by September 1890, as we know, the Chartered Company's forces had reached Mount Hampden and formally taken possession of the whole of Mashonaland. It was not until March of the following year that reports of a revival of the plot were again current. The support of the Transvaal Government could no longer be counted on, but the new plans were based upon a concession purporting to have been granted by two chiefs of Southern Matabeleland—Tshibi and Matibi—who claimed to be the independent rulers of the Banyai tribes. The concession was held by four Transvaal Boers, Dupreez the "field-cornet," Adendorff, Myer and Brummer, and was embodied in an imposing " Proclamation " wherein the chiefs appealed to the burghers of the Republic to come and reside in their country and to form a bulwark (*schijtsmeier*) between them and the rapacious Matabele raiders. They were to make this appeal known to " Her British Majesty the Queen of the Mighty and Free English Nation, and, in order to obtain the necessary help and assistance, to lay it, if need be, before the Powers and States of Europe asking their intervention." Upon the strength of this document Adendorff and Dupreez sent invitations to Boers of the Transvaal, Cape Colony and Free State to join in an expedition to occupy the rich pastures of Mashonaland. They were to assemble on the banks of the Crocodile (Limpopo) River during May, and on June 1st " a grand convoy "—so ran the invitation —" of five thousand armed Afrikanders, including the best fighting men South Africa could produce, viz. the Zoutpansberg Boers, who had grown old amid gunpowder smoke," was to cross the river. Their anxiety to include Boers of the Cape Colony was based on political reasons. Being British subjects their presence would cause the claims of the body of the trekkers to be treated with respect by the Portuguese and the Chartered Company. The prospectus went on to state that doctors of medicine, ministers of religion, journalists and all other professions were to be represented in the expedition. After crossing the Limpopo River the trekkers would proclaim the " Republic of the North " ; a provisional Government would be organised, and a constitution drawn up on the principles of the old Transvaal *Grondwet* of 1858. The frontiers of the Republic were to be the Zambesi and Limpopo Rivers, with Matabeleland on the west and Portuguese Africa on the east, corresponding with the boundaries named in the concession.

Representations were made to the Afrikander Bond, which, in April 1891, was sitting in Congress at Kimberley, with the object of enlisting its support to the expedition. In agreeing to the Swaziland Convention of August 1890, the Transvaal Government had withdrawn all claims to extend their territory, or to enter into treaties with the northern natives, but it was urged that this trek was independent of the Government, and to support this contention the organisers were most anxious that Cape Afrikanders should join them. But the Bond would have none of them. Mr. J. H. Hofmeyr, its President, took Counsel's opinion on the political issue, and was advised that England would never allow—would never be justified in allowing—the creation of an independent Republic north of the Limpopo, and that the Transvaal Government too was bound by the London Convention of 1884, as well as by the Pretoria Convention of 1890, to prevent its subjects from encroaching on territory outside the defined boundaries. The Bond held a meeting at Capetown on April the 20th, when Hofmeyr, who at that time was in close personal touch with Rhodes, announced that the Chartered Company would gladly encourage farmers from all the South African States to enter the new territory provided they accepted its laws and respected its flag, but would never tolerate an incursion by any body of men seeking to set up an independent form of government. A resolution of confidence in the Company was passed without dissent and the Bond thereby denounced the proposed trek.

Undoubtedly this was a great disappointment to Adendorff and his fellow-conspirators, who had counted on widespread Afrikander sympathy in any plot which threatened

British expansion.   But a worse blow was to follow.
Within a few days the High Commissioner issued a Proclamation cautioning those concerned that any attempt to enter
territories under Her Majesty's protection would be repelled
by force, while Krüger followed this up by a *Staats-courant*
extraordinary, prohibiting any movement from the Transvaal, and threatening confiscation of the lands of those who
disobeyed.   It was now apparent that their original hope of
peacefully entering Mashonaland in the old-fashioned way
with their wives and families would have to be abandoned.
Nevertheless, large numbers continued their preparations.
They were buoyed up by the knowledge that there was an
immense amount of sympathy in Pretoria with the idea of
" jumping the Englishman's claims," and that they would
have the secret support, if not the open assistance, of many
of the leading men of the Republic—General Piet Joubert,
at whose house meetings of the executive took place, and
whose son-in-law, Malan, was one of the ringleaders, being
their principal backer.

Meanwhile the Chartered Company were taking every
precaution against surprise.   Detachments of Police were
sent to each of the drifts on the river, where forts were built
and the British flag hoisted.   Similar measures were adopted
along the Protectorate border by the Imperial authorities.
Early in May Dr. Jameson (fresh from his encounter with the
Portuguese) and Sir John Willoughby, of the Company's
Police, went to Johannesburg, partly to pick up what news
they could, and partly to endeavour, by interviewing the
leaders of the trek and other prominent citizens, to dissuade
them from attempting a forcible entry.   The Company
secured an agent who got into touch with the trekkers'
head-quarters, and kept his principals fully informed as to
what was going on.   An old fighting Boer—Ignatius Ferreira,
who had served with the English in the Zulu war and had
been decorated by the Queen—was now elected as military
leader, and though the numbers of the force were reduced,
they were animated by the utmost determination to have
Mashonaland *coûte que coûte*.   In the Waterberg district a
large number of farms had been acquired by an *uitlander*

syndicate, and the Boers knew that sooner or later they would be ousted from their holdings. Practically every farmer from that district had thrown in his lot with the trek, looking upon it as the only chance of regaining freedom. At this stage probably a thousand men in all, with four hundred wagons, were participating, of whom the Waterberg men formed the bulk, with a few allies from Rustenberg and Middelberg, and seventy or eighty from the Free State. To stiffen their resolution, Adendorff openly affirmed that Rhodes had offered him £150,000 for his concession, which was, of course, a sheer fabrication, though it is probable that some of the shrewder ones—Ferreira amongst them—entertained hopes of being bought off. Krüger, interviewed by Jameson and Willoughby, was still emphatic that the trek would not take place. The Boers and wagons, he said, which were collecting at Pretoria, were intended for hunting expeditions, and he pooh-poohed the idea that there was any intention of raiding the Banyai country. He was probably sincere in his protestations, but Jameson felt that he had very little hold over the back-country Boers, many of whom were *bijwoners*—men who had no property in the Transvaal and everything to gain by escaping from it—and he determined that no pains should be spared to break up their organisation before they could do any mischief. He was aided in this object by the undisciplined character of their ranks. Dissensions were growing among the different leaders. The Company's agent, as a member of the Executive, was doing his best to split them up. Many of the Boers who had collected with their wagons at Pretoria and Pietersberg had no intention of acting on the initiative, and were merely watching the course of events. Some were prepared, if they could not get better terms, to accept the Company's rule and enter as authorised settlers. Others, again, were disgusted at the want of unanimity among the leaders—each of whom had his own axe to grind—and a few turned back. The transfer of a squadron of the Bechuanaland Police to Fort Tuli—enabling the Company to strengthen the detachments at the drifts—and the appointment of Colonel Sir Frederick Carrington to the general command, were convincing proofs that the Imperial Government meant to see the Charter through any trouble, and every day the number of waverers in the Boer camp increased. By the end of May it was clear that if the trek took place at all it would be on a much smaller scale than had at first been apprehended, and that it would be confined to Boers from the Waterberg and Zoutpansberg districts. Krüger, wherever his sympathies might lie, behaved with complete discretion, and, among other politic acts, sent for Dupreez, one of the leaders, and having first exacted an oath that he would not leave the Transvaal, despatched him on a land commission to another part of the country.

A certain amount of embarrassment was caused at this juncture by another body of Boers who were quite unconnected with the Adendorff trek. These men were led by one Van Reenen, a Pietersberg law-agent, who had obtained from Senhor Carvalho, the Portuguese Consul-General at Capetown, a promise of farms in Manicaland to as many farmers as would go there. They were to cross the Limpopo by the Waterval Drift, and merely wanted permission to pass through the Chartered Company's territory in order to reach Manica. They were speedily dealt with by Jameson, who arranged for them to enter as settlers under the Company, and to occupy land in the eastern portion of the Mashonaland high-veld under allotments of farms.

The remnant of the Adendorff trekkers brought matters to a head by attempting to cross the river in a body on the 24th June. Jameson, who was inspecting the various detachments of Police, at once rode to Main Drift, where the attempt took place, and found that a party of 112 mounted Boers, all armed, with thirty or forty wagons, but unaccompanied by their wives and children, had appeared on the Transvaal side, and that five of them, including their Commandant, Ferreira, had forded the river under the very muzzles of the Company's guns. Ferreira was at once arrested, whereupon his companions decamped, and in a state of considerable excitement made their way back to the opposite side. Upon Jameson's arrival he discussed the position in a friendly manner with the Boer Commandant, and having established pleasant relations, released him on parole and accompanied him to the trekkers' camp. Some hostility was at first displayed, but at Ferreira's bidding the Boers accorded him a fair hearing. Jameson explained the Imperial attitude towards the trek, reminded them that Krüger had forbidden them to cross, but assured them that Rhodes was perfectly ready to admit Transvaal Boers as settlers in the new country on an equal footing with men from the Cape Colony and the mother country, provided they agreed to come under the Chartered Company's laws. Other Boers had already been admitted upon these terms. He agreed to receive a deputation on the following day, and left Ferreira to talk the matter over. Just as he was leaving, some effect was produced by the arrival at the Chartered camp of Major Goold-Adams with reinforcements of the Bechuanaland Police.

Next day a number of deputations presented themselves— some disputing the Company's right to the country, others more amenable and anxious to come to terms. All of them were assured by Jameson that they would be fired on if they attempted to force a passage without undertaking to obey the Company's laws, and that none of them would be allowed to pass into the country until all signs of hostility had disappeared. Eventually two or three small parties who signed the required undertaking were admitted and the bulk of the trekkers dispersed. Ferreira, and a journalist named Jerome, who acted as his secretary, were kept under arrest, and sent with an escort to Fort Tuli, where they remained for some days as prisoners. Realising that the game was up, and that he could obtain a farm merely by agreeing to accept the Chartered Company's sovereignty, the old Commandant, without more ado, entered into an undertaking to keep the peace and obey the law, and was forthwith released. He was heartily sick of his connection with the trek, and being destitute of means he was only too ready to look about for suitable land to settle in. It was found that he had been in correspondence with Lippert, the German speculator, and from this and other evidence it was clear that there had been a considerable amount of political intrigue behind the movement.

So ended the famous Banyailand Trek, and with it died all the talk about the " Republic of the North." Jameson's tact, and the timely show of military force, had staved off a danger which at one time appeared more serious even than the Matabele or Portuguese. Some months later the Banyai Chief Tshibi was visited by Rhodes and sturdily denied having ever given a concession. He acknowledged Lobengula as his Paramount Chief and disclaimed all knowledge of Adendorff. This is only mentioned to show how little value can be placed upon documents purporting to have been signed by native chiefs. It is just as likely as not that he did sign the Adendorff Concession, and only repudiated it because he thought that it might get him into trouble.

For the information contained in this chapter the author has mainly relied on notes made in Mashonaland in 1891, and on conversations with the late Colonel Ferreira, Mr. Jerome and other principal actors in the events described. Reference has also been made to files of the Johannesburg *Star* for February, 1890, the *Transvaal Observer*, *Cape Times* and *Cape Argus*, March to May, 1891, and to the Cape of Good Hope *Government Gazette* for April 13th, 1891.

CHAPTER XIX

MASHONALAND BEFORE THE MATABELE WAR

HAVING made their boundaries secure against Boers and Portuguese the Company's officers were free to devote themselves to the settlement of Mashonaland, which now entered upon a brief period of comparative calm.

Up to the end of May 1891, the handful of Pioneers in the country had received few reinforcements from the south, for most of the parties that started in the early part of the year were still struggling with the obstacles of the long wagon route—incessant rains, swollen rivers and malaria. Consequently, in their efforts to repel encroachments from Manica and the Transvaal the Company had to rely upon the original Police force—augmented by a few recruits pushed up with extreme difficulty from Cape Colony at the end of the rainy season—and upon such volunteers from the disbanded Pioneers as were not engaged in working their gold claims. Although no exact record of the population is available, it is safe to say that the whites in Mashonaland at this time did not exceed a thousand,[1] for the provisioning of all of whom, it may be observed, the Company were more or less responsible, while the larger number were actually in the Company's pay.

By June the advance parties of the first prospecting expeditions from Kimberley and Johannesburg were beginning to arrive and the trickling stream of immigration soon swelled to respectable proportions. It became obvious that although no explicit authority to make laws had been obtained from Lobengula, the creation of an elementary machinery of government could not further be postponed.

[1] The Police Force was increased early in 1891 to a strength of 650 of all ranks; the ex-Pioneers numbered about 190, and 150 would be a liberal estimate of the number of other Europeans who reached the country before May 31st, 1891.

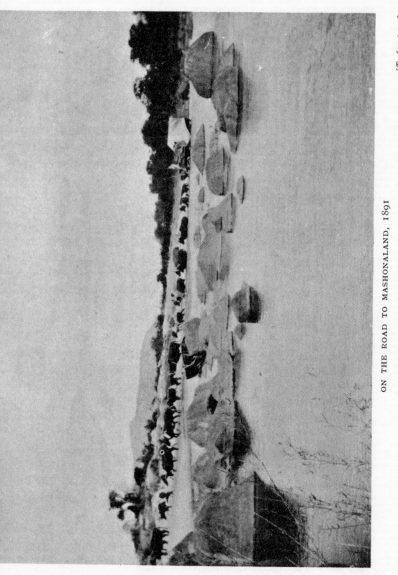

ON THE ROAD TO MASHONALAND, 1891

[To face p. 276.

Some judicial system must be adopted; magistrates, gold commissioners and revenue officers must be appointed; districts defined and township sites laid out; licences to carry on business enforced; a mail service instituted, and, as some of the new-comers were on the look-out for farms, a scheme of land-survey inaugurated. As to the last point, it will be remembered that the Company had so far acquired no land rights from Lobengula, but for the time being this deficiency was tacitly ignored and the privilege already accorded to the Pioneers of selecting farms was extended to the Police and the first civilians to arrive, subject to the condition of *bona fide* and beneficial occupation.

The exhilarating climate, now that the rains were over, the wide expanses of rich pasturage and the glowing reports of gold discoveries at Mazoe, Hartley Hill, Manica and later at Victoria, soon begat confidence, and a brisk trade sprang up in farms and claims—those who had a little capital buying the " rights " of less fortunate individuals at figures which to-day seem absurdly low.[1]

On the 9th May, 1891, the High Commissioner for South Africa was empowered by Order in Council to provide for the administration of justice, the raising of revenue, and generally for the peace, order and good government of the new settlement. In pursuance of these powers he shortly afterwards issued a proclamation applying the existing body of Cape Colony laws to Mashonaland, and, on the nomination of the Company, appointed a Resident Commissioner (Mr. Colquhoun) for the territory[2] with subordinate magistrates for Tuli, Victoria, Hartley, Salisbury and Umtali. Mining and revenue officers were also chosen from the material at hand, and so by the time the first settlers began to enter from

---

[1] The customary price for a " Pioneer right " to a farm was from £80 to £100, while an extra £25 would in most cases secure the additional licence to peg out twenty-five reef claims.

[2] Mr. Colquhoun was gazetted as " Resident Commissioner " by High Commissioner's notice of 29th June, 1891. A few weeks later the appointment was cancelled and he was gazetted as " Magistrate for Mashonaland." On the 18th September Dr. Jameson was appointed to succeed him as " Chief Magistrate for the Territory." These diversions of officialdom were, however, disregarded by the Company's Directors, who authorised their senior executive officer to assume the title of " Administrator," which was adopted by the Imperial Government three years later in the Order in Council of July 1894.

the south a rough-and-ready system of administration was already in existence. It was essentially a government of amateurs, and some of the procedure was calculated to horrify the trained officials of the old-established colonies of South Africa, but it answered its purpose, and on the whole nothing was done inconsistent with substantial justice.

Among the various expeditions which penetrated to Mashonaland in this year were two which are worthy of passing reference because, although vastly dissimilar in purpose, both contributed in some measure to the history of the country. The first was that led by Mr. J. Theodore Bent, F.R.G.S., for the purpose of investigating the ancient stone buildings which were reported to be scattered over the country, and which had piqued the curiosity of archæologists since the re-discovery of the Zimbabwe ruins by Adam Renders in 1868,[1] and the account of them by Karl Mauch published in 1874.[2] The existence of these remains was known to the Portuguese explorers of the sixteenth century, from whose accounts, based, it is true, on hearsay evidence, the contemporary historian de Barros was able to write a fairly accurate description of their massive fortresses and walls.[3] The misty legends of an ancient civilisation which had clustered round the kingdom of Monomotapa were founded largely on the Portuguese reports of the ruins, as also was the persistent belief in their connection with the miners of Ophir who supplied the gold which the Queen of Sheba presented to King Solomon. The expedition undertaken by Mr. Bent, who was accompanied by his wife, was supported by liberal subscriptions from the British South Africa Company, the Royal Geographical Society and the British Association for the Advancement of Science. He spent several months in research work among the ruins, unearthing many remarkable relics in the shape of carved stones, pottery and implements used for the extraction of gold, and gave the results to the world in a book in which he advanced the view that the ancient builders were

[1] *R.G.S. Journal*, 1891, February, p. 105.
[2] Petermann : *Geographical Communications*, Supplement, p. 37.
[3] *The Gold of Ophir*, by Professor Keane, p. 6.

Sabæans (Phœnicians) from Arabia.[1] But his conclusions have by no means been generally accepted, and the fascinating " Ophir theory " has its adherents to this day.

The second noteworthy expedition was that conducted by Lord Randolph Churchill, who, at the close of a chequered political career, made a sort of " Grand Tour " through Cape Colony, the Transvaal and Mashonaland, and published his impressions in a series of letters which appeared in the *Daily Graphic*. The object of his pilgrimage was obscure, but he appears to have undertaken it partly for sport, partly in the hope of picking up a gold mine, and partly with a view to acquring first-hand knowledge of South African politics. He was not fitted constitutionally or temperamentally to undergo the fatigues of a rough journey, still less to engage in a critical survey of the resources of a newly opened territory. He passed an unfavourable judgment on the prospects of gold-mining, laid stress on the dangers of malarial fever, and gave it as his considered opinion that as a field for emigration Mashonaland was unpromising. His articles, which gained a wide circulation, had a depressing effect on a public already somewhat disturbed by stories of the privations and disappointments encountered by the Pioneers in their first wet season. People were ready to assume that an ex-Cabinet Minister's pronouncements—on mining matters, for example—must be authoritative, and the extravagant optimism with which they had in 1890 regarded the Chartered Company's enterprise gave place for a time to an attitude of equally unjustified suspicion.

Early in August 1891, Colquhoun resigned his post— nominally on the score of ill-health. During his brief spell of office he had done valuable work—especially in connection with the Manica Concession—but his training as an Indian Civil servant was not the best preparation for the executive control of a South African colony in the process of making, and he found it difficult to adapt himself to the novel conditions. He was succeeded by Jameson, who was unversed in official routine, impatient of formality and always prone to take short cuts to achieve his purpose—defects

[1] *The Ruined Cities of Mashonaland*, by J. T. Bent, pub. 1892.

which were nevertheless an advantage in enabling him to deal expeditiously with the daily problems of the Pioneer community. For a short time he had the assistance of Rutherfoord Harris, the energetic South African Secretary of the Company, but the latter had to contend with a great deal of prejudice at the hands of the settlers, who saddled him with the responsibility for most of their grievances, especially for the failure of the food supplies during the preceding wet season. Before he had succeeded in living down this feeling an unfortunate accident put an end to his career in Mashonaland. While bathing in the Hanyani River he was attacked by a crocodile and so seriously injured that he had to leave the territory. Jameson then appointed the present writer (who had been a member of the South African staff of the Company since the beginning of 1890) as his Secretary.

The first of the Company's Directors to visit Mashonaland [1] now arrived on the scene—Mr. Alfred Beit, who, travelling from Johannesburg viâ Tuli, arrived in Fort Salisbury about the middle of August and spent several weeks in the country, during which he inspected some of the gold-reefs on which work was proceeding at Hartley Hill, Mazoe and near Fort Victoria. He was followed a few weeks later by Rhodes, who had made the journey in the company of Frank Johnson by way of Beira, an arduous and even perilous route in those days for anyone, and attended in Rhodes' case by special embarrassments because of the antipathy in which he was held by the Portuguese, who regarded him—not without cause—as the author of their recent humiliation.

Rhodes, like Beit, visited the gold districts, but was chiefly engaged in planning with the aid of the " Doctor " a programme of policy for the immediate future. There were several pressing matters to be settled. The provision of food supplies for the approaching wet season was one, for a recurrence of last year's break-down would have spelt

---

[1] Rhodes had travelled in November 1890 from the Cape Colony as far as Fort Tuli, but after crossing the River Shashi had been dissuaded from proceeding further owing to the imminence of the rainy season.

disaster, and no reliance could be placed on private importa-
tions. However, this was mainly a question of perfecting
the organisation which already existed, and was soon disposed of. More perplexing was the subject of finance. Of
the million pounds which formed the original capital of the
Company about one-half had already gone. £70,000 had
been spent in acquiring the concessions in Matabeleland,
Gazaland and north of the Zambesi; the construction of the
Pioneer Road had cost £90,000, and the extension of the
telegraph line—which was now nearing Fort Victoria—a
further £50,000. About £200,000 had been expended on
the Police Force, while the annual cost of maintaining it at
the strength to which it had been raised when the Boer trek
threatened could not be less than £150,000. Drastic re-
trenchment was called for, and it was eventually decided to
reduce the Police to the smallest limits compatible with the
bare requirements of law and order, retaining the field and
machine-gun detachments, which had been trained to a
high pitch of efficiency.[1] As a second line of defence in
case of emergency steps were taken to create a Volunteer
Corps (the " Mashonaland Horse "), with head-quarters at
Salisbury and companies at other centres, and in addition
to adopt the Colonial " burgher " system, under which every
able-bodied man was provided with a rifle and ammunition
and held liable to serve in the defence of the country.

The disbandment of the Mounted Police was not quite
such a risky step as might at first appear. It could reasonably be expected that a fair number of those discharged
would remain in the country, and every inducement was,
in fact, given for them to do so; but quite apart from these
a large proportion of the settlers had undergone military
training—many having served in the Warren expedition,
the Basuto war and other campaigns. Neither was there
any ground for serious anxiety on account of non-combatants,
for at this time there were barely a dozen white women and
perhaps half that number of children in the whole of Mashona-

---

[1] The Company had in the country three 7-pounder R.M.L. guns, one
1-pounder shell Maxim, five ·450 Maxims and four other machine-guns.
Great reliance was placed on the Maxims, which, although adopted by the
British Army in 1889, had not, in 1891, been tested in actual warfare.

land.[1]   The Imperial authorities offered no particular objection to the proposed reduction, but betrayed more anxiety
about the danger of inroads from the Transvaal Boers than
on the score of defence against the natives, and warned the
Company not to look to Imperial aid for protection of its
territories against aggression.[2]   This, however, did not
unduly depress Rhodes and Jameson, who knew full well
that the Government would be morally bound to repel
Boer attempts against a territory which had been placed
under the Queen's protection.   As regards danger from the
natives, to be sure there were the Matabele, with their
military organisation still intact, and, according to alarmists,
still chafing at the presence of the white men in their former
raiding grounds.   But a year had passed since the occupation and Lobengula had manifested no inclination to interfere.   Jameson had assured him that no prospectors would
be allowed to pass beyond the Shasha River, a few miles west
of Victoria, and called upon him to reciprocate by forbidding
raids to the east of that boundary, and although there is
no evidence that the chief ever pledged himself to this
arrangement, it is certain that for some months the Matabele
gave a wide berth to the districts in which white men were
at work.[3]   The Company's representative at Bulawayo
(Colenbrander) had taken care to keep the chief informed
of the military measures against his ancient enemies the
Boers and Portuguese, and the success of the Company's
troops in these encounters, following their well-organised
expedition into the country, had doubtless made a salutary
impression on Lobengula, and even on his headstrong young
warriors.

For the so-called " Mashona " clans in their immediate

[1] There were five English ladies engaged in nursing (three in connection
with the English Church Mission at Umtali, and two Dominican Sisters of
the Sacred Heart at Salisbury) ; two accompanied an expedition sent up
by the Salvation Army, and the remainder braved official discouragement
and came up with their husbands—one indeed having arrived close on the
heels of the Pioneer column disguised as a boy !

[2] Imperial Secretary to British South Africa Company, July 30th, 1891 ;
Lord Knutsford to Sir H. Loch, February 3rd, 1892.   *Blue Book* C. 7171,
pp. 5, 10.

[3] See letter from Colenbrander to H. Currey, dated May 1st, 1892,
which indicates the extreme eastern limits of Matabele military posts.
Blue Book C. 7171, pp. 29, 30.

neighbourhood few entertained any feeling other than contempt. Fifty years of Matabele oppression appeared to have reduced them to a state of abject pusillanimity. Although the chiefs preserved their rules of succession and many of the dynastic traditions which they inherited from the days when the Kalanga tribes were the powerful feudatories of the great Monomotapa, no one would have credited that they retained a spark of the old spirit which made them so formidable to Barreto and other Portuguese leaders of the sixteenth century. They were useful as hewers of wood and drawers of water; they were ready to barter their miserable produce for cheap blankets and other European trade goods, and could sometimes even be persuaded to work underground on the claims, but as fighting men they were deemed of no account. Accordingly Rhodes and Jameson decided without misgiving that the Police Force of 650 should be reduced by Christmas to 150 of all ranks, and the cost thereby brought down to £50,000 a year, and despite a few croakers who recalled previous native outbreaks in other parts of South Africa, there was no serious criticism of this decision.

For all that, it was not long before incidents occurred which would have led men of greater experience to suspect that the tranquillity of the Matabele was merely a cloak, and that even in the cowed and spiritless Mashona there lurked possibilities of mischief.

Before the occupation of 1890 the old chief Lomagunda, whose kraals were about seventy miles north-west of Salisbury, and whose only anxiety had been to keep on good terms with any who appeared to have the upper hand, be they Portuguese, Matabele or British, was in the habit of paying annual tribute to Lobengula, going on foot regularly to Bulawayo—over two hundred miles—for the purpose. In 1891 he failed to appear, and Lobengula sent a party of about forty *amatjaha* to investigate. These, after consulting a female witch-doctor (Mondoro) who practised in that district, proceeded to Lomagunda's own village, where, after interrogating him as to his relations with the white men, they killed him in cold blood, and with him a number of his family, including wives and daughters. In accordance with time-honoured custom they seized the remaining women and children in the kraal—eighty or ninety in number—and drove them off to slavery in Matabeleland.

Later in the year the same treatment was, by order of Lobengula, meted out to the important chief, Tshibi, whose district lay at the opposite end of Mashonaland between the Pioneer Road and the Crocodile River, and who will be recalled as the alleged grantor of the concession on the strength of which the Boer trek was organised.[1] Upon both occasions Jameson sent letters of expostulation and warning to Lobengula, but only elicited evasive replies disclaiming any intention of interfering with the white men. Other outrages of the same character followed, indicating either that Lobengula could not restrain his *amatjaha* from raiding, or else that he wished to see how far he could go without provoking reprisals from the European settlers.

The Administration had troubles also with some of the petty Mashona chiefs. A French prospector was murdered in the Mazoe district and, on a party of Police being sent out to arrest the culprits, resistance was offered and shots were fired, resulting in the deaths of several natives. Another small disturbance occurred in the Victoria district, where one chief raided another who appealed for protection to the Company. The Police came to the assistance of the injured party, and an affray followed in which the aggressor was killed. Finally, at Ngomo's village, a few miles south-east of Salisbury, an attempt to arrest the chief on a charge of theft and assault on a white farmer led to a fight of a more serious nature in which twenty-three natives lost their lives. These conflicts were in each case reported both to Lobengula and to the Imperial authorities, whose different points of view were curiously illustrated. The former, referring to the affair at Victoria, took exception to the Company's officers mixing themselves up in native disputes, and said, " What does it matter if the Mashonas fight among themselves? " The British officials were dissatisfied with the action of the Police in the case of the murdered Frenchman,

[1] See Chapter XVIII.

and expressed grave displeasure at the severity of the punishment administered at Ngomo's kraal, where, they pointed
out—not without some justice—the loss of life among the
natives was utterly disproportionate to the original
offence.

These occurrences were not sufficiently alarming to ruffle
the serene confidence of the local authorities or the white
settlers, and when we reflect how recent was the contact
between the savage tribes of Mashonaland and the restraints
of the new order, we must admit that cases of violence were
surprisingly few.   In other respects progress was unchecked
and rapid.   The purchase of the Lippert Concession [1]
enabled the Company to go ahead with the issue of titles to
farms, and to make larger land grants to syndicates and
companies in consideration of their introducing capital for
development.   The townships began to assume shape, the
old wattle-and-daub huts being gradually replaced by more
substantial buildings of locally made bricks.   The Government led the way with blocks of public offices at Salisbury
and Victoria, and private enterprise followed with hotels,
churches and stores.   A branch of the Standard Bank was
opened and cash began to circulate in lieu of cheques drawn
on Capetown and Mafeking.   A printed newspaper replaced
the primitive cyclostyle sheets which had hitherto done
duty, and as the telegraph line reached Salisbury in February
1892, the public were placed in touch with the outer world
and were able to read news despatched from England the
day before.   Prospecting and mining went on vigorously
and plenty of capital appeared to be forthcoming for new
ventures.   Even Lobengula himself was taking a hand, for
his representative, James Dawson, had registered a block
of claims in his name on a reef in the Umfuli district upon
which a small battery was erected, and the results, in the
shape of a substantial lump of gold, were in due course handed
to the chief at Bulawayo.

Of course there were grievances.   The cost of living due
to the enormous distance over which goods and machinery
had to be hauled from the railhead at a charge of £60 or £70

[1] See Chapter VII.

per ton for transport alone; the Company's claim to a half interest in all mineral properties; their failure to maintain a sufficient and steady supply of native labourers—all in turn provided grounds for public agitations. But hope was raised by the news that the earthworks of the Beira railway had been commenced at Neves Ferreira, while the Cape line was rapidly advancing towards Mafeking. The Company's reservation of a fifty per cent. interest was usually commuted on the flotation of a property, and it cannot be denied that the existence of this right acted as a check to fraudulent and reckless flotations. The scarcity of native labour was a matter largely in the hands of individual mine-owners, for the natives quickly grasped the value of money, and, though indifferent workmen, they were not unwilling to give their labour where they were assured of regular wages and good food. There were other minor complaints against the Company's administration, but generally speaking the community was a satisfied one. The gold prospects were encouraging and the omens for the future of the country were distinctly favourable.

This pleasant state of affairs was rudely disturbed early in July 1893, when the inhabitants of the little mining township of Victoria found to their amazement that a full-dress Matabele raid was being conducted, at their very doors, against the inoffensive local natives on whom they depended for their supply of labour.

To explain the origin of this incursion it will be necessary to go back a little. The story begins with the cutting, early in May, of the telegraph line on the Pioneer Road between Tuli and Victoria, and the removal of about 500 yards of wire. Investigation of the theft—which was not the first of its kind—produced evidence clearly implicating some natives under Gomalla, a headman of Setoutsi, one of the petty Maholi chiefs in the neighbourhood, and Jameson sent Police to order these men to surrender the culprits or to pay a fine of cattle. Gomalla, with an alacrity which should have raised suspicion, chose the latter course, and handed over a number of cattle which he described as his own, but which were in reality some that Setoutsi had received from

Lobengula for herding.[1] He then sent to inform Lobengula
that the Company's men had seized the royal cattle—news
which greatly incensed the Matabele chief, who wrote
indignant protests to the High Commissioner and to the
Company's officers at Tuli. On the true facts reaching
Jameson he at once ordered the cattle to be returned to
Lobengula, explained to him the trick which had been played
by Gomalla and took the opportunity of impressing on him
how serious a matter it was for his subjects to tamper with
the white man's telegraph line. Lobengula professed himself
satisfied, but transferred his resentment to Setoutsi, in whose
charge he had placed the cattle. Shortly afterwards he was
further embittered by the news that another petty chief,
Bere, fifteen miles from Victoria, had robbed him of cattle.
A small party of Matabele sent to recover them failed in their
purpose, but their presence so close to the township came to
the knowledge of Captain C. F. Lendy, the magistrate, who
rode out to interview them, and on learning from their
leader that a large *impi* was shortly to be despatched from
Bulawayo to teach the thieving Mashonas a lesson, deemed
it advisable to send a letter to Lobengula, with whom he was
on very friendly terms, pointing out the risk which such a
course might entail.

The *impi* nevertheless started from Bulawayo at the end
of June under an elderly Induna named Manyao (head of
the Enxa military kraal), with Umgandan, a young *matjaha*,
as second in command. It consisted of the Mhlahlanhlela,
the crack regiment of *amadoda*, and two others, together with
detachments from several military kraals—2500 fighting
men in all—and was augmented by a rabble of about 1000
Maholi who joined it on the way. Its departure was duly
notified by Colenbrander in a telegram to Jameson in which
he stated that Lobengula wished him to inform the Doctor
that he had sent the force to punish Bere and others for
various reasons, and that he had sent a letter to Lendy to the

---

[1] " It was the custom of Lobengula to distribute his cattle among his
various kraals to be herded by his subjects, who, in return for their services
were allowed to use the milk. These " King's " cattle could not, except
with the consent of the King, be slaughtered, and every death or casualty
amongst them had to be reported to Lobengula." (Report of Matabele
Land Commission, 1894. *Blue Book* C. 8130).

same effect, asking the white people at Victoria not to be alarmed, as there was no intention of molesting them. Colenbrander's telegram, however, did not reach the Doctor until July the 10th, and the letter from the chief to Lendy was not delivered by the messengers who bore it until too late to avert the mischief which ensued.

It should be stated, in fairness to Lobengula, that according to his way of thinking he was absolutely within his rights in sending an expedition to punish his own subjects for *lèse-majesté*, and there is, moreover, strong evidence that he had forbidden the *impi* to interfere with white men or their property. The raid on the Victoria natives was no doubt a desperate effort to re-assert the authority which he felt was gradually slipping away from him. There is something pathetic in his struggle against the force of circumstances. He was exposed to daily importunities from his soldiers to expel the white intruders, but while he felt their presence to be an inconvenience, and knew that the growing independence of his former serfs was due to it, he had a fair comprehension of the resources at the back of this handful of men. He knew the tenacity of purpose which characterised their race. He remembered Cetewayo, and was shrewd enough to realise that armed resistance would in the long run bring about the downfall of his own kindgom. What he did not perhaps so fully appreciate was the irritation which the slaughter of the wretched Mashonas would cause to Englishmen. The Mashonas were his property—his " dogs." He had been accustomed all his life to hunt them, kill them, ravish their women and seize their cattle. Why should he change his whole scheme of government because Jameson and a few gold-seekers had squatted among them and were using them as servants? These arguments could not, however, be expected to weigh with the Victoria settlers, who would hardly have been worthy of the name of Englishmen if they had tamely looked on at a revolting butchery or had stifled the impulse to put an end to the system which made it possible.

The history of South Africa shows that it is impossible for European civilisation and native barbarism to exist side by

side without a clash.   There was no reason why the occupation of Rhodesia should prove an exception to the rule,
and allowing that a conflict was, sooner or later, inevitable,
it is just as well that it came about early and in circumstances which are entirely free from discredit to our countrymen.

On Sunday the 9th July—to resume the story—several
farmers on the east of Victoria were disgusted to find that the
whole country-side was swarming with Matabele soldiers—
many wearing the war-plume—who were driving the unhappy
Mashonas before them, burning their villages, butchering
and mutilating all the men they could catch and making
prisoners of the women and girls.   The raiders appeared to
be beyond control.   They came on to the farms, appropriated
all the cattle—including those of the white men—and
assegaied the herds and native servants.   Later in the day
some, flushed with slaughter, had the audacity to carry their
depredations into the commonage, and Lendy and his Police
with a few mounted inhabitants had their work cut out to
keep them from entering the town and molesting the inhabitants.   One party indeed did come up to the houses,
and among other outrages carried off and murdered the
personal servant of the English chaplain.

The position was, of course, reported by telegraph to
Jameson, who decided at once to proceed to Victoria,
and in the meanwhile instructed Lendy to demand the
return of any cattle taken from Europeans, to order the
Matabele to get back over the agreed border, and failing
compliance to take his Police and expel them.   At the same
time he enjoined him to employ tact and to get rid of the
raiders if possible without collision.

The late Mr. Henry Labouchere, M.P. for Northampton,
for reasons which well-informed people could surmise,
cherished until his dying day the bitterest feelings against
Rhodes, the Chartered Company and all their works, and he
lost no opportunity of venting his spleen in Parliament and
through the medium of his widely-read journal *Truth*.
Among other favourite theories invented, and persistently
repeated by him, was the fiction that the Matabele war of

1893 was engineered on account of the collapse of the Mashonaland gold bubble, which led Rhodes and his "buccaneers" to provoke a quarrel with the Matabele as an excuse for invading their country, where the reefs were believed to be far richer.[1] By constant iteration this story gained credence in circles whose political ideas were far apart from those of Mr. Labouchere, as, for instance, among our old friends the Aborigines Protection Society,[2] who still cherished for the Matabele the affection begotten at the breakfast party given to Babyana and Mshete in 1889,[3] and who were deeply concerned at the breaking up of Lobengula's influence five years later. They overlooked the atrocities endured by the Mashona tribes (whom they had not had time to take under their wing), and were ready to believe that the Matabele were the victims of an outrageous conspiracy devised by Rhodes, Jameson and the greedy adventurers allied to them.

But Mr. Labouchere gave Rhodes and the Mashonaland settlers credit for a subtlety which they were far from

---

[1] The following quotations are typical of many paragraphs which appeared in *Truth* during 1893 :

"That the present war was provoked by the Chartered Company, no one, I suppose, who is neither employed by the Company nor interested financially in it, doubts. Equally certain is it that Lobengula and his people, although by no means desirable neighbours, have had a war forced upon them because Mashonaland is not a paying property, and the Chartered Company hopes that if it can get hold of Matabeleland, it will, whether it be really so auriferous as is stated or not, get British investors to believe that it is . . ." (*Truth*, October 26th, 1893.)

"Mr. Rhodes . . . the head of a gang of shady financiers who forced on a war with the man through whose kindness they have pocketed millions, conducted it on the principle that ' godless heathen ' ought to be mowed down with Maxim guns if they happen to inhabit a country where there may be gold, and their envoys murdered in order that a rotten Company might be saved from immediate bankruptcy, and the financing gang might be in a position to transfer more money from the pockets of British investors into their own." (*Truth*, November 30th, 1893.)

"I do not hesitate to say that never in our times had anything so wicked been done in Africa as what is now occurring. . . The war was forced on these people in order to rob them. The Queen's specific pledges to their King have been ignored. Hostilities have been waged with unrelenting cruelty." (*Truth*, December 14th, 1893.)

[2] *Cf.* Rhodes' speech at Capetown on January 5th, 1894 :—" One of the most amusing pictures that ever was seen is the member for Northampton and the Aborigines Protection Society in the same boat."

[3] See Chapter VII.

possessing. A few months before the Victoria incident the
former was congratulating himself and the Chartered shareholders, in language the sincerity of which is not open to
doubt, that the Company was on the most friendly terms
with Lobengula and that he had not the least fear of any
trouble with him in the future.[1] By the majority of the
settlers the existence of gold reefs in Matabeleland was
unsuspected. To those who had given the matter a thought,
the failure of the attempts to develop a payable mine at Tati
were sufficiently discouraging, while there were plenty of
reefs in Mashonaland to occupy their attention and new
discoveries were being made almost daily. The only interest which the Matabele had hitherto had for them was as
occasional, and exceedingly unsatisfactory, labourers at the
diggings; the only complaint against them was that from
time to time they outraged some inoffensive Mashona village
and thereby created uneasiness and a tendency to desert
among other native workers.

But the strongest proof of the fallacy of Mr. Labouchere's
theory was the absolute unpreparedness of the Company in
1893 for a trial of strength with the Matabele. Its military
forces had, as already shown, been reduced in the interests
of economy to the lowest possible margin consistent with the
maintenance of order. The Company's exchequer was low,
and the financial groups which controlled it had urgent need
to conserve their resources for purposes of railway development from Cape Colony and Beira. No more unpropitious
moment could have been selected for a costly war of aggression, and no more insane suggestion could have been made
than that anybody concerned in the country should have
desired to provoke such a war. " Labby " was neither
insane nor ill-informed, and unquestionably had his tongue
in his cheek when he spread the slander.

Within forty-eight hours of the arrival of Manyao and his
raiders every single native employed on the mines round
Victoria had deserted. Those on the farms—such of them,
that is, as had escaped the Matabele assegais—fled panic-

---

[1] Rhodes' speech at the meeting of Chartered shareholders, November
29th, 1892.

stricken from the district.   So too did the native drivers and
leaders employed by the transport-riders on the road, and
all movement of supplies and stores was paralysed. Naturally
business of every kind was brought to a standstill, but in
spite of their exasperation the inhabitants of Victoria and
the adjacent parts, confident that the authorities would
take immediate steps to relieve the situation, kept their
heads and preserved an admirable self-control. The first
duty was to ensure the safety of their women and children,
numbering about ninety, and the next to prepare for the
organised attempt which they felt assured would now be
made to put an end, once and for all, to the intolerable
position caused by the insolent savages on their borders.
All able-bodied men in the neighbourhood, therefore,
hurried to Victoria to enrol as Volunteers. The public
buildings and Police yard were put into a state of defence;
machine-guns were mounted on the walls, and pickets thrown
out by day and night to guard against surprise. In less
than a week a force of 400 burghers was under arms, actively
engaged in musketry and artillery practice, while those who
could find horses formed themselves into patrols under Lendy
and other leading inhabitants and did what they could,
pending Jameson's arrival, to keep scattered parties of
Matabele out of the commonage and to recover the cattle of
Europeans which they were driving off.

Not until the 14th of July was Lobengula's letter to Lendy
—announcing the purpose of the raid—delivered. The native
who carried it was escorted into the town by about a dozen
of the raiders, including their leader the Induna Manyao,
who, upon being brought before Lendy and learning that he
was the " White Chief," called upon him to hand over a
number of terrified refugees—men, women and children—
who had sought sanctuary within the fort, grimly adding
that he would not kill them near the river and so pollute the
water, but would have them despatched in the bush.   Lendy
gave the only possible answer to this impudent demand,
but the evidence goes to show that he behaved with great
self-control, abstained from any provocative language, and
informed Manyao that if he liked to bring a charge against
any Mashonas he was prepared to try it as Magistrate.

A few days later—on the 17th July—Jameson reached the scene, having made the journey from Salisbury in a Cape cart in the company of Mr. William Napier, a Victoria merchant. Before starting he had been disposed to make light of the affair. He had telegraphed to Rutherfoord Harris to contradict exaggerated reports which might reach Cape Colony. " The Victoria people," he added, " have naturally got the jumps; Volunteers called out, rifles distributed, etc. . . . Will wire you when I hear the Matabele have all cleared." From Charter, on the way down, he sent a similar message to Sir Henry Loch, the High Commissioner, who had suggested that he should keep in touch with the officer commanding the Imperial Police in Bechuanaland. " At present," he telegraphed, " this is merely a raid against the Makalakas round Victoria, and not against whites. . . . I hope to get rid of the Matabele without trouble."[1]   But as he neared his destination he began to realise that the raid was a rather more serious business than he had imagined. For the last few miles of the journey he saw villages burning on both sides of the road, and Matabele with shields and assegais driving mules (which could only be the property of Europeans) loaded with plunder. He lost no time in deciding on a course of action. No sooner had he arrived than he sent out a party of police to summon the Induna to meet him. On the following day Manyao with Umgandan and several of the leaders arrived, and after some little difficulty about leaving their arms behind, met the Doctor with a number of the principal white men about noon outside the gates of the fort, where an *indaba* was held.

Jameson did not mince his words. He told them in the plainest terms that in no circumstances would the Mashona refugees be given up, and that the Matabele *impi* must retire at once over the border. An insolent interruption from Umgandan led to an inquiry from the chief Induna as to whether he had lost control over the younger men. Manyao admitted that this was the case, and said that they would not go even if he ordered them. " Well," said the Doctor, " you go with those who will still obey you. With those that

[1] *Blue Book* C. 7171, pp. 50, 52.

refuse "—here he waved his hand towards the troopers and guns on the wall of the fort—" I will deal." He then told Mr. Napier, who was interpreting, to point to the sun and to a position lower down in the sky towards the west. " If you have not gone when the sun is there," he said, " we shall drive you." " Very well," muttered Umgandan. " we'll be driven ! " Manyao merely asked what Jameson meant by the " border " and rose to go.

The *indaba*, which had lasted twenty minutes, then broke up and Jameson ordered Lendy to have a mounted patrol ready in two hours' time to see that his orders were carried out. It would appear from what ensued that Manyao realised that he had gone too far and succeeded in persuading the bulk of his force to commence a retirement towards Matabeleland, but that Umgandan and some of the more defiant of his followers went on with the business of looting and made no attempt to carry out Jameson's orders. About 2.30 between thirty and forty of the Police and Volunteers under Lendy started in the direction of Magomoli's kraal, a few miles north of the town, where the Matabele main body had been encamped the day before. After proceeding at a walk for some three and a half miles they came upon bodies of the raiders near Makumbi's village moving with grain and cattle from another small village which they had just attacked. A shot was fired—probably by the advance guard, though some asserted that it came from the Matabele—and Captain Lendy gave the command to attack. The patrol advanced in skirmishing order and opened fire. The raiders after a faint show of resistance began to retire in the direction of the hills on the north. In ten minutes the affair was over. About a dozen of the Matabele, including the truculent Umgandan, lay dead, and the rest beat a rapid retreat. A reconnaissance on the following day showed that the whole *impi* had evacuated the district.

Elated by the easy success of Lendy's patrol, the settlers now loudly appealed for an organised effort to settle the Matabele question finally. Public meetings were held both at Victoria and Salisbury, at which resolutions were passed urging that a strong and efficient force should be raised to

teach Lobengula a lesson.   It was openly stated that, unless
the Company were prepared to move, a large proportion of
the inhabitants were determined to take the matter into their
own hands and themselves avenge their losses.   The gist of
these resolutions was sent on to Rhodes and Loch by Jameson
on the 21st of July.   Four days only had elapsed since his
arrival at Victoria, but in those four days he had changed his
whole view of the situation.   Before, his one aim had been to
smooth matters over; to induce the Matabele to retire from
Victoria without resorting to force and to persuade Lobengula
to see the reasonableness of putting an end to these raids in
the neighbourhood of European settlements.   Could this be
brought about he had hopes of gradually strengthening the
position of the Charter by a policy of peaceful penetration,
for the financial situation was uppermost in his thoughts,
and he knew that a campaign against the Matabele would be
ruinous to Rhodes' schemes of economy.   But after seeing
with his own eyes the extent of the damage done by the
raiders and noting the hostile demeanour of their leaders at
the interview on the 18th, it was borne in upon him that for
the future prosperity of Mashonaland it was vitally necessary
that the Matabele threat should be removed.   He did not
delude himself with the idea that the Matabele would tamely
swallow the rebuff they had received, and knew that even for
bare purposes of protection considerable expenditure would
now have to be incurred on horses, ammunition and equipment; but though this might possibly avert for a time the
danger of reprisals, yet in the long run, with such unruly
and aggressive neighbours, a conflict was inevitable.   Such
being his conviction, he argued that the longer the post-
ponement the heavier would be the expense involved.   All
round him were the settlers eagerly pressing to be allowed " to
go in and finish it."   They were confident in their ability
to do so, and Jameson also began to see that the soundest
policy was to follow up the affray at Makumbi's by a vigorous
and determined attack on Matabeleland itself.

For the moment he did no more than indicate to the High
Commissioner, in general terms, his belief that only by war
could the Matabele be kept within bounds, but he sent a

strong message through Moffat to Lobengula, informing him of the punishment inflicted on his *impi*, warning him that a repetition of the raid would lead to war, and stating that the white men's losses at Victoria would have to be made good. The High Commissioner also sent a solemn caution to the chief, adjuring him to respect the white men and their property, to punish the unruly soldiers who had brought about the trouble and to compensate those who had suffered loss.

On first hearing the news of the Victoria affair from Jameson, Lobengula displayed a certain amount of contrition. He expressed a hope that the cattle captured by his Indunas had been restored, and even went so far as to express satisfaction that his people had been ordered back, admitting that in allowing an *impi* to go so close to Victoria he had made a mistake. A few days later, however, Manyao and the other leaders of the *impi* returned and gave their version of the affair, which was to the effect that some of his people had been persuaded by the white men to leave their arms behind and attend a meeting at Victoria, and that thirty of them were then shot dead without any cause. On receipt of these reports Lobengula exhibited bitter indignation and sent a message (which was transmitted by telegraph) to the High Commissioner, refusing point blank to pay compensation for damage and loss of cattle, demanding the surrender of the Mashona refugees at Victoria, and expressing regret that he had not ordered his soldiers to capture and loot all they could lay hands on belonging to the whites.

The situation of the white people at Bulawayo was now highly critical. They consisted of Colenbrander (the Company's agent) and his wife, and eight or nine traders, including James Fairbairn. A few miles outside was an English missionary with his wife and children. The lives of all were in grave danger from the excited native population. From the chief himself they had nothing to fear in spite of his wrath (which was partly assumed to put himself right with his people), but he might be powerless to protect them. He, in fact, recognised this and recommended them to get out of

the way, and accordingly most of them, including the
Colenbranders, hastened to put themselves in a place of
safety and started viâ Tati for Bechuanaland.

Following his wrathful communication to the High Commissioner, the chief refused at the end of July to accept the
monthly payment of £100 due under the Rudd Concession,
and despatched messengers to recall an army of 6000 men
that had gone on a raiding expedition towards Barotseland.
In reality there was nothing he so much dreaded as war with
the whites, and in spite of these outward manifestations of
bellicose intentions he was casting about for means to avert
it.   A few days later he resolved to send a final secret message
of expostulation to the Queen, and he had this written by an
educated Colonial native who lived at Bulawayo, and en
trusted it to old Mshete, one of the two Indunas who visited
England in 1889.

In the meantime Jameson had returned to Salisbury and
began his preparations for organising a force of Volunteers,
which in case of emergency could take the field with the least
possible delay.   He had several telegraphic conversations
with both Rhodes and Loch, in which he explained his plans
and urged the necessity of sending an armed expedition to
Matabeleland.   The former at first advised caution—
recommended him to read Luke xiv. 31, and pointed out
the poverty of his resources, but ultimately saw the force of
his reasoning and busied himself in purchasing horses with
his own money and sending them forward for the mounted
force of Volunteers which it was proposed to raise.   Loch,
on the other hand, whatever his private opinions were—
and there is every reason to believe that he agreed with
Jameson—was obliged, in so serious a matter, to seek
inspiration from the Home Government.   The Secretary
of State for the Colonies was now Lord Ripon, who came into
office in 1892 with the fourth Gladstone Ministry.   His
despatches to Loch in connection with the Matabeleland
affair show that he was wholly out of sympathy with the
Chartered Company.   Ten years earlier, as Viceroy of India,
he had incurred great unpopularity by his tendency to
sacrifice British prestige in order to secure the goodwill of the

native populations, and apparently this idiosyncrasy still clung to him. Above all he was fearful of the possibility that if Jameson were allowed to cry " havoc " and attempt an aimed attack on Matabeleland, the course of events might involve the employment of the forces of the Crown, and in spite of the uncompromising message sent by Lobengula to Sir H. Loch, he gave orders that the Company's claim for compensation should be dropped and that no offensive movement should be undertaken unless the whites in Mashonaland were actually attacked. He was obliged to admit, however, that the Company were justified as a mere measure of prudence, in holding their Volunteers in readiness to repel attacks, and on hearing early in September that threatening movements were taking place among the Matabele, he was obliged also to sanction an increase in the Bechuanaland Police at Macloutsie, close to the southern border of Lobengula's country.

Reference has been made to the following authorities :

Blue Books C. 7171, C. 7196 and C. 7555.
Reports of the British South Africa Company, 1891–1893.

CHAPTER XX

THE MATABELE WAR

THERE was no lack of good fighting material in Mashonaland. Among the settlers were a number who had served
in previous South African campaigns, as well as several
officers of the British Army who had been seconded for
service in the Police or the Civil branches of the Company's
administration. The senior of these latter was Major
Patrick William Forbes—a captain in the Inniskilling
Dragoons—who, besides being Magistrate of Salisbury, was
in command of the Volunteer force and had given proof of
his level-headedness and resolution in the little affair with
the Portuguese at Umtasa's kraal in 1890.[1]   To him Jameson
decided to entrust the duty of organising and commanding
a field force for operations—should the necessity arise—
against the Matabele, and after various proposals had
been discussed between them, the following plan of campaign was arrived at : Three bodies, each of 250 mounted
Volunteers, were to be raised as rapidly as possible at
Salisbury, Victoria and Tuli. The two former were to
unite at a spot on the high veld on the eastern side of Matabeleland, and thence, following the watershed, to advance
on Bulawayo. The Tuli force was simultaneously to create
a diversion by entering Matabeleland from the south.
Each column was to have with it Maxim guns on galloping
carriages, and was to move with the least possible encum-
brance in the shape of transport.

With certain modifications this plan was adhered to.
The raising and training of the Salisbury contingent was
undertaken by Forbes himself, and of that at Victoria by
Captain Allan Wilson, an employé of the Bechuanaland
Exploration Company, who had served in the Cape Mounted

[1] See Chapter XI.

Police and in Basutoland, and was a man of strong personality with every qualification for a leader of irregular troops. For the command of the Southern force another good selection was made in Captain Pieter Johannes Raaf, C.M.G., a Dutch colonial who had rendered distinguished service in the Zulu war and had occupied an official post in the Transvaal during the British occupation. He was now Magistrate of Tuli and at once offered his services to the Company, which was fortunate in securing a man so experienced in native warfare and—as afterwards proved— so full of resource in difficult situations. A good number of recruits for the Tuli force was collected by Raaf at Johannesburg, and although President Krüger at first protested against this, a firm telegram from Sir Henry Loch induced him to waive his objections.

In September evidence began to accumulate that the Matabele were also making warlike preparations. Their regiments were reported to be mobilising and their wizards were said to be " doctoring " the roads leading into Mashonaland and Bechuanaland. The presence of bodies of fighting men was ascertained by European and native scouts at various points along a line extending from the Umniati River, which skirted the district of Lomagunda, past the head-waters of the Queque and Gwelo Rivers, to Chilimanzi and the Shasha River less than thirty miles from Victoria. Others were at the same time concentrating in the vicinity of the Mangwe Pass on the direct road from Bulawayo to Tati, their outposts being pushed forward in the direction of Tuli, thus threatening Khama's country and the line of communications with the south. The High Commissioner therefore arranged with the Chief Khama for a force of from 500 to 1000 of his best fighting men to co-operate with Major Goold-Adams [1] for the defence of the Protectorate. He also requested Jameson to gain as much information as possible as to the disposition of the Matabele *impis* by means of patrols along the border, but to avoid any move-

---

[1] At that time commanding the Bechuanaland Border Police; afterwards Sir Hamilton Goold-Adams, G.C.M.G., C.B., Governor of Queensland.

ment which might precipitate a collision.   It probably did
not occur to him that the Matabele would be unlikely to
draw a distinction between a reconnoitring patrol and a
hostile force.   His orders from Lord Ripon were to use his
utmost endeavours to avert a breach, and on October 1st,
in pursuance of this policy, he sent a final appeal to Logen-
gula to withdraw his regiments and to send some of his
Indunas to Capetown " to talk matters over so that there
may be peace."

The people on the spot, however, could hardly be expected
to view the situation with the mental detachment of a
Cabinet Minister in Whitehall.   To them the issue was
one of life and death.   Their occupations, their homesteads
—in many cases their wives and families were in jeopardy,
and no patched-up understanding with Lobengula could
give them any permanent security.   Neither the settlers
nor the Company's officials cherished any illusion as to
the intentions of the Matabele, and accordingly they united
in pushing forward their defensive preparations with feverish
vigour.   The horses bought by Rhodes in the Colony and
Raaf in the Transvaal were already on the road.   The
Salisbury Volunteers, who had been moved down to Charter
early in September, and the Victoria contingent were
rapidly completing their efficiency.   Among the latter a
question arose as to the terms of service in the event of
their taking the field.   If a campaign in Matabeleland were
undertaken, it would be as much for the protection of the
settlers as to safeguard the interests of the Chartered
Company.   The latter was not in a position to maintain a
paid force, but was prepared to guarantee all who served a
fair share in the results that might be expected to ensue.
Jameson, therefore, agreed that each member of the expedition should, if Matabeleland were occupied, have the right
to mark out a farm and claims for his own benefit on the
same terms as were already enjoyed in Mashonaland, and
that one-half of any loot captured should be divided among
them in equal shares.   When the Victoria force was enrolled,
a request was made that the terms should be committed to
writing, and Jameson signed a document which was pre-

pared by a committee of the Volunteers, but which, in the absence of a competent draughtsman, was so loosely worded that different constructions were afterwards placed upon its conditions. This was the notorious " Victoria Agreement," which, besides being productive of protracted disputes between the parties immediately concerned—the Company and the Volunteers—was denounced by the Company's opponents as a " secret compact " proving the existence of a plot to rob the Matabele of their country. There was in reality nothing novel to South Africans in an agreement of this kind, which—except in regard to the pegging of gold claims—followed the lines of similar contracts made on several former occasions when Volunteers were enrolled for war with troublesome native tribes,[1] and the suggestion of secrecy was of course ridiculous in regard to an agreement to which between 700 and 800 individuals were parties.

Jameson did not lose sight of the strategic importance of the force of Bechuanaland Police on the southern border of Matabeleland, and from the 17th to the 25th of September he was at Tuli conferring and planning routes with Goold-Adams, who met him there, and satisfying himself as to the progress of the Volunteers raised by Raaf. A scouting party of Europeans and natives under Captain the Hon. Charles White—the officer commanding the Company's Police—kept constant watch on the movements of the Matabele on the border along a frontage of fifty miles to the west of Victoria, while a detachment from the Bechuanaland Police patrolled the south bank of the Shashi River between Tati and Fort Tuli.

Until the first week in September Rhodes had been detained by parliamentary duties at the Cape, but had nevertheless played an active part in the despatch of supplies and remounts for the field force in Mashonaland. He too recognised that the presence of Goold-Adams' Imperial

[1] Sir Bartle Frere, discussing in 1879 the possibility of obtaining Boer support against the Zulus, speaks of " the ordinary *commando* terms— promise of cattle loot and of farms carved out of the conquered territory " (in a letter to the Under Colonial Secretary, quoted by Mr. Worsfold in his *Sir Bartle Frere*, p. 113).

troops in the Northern Protectorate was a valuable factor
in the situation, but he was by no means anxious that they
should take part in the actual advance into Matabeleland—
if such an advance became necessary. As soon as he
realised that war might be forced on the Company he had
placed £50,000 out of his private resources at its disposal,
at the same time informing the High Commissioner that
the Company wanted nothing and asked for no assistance
from Her Majesty's Government. This was not a mere
arrogant gesture on his part, though it may have been
provoked by the indecent anxiety of Lord Ripon to dis-
claim Imperial responsibility for the protection of the
Company's territories. Rhodes had his ears to the ground
and was suspicious that the Government, though willing
to allow the Company to bear the burden and cost of
defending themselves, might, if a war came about and
were successful, seek a pretext for dictating the terms of
settlement or even claim a share in the spoils. He therefore took a cue from Lord Ripon's ill-advised warning
and emphasised the Company's independence. Early in
September the Cape Parliament was prorogued and Rhodes,
in view of the critical position in the north, decided at
once to proceed to Mashonaland viâ Beira, hoping to be
able to take part in the military movements which he felt
were inevitable. Before he could reach Salisbury, however, matters had been brought to a climax by two open
acts of war on the part of the Matabele—nearly simultaneous, though occurring at widely separated points on
the border.

At the end of September Captain White, who was still
patrolling the border near Victoria, learnt that a party of
Matabele had crossed to the Mashonaland side and seized
some cattle, and he detached two of his scouts to follow the
spoor and endeavour to ascertain the strength and watch
the movements of the marauders. These men traced the
cattle to a village on the border, where they demanded to
see the Induna, and while waiting for his appearance were
fired on by a body of about fifty Matabele who suddenly
appeared on the rocks above the village. They returned the

fire and retired after satisfying themselves that the Matabele were on the border in considerable force. This was
on the 30th September, and five days later a small detachment from Goold-Adams' Police, while patrolling on the
Bechuanaland side of the Shashi River, was fired on by
about thirty Matabele—apparently a reconnoitring party
from a larger force in that neighbourhood. On these
incidents being reported to Sir H. Loch (who a few days
before had been advising the Company's officers, in view
of the approaching rainy season, to demobilise and endeavour
to arrive at a settlement with Lobengula), he realised that
the time for words was over, and sent a telegram to Jameson
authorising him, as soon as his force was ready, to advance
for the purpose of driving the *impis* to a safe distance from
Victoria, at the same time ordering Goold-Adams to occupy
Tati on the southern frontier of Matabeleland. Arrangements had already been made, as stated above, for the
Bechuanaland Police in such a contingency to have the
assistance of a force of Khama's people.

The Salisbury column of about 250 mounted men had
been moved from Fort Charter on the 2nd October, and,
when Loch's telegram arrived, was encamped a few miles
from the fort at the head-waters of the Umniati River,
which was recognised as the boundary in that locality
between Mashonaland and Matabeleland. It now advanced
in a south-westerly direction, the first objective being a
well-known landmark known as Sigala or Iron Mine Hill
(about thirty miles east of the modern town of Gwelo), at
which point it was proposed to effect a junction with the
Victoria column, which started to move on the same day.
In the neighbourhood of Iron Mine Hill were the villages
of a number of Holi chiefs and several of Lobengula's
easternmost cattle-posts. The two columns met on the
16th October, the scouts of each having been in touch with
the enemy during the last stages of the march, and skirmishes
having taken place, in one of which Captain J. A. L. Camp-
bell, an ex-officer of the Royal Artillery, attached to the
Salisbury contingent, was mortally wounded—the first
casualty of the war. From Iron Mine Hill the united

columns continued their advance, still in a S.W. direction, towards Bulawayo, keeping to the watershed, which was reported to be open and comparatively free from bush, along a line which lay a few miles south of the old hunters' road from Matabeleland.

The strength of the combined force, of which Forbes now assumed command, was approximately as follows :— [1]

Salisbury column : white men, 258 ; horses, 242 ; native contingent, 115 ; with two Maxim guns on mule-drawn galloping carriages, one Gardner machine-gun, one Nordenfelt, and one 7-pounder field-gun.

Victoria column : whites 414 ; horses, 172 ; Cape boys, etc., 78, and about 200 natives. Three Maxim guns (two with galloping carriages and horses), one Hotchkiss machine-gun and one 7-pounder. There were 16 ox-wagons for supplies and ammunition with the Salisbury, and 15 with the Victoria column.

Jameson himself arrived with the latter, accompanied by Major Sir John Willoughby, late of the Company's Police, who had come out post haste from England on the first news of trouble with the Matabele, and from now onwards acted—without, however, any definite commission —as the Administrator's military adviser and Staff officer. At the last moment Dr. G. W. H. Knight-Bruce, Bishop of Mashonaland, also joined the columns, being careful to explain that he did so, not as Chaplain to the British force " but as Bishop of the country in which both the contending parties lived," [2] an attitude which he would have found somewhat difficult to explain had he fallen into the hands of the Matabele.

Between Iron Mine Hill and the Shangani River, a distance of some seventy miles, the advance was com-

[1] Details of the personnel of the column are given by Forbes himself (in a narrative printed in *The Downfall of Lobengula,* by Wills and Collingridge), by Sir John Willoughby (in an official marching-out state printed in *Blue Book* C. 7196), by the Company (in the report presented to their shareholders on the 18th January, 1895), and in the Medal Roll. No two of these agree. The figures in the text are taken from the Company's report, which was probably based on the most accurate information obtainable.
[2] *Memories of Mashonaland,* by Dr. Knight-Bruce, p. 222.

paratively free of incident, but the column was kept aware of the close proximity of the enemy, and as several of the Matabele regiments were known to live near the route, the utmost vigilance was constantly maintained, *laager* being formed at every halt and scouts being invariably thrown out in front and on both flanks. At one stage in the march the expedition had to pass through the southern extremity of a belt of dense bush known as the Somabula forest, and additional anxiety was here felt owing to a thick fog which caused even the native guides to lose their way. It proved, however, to be a blessing in disguise, for, as they afterwards discovered, one of the strongest of the Matabele regiments—the Insukamini—had been lying in wait with the intention of attacking the column at this dangerous point, but missed them in the fog. Between here and the Shangani River the scouts had several brushes with small parties of the enemy, in one of which a valuable officer, Captain Edward Burnett, was shot with fatal results.

On the afternoon of the 24th October the column forded the Shangani River and formed *laager* in an open space in the thick thorn scrub on the western bank. Bush *scherms* or *zeribas* were built in rear of the troops for the protection of a number of friendly natives who had joined the force during the preceding few days, and for some Maholi women and children who had escaped from the Matabele and sought refuge with the white men, and about 1000 head of captured cattle were enclosed in kraals round the *laager*, the usual precautions being increased in the knowledge that bodies of the enemy were close at hand.

Before dawn on the morning of the 25th a few shots in rear announced that the expected attack had opened. The enemy, by accident or design, fell upon the camp of the friendly natives, who fled panic-stricken towards the *laager*. The wagons were quickly manned and the Maxim guns brought into action, but the defence was at first handicapped by the difficulty in the darkness—only partially relieved by a setting moon—of distinguishing the attackers from the friendlies, and some casualties occurred among the

latter owing to their running across the line of fire. The
Matabele pressed their attack with great courage. When
they surprised the native camp they did some cruel work
among men, women and children with their stabbing
assegais, and had they first stolen upon the *laager* in the
darkness and relied upon these—their natural weapons—
they would have stood a better chance of success.[1] With
their rifles they did very little damage, owing partly, as
was afterwards discovered, to an idea that by raising the
sights they would increase the deadliness of their fire!
The white troops, many of whom had never before been in
action, were remarkably steady, and the Maxims, skilfully
handled by Lendy and his well-trained gunners, were able
to prevent the *laager* from being rushed. As day began to
break the enemy fell back a few hundred yards, but a
mounted troop sent to clear the bush found them still in
great strength and was forced to retire. A second determined attack was made on all faces of the *laager* about
5.30 a.m., and further bodies of the enemy were seen to be
advancing from the *kopjes* a mile or so to the west. The
light now enabled the defenders to take better aim, and the
foremost parties of the Matabele were checked by the
Maxims and double line of rifle fire from the men both on
the wagons and under them, while the more distant bodies
were dispersed by a few shells from the 7-pounders. Mounted
troops were again sent out to reconnoitre, and about eight
o'clock came upon fresh masses of the enemy advancing
from three points at a distance of 1200 to 1500 yards from
the *laager*. These were the enemy's reserves and included
the Insukamini regiment, which had been hovering on the
flanks of the column for several days and had narrowly
missed it in the Somabula forest. This third attack was
frustrated, before it had time properly to develop, by well-
directed shells from the 7-pounder and Hotchkiss guns.
The enemy now fled in all directions, followed by a few
mounted men, and shelled by the guns as they scattered.

[1] It was afterwards stated by prisoners that the intention of the Matabele general had been to surround the *laager* in the darkness and to rush in
with the assegai without firing a shot, but the accidental discharge of a
rifle by one of his soldiers gave the alarm and spoilt the plan.

Some of the retreating Matabele were seen through field-glasses to fire at the shells as they burst, evidently with the idea that they were endowed with some diabolical form of life. Half an hour later—at 9.30 a.m.—mounted reconnoitring patrols reported that the enemy was in full retreat along the Shangani and towards the hills on the north.

As the Matabele in most instances removed their wounded and dead the extent of their losses could only be surmised, but from the number of bodies found on the field and from the reports of prisoners afterwards captured, it was estimated that their casualties—killed and wounded—amounted to between 500 and 600. One of the Matabele—identified as the commander of the Insukamini—was found to have committed suicide by hanging himself from a tree after having been disabled by wounds. The total strength of the enemy was computed at from 5000 to 6000. The casualties in the Company's forces were one white trooper and one " Cape boy " driver killed and six white men wounded. Forty or fifty of the friendly natives and a few of the women and children who had taken refuge in their camp were assegaied in the first rush, and some of the latter were barbarously mutilated.

The column continued the advance that afternoon without further molestation. During the next few days the route lay through the neighbourhood of many of Lobengula's military kraals, most of which were found empty of everything but grain, but the surrounding country was full of bands of the enemy on the move, and several minor engagements took place with detachments from the larger forces that were continually hanging on the flanks of the expedition. In one of these skirmishes Captain Owen Gwynydd Williams, in charge of a party of scouts, became separated from his men through his horse bolting and was never seen alive again, though his remains were found and identified many weeks afterwards. He was an ex-officer of the Royal Horse Guards who had originally entered Mashonaland as a member of Lord Randolph Churchill's expedition, and his military training and natural aptitude for scouting had rendered him a most valuable member of the force.

On the 31st of October the column found itself again in touch with a large force of Matabele, and although it was kept at a distance for the time being by occasional shell-fire, it was clear that another action was imminent. On the following day the usual halt was made on some high ground near the source of the Imbembesi River, and *laager* was formed with the right or Salisbury flank facing a large belt of bush 500 yards distant and with a good field of fire on the other sides. At about 1 p.m., while the animals were being watered, a very determined attack was opened on the Salisbury flank by a force of some 7000 of the enemy which advanced through the bush. The whole of the horses promptly stampeded and the Matabele made desperate efforts to cut them off, but were frustrated by a few gallant men who dashed out under heavy fire and by strenuous efforts headed the terrified animals back to the *laager*. A mounted picket at the edge of the bush was, however, surprised and one of the vedettes assegaied. While the main attack was directed against the right, several attempts were made to encircle the position, but as the enemy became more exposed in the open ground the Maxims were able to stop their rushes. On the bush side the engagement was fierce, and some of the Matabele advanced to within 150 yards of the wagons, but they could not long face the machine-guns and within an hour were driven back with heavy losses. The rout was made complete by parties sent out to clear the bush under cover of shell-fire from the 7-pounders.

In this fight at the Imbembesi the pick of the Matabele regiments were engaged, including the Ingubu, the Imbezu (which was estimated to have lost 500 in casualties out of a strength of 900) and the Insukamini, which had been present at the former battle on the Shangani. As on the previous occasion the majority of their dead were removed, but sufficient were found to show that their casualties had been very heavy. In the British force the losses were four men killed and seven wounded.

On the following day the column once more moved forward towards Bulawayo, now only about twenty miles distant.

On the morning of the 3rd November, soon after passing the Thabas Induna hill, they heard a heavy rumbling, as of thunder, in the direction of Bulawayo, and simultaneously saw a dense cloud of smoke rise into the air.   Scouts sent forward to investigate returned with the report that the great kraal had been fired in several places and that a large store of cartridges had been blown up.   They also brought the news that the chief had disappeared and that the native population had evacuated the place, but that two white traders, Fairbairn and Usher, were still there, alive and uninjured.   An officer and 25 mounted men were then sent forward and cleared Bulawayo of a few straggling natives who fled on their approach.   They found the two traders sitting on the roof of their stable, where they had taken up their quarters on the news of the battle of Imbembesi.   They owed their lives to the personal influence of Lobengula—a circumstance which must ever be remembered to his credit, for there can be little doubt that great pressure was brought upon him to hand them over as victims to the popular resentment against the white men.

At two o'clock on the 4th November the Mashonaland columns marched into the " Place of Slaughter," headed by an old Pipe-Major of the Royal Scots playing a lively air, and the Chartered Company's flag—the Union Jack with the lion badge in the centre—was run up on a rough staff fixed to a tree in the middle of the ruined town.

So far all had progressed satisfactorily.   Within a month from the date of crossing the Matabele border the settler-soldiers had met and routed the flower of the Matabele regiments, had destroyed many of their military strongholds, had occupied their principal town and had driven their great chief a fugitive into the wilds.   Though much remained to be done before the conquest could be regarded as complete, there could be no doubt that by their rapid and audacious *coup* Jameson, Forbes and their improvised little army had dealt a death-blow to the bloodthirsty tribe that for more than fifty years had been the main obstacle to the peaceful extension of South Africa.

But while these men of action were making history the

men of words in Whitehall were exercising themselves over a new problem. On the eve of the battle of Shangani, the Secretary of State telegraphed to Capetown that any negotiations with Lobengula were to be conducted by the High Commissioner and were to be under his complete control, and these instructions were in due course transmitted to Rhodes in Salisbury—Jameson himself being out of reach. Lord Ripon was probably within his rights under Clause VII of the Charter, but in view of the attitude which he had taken up during the preceding months, and judged by the actual event, the decision was regarded as preposterous. Rhodes at any rate was determined to keep the settlement of Matabeleland as far as possible in his own hands, and in a telegraphic conversation with Loch on the 1st November he begged the latter to inform Lord Ripon that the Company considered that it was entitled to administer the country, which it then hoped to win by its own efforts and the enterprise of the Mashonaland citizens. In private communications with his colleagues he was more outspoken. The Company, he said, had asked the Imperial Government for nothing, and if victorious claimed the right to settle the quarrel with Lobengula, subject to the approval of the Secretary of State.

A few days later, when the occupation of Bulawayo seemed assured, he followed up his protest by pointing out that the Company's troops had beaten the Matabele single-handed, that he himself had borne the expense of the expedition, that it was only right that the settlement of terms of peace should be left in his hands, and that he had the men and the means to govern the country. The correspondence was made public, and Rhodes' demands received general support in Cape Colony and other parts of South Africa and when Loch offered to leave the Bechuanaland Police in Bulawayo (which, by the way, they had not yet reached) until after the rains, Rhodes declined the proposal with thanks, saying that the Company was quite strong enough to look after itself.

But the Secretary of State was absolved from adherence to the strict letter of his instructions by the fact that when the Mashonaland Volunteers arrived in Bulawayo, Lobengula had vanished, and there was nobody to parley with, and so the question of negotiations, which had threatened to develop into a very pretty quarrel between Rhodes and the Imperial authorities, was tacitly allowed for the time being to drop.

It is possible that the Government had no real intention of interfering in the negotiations with Lobengula, but were anxious to conciliate the Radical Press and a few importunate members of Parliament, who, led by Labouchere, were determined that the Company should gain no further influence in Africa, and accordingly spared no efforts to distort the intentions of Rhodes and his " gang of adventurers." On the 9th November, when the news of the capture of Bulawayo had reached London, Labouchere moved the adjournment of the House of Commons in order to discuss the Matabele question, and delivered a violent harangue in which he subjected Rhodes and all concerned with the Company to the most malignant and scurrilous abuse. He found, however, that he had overshot the mark, for not only were his calumnies exposed and refuted by Rochfort Maguire—at that time Member for West Clare—but he was repudiated by Mr. Sidney Buxton,[1] and even by Mr. Gladstone himself, who denounced the unpatriotic attack in language of marked severity.

It will be observed that Rhodes claimed that the Company's forces had " beaten the Matabele single-handed." It is true that the Southern force, which was partly composed of the Bechuanaland Police, and was commanded by an Imperial officer (Lieut.-Colonel Goold-Adams), had been outstripped by several days in the race towards Bulawayo, but it is as well to remember that the presence of this force was a serious embarrassment to the enemy, and by drawing off a number of fighting men, who would otherwise have been able to join in the battles at Shangani and Imbembesi, materially contributed to the success of the expedition. As the reports issued at the time said next to nothing about the assistance rendered by Goold-Adams' column, it is only

[1] At that time Under-Secretary for the Colonies; now Earl Buxton, G.C.M.G.

right that a short account should be given here of its progress
and adventures.

Jameson's plan had been for Raaf and his Volunteers to
advance, with the hunter Selous who had joined them as
guide, from Fort Tuli towards the Mangwe Pass, which
commanded the old trade route from Tati to Bulawayo, but
this would have necessitated their marching through broken
and difficult country, and for so small a force would have
been an extremely hazardous operation. When, therefore,
it was decided in the first week of October that for the safety
of the Protectorate the Bechuanaland Police should themselves move forward and occupy Tati, Jameson readily fell
in with the proposal of Sir H. Loch that Raaf should place
himself and his men under Goold-Adams' command, and the
junction took place at Macloutsie on the 11th October,
immediately after which the combined force set out for
Tati, a sufficient garrison being left to secure the safety of
the base camp. The strength of the column was as follows :
Bechuanaland Border Police : 225 whites, 210 horses, four
Maxims, two 7-pounders, 14 wagons and 50 natives;
Chartered Company's Volunteers under Raaf : 225 whites,
191 horses, one Maxim and 11 wagons with their complement
of native drivers. The occupation of Tati (where there
were several English miners employed by the Concessions
Company) was the most pressing object, and to effect this
about half the force was pushed forward, the remainder,
with the transport, being left to follow as expeditiously as
possible in support. On reaching the Shashi River the column
was reinforced by 130 mounted and about 1700 dismounted
natives with 30 wagons supplied by the Bechuana Chief
Khama, who led them in person. The advanced troops
reached Tati on the 14th October—greatly to the relief of
the mining employees, whose situation had been rather
precarious—and the rear party and wagon-train joined them
on the 18th.

Now occurred an unfortunate affair of which much
political capital was made by Rhodes' enemies, though it
had not the slightest connection with the operations of the
Chartered Company. It will be remembered that on October

the 1st, just before his hand had been forced by the shots fired at the Company's scouts near Victoria and at the Police patrol on the Shashi River, Loch had sent a final appeal to Lobengula to recall his regiments and to send some Indunas to Capetown to confer with him for the purpose of arriving at a peaceful settlement.[1] This message reached Bulawayo on the 14th October and was delivered to one of the three white men remaining in the place—James Dawson the trader, who at once read it to the chief. Although Lobengula must by that time have been aware that Jameson's force was advancing on his eastern borders, he seized the opportunity presented to him as providing a chance of averting the crash which he felt was imminent, and detailed his brother, Ingubogubo, and two other Indunas to proceed to Cape-town, requesting Dawson to accompany them. They started at once on horseback, and reaching Tati on the 18th October found it to their surprise in the occupation of an armed British force, but instead of seeking the Commanding Officer immediately and reporting his important mission, Dawson foolishly left his native companions in charge of one of the mine foremen while he went to the Company's store to have a drink, and afterwards sat down with some friends to dinner. In the meanwhile Goold-Adams, in entire ignor-ance of Dawson's mission, but supposing that he had persuaded Lobengula to allow him to quit Bulawayo, and that the natives with him were simply an escort who would seek to return, took the obvious course of placing them under arrest, at the same time informing them that they had nothing to fear provided they made no attempt at escape. The In-dunas, dismayed at being made prisoners, thought that they had been led into a trap, and while being marched away one of them snatched the bayonet of a sentry and made a savage attack on his guards, two of whom he wounded. He was promptly shot dead, while the second Induna, who took advantage of the confusion to break away, was knocked on the head by a blow from the butt of a rifle which fractured his skull. Ingubogubo, the chief's brother, was sensible enough to remain quiet and suffered no injury. At a later

[1] See p. 301.

date he was allowed to return and join Lobengula. The mission, of course, came to nought. It is doubtful in any case whether it could have reached Capetown in time to stave off the catastrophe which was now quickly descending on Lobengula, but it is deplorable that his genuine if belated effort for peace should have been foiled by a blunder which must, in his eyes, have seemed to bear the stamp of treachery. The war was none of his seeking. The unhappy chief was the victim of circumstances and the fates had been against him from the start.

On the following day Goold-Adams continued his advance from Tati and at first met with no resistance, though his progress was retarded by the scarcity of water. On the 2nd November a party with a few wagons which, owing to this difficulty, had dropped a mile or so to the rear, while hurrying in rather straggled order to overtake the main body, was attacked by the Induna Gambo with 600 or 700 of the enemy, who were successful in seizing one wagon, which they looted and burnt, killing the native driver and a white corporal. The attack was eventually beaten off with heavy loss by reliefs sent back from the column, the casualties on the British side being two white N.C.O.s and three of Khama's men killed and about ten, including Selous, wounded. Soon after this—the only serious action in which the Southern column was involved—Khama and his contingent announced their intention of returning to Bechuanaland, making the excuse that smallpox had appeared among their families. Their real reason was that they had no stomach for fighting away from their own homes, and, now that the danger of an invasion seemed at an end, were impatient to get back to the more congenial occupation of attending to their crops and herds. Their desertion at first caused no little annoyance and embarrassment, but on November 5th all anxiety as to further attack was removed by the news of Jameson's successful occupation of Bulawayo. Goold-Adams then moved forward by easy stages, and ten days later joined the Mashonaland force.

From Fairbairn and Usher, Jameson gathered that Lobengula, accompanied by some of his " Queens " and

principal adherents, had trekked out of Bulawayo with
ox-wagons about the date of the battle of Shangani, and had
been followed in a panic by the rest of the population after
the rout of their fighting men at Imbembesi. Spies and
prisoners revealed that the Chief was still in the neighbourhood of Shiloh, a deserted station of the London Missionary
Society about thirty miles north of Bulawayo. It was of prime
importance that Lobengula's surrender or capture should
be effected without delay, for so long as he remained at
large there was no likelihood of any general submission
by his people. The heavy summer rains had already
commenced, and the prospect of a campaign prolonged
through the wet season, with increasing difficulties of
transport and the certainty of malaria and horse-sickness,
was one from which everyone shrank, including, of course,
Jameson himself. While on the line of march it had been
impossible for the Secretary of State's instructions as to
negotiations with Lobengula to reach him, and even after
he gained Bulawayo some days elapsed before he heard of
them. The nearest telegraph station was Palapye, in the
Bechuanaland Protectorate, whence all messages had to be
transmitted by runner or despatch rider. There was a
breakdown in the telegraph line at the end of October, and
he did not receive any messages from the High Commissioner
until the 18th November, long before which he acted, as he
invariably did, on his own responsibility. His first step was
to endeavour to open up communications with the fugitive
chief with the object of inducing him to surrender. It was
known that he had with him an educated half-breed named
John Jacobs, who acted as a sort of secretary, and Jameson
therefore wrote a letter which he entrusted to three plucky
Colonial natives who undertook to deliver it to Lobengula,
setting out on this hazardous errand on horseback on the
7th November.

The letter ran as follows :

" I send you this message in order, if possible, to prevent
the necessity of any further killing of your people or burning
of their kraals. I am here with my army by order of the
Queen, whose troops, as you must already know, started
from Macloutsie when my two armies started from Salisbury

and Victoria, and will be here immediately.   Now to stop
this useless slaughter you must at once come to see me at
Bulawayo, where I will guarantee that your life will be safe
and that you will be kindly treated.   I will allow sufficient
time for these messengers to reach you and two days more
to allow you to reach me in your wagon.   Should you not
then arrive I shall at once send out troops to follow you, as I
am determined as soon as possible to put the country in a
condition where whites and blacks can live in peace and
friendliness.   Hoping by coming in you will thus save the
lives of the rest of your people and that I shall be able to
report to the High Commissioner that you have done your
utmost at the earliest opportunity to repair the wrongful
actions done by your *impis* at Victoria, I sign myself your
former, and I hope your present friend, L. S. JAMESON,
Representative of the British South Africa Company, acting
under the orders of the Queen's High Commissioner."

Jameson's messengers were detained two days with the
chief, and on November 11th brought back a reply, in the
handwriting of John Jacobs, of which the following is an
exact transcription : [1]

" *To Dr. Jameson.*
" SIR,
       " I have the honour to inform you that I have received
your letter and have heard all what you has said so I will
come.   But allowed me to ask you were are all my men wh.
I have sent to the Cape such as Moffett and Joney and James.
And after that again three Goebogubo and Mantose, Goebo
these are names of the men which I have sent.   And if I
do come were will I get a house for me as all my houses is
burn down, and also as soon as my men come which I have
sent then I will come and you must please be so kind and
sent me ink and pens and paper.
                     " I am,
                          " Yours, etc.,
                              " KING LOBENGULA."

[1] From the original, which is in the author's possession.   The allusion
to " Moffett and Joney " is not clear, but " Joni " was the Matabele
nickname for the Rev. J. S. Moffat.   The native names refer to Ingubogubo
and the two Indunas who accompanied Dawson.   John Jacobs subsequently abandoned the chief and came to Bulawayo, where he reported
that immediately after dictating the letter the chief inspanned his wagon
and trekked in a direction away from Bulawayo.   But Jacobs was afterwards proved to be such an arrant scoundrel that neither the letter nor his
story can be accepted as *bona fide* evidence of Lobengula's intentions.

Several days passed and there was no further sign from the chief, but from various sources it was ascertained that while he himself was pursuing his flight northwards through the bush from Shiloh, a large body of the enemy, composed mainly of the remains of the regiments that had fought at Shangani, was concentrated at Inyati (or Mhlangeni), twenty miles to the east, and from that point was covering the chief's retreat. South and east of the line Inyati–Shiloh–Bulawayo the country was practically clear, save that an *impi*, which had not yet been engaged, was known to be collected in the Matoppo Hills under the old Induna Faku, but this could be held in check by the force left at Mangwe by Goold-Adams. It was decided, therefore, to despatch a strong patrol to reconnoitre the country between Inyati and Shiloh, starting from the eastern side, where the country was more open, and, if successful in driving back the enemy from this line, to endeavour to intercept the chief north of Shiloh. Volunteers were called for this duty, and on the 14th November—Goold-Adams' column having now arrived—a mixed force composed of detachments of the Bechuanaland Police, Raaf's Volunteers and the two Mashonaland contingents, all under Forbes, left Bulawayo, with three days' rations, for Inyati, which was another station of the London Missionary Society. On arrival there they found no large body of the enemy—merely a party of natives in charge of a mob of cattle. A few shots were exchanged, and the cattle, numbering 1600, were captured. The missionaries' quarters had been wrecked, their furniture smashed and their books and other belongings strewn over the veld. It was ascertained from prisoners that the chief had continued his flight and was now on the Bubye River, and thither the march was renewed, but after following the course of the stream for a few miles, Forbes, finding his rations exhausted and his horses knocked up, was compelled to fall back on Inyati. He was met by orders to make direct for Shiloh, where Jameson had sent reinforcements and further supplies, and to take up the spoor of the chief's wagons.

From Shiloh the scent was hot—freshly deserted Matabele

camps, the burnt remains of two of Lobengula's wagons and
his bath-chair, and other evidence indicating that he was
shaping his course for the Shangani River and could only be
a short distance ahead; but the progress of the troops was
slow owing to the heavy rain and the waterlogged condition of the track, and eventually Forbes found it necessary
to continue the pursuit with a flying column of 160 picked
men and to send the remainder with the wagons across to
Inyati to await his return.   On the afternoon of December
the 3rd, having seen very few natives, but having suffered
greatly from the incessant rain, the reduced force reached
the Shangani River.   A number of large *scherms* with the
fires still smouldering and various articles left lying about
proved that a big camp had been formed on the southern
bank and had only just been vacated—in fact a number of
natives and a large herd of cattle were seen hurriedly retreating up the river side as the column arrived.   Just before this
an incident occurred which was not brought to light until
months later, but which, had it come to the knowledge of
anyone in authority at the time, might at once have finished
the campaign and would certainly have prevented the
disaster which immediately ensued.

Lobengula, on reaching the Shangani with worn-out oxen
and disheartened followers, was only a short trek in front
of the column and came to the conclusion that the game was
up and that his only course was to surrender.   Summoning
his old Induna Mjaan, the commander of the Imbezu,
regiment, he gave him a bag of sovereigns and ordered him to
send it back to his pursuers with this message :—" White
men, I am conquered.   Take this and go back."   Two
messengers were at once despatched with the gold, but
misjudging the pace of the white troops, or possibly fearful
of approaching them from the front, found their spoor,
which they followed until they came in contact with the rear
of the column not long before it arrived at its halting-place.
They were seen by two troopers—batmen with pack-horses
straggling a little distance behind—to whom they handed
the bag of gold and repeated the chief's message, immediately
afterwards vanishing into the bush.   No one else had seen

them. The two white men were to all intents alone with a large sum of money—probably £1000—and a message the full import of which they doubtless failed to appreciate. At any rate the temptation was too much for them. The bag of sovereigns was hastily secreted and Lobengula's last overtures remained undisclosed.[1]

It was not clear to Forbes whether the chief had actually crossed the river, and he decided to form *laager* and to send a party forward along the spoor to find out in which direction it led. Major Allan Wilson was asked to pick a few of his men with the freshest horses, to ride ahead of the main body and to get what information he could as to the whereabouts of the chief, but to return to the column before nightfall. He started off with twenty-one officers and men, all eager for a duty which bade fair to be the culminating adventure of the war. As they cantered off, one of them called back and asked a messmate to see that some hot food was kept for him, as they would not be back till late in the evening. But it was long after dark before any news of them was received. At nine o'clock two of the party returned, reporting that the patrol had followed the spoor across the river, and a couple of hours later three more came back with the intelligence that Wilson had actually reached Lobengula's camp, but had found that his party was in danger of being cut off by a large number of natives protecting the chief, and had taken up a position in the bush with the intention of awaiting the arrival of the main body, which he hoped would follow before daylight.

[1] The full story afterwards came to light through native reports which reached the ears of Usher, the Bulawayo trader. Suspicion fell on two members of the B.B. Police who, at a time when there was hardly any specie in Matabeleland and no means of obtaining it, were seen at Inyati to be playing " banker " with heavy stakes in gold. It was found that on the day in question they had been riding in rear of the column. Popular feeling ran very high against them when it was realised that had they given up the money and reported the message to Forbes he would at once have halted the column and opened negotiations with Lobengula, and Wilson and Borrow with their companions would never have started out on their last fatal ride. The two men were brought to trial on the 20th May, 1894, before the Resident Magistrate of Bulawayo and four civilian assessors, and on conviction were sentenced to fourteen years' imprisonment with hard labour—a punishment undoubtedly measured by the indirect result of their crime. Two years later they succeeded in getting the conviction quashed by the High Court on the ground that the evidence against them was insufficient and the sentence *ultra vires* of the Magistrate's jurisdiction.

Forbes was now confronted with a most trying and difficult situation. The information sent back disclosed little more than that Wilson was in touch with a considerable body of the enemy which was within striking distance of the column. But Wilson asked that the column should proceed to support him. To have moved forward by night with his whole force (already much exhausted by a long march in bad weather) without further knowledge of the strength and disposition of the opposing Matabele would have been to act in defiance of military principles and to incur a grave risk, and Forbes was no doubt right in deciding not to do so. The other and more correct alternative was to send back Wilson's messengers with orders for him to return to the *laager* and make his report, but Forbes appears to have been reluctant to take this step, although Wilson had already disobeyed his instructions in failing to return by dark. He unfortunately chose a middle course, and one not defensible either on general military grounds or having regard to the special nature of the situation. He sent forward a further twenty men under Captain H. J. Borrow of the Salisbury Horse, with one of Wilson's messengers —Thompson—to guide them. As a mere reconnoitring patrol Wilson was strong enough without such support. To convert that patrol into a striking force far larger reinforcements were demanded. To increase his strength by a small party was to risk additional men without serving any good purpose and to tempt Wilson (as actually happened) to brave the overwhelming odds against him and make a splendid but hopeless dash to seize the person of the chief.

Borrow's party started off to join Wilson about midnight, and before sunrise the main column also moved forward. Almost at once heavy firing was heard from the further bank of the river on their right, and shortly afterwards they were themselves attacked by a large force of the enemy which kept up a sharp fire for about an hour from the bush on their left. It was noticed that the river was beginning to rise as the result of the heavy rains of the preceding few days, and before Forbes was able to extricate his force from its difficult position it was in full flood and unfordable. A slow retirement was effected under fire from both flanks, and with some difficulty the column regained a spot near the site of their previous night's *laager* with a loss of several men wounded and a number of mules and horses killed.   During their retirement they were joined by three scouts from Wilson's party who had crossed the river before it became impassable, and from them, and from native reports collected afterwards, the story of the ill-fated patrols was pieced together.   It appeared that Borrow's party joined Wilson before daybreak on the 4th December, and the two leaders after conferring made up their minds to try to capture the chief by a sudden assault on his *scherm*.   They succeeded in getting within a few yards of the wagons, but were received by such a heavy fusillade from all sides that they were obliged to fall back.   Wilson then despatched the three scouts, who with some difficulty and under heavy fire found a place where they could swim the river, leaving Wilson and his men still hard pressed by the natives and retreating into the bush.   But they were gradually hemmed in, and after firing away all their ammunition were rushed by the natives and killed at short range.   When the scene was examined two months later, the skeletons of thirty-two of the white men and several horses were discovered in a small open patch in the bush about fifteen yards in diameter, eight of the skulls and many of the bones showing bullet marks.   One body was found at a distance of ten yards from the rest.   The trees within a wide range were scored by bullets, showing the desperate resistance offered by the gallant band, who fell at the last literally shoulder to shoulder.[1]

[1] The full list of these dauntless men is as follows :
First Patrol :—Allan Wilson, Clifford Bradburn, Harold Alexander Brown, Frederick Crossley Colquhoun, Dennis Michael Cronley Dillon, Frederick FitzGerald, Harry Greenfield, Sidney Charles Harding, Harold John Hellet, Arend Hermanus Hofmeyr, George Hughes, William Joseph Judd, Argent Blundell Kirton, Alexander Hay Robertson, John Robertson, Edward Earle Welby.
Second Patrol :—Henry John Borrow, William Abbott, William Bath, William Henry Birkley, William Henry Britton, Edward Brock, L. Dewis, Harry Graham Kinloch, George Sawers Mackenzie, Matthew Meiklejohn, Harold Dalton Watson Money, Percy Crampton Nunn, William Alexander Thompson, Henry St. John Tuck, Philip Wouter de Vos, Frank Leon Vogel, Henry George Watson, Thomas Colclough Watson.

At the time no information as to the fate of Wilson and Borrow and their men could be obtained owing to the flooded condition of the river, which was now running bank high, but hope was still entertained that some, if not all of them, were safe and would find their way back to the main body.[1] During the night a terrific thunderstorm burst over the *laager* accompanied by a deluge of rain; the slaughter cattle broke loose and disappeared into the bush, and the plight of the column was wretched in the extreme. Although Forbes remained where he was until the following day on the chance of gaining some news of the missing patrols, further delay was impossible. All idea of advance had now to be abandoned, as it was out of the question to cross the river and it might be many days before it became fordable. Forbes' horses were in a bad state from overwork and shortness of fodder; he had several wounded men, and though he had plenty of ammunition, his provisions were nearly exhausted. The nearest point at which he could replenish his stores was Inyati—some eighty or ninety miles distant—and after consultation with his senior officers he decided that his only safe course was to retire in that direction, ascending the left bank of the Shangani River. At the same time he sent two mounted messengers across country to Bulawayo to acquaint Jameson of his intentions and to ask that he might be met with food, medical aid and reinforcements.

The retreat began on the 5th of December and was carried out, under the most trying and difficult conditions, for

Six men (Messrs. William Napier, Burnham, Ingram, Judge, Ebbage and Mayne) who originally set out with the first party, and three (Messrs. Landsberg, Nesbitt and W. L. Gooding) who started with Borrow were sent back at different times to report, and thus escaped the fate of their comrades. Of the thirty-four who fell, the majority were home-born, and of these over a dozen were English Public School and University men.

[1] When after several days no news of them reached the column, it was hoped that they might have made across country to Mashonaland. There was a persistent report for weeks that Lobengula had continued his flight in a north-easterly direction with Wilson's party in pursuit, and in the latter part of December the present writer was sent in charge of a patrol into the Lomagunda district to endeavour to get in touch with them. But although the natives in that part had heard the rumour and were nervously expecting the fugitive Matabele to descend upon them, it was apparent from the rain-sodden state of the country that the chief and his shattered army could never have got so far.

eight days.   Parties of the enemy were continually hovering on the flanks of the column and dogging its steps in rear. Heavy rain drenched the men daily, their boots were worn out and their clothing in rags.   Having no cattle they were compelled to eat horse-flesh, the weakest animals being killed for rations.   On three occasions there were sharp encounters with the enemy, the most serious being on the 10th December, when they were surprised while halted in broken country where the natives were able to creep up unobserved in the dense bush and attack from all sides at close quarters. Having extricated themselves after stiff fighting from this awkward position, Forbes and Raaf—the latter's experience, bravery and veld-craft were throughout the retreat of the utmost value—determined to shake off the enemy by a ruse. Leaving a few worn-out horses picketed at their halting-place, they moved the column stealthily by night into more open country, taking the Maxim guns from their carriages, which were abandoned, and slinging them in blankets.   All dogs were destroyed to prevent them giving an alarm; all orders given in an undertone, and every precaution taken to conceal their movements from the enemy.   They were fortunately aided by a violent storm which drowned any sounds that might have betrayed them.   As had been hoped, the natives remained unconscious that the white troops had slipped past them, and wasted some hours on the following morning firing at the horses tethered in the abandoned lines.   When they subsequently caught up the column it was in open ground where there was a better field of fire, and after maintaining a running fight for a few miles they drew off.   This proved the last engagement of the Shangani patrol and of the campaign.   The Matabele had probably been apprised of the approach of a relief force, whose presence, however, did not become known to Forbes' men until the evening of the 13th December, when they suddenly met two scouts—one of them F. C. Selous—who gave the welcome tidings that a strong column under Major Heany accompanied by Jameson, and by Rhodes himself, who had made his way round to Bulawayo viâ the Cape, was close at hand.   After the tense ordeal which the patrol had endured since leaving

the Shangani the reaction was indescribable. There was
now plenty of food, surgical aid for the wounded, whose
number had been increased during the retirement, and
horses to carry those who were too footsore—as most of
them were—to march. Within three days they were safely
back at Bulawayo.

The accounts of those who took part in this, the closing
episode of the war, bear unanimous testimony to the indomitable courage and endless resource of Raaf, to whom
during the most critical moments of the retreat Forbes
practically relegated the command and direction of operations. But his constitution had been sorely taxed by fatigue
and exposure. Shortly after reaching Bulawayo he was
imprudent enough to eat a heavy meal and was seized by an
illness to which a few days later he succumbed.

The failure of Forbes' expedition to achieve its principal
object had been almost entirely due to adversities caused
by the distressing weather conditions, and Jameson was
forced to realise that no further effective operations could
be undertaken until the rains had ceased. He therefore
decided to try to induce the natives round Bulawayo and
in the Matoppo Hills to surrender and to make another
attempt to send a message to Lobengula with the same
object. Fortunately, and somewhat unexpectedly, there
were signs that a number of the Matabele Indunas were now
in a submissive mood, and even before the return of Forbes'
force (on the 17th December) several deputations had come
in to Bulawayo to ask for terms of peace. Those experienced
in dealing with South African natives knew full well that to
convert this tendency into a complete acceptance of defeat,
to break up the military system, and to render the conquest
a real and permanent one, it was essential not only that there
should be a definite act of submission accompanied by the
surrender of such cattle as were regarded as their King's—
that is, their national property, but that they should be
made to give up their guns and assegais. Failure to exact
this penalty would have been construed by the Matabele
as a sign of weakness, would have encouraged them to
cherish hopes of renewing the struggle at a favourable

opportunity, and would have left them with the means of doing so. Jameson therefore let it be known that those—and only those—who delivered up their arms would be allowed to return to their villages—excluding the military kraals—and proceed with the sowing of their crops. In the eastern and southern parts of the country a good number of small parties of the Matabele complied with these terms, but no sign was made from those with the chief, who comprised the main military elements of the tribe, and it was natural that the general body of the population should be shy of making any overtures while their ruler was still capable of resisting. Demoralised though their armies were by their defeats, it would have been folly to assume that a tribe which had so recently regarded itself as invincible would tamely and all at once accept the new régime, and while any irre-concilables remained, it was essential to keep a strong white force in being to guard against any reorganisation. The Mashonaland Volunteers had originally been engaged for three months, and many of them were now anxious to return to their farms and businesses, but about 400 elected to remain, and from these was formed a Civil Police Force of 150 men, the remainder agreeing to undertake military duty in case of need : 400 of the Bechuanaland Police were also retained for the time being in the country. Garrisons were established at Inyati and several points on the outskirts of the Matoppo Hills, and short patrols were sent out from time to time to carry out the work of disarmament and to take possession of all cattle belonging to the chief, the latter being subsequently returned to the natives for custody pending a final settlement. At the same time preliminary steps were taken for selecting the site of a future township, and for the institution of an elementary judicial and administrative machinery.

It was perhaps too much to expect that the Company would be allowed to carry out the work of pacifying the country by these reasonable methods without interference from England. Whenever Englishmen have been engaged in conquering savage territories in distant parts of the world, there has generally been a faction of their countrymen ready to assume that they must be actuated by sordid and unworthy motives and capable of stooping to the grossest crimes. We have seen that the constituents of such a party were present in England during the early development of the Chartered territories, and that they had been stirred into activity by Labouchere, who never missed an opportunity of squirting venom at Rhodes and the Company. The voice of this " anti-Charter " group had been swelling during the Matabele campaign, and its malignity was intensified by the success of the Pioneers. Stories were circulated of the killing of prisoners in cold blood and of other barbarities on the part of Jameson's troops, and a section of the Press was quick to use these calumnies to serve its own political ends. Unfortunately the Government was not strong enough to resist the influences thus brought to bear. On December the 10th Lord Ripon telegraphed to Loch that newspaper reports had stated that Jameson was marking out townships in Matabeleland, one of which included the Bulawayo kraal; that patrols were seizing large numbers of cattle; that Lobengula's followers were dying of smallpox and starvation, and that the Matabele were being prevented from sowing until they surrendered their arms. Her Majesty's Government could not acquiesce in this treatment and in the continued seizure of cattle from people who had ceased to offer any effective or organised resistance.[1] " Such proceedings," he added, " greatly strengthen the opposition in this country to the Company and render it more difficult to arrive at a satisfactory settlement? "

Loch therefore gave Jameson instructions that the laying down of arms should be " construed in a very liberal spirit," and although the Doctor protested that without some disarmament the natives would never understand that they were conquered,[2] he was compelled to bow to the decision of the authorities and to countermand the steps for the seizure of arms. A large number of rifles, assegais and other

---

[1] *Blue Book* C. 7290, p. 24. There is tragic irony in the fact that these words were penned less than a week after the massacre of Wilson's patrol, and on the very day that Forbes and his little column were painfully struggling to escape from the masses of the enemy who had surrounded them during their retreat from Shangani.   [2] *Ibid.*, p. 63.

weapons were concealed by the Matabele for use on a future occasion, and to what purpose they were put we shall see in a later chapter.

Authorities referred to :

Blue Books C. 7196, C. 7284, C. 7290.
Published Reports of the British South Africa Company.

CHAPTER XXI

THE SETTLEMENT OF MATABELELAND

WITH the lesson of Bechuanaland engraved in his memory Rhodes was not disposed to allow the future of Matabeleland to be further imperilled by hesitating politicians in Downing Street, and early in the New Year he hurried off to Capetown to open discussions with the High Commissioner as to the settlement, leaving Jameson in Bulawayo— as he put it, " to hold the fort." He meant to fight hard to secure a free hand for the Company and he had strong arguments in his favour. From the first Matabeleland had been included within the ambit of the Charter, which had, in addition, acquired by concession both the mineral and the land rights; it had now been occupied by Chartered troops; the Charter had, close by, the necessary machinery of government which could readily be expanded, and— what was most likely to weigh with the Ministers of the Crown—the Charter could command the means to administer and develop the new territory without cost to Great Britain. Before leaving Bulawayo, Rhodes addressed the disbanded Volunteers and congratulated them on carrying out a task which the highest military authorities had predicted would require 10,000 men. He also paid a somewhat tardy tribute to the assistance rendered by the Bechuanaland Police. He told his audience that after provision had been made for native reserves the remainder of Matabeleland would be public land, and that they as Pioneers would be allowed the first selection of farms. " It is your right," he said, " for you have conquered the country." He added that his immediate concern was to find fresh capital for railways and public works in the new territory. By these words and in other ways he showed his determination that the Company's authority in Matabeleland should be recognised as a *fait accompli*. Although he expected a rush of immigrants now that danger from the natives was past, he knew that it could not commence on a serious scale until the dry season opened. That gave him till April, and by April he felt confident of concluding a satisfactory bargain with the Crown.

In the next few weeks he was materially assisted by the course of events. In the first place public feeling at home had been stimulated in favour of the Company by the spectacular march on Bulawayo. That a handful of British settlers should in a couple of months have conquered a country as large as France and have broken down a military despotism which for fifty years had been the terror of its neighbours—white and black—appealed strongly to the gallery of national sentiment. True, the closing stages of the campaign were shadowed by the grave anxiety as to the missing patrol, but hope for its safety did not entirely die down until some weeks later, and in the meantime the uncertainty served to keep alive the general interest. In the middle of January all doubt was removed by the publication in London of a telegram from Loch giving a circumstantial account, gleaned from native eye-witnesses, of how Wilson and his men died. Additional pathos was lent to the story by details—embroidered maybe in the telling—of the last moments of the doomed party—how, when a bare half-dozen sorely-stricken men remained alive, they struggled to their feet and sang the National Anthem, and then how, just before the final rush, they were seen to be writing farewell messages on scraps of paper. Not since the disaster of Isandhlwana—though that indeed was a massacre on a far larger scale—had any episode of British arms more profoundly stirred the public. The glory of their fight against overwhelming odds spread a glamour over the whole achievement and raised Jameson and his Volunteers to the highest pinnacle of popularity.[1]

---

[1] The first white man to visit the scene of Wilson's fight was James Dawson, who in February 1894 undertook to convey a message to Lobengula, and discovering that he was too late—for the chief was already dead—proceeded to the north bank of the Shangani, where he found the remains of the whole of the party as already described. He collected

[Photo by the late Sir R. Coryndon

THE TREE MARKING THE SPOT WHERE WILSON'S PARTY FELL

[To face p. 331.

Labouchere and his clique were powerless to check the growing feeling in favour of the Company; in fact the former's attacks—by their very extravagance—may have helped it on. He had been mainly responsible for the reports that wounded and unwounded prisoners had been murdered by the Company's troops, whom he described, in the columns of *Truth*, among other choice phrases, as " border riff-raff " engaged in fighting for loot, selling their claims and spending the proceeds in drunken orgies at Bulawayo, and " shooting natives with as little qualm as an English squire shoots a partridge." There was much more in the same strain, so manifestly prejudiced, and founded on such tainted evidence, that it produced a result quite opposite to what he intended. The immediate effect of his attacks was to give a splendid opening for retaliation to several of those whom he libelled, who had returned to England fresh from the war—notably to Selous, who published a vigorous *démenti* in *The Times*, categorically exposing the falseness of the charges and holding their author up to well-merited scorn.

Another circumstance which helped the Company was the death of Lobengula, for it had the double advantage of solving the difficult question of how to dispose of him, and of inducing the remainder of the Matabele Indunas to surrender. After the pursuit by Forbes had been given up the unhappy chief, with three of his sons and a few other faithful adherents, continued the retreat in the direction of the River Zambesi on horseback, their wagons having been rendered useless by the boggy condition of the country. They were followed by an assortment of Lobengula's wives —the so-called " Queens "—with slaves and cattle. On reaching the Mlindi stream, a tributary of the Zambesi, they found themselves in a belt of tsetse fly which proved fatal to their horses and oxen. The chief, broken in spirit

---

their bones and interred them on the spot close to a large *Mopani* tree, on the trunk of which he carved a cross and below it the inscription " TO BRAVE MEN." The remains were afterwards removed by Rhodes' directions, and at his expense, to consecrated ground near the Zimbabwe ruins, and ultimately to the Matoppo Hills, where they rest, under a massive granite monument, in close proximity to Rhodes' own grave.

and exhausted by the unwonted fatigues to which he had been exposed since his flight from Bulawayo, was unable to drag his massive frame further, and when, a little later, smallpox broke out in his camp, he fell an easy victim.

So passed from the stage a remarkable figure whose misfortune was that he lived to become an anachronism. It is significant that he was regretted not so much by his own people as by the few Europeans who had come into contact with him in the days when he was supreme from the Limpopo to the Zambesi. They had enjoyed his protection and in some cases even his friendship, and, savage though he was, relentless to his enemies, merciless to his subjects, not one of these white men but testified to his outstanding ability as a ruler and to the dignity with which he maintained the unequal struggle against the inexorable force of civilisation.

Lobengula's death did not become known at once, in fact no authentic news of him had reached Bulawayo since the return of Forbes' patrol, and Jameson was still anxious to open up communication with him. On February 1st James Dawson, the trader, with one white companion undertook the delicate and dangerous errand of conveying a message to the chief, but a few days later, on arrival at the Shangani River, they obtained positive and convincing information of his end, and gathered some particulars of the event, which appeared to have taken place in the latter part of January. Under the supervision of Mjaan, the Commander of the Imbezu regiment, the body of the chief was wrapped in the hides of two newly-flayed oxen, and after being kept till decomposition was far advanced was buried where he died. The wagons abandoned during his retreat were plundered, but such articles as escaped were appropriated by his principal consort, Losikeyi, who, together with his other wives, was afterwards looked after and provided with a safe asylum by the Company. The chief's younger sons Njube, Mpeseni and Nguboenja, were taken by Rhodes under his protection and educated in Cape Colony at his expense.[1]

[1] Lobengula left six sons in all—Nyamanda, Sintinga, Sidotjiwa,

Before we take leave of Lobengula, mention may be made of the persistent belief, which to this day has not entirely died down, that he had accumulated a rich hoard of uncut diamonds, ivory and gold coin which he deposited in a safe and secret hiding-place at the time of his flight. The Company has frequently been approached by persons professing their readiness—for a consideration—to disclose the whereabouts of this cache, but the source of their information has generally been traced to John Jacobs, the rascally half-breed who posed as "the King's secretary," and who for years traded on a pretended knowledge of the exact spot where the treasure lay hidden. That it existed and was concealed is not inherently impossible. Diamonds were quite likely to have been carried to Bulawayo by the many Matabele who worked at the Kimberley mines, and most great African chiefs owned stores of ivory handed to them as tribute by their vassals. But it is hardly credible that those who really possessed the secret should not have turned it to practical account, and the inference is that any natives whom Lobengula may have taken into his confidence have long since died.

With the death of Lobengula the way to a settlement was open, and by the middle of February Rhodes and Loch were in agreement as to its terms, which only remained to be approved by the Secretary of State. It was proposed that the control of Matabeleland and Mashonaland should be vested in the Company, and that the new constitution should embrace a court for the demarcation of the land to be set aside for native locations. Provision was also made for nomination by the Company of a Council to assist the Administrator, for the appointment of a Judge and for the imposing by ordinances of the Company of such taxation as might be requisite for the order and good government of the territory, as well as for the creation of the Company's revenue. The approval of the British

---

Njube, Mpeseni and Nguboenja. The first three lived for years in Rhodesia; Njube, who was regarded as the successor to his father, died leaving two sons, Alban and Rhodes, who were educated in the Union; Mpeseni died in boyhood, and Nguboenja, who was mentally deficient, was cared for by the Administration.

Government having been obtained, the terms were embodied in an agreement executed on May 24th, and their details given effect to by the Matabeleland Order in Council of July 18th, 1894.

Rhodes had pressed for the insertion in the Order in Council of a provision restricting the imposition of Customs dues on British goods imported into the Company's sphere to the rates at that time in force in the South African Customs Union, which, he urged, were levied there—not for protection but for purposes of government. This would have given British manufacturers a low tariff for all time, and the idea was inspired by a desire to strengthen the commercial ties between the new territories and the Mother Country. But the Government were horrified at the novelty of the proposal, which, Lord Ripon said, would involve a departure from the course pursued by them now for many years. They scented Protection, and strongly resented a suggestion made by Rhodes that the policy of giving complete financial and fiscal freedom to the Colonies had been mistaken. In spite of their refusal to meet his wishes, Rhodes clung with extreme tenacity to his purpose. He bided his time, and four years later, when the presence of Mr. Joseph Chamberlain at the Colonial Office offered a more favourable opportunity, he returned to the charge and got his way.[1]

The next few months, though not marked by any outstanding events, were crowded with activity. During the dry season a steady stream of prospectors, diggers, mining engineers, speculators, traders and the like flowed from Kimberley and Johannesburg, the two nearest centres of white population, towards Matabeleland, but the distance and the expense of the journey prevented anything like a " rush " and kept back to a great extent the undesirable elements which are a common feature of early mining settlements.

---

[1] The Order in Council of 1898 contained the well-known " Rhodes Clause," under which the colonists of Rhodesia continued to enjoy the tariff rates of 1898, although higher duties were subsequently levied by other parties to the Customs Union, and which has also had the effect of leading them to transact the bulk of their import trade with Great Britain.

Only a bare outline can be given of the steps taken by the Company to consolidate its position under the agreement with the Crown, to provide for the needs of the new population and to carry out its obligations towards the old. The latter appeared thoroughly resigned, and as early as May it was thought that the requirements of law and order could safely be met by the new Police Force which the Company had raised. The contingent of Bechuanaland Police was accordingly released, though some took their discharge and remained in the country. Shortly afterwards a Commission composed of Mr. Joseph Vintcent, the newly-appointed Judge, and two other members—one of them a nominee of the Company—was appointed to set apart suitable areas for tribal occupation by the conquered natives, as required by the Order in Council, and to arrange for the distribution among them of a fair proportion of the large herds of cattle which, according to Matabele custom, had been regarded as belonging to the Paramount Chief, and had therefore reverted to the Company by right of conquest. In both respects the decisions of the Commission were unfortunate. After a somewhat perfunctory inquiry they recommended the creation of two huge reserves, one of about 3500 square miles on the Shangani River, to which they paid a hasty visit, and the other, nearly as large, to the west of the Gwaai River, in a locality which they did not even inspect, but as to the character of which they accepted native testimony. The latter area proved quite unsuitable, the bulk of it being waterless, and the natives never settled in it except on a small portion along the banks of the river itself.

The cattle question was left in an equally unsatisfactory position. In Lobengula's days very few individuals possessed cattle of their own—in fact it meant death to be the owner of large herds. It was the chief's custom to distribute breeding stock among various kraals to be tended by his subjects, who in return used the milk. These " King's cattle " could not be slaughtered, and any casualties among them had to be reported to him. After the occupation large numbers were stolen by the Maholi, or slave tribes, and taken to Mashonaland, and many of the Matabele claimed as their private property, or else concealed, beasts which had undoubtedly belonged to the " royal " herds, so that it became impossible to say which were the " King's cattle " and which were not. An attempt was made by the Commission to dispose of this thorny question by the acceptance of a proposal that the leading Indunas should at once be allotted a certain number of head as their private property, and that the *dominium* over the remainder should be vested in the Company, it being understood that these latter—in number about 70,000—should be left in charge of the natives, but regarded as a stock upon which to draw for distribution from time to time to given kraals and portions of tribes. A clear-cut settlement—even one that might have appeared less generous to European eyes— would have been better comprehended by the natives and preferable to a compromise that left the Company's ultimate intentions in doubt. The periodical withdrawal of small numbers of cattle subsequent to the first confiscation became a perpetual source of irritation and probably contributed to the unrest which culminated in the rebellion of 1896.

The most pressing need of the white population was the improvement of communications, and Rhodes lost no time in proceeding with his programme of railway and telegraph development. The first section of a light line to connect Mashonaland with the River Pungwe and Beira—75 miles in length—had been completed in October 1893. This traversed the tsetse fly belt—a peculiarly unhealthy strip of country—and brought Salisbury within 260 miles of the rails. In the same month the standard-gauge line from the south was opened as far as Mafeking, and preparations for the further extension of both lines were now taken in hand. The telegraph wire, which had been laid from Palapye to Tati during the war, was carried up to Bulawayo, and further construction in the direction of Salisbury was now commenced. The linking of South and North Africa by means of a trans-continental telegraph—first mooted by Rhodes at a meeting of the Company in 1892—began to assume practical shape. An independent Company was formed, and by the end of 1894 had constructed over 300 miles of line, including the sections from the Portuguese settlement at Tete on the Zambesi to Blantyre in Nyasaland, and from Salisbury towards Tete as far as Mazoe.

Mining work was actively resumed in Mashonaland immediately after the close of the war, but for the time being this part of the country suffered a partial eclipse, and the focus of interest was transferred to Matabeleland, where enthusiasm was kept alive by the constant discoveries of gold-reefs with abundant remains of old workings. " Experts "—of whom there was no lack—affirmed that although millions of pounds worth of gold had been removed by the ancient miners, the country as a whole had merely been " scratched." Of course the high cost of transport, with the rail-head still so many miles away, made it difficult to import mining machinery on any considerable scale, and the value of the discoveries consequently remained largely conjectural. Nevertheless development work was carried on energetically and hopes ran high.

A township was laid out on most ambitious lines about three miles south of Lobengula's kraal of Bulawayo, and Government buildings of brick, and stores and business offices—mainly of galvanised iron—sprang up like mushrooms. On the actual site of the chief's old kraal Rhodes erected for his own use a roomy house on the model of a better-class Boer homestead. In choosing this site he was influenced no doubt by sentiment and an eye for effect, for the selection was not without significance to native minds.

Now that Mashonaland and Matabeleland were united under one administration, the need began to be felt for some comprehensive label to include both. " Zambesia " and " Charterland " had been suggested—the former by Rhodes and the latter by Jameson,[1] but neither term achieved currency. " Rhodesia " had been employed in the title of

---

[1] " Zambesia " was used by Rhodes in a speech to the Company's shareholders on November 29th, 1892, and " Charterland " by Jameson on a similar occasion in January 1895.

the first printed newspaper in Mashonaland as far back as October 1892, and the editor in appropriating it stated that it had been in common use by the leading Colonial papers since the early months of 1891. It was officially adopted by the Company in May 1895, when a " proclamation " by the Administrator opened with the following clause :

> " The territories now or hereafter placed under the control of the British South Africa Company shall be named collectively ' Rhodesia.' " [1]

Rhodes, who was not given as a rule to personal vanity, was unmistakably gratified by the use of his name for the country he had founded, and in a speech to the shareholders after his re-election as a Director in April 1898, alluded more than once with evident feeling to the compliment.

[1] The word was not, however, accorded Imperial recognition until the promulgation of the Southern Rhodesia Order in Council of 1898.

Authorities referred to :

Blue Books, C. 7290, C. 7383, C. 7782, C. 8130.
Colonial Office White Papers, Nos. 177 and 512.
Files of the Bulawayo Chronicle, 1894.
Published Reports of British South Africa Company.

CHAPTER XXII

SUNSHINE AND SHADOW

DURING the next eighteen months Rhodesia basked in the sunshine of popular favour. The progress made in Matabeleland outstripped the most sanguine expectations. The dramatic incidents of the occupation had afforded what we should to-day describe as " excellent publicity," and money was freely forthcoming in England for the flotation of the numerous companies and syndicates launched for the exploitation of the reputed mineral wealth of the new territory. By the middle of 1895 the number of such companies was approximately 200; 45,000 gold claims had been pegged in Matabeleland alone, and while in the absence of milling machinery no actual output of gold was possible, confidence was maintained by the knowledge that several batteries were under order and would be sent forward as soon as the railway arrived within reasonable distance of the mines. Bulawayo was thronged with highly-paid company-managers and their staffs, and with speculators in land, gold claims and shares. By August there were 12 hotels, over 100 general merchants, 26 share-brokers, 9 solicitors, 3 banks and 3 printed newspapers.[1] There was an exhilarating atmosphere of prosperity, and the white population, numbering already over 2000, were engrossed in the fascinating pursuit of easily gotten wealth. The distance over which the necessaries of life had to be dragged by wagons from Mafeking or Johannesburg, and the exorbitant prices charged for all imported merchandise, were forgotten in the excitement of the " boom."

Forgotten also—by the majority, at any rate—was the old fear of the Matabele—but two years earlier the most dreaded and formidable tribe of savages in Africa. The Directors of the Chartered Company were struck by the

[1] Report of Directors of Company for 1895.

tranquillity with which this race of natural warriors appeared
to accept the new régime, and we find them in their Annual
Report congratulating themselves and the shareholders on
the formation of a corps of Matabele Police largely composed of men from the late Lobengula's crack regiments,
the Imbezu and the Insukamini. At the same time it was
suggested by Rhodes and Jameson, and recognised by their
colleagues, that it was desirable to have a European force
as an insurance against native trouble, and early in 1895
steps were taken to organise a permanent body of Volunteers
to be styled the " Rhodesia Horse," with divisions in
Mashonaland and Matabeleland.

Although regarded merely as a measure of general precaution, this Volunteer movement was at first received with
enthusiasm, especially in Bulawayo, and some hundreds
of men enrolled themselves and engaged vigorously in the
musketry competitions, field-days and other exercises
instituted in connection with it. But military training
without a definite purpose in sight was not likely to appeal
for any length of time to the adventurous class of which
the early population of Rhodesia was mainly composed,
and it must be admitted that the obligation of preparing
themselves to meet a vague emergency did not weigh very
seriously with the bulk of the settlers. The pegging-out
of claims and flotation of syndicates were occupations too
absorbing to allow much time for the dull routine of drill
and manœuvres.

The formation of the Rhodesia Horse, however, had a
deeper significance than was suspected. It was revealed
afterwards by Jameson that it had an intimate connection
with the " plan " which, as early as October 1894, he was
discussing with Rhodes, for giving armed support to a possible
revolt in Johannesburg. According to his statement before
the Parliamentary Committee which inquired into the Raid,
it was then agreed that the military forces of the Company
should be made as efficient as possible in order to be prepared for eventualities in the Transvaal. The Rhodesia
Horse was the outcome of the discussion.[1]

[1] Evidence of Dr. Jameson before the Select Committee on British
South Africa : Question No. 4513. (*House of Commons*, No. 311, 1897).

It is hardly necessary to explain that no inkling of this ulterior purpose was allowed to reach either the Directors of the Company or the settlers in Rhodesia. The former were informed by Rhodes and Jameson in December 1894 that a Volunteer organisation was advisable " in view of the extension of the Company's responsibilities north of the Zambesi, and the necessity for maintaining a properly equipped force in its territories." [1] This advice, on the face of it eminently sound, was adopted, and steps were at once taken to provide the necessary equipment and arms— admirable material in the shape of men being available among the settlers, of whom many had served in the expeditions of 1890 and 1893. Lord Gifford, one of the Directors, who possessed great experience, gained in two African campaigns, of native warfare, and had been awarded the Victoria Cross for gallant conduct in the Ashanti Expedition, threw himself warmly into the proposals, and, probably at his instance, sufficient rifles were ordered for between three and four thousand men, besides a number of Maxim guns.[2]

In Rhodesia, as already mentioned, the raising of a Volunteer force was not at first regarded as having any special or definite purpose, and after its novelty had worn off, interest in the movement showed signs of flagging. Later in the year, when people saw the scale on which the organisation proceeded and the earnestness with which equipment and armament were pushed forward—particularly when a number of horses arrived for the corps— an impression got about that something was in contemplation beyond the mere insurance against danger from the local natives.[3] The Matabele, it was argued, had been handsomely beaten in 1893 and had accepted their defeat. In Mashonaland the natives had never been regarded as a

---

[1] Evidence of Duke of Abercorn : Select Committee, Questions 7472– 7476.

[2] Evidence of Lord Gifford : Select Committee, Questions 7747, 7798, etc.

[3] It must be remembered that a considerable portion of the rifles and Maxim guns was diverted at Capetown and forwarded to the Reform Committee at Johannesburg in accordance with the revolutionary plan. See *Report of Select Committee :* evidence of Dr. F. R. Harris, Question 6291. Even so, however, a large amount of ordnance reached its legitimate destination, Rhodesia.

menace; nobody troubled to carry arms, even in outlying districts, except for hunting game, and any white man would cheerfully have ridden alone into the largest native kraal with no more deadly weapon than a *sjambok*. On the other hand, the successful expeditions of the last five years had whetted the appetite for pioneering, and the occupation of new territory had come to be regarded as part of a regular routine. Gradually the welcome conviction grew that some new adventure was being prepared, and much rumour and speculation ensued as to what direction it would take. One suggestion, based probably on gossip that had leaked out as to the recommendation made by Rhodes and Jameson to the Board of the Company, was that there was to be an expedition to the unknown regions north of the Zambesi, while others thought the authorities might possess evidence of hostile intentions from Khama and other Bechuana chiefs, who were known to be strongly opposed to any extension of the Company's influence over their territories. Whatever Jameson's ideas may have been as to utilising the Rhodesia Horse in connection with possible troubles in the Transvaal, it is certain that up to the last moment neither the Chartered Directors in authorising the creation of the force, nor the settlers in joining it, had any suspicion of an ulterior purpose.

A digression must now be made to explain what was going on in the Bechuanaland Protectorate, as it bears closely on subsequent events in Rhodesia.

In the autumn of 1895, in furtherance of Rhodes' plan for carrying the railway line from Mafeking towards Bulawayo, the Railway Company made an issue of £900,000 worth of debentures (the interest on which was guaranteed by the Charter). At the same time Rhodes approached the Imperial Government with a request for certain land grants along the proposed route—which lay in close proximity to the Transvaal border—and offered to place a portion of the Company's white Police Force at Gaberones, about 100 miles north of Mafeking, to afford the necessary protection during the work of construction. The Imperial Government on their part were anxious to reduce the heavy expenditure

involved in the administration of the Protectorate—a vast
territory which produced next to no revenue—and welcomed
a proposal which simultaneously offered a means for increasing trade and an opportunity for cutting down the costly
Police Force which they had hitherto maintained. They
were impressed also by the success which seemed to have
crowned the Chartered Company's efforts to develop and
govern the new territories in the north, and so far from
showing unwillingness to meet Rhodes, they went even
further than he had asked. In the latter part of 1895, in
spite of protests from Khama and other Bechuana chiefs,
Mr. Chamberlain and Sir Hercules Robinson were busily
engaged in negotiations [1] for transferring the administration
of a large strip of the Protectorate to the Company, native
objections being soothed by the creation of Reserves for the
tribes through whose territories the projected railway line
would pass. The proposals regarding police were at the
same time amplified by an agreement whereby the Company
undertook to absorb into their own forces as many of the
officers and men of the Bechuanaland Border Police as were
willing to be transferred, and the whole of the stores and
equipment in their possession.

In pursuance of these arrangements Jameson was on the
18th October, 1895, gazetted Resident Commissioner of the
territories of the two chiefs Montsioa and Ikaning, which
covered the section of the railway route immediately north
of Mafeking, with the understanding that the Company's
administration should later be extended up to Khama's
borders, and that they should have the right of carrying the
railway through the country of the last-mentioned chief as
far as the boundary of Matabeleland. The Native Reserves
were to be retained under the supervision of an Imperial
officer, and Major Goold-Adams of the Bechuanaland Police
was selected to fill this appointment.

Apart from the encouragement which they derived from
the news of the proposed railway extension, these changes
did not distract the attention of the Europeans in Matabeleland from the immediate business of speculation. Even

[1] *Blue Book* C. 7154.

the removal from Bulawayo to the Protectorate at the end of October, of about 280 men, forming the major part of their European Police Force, was hardly mentioned in the local Press, and does not seem to have aroused any misgivings. The settlers appear to have been satisfied that the interests of law and order were safe in the hands of the remaining 40 white police, aided by the smart black constabulary distributed over the various districts, while, if the possibility of native unrest ever crossed their minds, the existence of the Rhodesia Horse was sufficient to allay any apprehension.

The atmosphere then in Matabeleland at the close of 1895 was one of confident security, flavoured in some degree with pleasant anticipation, when suddenly, in a wholly unexpected quarter, the explosion occurred which shook, not Rhodesia alone, but the whole sub-continent and even the Empire. On the evening of Sunday, the 29th of December, Dr. Jameson, the Administrator of Rhodesia, left his camp at Pitsani and broke into the Transvaal with a small body of 500 men composed mainly of Rhodesian and Bechuanaland Police. A few days later the world knew that he had been defeated in action by the Boer burghers in an attempt to force his way to Johannesburg.

It is entirely outside the purpose of this book to give any account or attempt any explanation of the Raid. It is referred to solely because of its immediate effects upon the progress of Rhodesia and its bearing upon the subsequent history of that territory. These effects were far-reaching and have perhaps never been fully appreciated. The question whether the native rebellion which followed a few weeks later was a direct result of the Raid will be discussed in its proper place. But one less obvious consequence may be mentioned at once. In spite of the verdict of the Parliamentary Committee which sat in England in 1897 and expressly exonerated the Company, as a corporation, and by implication the settlers as a community, from complicity in the affair, a cloud of suspicion was created which clung for years round both. In official circles especially the change was noticeable. In 1895 the Government were eager to increase the scope and activities of the Company and to delegate to it more and more of what were, admittedly, Imperial obligations. Immediately after the Raid that spirit disappeared and was replaced by one of mistrust. The policy of the Colonial Office towards those who were doing its work in Rhodesia was ever afterwards one of restriction and interference rather than of encouragement and assistance. Whatever justification may have existed for the change of attitude in 1896, its perpetuation was grossly unfair.

Jameson's force crossed the Transvaal border in two detachments during the afternoon and evening of Sunday, the 29th of December, 1895. The news reached Bulawayo by telegraph on Monday morning, but previously to that at least two persons—Captains Napier and Spreckley, the senior officers of the Rhodesia Horse—had received a direct communication from Jameson himself bidding them to be ready, if necessary, to come to his assistance with Volunteers. Captain Napier had shown the message to several of his intimate friends, so that Jameson's intentions were known to a select few as soon as, if not actually a few hours before, the movement took place. On Monday the Press telegrams made the affair public and intense excitement at once took possession of the people. A mass meeting was held outside the Magistrate's office at which Napier read the telegram, and speeches were made by the veteran hunter Selous, by Digby Willoughby, of Madagascar fame, and by other leading citizens, in which Jameson was held up as the saviour of the oppressed British in the Transvaal, and the manhood of Bulawayo was urged to rally to his support.[1] Much wild talk followed as to the immediate formation of a flying column to support him, and in the end a resolution pledging the despatch to the Transvaal of 1000 Volunteers if necessary to aid in the protection of *uitlander* lives and interests was unanimously carried amid a hurricane of cheers. The impossibility of mounting and equipping such a force and of its reaching Johannesburg in time to be of any real assistance did not, apparently, occur to any of those present. The rights or wrongs of Jameson's incursion did not trouble

[1] *Bulawayo Chroncile*, 4th January, 1896.

them. All they knew was that their leader in other hazardous adventures was engaged in a new escapade and was said to need them, and with characteristic devil-may-care they were ready to answer the call.

Within three or four days—before the organisation of the flying column had had time to take shape—came the crushing news of Jameson's surrender at Doornkop! The enthusiasm of Monday gave place to sullen dismay, and even the most bellicose realised that all idea of military assistance from Matabeleland must be abandoned. In the meantime, however, reports of their intentions reached President Krüger through exaggerated and circumstantial telegrams communicated to the Johannesburg Press by correspondents at Bulawayo. According to these, all arrangements were complete for the immediate despatch to the Transvaal of the whole available force of the Rhodesia Horse under Captains Napier and Spreckley. It was stated that the expedition would consist of 1000 mounted men with all the Maxim guns in Bulawayo and a 12-pounder field-gun; that it would proceed viâ Tati and Mafeking, and that all arrangements for provisioning the force *en route* had already been made. After what had occurred, Krüger can hardly be blamed for taking a serious view of these reports and for repeating them by telegram to the Secretary of State; and it must be admitted that in the circumstances the tone of his communication was moderate and dignified.[1] It is all the more regrettable, therefore, that Mr. Chamberlain, without further inquiry, should have sent off hasty orders and telegrams which suggested nervousness and loss of balance. He directed the Chartered Company in London to telegraph at once to their representative in Matabeleland to " stop the intended movement," as if an order transmitted from City Directors 6000 miles away was likely to carry weight with a body of adventurous colonists excited by a passionate outburst of patriotism! He also instructed the High Commissioner to send a Mr. Ashburnham, a Bechuanaland Civil official, to order the force back in the Queen's name and to warn any officers holding the Queen's commission that

[1] *Blue Book* C. 7933, p. 11.

they would be cashiered if they disobeyed. Before these
futile injunctions could reach Bulawayo all danger of
further aggressions had been removed by the collapse of the
Raid, but Chamberlain was taking no risks, and at the
instance of Krüger ordered that a high military officer should
follow Ashburnham and should demand, in the Queen's
name, the surrender by the Chartered Company of all
ordnance and reserve ammunition.[1]

Sir Hercules Robinson was fully aware that the movement
in Bulawayo had died down, and that no recrudescence was
likely unless Jameson's life were forfeited. Still, to satisfy
Chamberlain, he ordered the G.O.C. to send an officer, and
the selection fell on Major Herbert Plumer,[2] of the York and
Lancaster Regiment, who was given the local rank of Lieut.-
Colonel and left for Bulawayo on the 12th January. This
was Colonel Plumer's first connection with the country where
he was shortly afterwards to prove the magnificent organising and fighting powers which have since carried him to one
of the foremost positions in the British Army. Soon after
taking over the guns and ammunition he was relieved by
Captain John Sanctuary Nicholson[3] of the 7th Hussars,
who remained in charge until the outbreak of the Rebellion,
when he was actually the only Imperial officer on the spot.

Though it would have been natural to expect that the
Transvaal imbroglio, implicating as it did many prominent
citizens of Rhodesia, besides the Company's Managing
Director and the Administrator, might recoil to the detriment
of the territory, Matabeleland, to outward appearances,
soon returned to normal conditions. Whatever the indirect
political consequences of the Raid, it did not at the time
impair the credit or damage the nascent industries of
Rhodesia. Gold-mining went on as before; agricultural
development continued, and the white population, while
profoundly stirred at the danger which overshadowed some
of its popular heroes, was inclined on reflection to admit that
it would be wise to abstain from meddling with the politics
of an adjacent State. In the absence of any inner knowledge

[1] *Blue Book* C. 7933, p. 14, 29.
[2] Now Field-Marshal Baron Plumer, G.C.B., etc.
[3] Afterwards Brigadier-General Nicholson, D.S.O., M.P., etc.

of the intrigues which had led up to the Raid, the interest of the settlers was of a personal character and was limited to a strong sympathy with Jameson himself and his officers. With their removal, in January, to England for trial all immediate anxiety as to their safety was relieved, and the citizens of Bulawayo were content to wait calmly, in the conviction that their remarkable exploit would be justified, and their honour vindicated, by British courts of justice. At the moment there was no other cloud on their horizon, and not the faintest forewarning of the two impending catastrophes nearer home which were shortly to cause the Raid to be forgotten, and the combined effect of which was to imperil the very existence of the little European community.

The first blow was the outbreak, in the latter part of February, of rinderpest, which had for some time been known to exist in Central Africa and, conveyed no doubt through the agency of buffaloes, eland and other large antelope, had been gradually creeping southwards. No serious apprehension had been felt in Rhodesia, and no precautions appear to have been taken to guard against the pestilence, until cases of sickness suddenly appeared in the Bulawayo district among some transport oxen belonging to a Boer who had been on a hunting and trading expedition north of the Zambesi, and had crossed the river with his wagon on his return journey early in the year. There were large numbers of cattle owned by transport-riders, farmers and natives in the neighbourhood, and the contagion soon reached these and spread with alarming rapidity throughout the territory despite the hasty and drastic steps taken in a vain effort to check its progress. Bulawayo and the adjacent gold districts were dependent on ox-transport for almost all the necessaries of life, and the disorganisation which was caused, not only by the death of numbers of cattle from the disease, but by the ill-advised measures adopted to arrest its course, speedily paralysed all industry and threatened the country with famine. The Veterinary Officers of the Government advocated the destruction of all teams and herds of cattle in which the infection showed itself, and unfortunately this advice was followed. Thousands of healthy cattle were shot, including many of those which had been allotted to the natives under the recommendations of Mr. Vintcent's Commission.

Anyone who has had experience of the peculiar regard in which African natives hold their cattle will appreciate the bitter feelings engendered among the Matabele by this action—well-intentioned, no doubt, but useless for its object —on the part of the Government. It added one more grievance to the mass of troubles which had been accumulating since the occupation, and all of which were attributed to the presence of the British. An unprecedented drought had commenced simultaneously with their arrival, and, by a sinister coincidence, locusts in swarms of unusual dimensions had at the same time begun to ravage the native crops. The Matabele chafed at the growing demand for their labour at the mines, and still more at the methods adopted to meet it by some of the officials, who used to send their black police into the districts for recruiting purposes. The latter, dressed in a little brief authority, abused their powers and strutted through the villages, ordering the young men to come and work and sometimes compelling them by physical force.

Faced with a grain famine, robbed of their newly-acquired cattle, importuned in season and out of season to provide unaccustomed labour, bullied by their former tribesmen and slaves who had enlisted in the Police Force—and yet with the old spirit of war and bloodshed still burning in their hearts—what wonder if the Matabele Indunas began to seek a short cut out of their troubles !

It will be remembered that, even before the downfall of Lobengula, there had been two factions among the tribe— one, composed mainly of the older men, which sought to live at peace with the European new-comers, and the other which cherished an implacable resolve to be rid of them. Although after the collapse of their best regiments in 1893 the militant section appeared to accept defeat and returned to their fields and their flocks, they continued to brood in secret over the loss of their old freedom to raid where they liked and make slaves of their neighbours, and only awaited a favourable moment for attempting to regain it. This section comprised not only the witch-doctors, who saw their influence disappearing, but some of the leading Indunas of the Matabele—among the latter Mlugulu, a representative of the priestly family, who during Lobengula's reign had been the principal actor in the ceremonies connected with the annual war-dance, during which he had temporary control of the whole nation. He was in fact the chief " Dance Doctor." [1] The late Mr. David Carnegie, one of the earliest established missionaries in Matabeleland, was informed on trustworthy native authority that Lobengula, shortly before his death, had given special injunctions to this man to keep alive the Great Dance, the political and military significance of which was fully appreciated by all the Matabele leaders.[2]

Mlugulu's head-quarters were about thirty miles south-east of Bulawayo on the outskirts of the Matoppo Hills, and in the same neighbourhood were the kraals of several relatives of the late King who were equally determined to preserve the traditions of the tribe. They included Mfezela, own brother to Lobengula and a likely candidate for the succession, Mlugulu having earmarked for himself the post of chief adviser or Prime Minister. These two resolved to revive the Great Dance at the full moon at the end of March, and they saw in the growing discontent around them a means by which it might be made the occasion for working up a general revolt. They found willing conspirators in some of those beings to whom the name " Mlimo " has been loosely and incorrectly applied. The cult of the Mlimo was of Kalanga origin, and existed in various forms among most of the tribes occupying Rhodesia long before the Matabele first entered the country. Mr. W. E. Thomas, whose early childhood was spent in Matabeleland, and who long held an important position in the Native Department, gave the authorities in 1896 the following communication, which

---

[1] See Chapter IV.
[2] Letter from Mr. Carnegie to Sir R. Martin, *Blue Book* C. 8547, p. 32. (The spelling of native names in this letter has suffered at the hands of the printer.)

shows how a harmless superstition was converted into a
powerful agency for mischief :

" As far as I can recollect I have, from the days of my
boyhood, heard the Matabele talk of the ' Ngwali ' as
the Makalanga ' M'Limo ' or god, whom they found the
Makalanga worshipping when they (the Matabele) first
entered the country under Mziligazi. This Ngwali was
supposed to be a spirit invisible to the human eye, who
sometimes elected to speak from trees, stones, caves, etc.,
having the place of his high priest's chief abode in the
Matoppo Hills.

" He was more especially the god of the seasons and
crops, and as such was propitiated by offerings of
cattle, beer and other native products and food—the
seed often being taken to his temple (or head-quarters)
to be blessed. He was represented by so-called sons of
god (*abantwana bomlimo*) or priests—all of whom being
Makalanga people—who underwent a severe and
rigorous course of training before being admitted to
the order of priests. . . . Ngwali was a god of peace
and plenty, and never in the knowledge of the natives
has he posed as the god of war; for not when Mziligazi
entered the country did he help the Makalanga to
withstand the Matabele; nor did he ever pretend in
any way to assist the Matabele *impis* which went to
war during Lobengula's time; nor did he ever assist
Lobengula (or ever pretend to do so) when the whites
advanced against him in 1893. He blossomed forth
as a god of war for the first time during the late Matabele rising in this present year, and even to this day
the natives in Matabeleland say, ' Who ever heard of
Ngwali being a god of war or armies? ' Again, the
Makalanga, whose tutelary deity and special property
this M'Limo is, did not as a tribe join in the rebellion.
The deduction I make from the foregoing facts is this,
viz. that the Matabele, having imbibed gradually some
of the Makalanga ideas with reference to the M'Limo,
and, having often striven to propitiate him with offer-

ings, that they might reap good crops and be kept from sickness and harm, had learned in a great measure to participate in the Makalanga faith in him; the Indunas, knowing the people had this faith, and circumstances combining to assist them, persuaded one or two of the *abantwana bomlimo*, or priests, to co-operate with them and proclaim as the will of the M'Limo (or god) what was really the will of the Indunas : hence the rising. I do not think that there is any man who actually personates M'Limo and is known as such by the priests, but I think the priests pretend to hold converse with M'Limo, and thus hoodwink the people, probably believing thoroughly in their rites themselves."

One of the Mlimo priests (probably Siginyamatche, though his identity is not certain), who may have been acting in co-operation with others of the hierarchy, resided and practised as a " witch-doctor " in the Matoppo Hills not far from Mlugulu's village, and the sermon which he undertook to preach to the Matabele was, according to evidence supplied by natives to Mr. Carnegie, on the following lines :

> " These white men are your enemies; they killed your father (Lobengula), sent the locusts, this disease among the cattle, and bewitched the clouds so that we have no rain.   Now you go and kill these white people, and drive them out of our fathers' land, and I will take away the cattle disease and the locusts and send you rain." [1]

Thus the Mlimo, originally a god of peace and plenty, was employed as a means of bringing about war.

Particular attention was paid to the Native Police, and strong, and in some cases successful efforts were made to induce them at the appointed time to throw in their lot with the rebel party. These inflammatory propaganda to a certain extent defeated the objects of the conspirators, by

---

[1] Statement by Mr. Carnegie dated 29th March, 1896.

creating a feeling of excitement which was liable to break into violence prematurely, as actually happened.

In view of the prolonged dispute as to the causes of the Rebellion which afterwards took place between the Imperial Commissioner (Sir Richard Martin),[1] the Company's officials, and various missionaries and settlers prejudiced in one direction or the other, and of the efforts which have been made in later years to attribute the rising to gross oppression of the natives by the Government, or the settlers, or both, it may be as well to state here that a close study of the question based on evidence taken at the time and in the country has convinced me that there is no justification for incriminating individuals or for seeking recondite causes.

Prior to 1893 the Matabele as a tribe practised bloodshed as a means of livelihood. They had not by any means been subdued in 1893. Two or three of their best regiments had, it is true, received a severe chastisement at Shangani and Imbembesi, but the bulk of the fighting force had never come into actual contact with the white troops. For the moment they were stunned, and had Jameson's victory been pressed home then and followed by stern control for a number of years, it is possible that the Matabele might gradually have settled down without a further trial of strength. It is possible, I say, and it might appear as if in the last twenty-five years that possibility has been realised, but it would be hazardous to assume of any tribe of African natives that an outward calm betokens a permanent acceptance of what to them is always an irksome restraint. However, the " conquest " of 1893 was in no sense complete, and even the comparatively lenient measures of disarmament that the Company wished to adopt were vetoed by the Imperial Government, with the result that large numbers of guns and other arms were carefully hidden by the natives for use on a future occasion.[2]

There were many sources of irritation which led to the trouble coming to a head when it did. No discrimination

---

[1] Sir Richard Edward Rowley Martin, K.C.M.G., Deputy Commissioner of Rhodesia 1896–1898. Died in 1907.

[2] See p. 327.

was made by the authorities between the proud high-class Matabele and the Maholi. All were urged to work on the farms and mines and all were treated alike when at work. To the former as a fighting race the idea of settled labour was odious. Especially did they hate being bullied to become labourers by their fellow-tribesmen, now swaggering as members of the new Police Force. Moreover, there can be no doubt that there were cases of victimisation by a few unscrupulous white men who cheated their labourers of their wages and in other ways made the work hateful to them. The injudicious handling of the cattle question was another grievance. Though few had possessed cattle of their own during Lobengula's reign, they were assured that the distribution in 1895 gave them actual ownership, and consequently were suspicious of the branding regulations, which they interpreted as meaning that the Company would some day break their promise and take the cattle away. Still less could they grasp the reasons for the wholesale slaughter which took place in the effort to stamp out rinderpest. Finally, they were greatly swayed by the influence of the priests of the Mlimo, who saw that their own prestige was doomed under civilised rule and spared no efforts to foment disaffection.

The conspirators looked round and saw the white men unsuspecting—unarmed—at their mercy. They heard that Jameson's soldiers—the very men, no doubt, who had beaten them in 1893—had themselves been " wiped out " by the Boers.[1] The time seemed ripe for a blow for freedom.

Such evidence as has been obtained points to their having fixed on the full moon, on the 28th March, as the signal for a general uprising, to commence with a massacre of all white

---

[1] Sir Richard Martin, who was sent by the Home Government to Rhodesia after the outbreak and ordered to inquire into the causes of the rebellion, stated that the withdrawal of the police by Dr. Jameson, though not actually a cause, afforded the opportunity for the rising. In the opinion of men who were in the country at the time, and had a better opportunity to judge than Sir R. Martin (who arrived at his conclusions without taking any native evidence), the withdrawal of police—some 280 in all—which took place in October 1895, *i.e.* some months before the outbreak, was not specially noticed by the natives. What really weighed with them was the surrender of Jameson's force at Doornkop, for it taught them that the men whom they had feared were by no means invincible.

people who could be attacked singly or in small parties in the outlying districts, and they no doubt hoped that they could then surround the townships and have their inhabitants at their mercy. But the smouldering fires they had been fanning unexpectedly burst into flame. A quarrel arose on the 20th March between some Matabele villagers and a small detachment of Native Police on patrol, and one of the latter was shot dead. The excited Matabele rushed to a neighbouring kraal, where they found another black policeman, whom they assegaied in cold blood. The lust of carnage was now thoroughly aroused and spread like wildfire among the natives. On Monday the 23rd armed Matabele suddenly appeared at several camps and stores of white men in the Insiza and Filabusi districts, and catching their owners unawares stabbed or bludgeoned them to death. Before the sun set on that Monday evening practically the whole Matabele nation had embarked on an open and bloody rebellion.

Authorities referred to :

Blue Books C. 7154, C. 7782, C. 7933, C. 7962, C. 8063, C. 8547.
Report of Select Committee on British South Africa.
Files of the *Bulawayo Chronicle* and *Matabele Times*, 1895, 1896.
Published Reports of British South Africa Company, 1895.

CHAPTER XXIII

THE REBELLION

THE reports of the murders of native policemen did not reach Bulawayo until the 23rd March and caused no serious apprehension, but much more disquieting information was brought early on the following day by a Mr. Cummings who had ridden hard through the night from his store—fifty miles off in the Insiza district—with the news that a well-known miner, Thomas Maddocks, had been killed, and two other white men badly wounded, by Matabele at the Nellie Mine on the previous evening, and that a number of residents in the neighbourhood were forming *laager* at the store. This intelligence caused grave anxiety for the safety of the scattered Europeans known to be at work in the districts immediately to the east of Bulawayo, for those experienced in the native character knew that unless instantly and sternly repressed the murderous spirit might spread far and wide through the country with dire results for the settlers.

The senior representative of the Company in Matabeleland was Mr. Andrew Henry Farrell Duncan, a retired naval officer, who had recently returned from leave in England and had been engaged in fighting the rinderpest. He was quick to grasp the necessity for firm action, and as a preliminary step arranged that a Justice of the Peace—the Hon. Maurice Gifford—should ride at once to the scene of the outrage to ascertain all the facts, and that he should be accompanied by an escort of Police and Volunteers, whose first duty would be to relieve any Europeans in danger of their lives. Duncan also telegraphed to the High Commissioner for the release of sufficient ammunition to arm this and any further patrols that might be necessary, and as no reply was immediately forthcoming he resumed control of the Company's arsenal with the concurrence of Nicholson, the

356

Imperial officer in charge, who recognised that this was no time for red-tape scruples. A stronger body of mounted men under Captain Napier left the same evening (March 24th) to support Gifford and make a demonstration of force in the disturbed area.

Next day the worst anticipations were realised. Reports came in from the whole countryside of the murders—aggravated in many cases by the hideous mutilations with which savages gratify their blood-lust—of isolated parties of Europeans, including some women and children, and by the end of the week the list of victims had swollen to 130.[1] In addition a number of Colonial natives in the employ of white men were done to death, stores and camps were burnt and looted, mules, donkeys and other stock slaughtered, and incalculable damage done to the mines, farm homesteads and other property of the unfortunate settlers. It is safe to assert that by the first week in April, with the exception of those who had managed to reach Bulawayo, Gwelo, Belingwe or the two or three other centres where *laagers* were hastily formed, not a single European was left alive in the whole of Matabeleland.

The full extent of these horrors was not, of course, revealed at once, but the news on the 25th March was sufficiently alarming to show those in control that they were face to face with an almost overwhelming crisis, and it is greatly to their credit that they made their preparations to meet it collectedly and without the slightest trace of panic.

It is not proposed to embark on a detailed narrative of the events which followed. The early history of the outbreak in Matabeleland has been faithfully and graphically told by the late F. C. Selous, and that of the subsequent military operations in books by Plumer, Baden-Powell and Laing, and in the published reports of the Company.[2] All that will

---

[1] The official records show that during the last week in March 122 white men, five women and three children were butchered in various districts of Matabeleland. During April there were thirteen more murders including three women and five children. Among the most terrible cases was that of a family of eight (the Cunninghams), murdered at their homestead in Filabusi, and one of seven, including five young children, at the Tekwe River. The number of white men who escaped wounded was comparatively small.

[2] *Sunshine and Storm in Rhodesia*, by F. C. Selous; *An Irregular Corps*

here be attempted is a general outline of the campaign, which, though brought to a successful conclusion in Matabeleland in less than six months, was prolonged in Mashonaland until late in the following year.[1]

At the commencement of the rising the position in Matabeleland was that the military organisation, designed two years before to meet just such an emergency, had been thrown out of gear by events connected with the Raid. The bulk of the white police, taken prisoners at Doornkop, had been sent in a body to England, and the remnant of the Corps—a mere handful—was scattered in small detached posts, and was useless as a striking force. The loyalty of the Native Police could not be relied upon. Many of the Rhodesia Horse Volunteers were, of course, still in Bulawayo, and could be trusted to give a good account of themselves, but although there were ample supplies of ammunition, rifles could only be provided for about half of the 800 or 900 men capable of using them, and there were not at that time more than 100 horses available for patrol work. There were eight or nine machine-guns—several of them in bad repair—and three field-guns.

The two most pressing needs were to search for and bring into safety any white people who might have escaped massacre, and to put Bulawayo itself, where there were about 600 women and children, into a proper condition of defence. By the exertions of the inhabitants both these objects were attained within the first seven or eight days. Without any very definite or co-ordinated plan, relief parties of thirty or forty men—the paucity of horses precluded stronger bodies —rode out daily into all districts within a radius of thirty miles to rescue those whose retreat had been cut off. Daring

---

in *Matabeleland*, by Lieut.-Col. H. Plumer; *The Matabeleland Campaign*, 1896, by Col. R. S. S. Baden-Powell; *The Matabeleland Rebellion*, 1896, by Major D. Tyrie Laing; *Reports on Native Disturbances in Rhodesia*, 1896–7, issued by the British South Africa Company.

[1] Of the rebellion in Mashonaland no adequate account has ever been published, though a portion of the military operations was described by Colonel (now General Sir E.) Alderson in his book, *With the Mounted Infantry in Mashonaland*. For the early incidents of the rebellion, *quæque ipse miserrima vidi*, I have been permitted to refer to official documents kindly placed at my disposal by the Board of the Chartered Company.

and capable captains—all experienced pioneers and possessed of the capacity to lead—were at once forthcoming : men such as Selous, George Grey, Maurice Gifford, Ronald Macfarlane (an old cavalry officer), the two Boer commandants, van Rensburg and van Niekirk, William Napier and Jack Spreckley—to mention a few only of those who in those early days raised companies of Volunteers which dashed out unsupported to every part where white men were known to have been working. Sometimes they were successful in effecting rescues of small parties, but more often they were too late to do more than give decent burial to the remains of foully murdered and mutilated men, women and children who had been caught unawares in the horrible trap prepared for them. In almost every instance the relief parties encountered fierce opposition from bodies of well-armed and determined Matabele and sustained many casualties in beating them off.

These hastily organised patrols were of the greatest value in ascertaining the strength and general disposition of the rebels and in preparing the way for more concerted efforts to attack them. It was found that the enemy forces were concentrated mainly on the north, east and south of Bulawayo in a crescent extending from Shiloh round to the Matoppo Hills at a distance of from twenty-five to thirty-five miles from the town, towards which they were gradually converging. The western side was left comparatively open —doubtless owing to the fact that Gambo, the principal Induna in that quarter, with twenty of his headmen, had been in Bulawayo on business connected with the cattle plague at the time of the outbreak and had been promptly placed under close surveillance. For some reason, never clearly explained, the rebels made no attempt to occupy the coach road through Mangwe and the western defiles of the Matoppo Hills, although that was the white men's principal line of communication with the south. Fortunately also news was received that Gwelo, where there were about 250 Europeans, could defend itself without assistance, and that a sturdy little group of forty or fifty miners had collected at Belingwe, ninety miles east of Bulawayo, under

Tyrie Laing, an old soldier, and were confident of holding their own, while another small party was strongly laagered at Mangwe.

In the meanwhile in Bulawayo the authorities, using the Rhodesia Horse as a nucleus, proceeded with the formation of a Field Force composed of all civilians capable of bearing arms, and British and Boers alike came forward eagerly to serve in face of the common danger. A committee of influential citizens was formed to assist Duncan, and at once assumed control of arms, food supplies and liquor saloons, organised a system of pickets round the town and tackled the various problems incidental to a sudden state of siege. A strong *laager* fortified by machine and field guns was constructed round the Market Hall, providing fairly comfortable quarters for the sick and wounded, women and children, and other non-combatants. The importance of keeping open the route from the south was fully realised, and steps were taken to erect a chain of forts along the road to the border in order to ensure the safety of food convoys.

When the first outrages occurred, Rhodes was at Umtali, having just returned from a flying visit to England.[1] On the 25th March Duncan got into telegraphic conversation with him, reported the steps he had taken on his own responsibility and obtained full confirmation of his actions and a free hand for any further measures he might deem desirable. Rhodes also arranged for the immediate despatch by coach from Salisbury of a supply of arms and ammunition for Gwelo, with a small escort of Volunteers under Captain J. A. C. Gibbs (of the Duke of Wellington's Regiment), Adjutant of the Rhodesia Horse. On arrival this officer found that the townspeople there had taken refuge in a rough wagon *laager*, and he assumed command, organised the able-bodied men into corps, built a strong stone fort between Gwelo and Iron Mine Hill, and commenced an active system of patrols which was maintained until the close of hostilities.

Simultaneously steps were taken at Salisbury for despatch-

---

[1] During this visit he had tendered his resignation as a Director of the Company, but his colleagues on the Board had postponed acceptance for the time being.

ing reinforcements on a larger scale to Matabeleland. The
Rhodesia Horse—about 200 in all—volunteered in a body,
but the strength of the relief force had to be limited by the
necessity of retaining a few men for the protection of the
women and children (though no danger was at that time
apprehended), and by the scarcity of transport owing to the
ravages of rinderpest. Nevertheless on April 6th—less than
a fortnight after the news of the outbreak reached them—
a well-equipped contingent of 150 white troops under Lieut.-
Colonel Robert Beal started for the front, taking with them
in addition to their own rations, food supplies to be left at
Gwelo *en route*. With them went Rhodes himself. He had
barely recovered from an attack of low fever caught on the
way up from Beira, but he shared in all the hardships of the
long march and was present at several engagements which the
Salisbury column fought with various bodies of rebels on the
road to Bulawayo.

At the commencement of the rising it was Rhodes' hope
that as soon as all isolated parties of white men had been
rescued the local troops would be able to assume a vigorous
offensive. For the settlers to remain cooped up in two or
three *laagers* would in his opinion be to encourage the rebels
to think that they had the country at their mercy. He was
anxious that the insurrection should if possible be crushed
without outside assistance, and with this idea he urged
Duncan in conversations over the telegraph wire to " hammer
away " at the Matabele with patrols and give them no rest
until the Salisbury contingent arrived, when the combined
force could sweep the Matoppo Hills, the principal rebel
stronghold.

But to Duncan and his military advisers who were in
close touch with the situation it very early became clear that
even with the promised assistance the forces at their command would be insufficient to undertake any serious aggressive operations, and that until the Salisbury men reached
Matabeleland, nothing much could be done beyond defending
Bulawayo itself, for which 200 men at least were necessary,
and establishing forts along the southern road so as to keep
it open for the maintenance of supplies. The utmost that

could at any time be provided for patrol duties was about 200 mounted men and 100 Colonial natives and so small a force could make little impression on the Matabele hordes now threatening Bulawayo from three sides. Moreover, a section of the white community was restless and began pressing for further reinforcements from the south. A petition to the High Commissioner with this in view was being prepared, and there were some who openly asserted that the present emergency proved the incapacity of the Company to govern and clamoured for direct Imperial control.

On the 31st March the telegraph line between Bulawayo and Gwelo was cut by the rebels, and communication with Salisbury was interrupted for several days. Just before this, however, Rhodes and Vintcent, the Acting Administrator, arrived there from Umtali and held a conversation over the wires with Duncan, who laid the whole position before them and plainly stated his conviction that a further 500 men would be required to cope with it. Rhodes at once authorised him to take steps to obtain them, and the authorities at Capetown acted with admirable promptitude. It was arranged that the necessary men should be recruited in Cape Colony and the Transvaal and mustered and equipped at Mafeking, the terminus of the railway, the Home Government giving their consent subject to the command being vested in an Imperial officer. On April 2nd Major Plumer, Assistant Military Secretary at the Cape, was appointed to raise and command the force which was to be pushed forward to Bulawayo as rapidly as possible, and was to include the members of Jameson's Police then on their way back to South Africa from England.

Plumer started buying horses at once, and opened recruiting offices at Kimberley and Mafeking, which in a few days were besieged by eager applicants. The best of them only were accepted, including a fair proportion with previous experience of soldiering, but so expeditiously did the organisation proceed that the first detachment of the " M.R.F." (Matabeleland Relief Force) left Mafeking, horsed and equipped, ten days after recruiting commenced, and by the end of the month the whole force of about 800 men was on the road to Bulawayo.[1] In addition to the M.R.F. a mounted troop of Volunteers was raised at the end of May in Natal, and, with the consent of the Portuguese authorities, sent to Rhodesia by way of Beira.

While these preparations were in train the Volunteers at Bulawayo were doing their utmost to keep the enemy on the move. Patrols were sent out almost daily to drive his outposts back, but in spite of heroic efforts it was seen that his *impis* were gradually closing in on the town. In fact the rebels from Shiloh and Inyati pressed on until ultimately they established themselves on the Umguza River not far behind Rhodes' house, and only four or five miles north of the *laager*. Several attempts were made to dislodge them, but without success until April 28th, when they were completely routed by a small column of 115 mounted white Volunteers and 70 Colonial natives, led with admirable dash and judgment by Captain Ronald Macfarlane, an ex-officer of the 9th Lancers. Their heavy losses in this, their first real reverse, had a marked effect on the morale of the rebels, and although Macfarlane's success could not, owing to the shortness of supplies and the poverty of the horses, be followed up by more extended operations, it freed Bulawayo from the danger of attack and enabled preparations to be made for the despatch of a strong party to meet the Mashonaland column advancing through Gwelo. This patrol, which was commanded by Napier, started on May the 11th, and after dispersing an *impi* which was collected to oppose it at Tabas Induna, twelve miles out, marched forward and effected a junction with Rhodes, Beal and the Salisbury contingent near the Shangani River on the 21st. The combined force then made a successful sweeping movement through the Insiza and Filabusi districts, the scene of the first outrages, and reached Bulawayo on June the 1st.

In the meanwhile Earl Grey, who had been appointed by his colleagues on the Directorate of the Company to succeed Jameson as Administrator, and had left England before there had been any sign of native trouble, reached South

---

[1] The number originally sanctioned was 500, and this was subsequently increased to 750, but Plumer recruited a few men in excess of the authorised establishment.

Africa, and on learning of the new crisis hastened to Mafe-king, where he threw himself with all the energy he possessed into the preparations for the relief force and the problem of organising the conveyance of arms, ammunition and food-stuffs over the 600 miles of road to Matabeleland—a supremely difficult matter now that the majority of the draught oxen had perished from rinderpest. He also made arrangements for recruiting and arming an additional corps of about 250 of Khama's natives, and for raising a further contingent of the same number of Colonial natives at Johannesburg.[1] While at Mafeking he learnt that the Home Government, influenced, no doubt, by private representations from some of the settlers, had made plans for supplementing the Volunteer reinforcements by Imperial troops on a scale which at the time was almost embarrassing, though providential in the light of after events. During April they offered to transfer 300 of the cavalry (7th Hussars) and 200 of the mounted infantry (West Riding and Yorks. and Lancs. Regiments), with a section of the 10th Mountain Battery, R.A., then stationed at Pietermaritzburg, to Matabeleland viâ the Cape, and ordered four specially trained companies of mounted infantry under Lieut.-Colonel Alderson[2] to be sent from England to South Africa to be in readiness to proceed up-country if the necessity arose. Having given all the assistance in his power to Plumer and having entered into important supply contracts, Grey hurried on by coach to Bulawayo, where he arrived on May 2nd, took over the control of affairs from Duncan, and made himself fully acquainted with the situation on the spot. He realised the advantage of having Imperial troops within reach, though, as the Government had expressly stated that their cost if employed on active service would fall on the Company, he devoutly hoped that the irregular forces now available would be sufficient to finish the business and render it unnecessary to incur this heavy additional burden of expenditure. In accepting the Government's offer, therefore, he asked that, in view of the

---

[1] Major Robertson's " Cape Boy Corps," which afterwards rendered most valuable service in the field.

[2] Now Lieut.-General Sir E. A. H. Alderson, K.C.B., etc.

acute difficulty of maintaining the regular transport of supplies through Bechuanaland, no detachment should be sent north of Mafeking until Plumer's force had got well ahead. To this the Imperial authorities agreed, but they were now thoroughly determined to take control of the operations in Matabeleland, and having convinced themselves that regular troops were necessary, they next announced that the conduct of the campaign " must be placed in the hands of a general officer on full pay." [1]

Soon after the Raid it had been decided that there must in future be an Imperial watch-dog in the Company's territories, and the Colonial Office had appointed Colonel Sir Richard Martin, formerly of the 6th Dragoons, to be Deputy Commissioner and Commandant of all military forces in Rhodesia. The present emergency, however, seemed to the Government to demand an officer with special qualifications, and they selected Major-General Sir Frederick Carrington, whose reputation in native warfare dated back to 1875, but who was now possibly somewhat past his prime, for the supreme command of all the forces engaged.

Martin reached Bulawayo on the 21st May, and Carrington, with a staff which included Col. R. S. S. Baden-Powell, superseded him on the 2nd June. Rhodes, who had arrived the day before, had, of course, no official status in the country—he had even resigned his position as a Director of the Company [2]—but he was nevertheless recognised by the natives as the " Great Induna " of all the white men, and was still regarded by the settlers as the guiding spirit of their destinies. For the time being he played the rôle of onlooker, but held himself ready to take a hand when a favourable opportunity occurred.

From the forces on the spot [3] Carrington decided to send

---

[1] C. 8060, Mr. Chamberlain to Sir R. E. R. Martin, April 25th, 1896.

[2] The resignation was formally tendered in a letter from his solicitor, Mr. Hawksley, dated 3rd May and published in the London Press. Rhodes' colleagues at first hesitated to accept it and cabled to him to that effect. He was then on the way to Bulawayo and sent his historic reply, " Let resignation wait; we fight the Matabele again to-morrow." It was eventually accepted on June the 26th.

[3] When Carrington assumed the command he had in Rhodesia or close at hand over 2000 irregular white troops and about 600 " Cape boys "

out three columns to clear the country west and north of
Bulawayo, postponing for the time being any operations in
the Matoppo Hills.   Two of the columns failed to come in
contact with any considerable body of rebels.   The third,
owing to a delay in starting, was able, in combination with
Beal's force, to inflict a severe defeat on a large *impi* which
unexpectedly appeared about six miles from Bulawayo on
the further bank of the Umguza River, where they had been
assured by the Mlimo that they would be safe from the white
troops, who would be struck blind if they ventured to cross !
They were taken by surprise and completely routed with a
loss of 300 killed, and so great was the moral effect of this
encounter that from that time forward the Matabele were
exceedingly wary of fighting in the open or of attacking any
but small bodies of the British forces.

All was now ready for a combined movement on the
Matoppos, when the plan of campaign was entirely upset

---

and native levies.   He also had the call on a further 1000 Imperial troops
from the south.
Approximate details were as follows :

Irregular white troops :

Bulawayo Field Force	(under Napier) . . .	700
Gwelo ,, ,,	(Gibbs)	336
Belingwe ,, ,,	(Laing)	44
Salisbury column, Rhodesia Horse	(Beal)	150
Remainder of R.H. in Mashonaland	(MacGlashan) . . .	50
M.R.F.	(Plumer)	800
Natal Volunteers *en route*	(Turner)	60
Total white troops		2140

Colonial natives at Gwelo	. . . .	53
Khama's natives	(Coope)	225
Colonial natives from Johannesburg	(Robertson)	200
Colonial natives at Bulawayo	(Colenbrander) . . .	125
Total coloured troops		603

Regular troops—At Mafeking :

7th Hussars	(Paget)	300
Mtd. Infantry	(Rivett-Carnac) . . .	200
Detachment 10th Mountain Battery R.A.	(McCulloch)	36

At Capetown :

Mtd. Infantry	(Alderson)	480
Total regular troops in reserve .		1016

by the grave news from Mashonaland that large numbers of white settlers had been attacked and murdered by the natives who had suddenly and simultaneously risen in almost every part of that province, and that the remaining inhabitants had hurriedly formed *laagers*, where they were defending themselves against heavy odds. Within a few days it was clear that a substantial portion of Carrington's forces would have to be sent with the utmost despatch to their relief.

There was nothing at that time—no rankling grievance or hatred of the white man—to account for this startling departure on the part of the Mashonaland tribes, who were generally regarded as cowardly by nature and incapable of organisation. It was not until afterwards that their revolt was found to have been engineered by the same devilish agency as had already wrought such terrible mischief in the sister province—the Mlimo. This mysterious being was supposed to have his head-quarters in a cave in the fastnesses of the Matoppo Hills,[1] and to be inaccessible to the general body of natives. The oracle was worked by a select body of " priests," of whom the most notorious were Mgwati [2] and Siginyamatche. Both of these worthies were intimately concerned in the propaganda which led to the Matabele outbreak. One, or perhaps both, were at Jingen's kraal, to the north of the Insiza district, at the end of March, but although that locality was immediately visited by Napier's patrol, and the villages burnt, the evil wretches escaped. They appear next to have betaken themselves to Tabas-

---

[1] In June 1896 two members of the Bulawayo forces—one of them a native commissioner—persuaded Carrington that they knew the actual hiding-place of the priest of the Mlimo and obtained permission to go and kill him. On their return they were greatly applauded for having achieved their dangerous errand, but some time later, when it was found that the Mlimo was still at work, an official inquiry was held, with the result that the whole affair was exposed as an elaborate hoax.

[2] Probably this was an assumed name. It is a variant of Ngwali, referred to by Mr. Thomas as the traditional name for Mlimo among the Makalanga tribes (see p. 351), and has also been spelt Mgwari, Mkwati, etc. The name of the man who acted as the Mlimo's principal agent in instigating the Mashonas to revolt was given to the author by several trustworthy natives as Bonda, and their evidence pointed to his being identical with Mgwati. Siginyamatche (the stone-swallower) is mentioned by Lord Grey in his printed report as Siginyamabele, which is undoubtedly a typist's error. The careless spelling of native names in official reports is most bewildering.

imamba, about twenty miles north-east of Inyati, a group of precipitous rocks riddled with caves and gorges and forming an almost impenetrable stronghold. Here they were consulted by the rebel leaders, who took orders from them as to the conduct of their operations. Here also was collected a large portion of the stores, fire-arms and cattle looted from white men in the early stages of the rebellion. It was, in fact, the central depot for this purpose.

During May it must have dawned upon Mgwati that the Rebellion in Matebeland was not proceeding according to plan, and that a diversion must be created, for he made overtures for assistance to others of his fraternity residing further afield—notably to Kagubi, the Mandoro or " liongod " of Western Mashonaland, and Nyanda, a witch of great repute and power in the Mazoe district. These readily agreed to use their influence in fomenting trouble. They went or sent messengers to every important chief in Mashonaland—even to Mtoko in the extreme north-east near the Portuguese border, and to Makoni on the Manica side— spreading the report that the Matabele had " wiped out " Beal's column, had killed all the white folk in Bulawayo and were now coming to do the same in their old raiding grounds in Mashonaland. They bid the people sharpen their assegais and make ready to join the movement on an appointed day, and warned them of the consequences of standing aside. They pointed out that there were no white soldiers left and that the settlers were scattered in small bunches all over the country—an easy prey. By such cajolery and threats Kagubi and Nyanda speedily gained over the credulous natives, more especially those of the Hartley, Salisbury, Charter and Manzoe districts, where their influence was strongest, and which were afterwards the first in which murders occurred.[1]

At Hartley, which was close to the Matabele border, the

---

[1] For some months after the rebellion the present writer was engaged as Magistrate, in investigating the numerous murders which took place in the Salisbury, Charter and Mazoe districts, and the above facts were elicited during the examination of some dozens of Mashona witnesses, and from the officials of the native department, who collected a mass of corroborative evidence from every part of the country.

miners and Civil servants—about a score in number—had thought it prudent, on the outbreak of the Rebellion, to build a *laager*. The Company's officials sent them a supply of rifles and ammunition and urged them to fall back on Salisbury, but they preferred to remain and were confident of being able to hold their own. In consequence of reports of a prospector being murdered in the neighbourhood and of the appearance of a number of Matabele, ostensibly seeking work, they took up their quarters in the *laager* towards the end of April, and were thus comparatively safe when the Mashonas rebelled. In all other parts the European settlers were caught unawares. On the 15th June the natives in every district suddenly began attacking them with battle-axes and assegais, and within a day or two they had hacked to death practically every isolated family and individual within a radius of eighty miles of Salisbury.[1]

In all Rhodesia's chequered history this was the blackest hour !

The main body of white people was, of course, at Salisbury, and a strongly fortified *laager* was quickly constructed round the brick gaol, the usual occupants of which were temporarily displaced—there was no danger of their attempting to escape !—in order to make room for the women and children, numbering about 250, who were brought from their houses and unceremoniously huddled into it. There were some 300 men capable of bearing arms, of whom about 60 were members of the Rhodesia Horse. The remainder of this regiment had gone off to Matabeleland with Beal, who had also taken with him his column the pick of the available horses and most of the rifles, of which there was now a lamentable shortage, but notwithstanding their small numbers and scanty resources the settlers immediately organised patrols for the relief of those less fortunately situated in the surrounding districts, and by this means several little groups of people who had managed to get together and defend themselves in hastily fortified stores or rough *laagers* were brought into safety. These early patrols

---

[1] In the first few days of the rebellion in Mashonaland 119 Europeans (including several women and children) and a number of Colonial natives were caught and massacred.

furnished many instances of conspicuous bravery. Perhaps the most brilliant exploit of the whole campaign was a sortie by twenty-two Salisbury Volunteers in two detachments (led respectively by Lieut. D. Judson of the Rhodesia Horse and Inspector R. C. Nesbitt of the Police), who rode out twenty-seven miles to the aid of a party of fourteen white people, three of whom were women, cut off at the Alice Mine in the Mazoe district, where they had managed to improvise a sort of *laager* on a stony *kopje*, and were holding out against some hundreds of natives armed with rifles. Five of the beleaguered party had lost their lives before the arrival of the relief, including two telegraph clerks [1] who heroically left the *laager* in the face of the enemy and made their way to the telegraph office a mile off. They were successful in sending an appeal for help over the wire to Salisbury, but were killed within view of the *laager* on the return journey.   During the retirement of the Mazoe refugees with their rescuers to Salisbury the whole party was exposed for ten miles to a murderous fire, and three of the patrol were shot dead, besides a number wounded. The ladies were placed in a wagonette ingeniously protected by sheets of iron and reached Salisbury unhurt, though in a state of exhaustion.

In addition to those rescued by patrols from Salisbury there were several remarkable escapes from death by individual white men who found their way, some to Salisbury, others to Charter or Umtali, where *laagers* were also formed, on the first news of the outbreak. Most of these were wounded, and the story of their adventures would fill a volume.

Martial law was proclaimed throughout Mashonaland and a citizen force organised in which all able-bodied men, irrespective of age or calling,[2] at once enrolled themselves.

[1] John Leonard Blakiston and T. G. Routledge, whose fine act of self-sacrifice was the means of summoning relief to their friends and so saving their lives.

[2] To illustrate this it may be mentioned that among those enrolled as troopers in the Salisbury Field Force were a former Prime Minister of Cape Colony (Sir Thomas Scanlen, K.C.M.G.) and a distinguished French officer who had served as *aide-de-camp* to Marshal MacMahon in the Franco-Prussian war (the Vicomte E. de la Panouse).

Judge Vintcent, who was acting as Administrator, took steps
to intercept and recall the troop of Natal Volunteers which
was making its way across country to Matabeleland and was
nearing Charter.   This with its two Maxim guns was a
valuable accession to the local forces, but no effective steps
to clear the country or settle accounts with the rebels could
be undertaken without far larger reinforcements, and
Carrington immediately arranged for additional men to be
sent forward. Beal's Salisbury column, and a troop of
70 scouts originally raised by George Grey, but now commanded by the Hon. Charles White, were the first to start,
and arrived at Salisbury about the middle of July.   A
detachment of 100 of the M.R.F. under Major Watts (Sher-
wood Foresters) was also sent from Bulawayo to clear the
Charter district.   To make good these withdrawals the
regular cavalry and mounted infantry, which had so far
been detained at Mafeking, were moved up-country.[1]
Simultaneously Colonel Alderson with 250 of his mounted
infantry embarked at Capetown for Beira (where he was
joined by some R.E. and other details), and with the generous
co-operation of the Portuguese authorities entered Mashonaland from the eastern side.   He engaged the rebels successfully at two points on the road and reached Salisbury on the
9th August.   On the arrival of these forces all danger of
attack was removed and the *laagers* were broken up.   It was
not possible, of course, for white men, other than armed
bodies, to move freely beyond the townships, still less to
resume their occupations in the outside districts, and the
pacification of the country was still a long way off, but after
the first orgy of slaughter the transient courage of the
Mashona natives had oozed away and when they saw that,
so far from scuttling out of the country as their witch-
doctors had predicted, the white men were bringing in
hundreds of fresh soldiers, they began to slink back to their
rocky hills and caves and remained on the defensive.

And now a new enemy had to be reckoned with, namely
famine.   The food supplies throughout Mashonaland had

---

[1] To Macloutsie in the first instance. Two hundred of them were
despatched to Bulawayo about the middle of July.

been greatly reduced owing to the loss of cattle—draught as well as slaughter—through rinderpest and the interruption in communication between Salisbury and the Eastern railhead during June and July, and the scarcity was made more acute by the arrival of so many troops with a limited commissariat. The solution of this difficulty was placed in the hands of Mr. H. Wilson Fox,[1] the quartermaster of Beal's column, who was given charge of all transport and supply. In the face of immense obstacles he organised a combined mule and carrier service from the railhead, by which means regular supplies were introduced, and although the civilian population were on short rations for several weeks, the situation was saved.

Early in July a column of 750 men under Plumer attacked Tabas-imamba, sixty miles N.E. of Bulawayo, a confused mass of granite forming an extensive natural stronghold in which, as already stated, Mgwati the priest of the Mlimo had made his head-quarters, and where he was joined by a considerable force of rebels. They were taken by surprise, but made a stubborn and protracted resistance, and their dispersal cost Plumer a good many casualties in killed and wounded. The elusive Mgwati again escaped and was found later to have fled to Matshayangombi's kraal, another rocky fortress in the Hartley district, where he remained until the place was stormed and blown up a year later. A large quantity of loot, identified as the property of murdered settlers, was found at Tabas-imamba, and some hundreds of cattle and sheep and many women and children were captured. After this engagement the resistance of the Matabele showed signs of weakening, though their tactics continued to be embarrassing. The bulk of their forces was now concentrated in the broken granite country forming the Matoppo range of hills, from which it seemed almost hopeless to dislodge them. The rocks, honeycombed as they were with caves and intersected by labyrinthine passages, provided their occupants with innumerable hiding-places and *points d'appui*, and as soon as they were driven out of

---

[1] Afterwards a Director of the Chartered Company, and, at the time of his death in 1921, M.P. for Tamworth.

one quarter they took refuge in another. Several actions
took place in these hills without any conspicuous success
and with somewhat heavy losses to the troops, who were
always fighting at a disadvantage.

Rhodes and Grey saw with dismay that the campaign
was resolving itself into a guerilla war which might be prolonged until the natives were starved into submission, and
would certainly cost many valuable lives. Meanwhile
mining and other industries would remain paralysed, and
the grievous burden of expenditure already piled on the
shoulders of the Chartered shareholders would be swollen
to proportions which would drag the Company into bankruptcy. With this disturbing prospect before them they
debated the possibility of getting into touch with the rebel
chiefs and persuading them of the ruin they were bringing
upon themselves by keeping up the contest.

An accident placed in their hands the means of opening
negotiations. In the course of a reconnaissance in the
Matoppo Hills there fell into the hands of the troops an old
woman who proved to be the mother of one of the principal
Indunas of the Matabele. Information given by her indicated that many of the rebels were tired of fighting but
afraid to surrender, and Rhodes determined to use her as a
medium for opening up communications with them. By
this means he succeeded after some difficulty in arranging a
meeting. The chiefs were far too suspicious as yet to trust
themselves within reach of the white soldiers, but made it
known that if Rhodes personally would come into the hills
they would parley with him. With great courage he undertook this dangerous errand, and on August the 21st, accompanied only by Dr. Hans Sauer (an old Kimberley friend),
Mr. V. Stent (special correspondent of the *Cape Times*),
Colenbrander to interpret, and two of his Colonial natives
well known to the Matabele, he rode five miles into the hills
to confer with any who might be there to meet him. The
party carried no arms save revolvers and were absolutely
at the mercy of the rebels, who were crowded on the surrounding rocks intently watching their movements. Any
gesture of precaution or suspicious movement on the part

of the white men would infallibly have cost them their lives. But in spite of the tension of the moment they preserved a calm demeanour, tied their horses to tree-stumps and waited. Presently, after a little hesitation, Mlugulu, Sekombo and about forty other Indunas and headmen advanced out of the rocks to meet them. Formal greetings were exchanged and the *indaba* opened. As usual with African natives, petty grievances were aired and crucial matters avoided, but the ice had been broken, and in the end the Matabele delegates admitted their desire for peace, though they asked for time to ascertain the feelings of the body of the rebels.

This meeting, which lasted several hours, was the prelude to many others. All military operations were suspended, and Rhodes made a camp at some distance from the troops, where for two months he patiently remained, interviewing one chief after another, gradually winning their confidence and overcoming their apprehensions of the large force which Carrington felt it his duty to maintain on the outskirts of the hills. On the 9th of September the meetings assumed a more official tone, and Rhodes, after consultation with Grey the Administrator and Martin the Imperial Commissioner, formally stated the terms on which peace would be agreed to. They stipulated that those Matabele who had been guilty of murder should be brought to trial, and that all arms should be surrendered. On these conditions being accepted the troops, apart from a permanent Police Force, would be demobilised; a limited number of influential Indunas, including Gambo and two others who had taken no part in the Rebellion, would be officially recognised by the Government and would receive salaries during good behaviour; certain admitted grievances of the native population would be redressed, and the natives generally would be helped with food and provided with seed for next season's crops. The terms were finally accepted at a second official meeting on the 13th October, immediately after which, the Imperial authorities having satisfied themselves that the organisation of the new Police Force was proceeding smoothly and that all fear of further hostilities was, so far as the

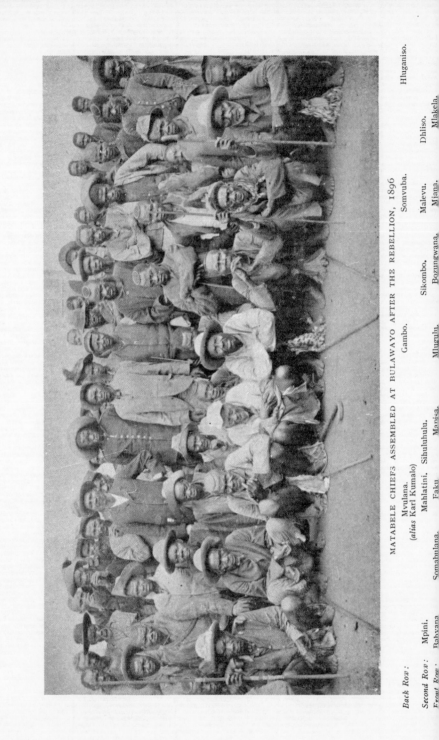

MATABELE CHIEFS ASSEMBLED AT BULAWAYO AFTER THE REBELLION, 1896

Back Row : Hluganiso.

Somvuba.

Mvulana. Dhliso.
(alias Karl Kumalo)

Gambo. Malevu. Mlakela.

Mahlatini. Sihuluhulu. Miana.

Sikombo.

Faku Marisa. Bozungwana,

Second Row : Mpini. Mlugulu,

Front Row : Somabulana. Rabyana

Makela.

Matabele were concerned, at an end, sanctioned the disbandment of Plumer's column.

During these arduous and delicate negotiations Rhodes
had maintained his camp at some distance from the troops,
on the edge of the Matoppo Hills and in the immediate
vicinity of the rebel head-quarters. Unprotected by any
guard he held conversations almost daily with the native
leaders, and by infinite patience succeeded in winning their
confidence. He was rewarded by acquiring an influence
over the Matabele which he never lost. Thenceforward
they looked upon him as their protector, their " Father,"
and his just and sympathetic attitude towards them begat
a feeling of trustfulness which was soon extended to the
Company's administration generally, grew steadily with
succeeding years, and, be it here said, was at no time
betrayed.

In coming to terms with the Matabele, Rhodes and Grey
had the advantage of dealing with an unanimous tribe which
still retained much of its ascendancy over the surrounding
native population. Consequently the decision to lay down
arms was accepted and given effect to without delay in all
parts of Matabeleland proper, and within a few weeks of
the final *indaba* of October the 13th the submission of the
rebels was complete. In the meanwhile the settlers began
boldly to resume their interrupted occupations of prospecting,
mining and farming in the disaffected districts, and were
joined by many of the members of Plumer's column, which
had been taken down to Mafeking and there disbanded.
So far from causing uneasiness among the natives, this
display of confidence had the result of speeding up the
settlement. The salaried Indunas were loyal to their
pledges and gave ready assistance to the Native Commissioners in bringing about the surrender of arms, the capture
of known murderers and the restoration of order among the
people. For some months the Matabele suffered severely
from famine, but the Company generously came to their aid
by distributions of grain both for food and seed,[1] and though

---

[1] In addition to supplies for the Police Force and the troops still retained
in Matabeleland, the Administration imported from the south, for free

there were many deaths from starvation, the natives realised that their distress was due to their own folly and that the authorities were making genuine efforts to give them a fresh start. Meantime the organisation of the new Police Force proceeded smoothly and rapidly; the various irregular corps were broken up and the Imperial troops, with the exception of 200 of the 7th Hussars, were withdrawn from the country.

In Mashonaland, unfortunately, the case was very different. To begin with, the natives of this part of Rhodesia, though known collectively to Europeans as " Mashona," were not in reality one people but a congeries of semi-independent tribes of various origins under petty dynastic chiefs. Some of them had occupied the same localities for many generations, and were lineally descended from the more robust Makalanga, who proved such formidable opponents to the Portuguese adventurers of the sixteenth century. Others were the survivors of a series of incursions by various wandering hordes which had drifted into Mashonaland from time to time—Swazis and Shangaans, for example, from the south, Varoswi (aba-Lozi) from beyond the Zambesi, and many others—and had never assimilated with the older inhabitants or with one another. Though all had been preyed on indiscriminately by Mziligazi and Lobengula, no mutual confidence had thereby been engendered. Even when, under the influence of the witch-doctors, the various groups made common cause in 1896, the combination was a fortuitous and artificial one, which rapidly broke up when confronted with organised resistance. The result was that in Mashonaland no opportunity presented itself for a comprehensive settlement. Each of the petty tribes had to be tackled separately, and, as most of them were implicated in the Rebellion, the process of pacifying the country was tedious and protracted.

Their tactics were of a most baffling description. With the instinct of wild animals, sharpened by a long experience of

---

distribution to the natives, about 1400 tons of grain, all of which reached the country before the end of October. The cost of transporting this from the railhead was approximately £50,000.

Matabele raids, they soon abandoned all pretence of fighting
in the open and, on the approach of white troops, withdrew
to their stockaded villages, which were usually situated in
close proximity to clusters of granite *kopjes*, constituting an
almost impenetrable second line of defence.   The gigantic
rocks piled up in confused masses formed countless caves
and hiding-places known only to their native denizens and
provided cover which they were expert at turning to advantage.   Ensconced in inaccessible crevices and crannies they
were able, without exposing themselves, to use their Tower
muskets, flint-locks and antiquated blunderbusses at close
range with deadly effect.[1]   Military science could devise
no means of dealing expeditiously with such methods, and
it seemed that only a wearing-down process would reduce
the rebels to submission.

For nearly four months Alderson's mounted infantry,
acting in conjunction with the local forces, endeavoured to
force a decisive engagement.   They were successful in breaking the resistance of Makoni and a few less important chiefs
and in opening up the lines of communication between the
principal European centres, but they were at all times
hampered by the shortness of supplies, which prevented
them from undertaking any extensive operations.   It was
grudgingly admitted that the work of pacification would
be a task better left in the hands of the new Police
Force, the organisation of which was now proceeding apace,
and that it would be desirable to get as many of the Imperial
troops as possible out of the country at once, for if retained
during the rainy season they would be compelled to remain
inactive and would be exposed to the risk of malarial fever.
Accordingly Alderson's force left viâ the East Coast early
in December, and was followed by Carrington with the Head-
quarter Staff and the Natal Volunteers.

The supreme command was then resumed by the Deputy
Commissioner, Sir R. Martin, and the Police divisions in

[1] The Mashonas were largely armed with old muzzle-loading fire-arms,
the proceeds of generations of trading.   In these " family guns," as the
settlers called them, they used home-made powder and ammunition of a
most miscellaneous description, such as short lengths of telegraph wire,
nails and the glass balls from soda-water bottles—all capable of inflicting
ghastly wounds at close quarters, though useless for long-range purposes.

Matabeleland and Mashonaland were placed under Lieut.-
Cols. J. S. Nicholson and the Hon. F. R. W. E. de Moleyns [1]
respectively. About 400 of the Volunteers and 120 of the
native contingent were also retained under de Moleyns for
the operations in Mashonaland.

During the first three months of 1897 his force suffered
greatly from fever, aggravated by poor diet and constant
exposure to the heavy rains, and de Moleyns could do little
beyond establishing posts in the principal centres of rebellion
while keeping up harassing tactics, such as the destruction
of growing crops, but as soon as the dry weather set in he
was reinforced by the Hussars and detachments of Police
and " Cape boys " from Bulawayo, and towards the end of
April, his own Police having in the meantime been brought
up to full strength, he was able to undertake effective operations on a concerted plan. One petty chief after another
was attacked and forced to submit. Matshayangombi's
kraal was stormed on the 26th July, the chief himself and
many other rebels killed and the caves blown up by dyna-
mite. The breaking up of this important stronghold, which
for twelve months had been the head-quarters of Mgwati,
Kagubi and other witch-doctors and the central rallying
point of the rebel leaders, was the turning-point in the
campaign and was soon followed by the surrender of most
of the remaining chiefs. All their natives offering submission and complying with the demands for the surrender
of their guns were forthwith located in suitable places in
the open and ordered to build new kraals and prepare land
for the next season's crops.

By the end of September the long-drawn-out campaign
was over. The Volunteers were disbanded and the Hussars
marched to Maçequeçe, whence they proceeded by train to
Beira and embarked for Durban. Of the witch-doctor
Mgwati no more was heard. Probably he was among those
killed at Matshayangombi's. His Mashonaland colleague
Kagubi, after escaping from that kraal, fled with his women
from one chief to another, but found everywhere that his
prestige was gone and that his presence was resented by

[1] Afterwards Lord Ventry. Died September 22nd, 1923.

KAGUBI : THE PRINCIPAL WITCH-DOCTOR

[*To face p.* 379.

those who had formerly been his willing tools. At last, realising that he could no longer elude capture, he surrendered unconditionally to one of the Native Commissioners on October the 27th. Nyanda, the Mazoe witch, followed suit a few days later. The couple were tried and condemned at Salisbury and were executed on the 27th of April, 1898.[1]

With their surrender the last elements of the Rebellion disappeared and the Company was in a position to devote its attention to the settlement of the natives in areas where they could be kept under supervision and deprived of the opportunity of hatching further plots. Large tracts of country were selected for reservations and the building of kraals in rocky and inaccessible positions was prohibited. The constitution of the native department was overhauled and commissioners of proved capacity, supported at the outset by detachments of Police, were sent to all the principal centres of population.

In framing a new native policy and in setting their house in order generally the Company were fortunate in securing the assistance of Mr. William Henry Milton,[2] who had held important posts in the Cape Colony, where he had been closely associated with Rhodes in the preparation of the famous Glen Grey Act. While recognising what Rhodesia owed to the handful of pioneer commissioners and magistrates—whose time, however, had hitherto been occupied nearly as much in soldiering as in the normal duties of administration—he saw that they needed a leaven of trained

---

[1] Official lists compiled at the time show that the number of European casualties due to the Rebellion was 638. In addition to 261 (inclusive of women and children) murdered or missing, 189 died through wounds and other causes, bringing the total number of deaths to 450. The number of wounded was 188. Omitting the casualties among the relief forces, the Imperial troops and the Police, the returns show that of the settlers in the country at the time of the outbreak 372 lost their lives and 129 were wounded, or nearly 10 per cent. of the white population. The figures given in the report issued by the Directors of the British South Africa Company in April 1898 are slightly inaccurate.

[2] Mr. Milton (now Sir William Milton, K.C.M.G., K.C.V.O.) assumed office as Chief Secretary in July 1896, and a year later, on the retirement of Earl Grey, was appointed Administrator, being assisted at the outset by a deputy Administrator at Bulawayo, the Hon. Arthur Lawley. He filled this post of increasing responsibility with credit and success for seventeen years, retiring in 1914, and leaving to his successor a legacy of high efficiency.

Civil servants, and gradually reinforced them by selected officials transferred from the older South African colonies. Thus under his discreet guidance the rough-and-ready methods inaugurated by Jameson soon gave place to a settled system of government.

In other respects also the suppression of the Rebellion marks the close of the first chapter in the history of Southern Rhodesia. The era of romance, adventure and novelty came to an end. Trials, indeed, and adversity were in store for the small white community, but of a kind incidental to the opening up of all new colonies and with little of the dramatic interest which had kept the settlers at fever-pitch since the occupation of 1890.

These first seven years had bred in them a fine spirit of self-reliance and pride in the country they had won. Newcomers speedily absorbed the same feelings, and as the years passed there grew up that remarkable exclusiveness which ultimately led Rhodesians to reject the prospect of comfortable quarters under the roof of the great South African Union and to choose the more difficult course of housekeeping for themselves.

Authorities consulted :

Blue Book C. 8060.
Files of various Rhodesian newspapers from 1896 and 1897.
Published reports of the British South Africa Company.

Other authorities are quoted in foot-notes.

CHAPTER XXIV

EARLY SETTLEMENTS NORTH OF THE ZAMBESI

(i) *North-Eastern Rhodesia*

IN a former chapter [1] the story of North-Eastern Rhodesia was brought to the point when the Chartered Company's agents, Sharpe and Thomson, acting in conjunction with Consul Johnston, had secured " treaties " in favour of Great Britain from all but two of the important native chiefs in the region lying between Nyasaland and the Luapula and Kafue rivers—the exceptions being Msiri, whose country, now known as Katanga, was annexed to the Congo Free State by Stairs in 1892, and Mpeseni, the chief of the Angoni, in the south-eastern corner of the territory, who had consistently repelled all overtures for an understanding with the British. The latter was a ruler of the type of Lobengula, and lived by raiding his weaker neighbours and by selling to Arab slave-traders such captives as he did not require for incorporation into his own tribe. His status as a territorial chief was, however, not recognised by Johnston, who maintained that he was an alien invader and that his refusal to fall into line could be ignored until an opportunity occurred for reducing him to submission.

Shortly before Thomson's return to Blantyre in March 1891, the Chartered Company's field of operations was extended, by agreement with the Foreign Office, so as to cover the whole of this great tract of country, with the stipulation that powers of government should for the time being be exercised, on behalf of the Company, by H.M.'s Commissioner for Nyasaland, who should receive from the Company an annual contribution of £10,000 for the maintenance of a Police Force and such further amounts as might be required for the expenses of government in the Chartered

[1] Chapter XVI.

sphere. It was also laid down that the administration of justice should be carried out by means of Consular Courts as provided in the Africa Order in Council of 1889.[1]

At one time the Foreign Office seemed disposed to bring Nyasaland itself under the Charter, but it was eventually constituted a separate British Protectorate, the extensive land and mineral rights acquired by Rhodes from the African Lakes Company being confirmed subject to proof of valid title.[2]

No real advance could be made by the Company either towards assuming the direct responsibility of government or turning to account the agreements with the native chiefs of this immense territory until law and order had been established in the neighbourhood of Lake Nyasa, and its annual subsidies were for two or three years expended by Johnston mainly in maintaining a force of Sikhs and Zanzibaris, who were employed in the suppression of the slave trade in the Lake area and in reprisals on certain chiefs guilty of outrages on British subjects. Although they have an intimate bearing on the subsequent history of North-Eastern Rhodesia, considerations of space preclude any account in the present narrative of these encounters with the various marauders and freebooters who then infested Nyasaland. The protracted struggle of the Pioneer settlers and the " nightmare of responsibility," as he calls it, endured by Johnston himself are graphically described in his *British Central Africa*, to which the reader must be referred.

To play a waiting game while such heavy demands were being made upon his Company's funds,[3] largely for the benefit of the adjoining Protectorate, did not accord with

[1] *Blue Book* C. 7637.

[2] The African Lakes Company (see Chap. XV) was in 1890 in financial straits owing to the exhausting struggle which it had maintained for some years against the Arab slave-traders. Rhodes came to its rescue by offering to absorb it in the Charter by means of an exchange of shares. Though accepted in principle, the arrangement was not completely brought into effect until 1893, when the Lakes Company transferred the benefits of its concessions and treaties to the Charter and its trading business to a new concern formed for the purpose—the African Lakes Corporation—which has since had a prosperous career.

[3] During the years 1890–1894 no less than £75,000 of the Company's money was expended in Nyasaland mainly in the suppression of the slave trade.

Rhodes' habit of rapid action, nor had the possession of a Charter for the unoccupied districts north and south of the Zambesi, huge as they were, appeased his appetite for British expansion in Africa. As each point was gained his horizon widened, and while Johnston was hammering away at the Arabs, Rhodes discerned a danger signal further north. It was in Uganda, where the British East Africa (Chartered) Company had exhausted itself in an unequal contest against opposing French, Islamic and other influences. In 1892 a section of the English public were for abandonment, and this course was favoured by certain elements in the new Gladstone Ministry.[1] Rhodes felt that he must throw what weight he could on the side of those who opposed the policy of scuttle, and during a short visit to England in that year he evolved a scheme for an overland telegraph line from South Africa to Egypt. He sketched out his plans naïvely and almost apologetically—he called it a " personal " matter— at a meeting of Chartered shareholders in November. He told them that he was prepared to " build a telegraph to Uganda," with confidence that once there he could get through to Wady Halfa. Rapidly and airily he gave them figures (which nobody at the time was in a position to dispute or even analyse) to show that when his line was complete, telegrams between England and South Africa would cost 2s. 6d. a word as against the current rate of 9s. 6d. Obstacles such as the Mahdi,[2] the lack of knowledge of much of the country to be traversed and of the native tribes to be encountered were dismissed in a sentence, and a scheme which on sober reflection must have appeared chimerical was hailed with shouts of applause.

The immediately practical part of this project was to carry the wire from Salisbury in Mashonaland northwards, across the Zambesi and the intervening belt of Portuguese territory, to Blantyre in Nyasaland, roughly 400 miles, and this was

[1] The idea did not originate with the Radical Government, for Lugard had actually in December 1891 received orders to evacuate Uganda. He succeeded in gaining a reprieve, which was later utilised by the Portal mission to obtain a reversal of the decision.

[2] The Khalifa, Abdallah, whose influence still blocked the way across the Sudan between Uganda and Egypt.

actually taken in hand at once.   Six weeks after Rhodes'
speech the African Trans-continental Telegraph Company
was launched, sufficient material ordered for the first section,
and Portuguese consent obtained—the last a difficult
engineering feat in itself.   During 1893 and 1894 surveys of
the route were made and active construction commenced
from both ends simultaneously with the object of linking
up at the ancient Portuguese settlement of Tete on the
Zambesi.   The work of the northern section was placed early
in 1894 under the supervision of Major Patrick Forbes—
not a very generous return, perhaps, for his services in the
south, but although Forbes' conduct of the Matabele campaign had been marked by his habitual courage, it was
obvious that his prestige had been injured by the unfortunate
outcome of his pursuit of Lobengula.

Towards the close of that year the end of Johnston's
dogged struggle against the Arab influence in Nyasaland was
in sight, and Rhodes intimated to H.M.'s Government that
the Company would be ready to undertake the independent
administration of its new territory in June 1895, a proposal
which was accepted and embodied in a second agreement
with the Foreign Office.[1]   Advantage was then taken of
Forbes' presence on the spot to appoint him Deputy Administrator with head-quarters temporarily at Blantyre in the
Protectorate.

Some time previous to this, Johnston, on behalf of the
Company, had established a station or fort near the south
end of Lake Tanganyika which he named Abercorn, and
another—Fife—midway between that point and the north
end of Lake Nyasa, thereby extinguishing Germany's aspirations to control the great water route from south to north.
Similarly stations were founded by Captain Crawshay of the
Nyasaland Consular Service at two points on Lake Mweru,
one of which, now Kalungwisi, was at first called "Rhodesia."
But the occupation of these stations had been intermittent,
and the officers who from time to time were placed in charge
of them with small detachments of Sikhs and Native Police
could do little more than play the rôle of sentries, though

[1] *Blue Book*, C. 7637.

they strove gradually to establish friendly relations with the
restless and quarrelsome tribes around them, and so far as
possible to throw obstacles in the way of the slave traffic.
The most important post was Abercorn, where Mr. Hugh
Marshall arrived as Consular officer in 1893.   To the south
of him were the Awemba, an exceptionally cruel and
aggressive tribe through whose country the Arab slavers
passed regularly *en route* for Zanzibar viâ German East
Africa.

In the hope of destroying this traffic, Forbes' first step
was to strengthen the detachments at Abercorn and Fife
and to create a sub-station at Nyala, further east along the
Stevenson road.   These measures were partially successful,
and during 1896 several caravans were intercepted and broken
up by the Company's officers before they could reach the
German border.   For a time, it is true, there were many who
evaded their vigilance by adopting a southerly route through
the country of the Asenga, a more or less peaceful tribe.
For a time too the Awemba kept up their raids and showed
their resentment of interference by constant attacks on any
natives who evinced a disposition to help the white officials,
their favourite victims being the same Asenga, whose district
was thus doubly afflicted.   But by degrees the influence of
Marshall and his colleagues spread and the feeling of security
inspired by their presence increased.   Sir Lawrence Wallace,
who was at Abercorn in 1896, says that at that date, *i.e.*
within three years of the arrival of the first Consular
officer, " the safety and content that came with the new
Government, and especially the feeling that it was gathering
power, were strong forces acting in its favour.   There was
still some sitting on the fence by some of the more distant
chiefs, and by some of the Arab villages, remnants of the old
slave-trading stations.   The Awemba, though they still
would allow no European to visit their country, showed
some respect, and had evidently become afraid of raiding.
Rumours and alarms of raids were not uncommon, but no
more raids came off.   The people of this tribe too, without
the excitement of successful war, were getting tired of the
cruelty of their chiefs and, seeing the safer conditions near,

were beginning to desert, a few at a time, and to ask to be allowed to settle near the Europeans."[1]

A last desperate effort to regain their waning power was made by the Arabs, in conjunction with the Awemba, in September 1897, when they advanced on a friendly Senga chief called Chiwali, whose kraal was not far from one of Forbes' new posts, Mirongo. Mr. R. A. Young, the Company's Collector, on being appealed to by the chief acted with great promptitude. With his small force of ten Native Police he marched to the rescue of Chiwali and kept a large body of the attackers at bay for five days while reinforcements were being hurried up from Fife and Nyala. With their assistance a salutary lesson was inflicted upon the Arabs and their allies. A large number were killed, many villages freed from their presence and numerous slaves liberated. By this rapid and effective action the Company's forces succeeded in breaking up for good the influence of the slavers who for generations had preyed upon the native tribes, and in stopping the external raids of the savage Awemba, who thereafter confined their murders and mutilations to their own tribesmen.

The first attempt at European settlement in the ordinary sense was made, not in the neighbourhood of the Company's stations on Lakes Mweru and Tanganyika, but in the southern portion of the territory, where a fertile and promising district, consisting of a plateau from 3000 to 4000 feet in altitude, drained by the Loangwa River and its tributaries and abounding in cattle, was dominated by Mpeseni the Angoni chief.

Reference was made in Chapter XVI to the presence at this man's town at the time of Sharpe's visit in 1890 of a German called Karl Wiese. At that date he was an ivory trader working in co-operation with the Portuguese, but on their withdrawal from the district in 1891 [2] he employed his talents in strengthening his personal influence with the local chiefs, with the object of acquiring private interests,

[1] Paper read by Sir Lawrence Wallace before the African Society and printed in the Society's Transactions for April 1922.

[2] In consequence of the Anglo-Portuguese agreement of 10th June, 1891, which threw Mpeseni's country into the British sphere.

and when the time was ripe, that is to say, in 1894, when the Chartered Company was preparing to assume direct responsibility for North-Eastern Rhodesia, he produced a number of written concessions in his favour, all of which included the grant of mineral and some of them of land rights as well, in areas within the Company's sphere. His trump card was a concession which purported to have been executed by Mpeseni himself, but, apart from other defects, this document lacked the chief's sign-manual, the omission having been obligingly rectified by the autograph of one Auguste de Fonseca de Mesquita e Solla, who was stated to have drawn up the deed at the request of the chief.

Wiese had previously made several attempts to secure recognition of his concessions from the British authorities, but both the Foreign Office and Johnston consistently refused to admit their validity without supporting evidence, the latter pointing out *inter alia* that Mpeseni, who was described in his concession as " Paramount Chief of the Angoni and Sovereign Ruler of Maravia and Western Nyasaland," was in reality merely a Zulu raider; that he had on several occasions refused point-blank to enter into friendly relations with the British, and that his assumption of authority over local tribes was entirely unwarrantable. But although not ratified, Wiese's claims were not expressly repudiated by the Government. He succeeded in floating a company in which his concessions constituted the principal asset, and they remained a bone of contention until eventually, to save further trouble, the Chartered Directors agreed to make a grant to this company of a large tract of land with mineral rights in Mpeseni's country on condition that a new company, in which the Charter should have a substantial interest, should be formed to develop it and that the concessions should be surrendered.

The North Charterland Exploration Company, as it was called, lost no time in equipping an expedition to proceed to Mpeseni's country and in embarking on a somewhat ambitious programme of agricultural and mineral development. But the command was entrusted to an officer from Natal who started with the mistaken idea that his company was entitled to exercise powers of administration—an impression which led to friction with the Foreign Office, with the Chartered Company and ultimately with Mpeseni and his Angonis. In justice to this chief it must be admitted that he wished to live at peace with the British settlers, but he was now an old man and had lost control over his hot-headed young warriors, who resented any interference with their customary raids and cattle-looting expeditions. The trouble culminated in December 1897, when the Angoni rose in rebellion under Singu, the chief's eldest son. They were flushed with the success of some local forays and began to mass in a threatening manner round Loangweni, a station of the North Charterland Company, where four white men, including Wiese himself, were quartered. The position of these and of Mr. Worringham, the Chartered Company's Collector at Fort Jameson,[1] became extremely precarious, and on the situation becoming known to Colonel Manning, the Acting Commissioner of Nyasaland, he decided that the time for half-measures was past, and that in the interests of the Protectorate as well as of Rhodesia the depredations of the Angoni must be stopped once for all. It was not a favourable moment for sending troops across country, as the rainy season was at its height. Nevertheless an advance detachment of B. C. A. Rifles, with some Sikhs (400 men in all, with two 7-pounders and two Maxims), was despatched from Nyasaland under Captain Brake, R.A., of the Pro-tectorate forces, while Colonel Manning himself with further troops moved forward in support. Brake reached Fort Jameson on the 17th January and learnt that Wiese's party was surrounded by about 10,000 of the rebels, whose number was daily increasing. Although it meant moving through an unfamiliar country at a distance from his supports, he courageously decided to proceed with his small army, and by forced marches covered the fifty miles of alternating forest and swamp that lay between Fort Jameson and Loangweni in two days, driving off several bodies of the enemy *en route*. His rapid movements took the rebels by

[1] Not the present Fort Jameson, which was laid out later by Mr. Codring-ton, but a station about fifty miles from Mpeseni's chief town.

surprise. They were concentrating for a final assault on Loangweni, which Brake was fortunately able to reach in the nick of time. After relieving the beleaguered white men he boldly took the offensive and for eight days kept the rebels on the move, fighting several engagements in most difficult country and doing good execution with his field-guns and Maxims. He was then joined by the main body under Manning, who divided the force into several columns which swept the hills in different directions. The Angoni at first put up a stiff resistance, but fortunately their leader Singu was captured, tried by court-martial and shot, after which they became somewhat demoralised. By February the 6th they were broken up into small bodies, all of which were on the run. About 12,000 of their cattle were seized, many of their kraals destroyed and a number of prisoners taken. The casualties on the British side were comparatively slight. Mpeseni himself fled to the hills, but surrendered voluntarily on the 18th February, and on promise of good behaviour was allowed to remain in the district and to retain a nominal chieftaincy.

This little campaign had an excellent moral effect not only on the Angoni, but on all the restless elements in the heterogeneous native population. The former, as usually happens with Zulu tribes, took their chastisement stoically and submitted to the inevitable. Indeed within a few months 150 of them enlisted for service with the native regiment then being raised for duty in Mashonaland, where by careful handling and discipline they were converted into efficient military policemen.

Forbes, who had resigned on the ground of ill-health shortly before the Mpeseni rebellion, was now succeeded by Mr. Robert Codrington, a former member of the Bechuana-land Police who had served in the Matabele war. Under his strong guidance the Company's administration rapidly took shape. The country was divided into districts, the little staff of experienced but overworked officials was reinforced by fresh blood from England, and order and good government began to prevail in the land which had so recently been terrorised by raiders and slave-traders.

During the two succeeding years the Company's influence was gradually extended and consolidated; a small township was laid out at Fort Jameson; the Stevenson road between Lakes Nyasa and Tanganyika, hitherto little more than a rough clearing, was completed, and seven or eight hundred miles of other roads constructed. The telegraph line was steadily pushed forward, and by the end of 1899 reached Lake Tanganyika, which was thus brought into direct communication with Southern Rhodesia. By the North-Eastern Rhodesia Order in Council of 1900 the scope of the Administration was enlarged so as to include a considerable area in the south-west bordering on the Zambesi and Kafue Rivers and reaching as far as the nominal boundary of the Barotse king's influence. At the same time the old Consular courts were replaced by a judge and district magistrates, and provision was made for the imposition of a hut tax.

But although a good deal of quiet spade-work was being accomplished and a marvellous transformation had been effected in the general well-being of North-Eastern Rhodesia, it remained purely a native territory. With the exception of the embryonic settlement round Fort Jameson no attempt at colonisation had taken place. There was little or no agriculture save of an experimental nature. Here and there indications of gold were found, but no such mineral discoveries as had induced Englishmen to triumph over the physical difficulties of occupying Mashonaland and Matabeleland. The progress of the territory was hampered by its inaccessibility, the only means of approach being an uncertain steamer service from Chinde viâ the Zambesi and Shiré Rivers, followed by a long road journey with native porters. This will explain why as late as 1911, when North-Eastern and North-Western Rhodesia were united under a joint Administration, the white population of the former, save for a few traders and missionaries, was purely official, and numbered all told less than 500 souls.

(ii) North-Western Rhodesia.

Very different was the course of events in the west, where the active work of the Chartered Company did not begin

until the arrival of Coryndon in the Barotse valley in October
1897.[1] In order to meet Lewanika's hankering for a direct
representative of the Queen, this young Commissioner—he
was only twenty-seven when he took up his duties—was
accredited by the Foreign Office as British Resident and
also held a warrant as a judicial officer under the Africa
Order in Council, but his principal tasks were to prepare the
way for direct control over the Barotse and their tributary
tribes, to secure to the Company some effective means of
dealing with the expected influx of white prospectors and
traders, and, with these objects in view, to persuade the
Paramount Chief to grant more liberal powers than were
contained in the concession obtained by Lochner in 1890.
He played a difficult part patiently and with great consideration for Lewanika and his Council of Indunas, thereby
restoring their confidence in the Company, whose *bona fides*
had fallen under suspicion owing to the length of time
which had been allowed to elapse since Lochner's visit.
Eventually he induced the chief to undertake a journey to
the Victoria Falls to meet the Company's senior representative in Matabeleland, the Hon. Arthur Lawley,[2] who
travelled up from Bulawayo to meet him there, and afterwards published a graphic and amusing account of his
experiences. The proceedings were conducted with fitting
ceremonial. Several days were spent in the discussions so
dear to African natives, and finally, on the 25th June, 1898,
Lewanika agreed to grant to the Company very wide powers
of administration and jurisdiction, and exclusive privileges
in respect of mining and commerce within certain defined
boundaries. He also undertook to use his best endeavours
to suppress slavery and witchcraft. In return Lawley and
Coryndon pledged the Company to assist in the education
and civilisation of the chief's subjects, to reserve large
specified tracts for the sole use of the Barotse people, and
to pay an annual subsidy which was to include the royalty
due under the Ware Concession acquired by Rhodes in

---

[1] See Chapter XIV.
[2] Afterwards Sir Arthur Lawley, G.C.S.I., etc., Governor of Madras
For the account referred to see *Blackwood's Magazine* for December 1898.

1890.[1] At a later date this agreement was embodied in a formal document to which the chief put his signature—not his mark merely, for he was distinguished from other African rulers by being able to write his name in English characters— and which was also attested by the signatures or marks of his " Prime Minister," his son Litia and five of his principal Councillors, Coryndon signing on behalf of the Company.

But Her Majesty's Government was not disposed at once to give the Company a free hand. The frontier between Barotseland and Portuguese West Africa (Angola) had not yet been determined, and it was considered advisable, pending the settlement of that question, that the control of the Imperial authorities should be closer than it would be if the direct administration were given to the Company, as had been done in North-Eastern Rhodesia. It was decided, therefore, that the western province should be administered by the High Commissioner for South Africa acting under the direction of the Secretary of State for the Colonies, though the Company was permitted to nominate an Administrator and other officers, and, it may be added, was also permitted to bear the cost of government. Effect was given to this arrangement in 1899 by an Order in Council, but the ratification of the agreement which Lawley and Coryndon had negotiated with the chief was delayed, on various pretexts, until November 1901—more than three years after its terms had been settled at the Victoria Falls.

Between 1898 and 1904, when the railway from the south reached the Victoria Falls and the country was made accessible to white settlement, the history of North-Western Rhodesia is the record of an uphill struggle by an isolated handful of earnest and stout-hearted officials, far removed from the advantages of civilisation, to consolidate their position with the natives, to wean them from their barbarous and superstitious practices and to teach them to lean on British support. As in North-Eastern Rhodesia, the task was complicated by the diversity of tribes and their inability, after centuries of strife and upheavals, to comprehend any system of government which was not dictated by brute force.

[1] See p. 214.

But Coryndon and his assistants, conspicuous among whom were his Chief of Police, Major Colin Harding, and his Native Commissioner, Mr. Frank Vigers Worthington, were aided by the intelligent co-operation of the Paramount, Lewanika, who, next to Khama, was probably the most far-seeing native ruler that the nineteenth century produced in Africa, and who, as soon as he grasped the advantages of the new arrangement in stabilising his own position developed a genuine ambition to help his people to advance towards peace and prosperity. The Company's officials were loyally supported also by the French missionary Coillard, who spared no effort to instil into the Barotse the advantages of a settled life under a British régime. It is hardly an exaggeration to say that his influence during the first few years of Chartered administration was the principal factor in smoothing the way for the reforms which Lewanika gradually consented to introduce.

The outstanding events of those years were the visit of the chief to England in 1902; the settlement of the western boundary of his kingdom; the suppression of slavery; the discoveries of base metals in the basin of the Kafue River, and the advent of the railway. Each of these events contributed in greater or less degree towards lifting North-Western Rhodesia out of savagery and setting it on the path to colonisation, and each demands a brief reference.

From the date of Coryndon's arrival the chief had expressed a strong desire to visit England and to see with his own eyes the " Great White Queen." Her Majesty's death in January 1901, while it caused some dismay in the chief's mind, as was the case with millions of her black subjects who had for years invested her personality with almost divine attributes, by no means damped his longing to undertake what was, in those days, an almost unheard-of pilgrimage for a Central African king. The organisation of the journey and the supervision of the chief and his native attendants presented no small difficulties, but in 1902, with the consent of the Colonial Office, the Company decided to gratify his wish, and arranged for him to take part officially in the Coronation of King Edward VII. The visit, which included a special audience granted by His Majesty to the chief, was carefully planned and passed off without contre-temps. The novelty and constantly increasing interest of the scenes which he encountered during his long journey by canoe, road, railway and steamship, his tour through dock-yards and manufacturing centres in England and the culminating splendour of the Coronation ceremonies, pro-duced in the chief an overwhelming impression which was manifested later in the eagerness with which he welcomed suggestions for the betterment of his own nation and in his ready acceptance of decisions emanating from the King's Government.

A striking instance of this was seen in 1905, when the result of the arbitration as to his western boundary was announced. Disappointing as that result was to him, he acquiesced because he had come to realise that wider interests than his own existed, that the welfare of himself and his people was in good hands and that every effort had been made to secure an equitable decision.

It should be explained that Lewanika had long asserted sovereignty over an immense belt of country to the west of the Zambesi covering practically all that lay between the Congo Free State on the north and German territory on the south as far as about the 17th degree of East Longitude. But his authority over many of the people on the outskirts of this area was tenuous and intermittent. Occasional presents of ivory or guns on the part of some one of the tribes; the presence in their villages of a Barotse headman, and their practice, on the death of a chief, of consulting Lewanika as to the choice of a successor, were some of the facts cited to show that these tribes were his tributaries. But compli-ments and relations of this character were not unusual between chiefs of adjoining districts. They did not necessarily betoken submission, but arose from a desire to conciliate and live at peace with a powerful neighbour. The Portuguese, on the other hand, could point to more substantial arguments in the shape of forts and garrisons which they had established a long way east of the boundary claimed by Lewanika, and which in some cases had existed

LEWANIKA, " KING " OF BAROTSELAND, AT HOME, 1903

Seated : Mr. F. V. Worthington, The Author, Lewanika.
In front : Litia (now the paramount chief Yeta III)

BAROTSE FEMALE CHIEF : (THE MOKWAE AKANANGISOA)
(*see* p. 207)   [*To face p.* 394.

for years. The masses of conflicting evidence were in the end submitted to the King of Italy, whose decision was delivered in May 1905. His award very pertinently referred to the "notorious instability of these remote tribes and their frequent intermingling," which made the fixing of a frontier according to natural lines impracticable and necessitated the adoption of a conventional boundary following degrees of longitude and latitude. There was assigned to the Barotse chief a strip of about 200 miles in width roughly parallel with the Zambesi River along its western side from the Congo State to the German border, and all beyond this strip was thrown into Portuguese West Africa. Although arrived at in somewhat arbitrary fashion, and although it caused intense chagrin to Lewanika, there can be little doubt that the partition was in the main an equitable one.

The Chartered Company's commercial rights were not directly affected, as the Directors had never contemplated extending its operations to these distant and inaccessible regions.[1] Indirectly, however, the boundary dispute was of importance to the Company because of its close bearing on the struggle which, in accordance with the obligations imposed by the Charter,[2] it was waging against the slave trade.

Reference was made in an earlier chapter [3] to the activities of the slave-dealers in the districts lying immediately to the north and west of the Barotse country at the time of the Lochner mission, and it may here be added that at the close of the nineteenth and during the opening years of the present century they were still openly plying their evil business throughout the disputed territory, and sometimes even ventured into districts whose inclusion in the British sphere was not open to doubt. Before 1898, when North-Western Rhodesia was officially brought under British protection and the nucleus of the Chartered Administration first

---

[1] The Company subsequently agreed that the additional strip of country now definitely assigned to the Barotse should be added to the area reserved against white occupation. In return for this the chief granted to the Company substantial land rights in the remainder of North-Western Rhodesia (the "Wallace" Concession of 1909).

[2] Article 11 of the Royal Charter.

[3] Chapter XIV.

established, nothing could be done to check the traffic, though its horrors had been made public by Commander Cameron, by Selous, by Major Gibbons and by other explorers who visited Barotseland.[1] The main slave route lay from the head-waters of the Zambesi—in the " no man's land " where the territorial limits of the British, Belgian and Portuguese spheres had not been accurately defined—in a westerly direction to Bihé, an important caravan centre in the Portuguese colony of Angola, whence the gangs of captives were passed on, under the guise of porters, to Benguella on the West Coast. The actual " trading " was carried on by Mambari natives, many of whom had an infusion of Portuguese blood. Whenever encountered by the rare British who penetrated to this part of the interior, these purveyors of human flesh professed to be engaged in the collection of indigenous rubber, but the desolation left in their track, the discarded yokes and shackles and the skeletons and rotting remains of slaves who had dropped exhausted by the way were abundant evidence of their real business. The usual medium of purchase was calico, but Martini and Snider rifles and ammunition were also employed, and to obtain the means of acquiring these coveted articles— all of which, be it noted, were of British origin—the native tribes were engaged in a constant system of mutual raids. On the smallest pretext a strong chief would attack the villages of a weak neighbour, and would keep any prisoners he might secure for sale to the villainous Mambari, parties of whom were generally hovering round on the look-out for such opportunities, and even ready to provoke them if supplies of " black ivory " were short. Not only was this traffic winked at by the Portuguese, but there can be little doubt that some of the forts which they established in the Lunda, Lovale and Mbunda districts (all claimed by Lewanika) were for the express purpose of intercepting runaway slaves. There was a chain of these forts along the main caravan route and slave-gangs regularly passed under

---

[1] *Across Africa*, by V. Lovett Cameron, 1885; *Travel and Adventure in South-East Africa*, by F. C. Selous, 1895; *Exploration and Hunting in Central Africa*, by Major St. Hill Gibbons, 1898. See also *Garenganze*, by F. S. Arnot, 1889.

their very shadow—sometimes headed by the Portuguese flag flying from a long pole. Mambari traders frequently appeared at Lewanika's capital, but only to barter guns, calico and the like for ivory and skins, for the chief gave no countenance to slave-dealing.

So long as this traffic was confined to the disputed territory the Chartered officials could take no steps to repress it, but on learning that the Mambari occasionally made excursions over the established boundary into the British sphere, Coryndon placed a Commissioner at Kasempa, near the border, with instructions to keep a sharp look-out for offenders. This officer with a few Native Police maintained a system of patrols, and in 1903 was able to intercept and break up several caravans and to release the wretched men, women and children collected from villages in the vicinity. The presence of the small Police Force and the arrival of miners to investigate the copper discoveries at Kanshanshi were sufficient to check the activities of the slavers, and the settlement of the boundary saw their final disappearance from British territory.

Although the " slave trade " in the accepted sense of the term was discouraged by Lewanika, slavery was a time-honoured institution among his people and survived until some years after the British occupation. The Barotse " aristocracy " depended for their crops, their canoe transport and all the necessaries of life upon slave labour, reserving for themselves the more congenial occupations of hunting and palavering. Large numbers of slaves had been acquired by raiding parties in previous years, and the supply was maintained by others who were, even after the arrival of Coryndon and his officers, brought to Barotseland as tribute by conquered tribes. M. Coillard has left us a description of the painful scene when such a party, consisting of young women and children only, to the number of some hundreds, was distributed by Lewanika among the Barotse to become their chattels.[1]

The slave raids were firmly repressed by Coryndon as soon as his status as British Resident was established, but the

---

[1] *On the Threshold of Central Africa*, by F. Coillard, pp. 471, 472.

abolition of slavery as an institution, and the emancipation
of the slaves themselves, were undertakings demanding much
careful preparation, and were not achieved for several years.
In the long run they were brought about by a combination
of events. Lewanika had consented to the imposition of a
general hut tax and had agreed to forego the collection
of annual tribute from the vassal tribes provided that a fixed
proportion of the tax received from them was paid to him
for his own use, and a further proportion devoted to certain
purposes of national benefit such as education. But the
tax was applicable also to Barotseland proper, where a large
proportion of the inhabitants consisted of slaves with no
means of paying, as they could own no property. Among
these latter there was now a growing tendency to desert and
return to their tribes, and Lewanika and his councillors were
well aware that the Company's officials would not allow any
steps to recover them by force. They realised with anxiety
that unless they accepted some compromise the time was
fast approaching when they would not only lose the means
of meeting their tax, but would become destitute for want
of labour. Furthermore, the lessons of his visit to England
had not been lost on Lewanika. Both he and his intelligent
Prime Minister, who had accompanied him, knew that
throughout the British Empire, of which their country was
now a unit, the idea of slavery was odious. They determined,
therefore, to make a virtue of necessity, and, having brought
the National Council to the same way of thinking, announced
that a ceremonial *pitso* would be held at which the Paramount
Chief would formally and solemnly "abolish slavery."
The Company's officers were alive to the importance of this
occasion. The Secretary for Native Affairs (Mr. Worthington, who had been mainly instrumental in convincing the
chief of the necessity for the step) was present, and was
supported by the district officials and by the full strength
of the local detachment of Police. Many thousands of
natives assembled to hear the proclamation read. It contained certain saving clauses reserving to the chief the right
to call upon his people to provide free services to himself
and his household for a limited number of days in each year,

and giving similar privileges to the Indunas and headmen
in respect of duties for the benefit of the community.   All
other work or services were to be paid for at a minimum wage,
and existing slaves from other tribes were to be allowed
forthwith to purchase their freedom by a small payment.

With this proclamation (October 1906) the last relics of
slavery disappeared from the territories governed under the
Royal Charter.

So far we have been dealing with domestic affairs and
native reforms, but the circumstances which finally determined the future of North-Western Rhodesia were the discoveries of base-metal deposits—not only in the Territory
itself but in the Belgian Congo further north—and the
resulting impetus given to railway extension.   It was some
time before the mineral possibilities of these northern
regions began to attract serious notice.   It was difficult in
the 'nineties to think of anything but gold, the pursuit of
which absorbed all the energy of the Pioneer settlers in
Southern Rhodesia.   But there were shrewd men there who
had not lost sight of the old reports of the copper lodes of
Katanga, and who saw no reason why similar deposits should
not be found on the Rhodesian side of the frontier.   Between
1899 and 1902 two or three expeditions were formed in
Bulawayo to explore these parts.   One of them, organised
by Mr. Robert Williams and commanded by the late Mr.
George Grey—both pioneers of mining development in
Mashonaland and Matabeleland, and the latter a prominent
leader during the Rebellion [1]—demonstrated the immense
importance of the Katanga copper-fields and the existence
of similar formations in Rhodesia at Kansanshi and elsewhere.   Further south, in the hook or bend of the Kafue
River, other prospectors discovered certain indications of
copper and other minerals at several different points,
together with evidence—in the shape of shallow excavations
and old smelting tubes—that a considerable industry had
at some earlier date been carried on in working them.   In
fact the local natives were still, with their primitive methods,
producing copper for trading purposes and for manufacture

[1] See p. 359.

into implements and ornaments for their own use. Systematic prospecting revealed the existence of galena with lead and zinc deposits some distance to the east, in what was then North-Eastern Rhodesia, and in 1902 mining was started at a property which, from its resemblance to the famous Australian mine of similar formation, was called the " Rhodesia Broken Hill." Discoveries further north, at Bwana Mkubwa near the Congo border, of a valuable copper lode left no doubt that the anticipation of mineral wealth in North-Western Rhodesia had been well founded.

It had always been Rhodes' intention to extend the railway from the south across the Zambesi River. Originally his plan was to make Lake Tanganyika the objective, to build a line from Bulawayo to Salisbury and to carry the rails from Gwelo, a midway point, in a northerly direction to Kariba Gorge, tapping on the way a coal-field which was known to exist in Northern Matabeleland. Later it was found that the difficulties of construction by this route would be very great, especially beyond the Zambesi River. On the other hand, the coal deposits further west, at Wankie, seventy miles from the Victoria Falls, were proving to be of great extent and value, while the country to be traversed between Bulawayo and Wankie (200 miles) offered no engineering difficulties. The possibility of opening the Falls to tourist traffic was another point which claimed consideration. For these reasons it was decided in 1900 that the course of the northward railway extension should be from Bulawayo viâ Wankie to the Falls, where the throwing of a bridge over the narrow gorge would be less costly than the construction of the line across the deep wide valleys further east. The idea of this bridge stirred Rhodes' imagination and was constantly present to him during the last months of his life. It was his wish that it should be built as close to the Falls as safety would permit, and he pictured the train passengers being drenched by the clouds of spray which at all times hang over them. This conception was realised, but not by Rhodes. He was never able to undertake the journey to the Zambesi by road, and he died two years before it was reached by the railway. But although his direct guidance was no longer

AFRICA SOUTH OF THE EQUATOR
AS CECIL RHODES LEFT IT

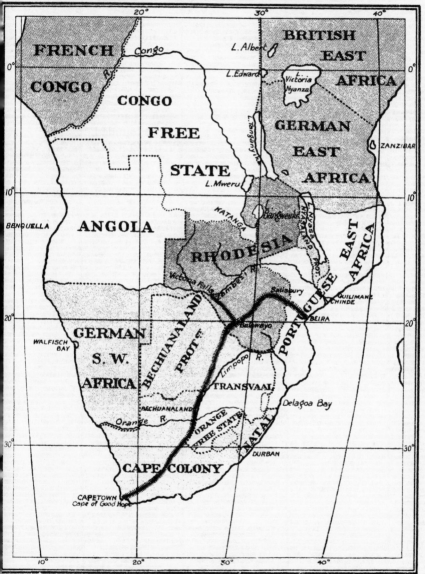

there his inspiration remained, and the work which he had
marked out for himself was faithfully pursued by those who
came after.

The railway arrived at Wankie in September 1903 and at
the Falls in 1904. By this time further objectives were in
sight—Kalomo, the head-quarters of the North-Western
Administration, the Broken Hill mine and the copper-fields
of Katanga, which assured a profitable market for Wankie
coal and a constant freight for the railway. A future of
boundless industrial development opened out for the land
which, less than a decade before, had been one of the waste
places of the earth.

Here this chronicle may fittingly be brought to a conclusion. The recent history of the sister Colonies of Rhodesia
is public property in the sense that it is accessible to anyone
who cares to turn to the contemporary Press or to books of
reference. But the living links with the pioneer days are
now few in number; human memory is treacherous, and
even documentary records tend to become obscure or to lose
their coherence as time rolls on. One who has been privi-
leged to live in those days, and to know most of the people
concerned in the " Making of Rhodesia," may therefore be
forgiven for attempting to piece the story together.

South of the Zambesi the years between the Rebellion
and the present time have been notable for the determination
of the settlers in surmounting the difficulties of their
geographical position and for the steady growth among them
of representative institutions—beginning with the infant
Legislative Council of 1899, with four members elected
by the people, and terminating with full parliamentary
government in 1923.[1]

[1] Thus realising Rhodes' prophecy of thirty-two years before. In a
speech at the Congress of the Afrikander Bond in 1891 he said :—" These
territories possess a sufficient amount of wealth to demand, in time, the
principle of self-government. . . . There is an extraordinary flight of the
imagination, that there must be a self-governing white community up to
the Zambesi in connection with the United South."

Those years brought many set-backs, many disappointments, but the dogged resolution of the colonists triumphed and enabled them, not merely to make sure the hardly earned position within their own borders, but to play a worthy part in the wider sphere of Empire. During the crisis of the South African War, and again in the World War, Rhodesian citizens bore their share, and more than their share, of military service under the British flag. Few in numbers they have—perhaps unconsciously—cultivated a national character, the seeds of which were sown amid the trials and hardships of the early occupation. With the dawn of settled institutions the " heroic age " gradually faded, and, while the self-reliance bequeathed by the Pioneers remains, their successors of to-day follow the path of commercial progress unembarrassed by adventure. A great part of Northern Rhodesia may be still in the twilight, but there too the glare of civilisation is gradually driving back the shadows which only yesterday shrouded the country in seclusion and mystery.

Looking back one must admit that, in the building up of these Colonies, though mistakes were undoubtedly made and opportunities may have been missed, the foundations were well and truly laid by the old Company and the adventurous spirits who clustered round it. Looking forward, what better prayer could one utter than that which the Southern Colony has adopted as its national motto—
Sit nomine digna !

Authorities consulted :

    The Great Plateau of Northern Rhodesia, by C. Gouldsbury and H. Sheane, 1911.

    Blue Book C. 7637.

    Published reports of the British South Africa Company.

Other authorities are quoted in the text or in foot-notes.

APPENDIX I

1889.	*The Duke of Abercorn, K.G., President .	died	1913
,,	*The Duke of Fife, K.T. . . .	resigned	1897
,,	*Hon. Cecil John Rhodes . . .	died	1902
,,	*Lord Gifford, V.C.	died	1911
,,	*Alfred Beit	died	1906
,,	*George Cawston	resigned	1908
,,	*Albert Grey (afterwards Earl Grey) .	resigned	1903
,,	Horace Farquhar (afterwards Sir Horace)	resigned	1897
1898.	Sir Sidney Shippard, K.C.M.G. . .	died	1902
,,	James Rochfort Maguire, President 1923	died	1925
1899.	Philip Lyttelton Gell, President 1920 .	resigned	1925
1902.	Leander Starr Jameson, C.B. (afterwards Right Hon. Sir Starr Jameson, Bart.), President 1913	died	1917
,,	Hon. Sir Lewis Loyd Michell, C.V.O.		
1905.	Henry Birchenough, C.M.G. (afterwards Sir H. Birchenough, Bart., K.C.M.G.), President, 1925.		
1907.	The Marquess of Winchester.		
1910.	Otto Beit (afterwards Sir O. Beit, Bart., K.C.M.G.)		
1913.	Baron Emile Beaumont d'Erlanger.		
,,	Henry Wilson Fox, M.P. . . .	died	1921
,,	Brigadier-Gen. Hon. Everard Baring, C.V.O., C.B.E.	resigned	1925
,,	Dougal Orme Malcolm.		
,,	The Duke of Abercorn, K.P.		
1919.	Major Percy Sidney Inskipp, O.B.E. .	resigned	1922

* Directors appointed under the Charter.

APPENDIX II

I. SOUTHERN RHODESIA.

Administrators.

1891. Archibald Ross Colquhoun (Mashonaland).

,,   Leander Starr Jameson (Mashonaland; 1894, S. Rhodesia).

1896. Right Hon. Earl Grey.

1898. William Henry Milton (afterwards Sir Wm. Milton, K.C.M.G., K.C.V.O.)

1914. Francis Drummond Percy Chaplin (afterwards Sir Drummond Chaplin, G.B.E., K.C.M.G.)

Acting Administrators.

1893. Andrew Henry Farrell Duncan.

1894. Col. Francis William Rhodes, C.B., D.S.O.

1895. Hon. Joseph Vintcent.

1897. William Henry Milton.

1898. Hon. Sir Thomas Charles Scanlen, K.C.M.G. (and on several later occasions).

1899. Hon. Arthur Lawley.

1902. John Gilbért Kotze, K.C.

1909. Francis James Newton, C.M.G., afterwards Sir F. Newton K.C.M.G., C.V.O. (and on several later occasions).

1919. Clarkson Henry Tredgold, K.C.

1922. Ernest William Sanders Montagu.

1923. Percival Donald Leslie Fynn.

II. NORTH-EASTERN RHODESIA.

Administrators.

1896. Major Patrick William Forbes.

1898. Robert Edward Codrington.

1907. Lawrence Aubrey Wallace.

Acting Administrators.

1897. Captain Henry Lawrence Daly.
1901. Christian Purefoy Chesnaye.
1905. Leicester Paul Beaufort.
1911. Hugh Charlie Marshall.

III. NORTH-WESTERN RHODESIA.

Administrators.

1897. Robert Thorne Coryndon.
1907. Robert Edward Codrington.
1909. Lawrence Aubrey Wallace.

Acting Administrators.

1899. Major Colin Harding, C.M.G.
1903. Hugh Marshall Hole (and again in 1907).
1904. Frank Vigers Worthington.
1906. Francis James Newton, C.M.G.
1906. Ernest Charles Baxter.
1907. Lt.-Col. John Carden.

IV. NORTHERN RHODESIA (after the amalgamation).

Administrators.

1911. Lawrence Aubrey Wallace, afterwards Sir L. Wallace, K.B.E., C.M.G.
1921. Sir F. D. P. Chaplin, K.C.M.G.

Acting Administrator.

1922. Richard Allmond Jeffrey Goode, C.B.E. (and again in 1923).

INDEX

ABERCORN, station on Lake Tanganyika, 384

Abercorn, Duke of, original Director of Chartered Co., 103

Aborigines Protection Society, entertain Matabele envoys, 81; letter to Lobengula, 84; effect of letter, 112

African Lakes Co., subsidised by Chartered Co., 95

Alderson, Lt.-Col. E. A. H., in command of mounted infantry for defence in rebellion, 364, 371, 377

Ancient gold-workings in Rhodesia, 3, 4, 176

—— copper-workings in N. Rhodesia, 399

Andrade, Paiva d', efforts to save Portuguese colonies, 8; at Maçequeçe with armed force, 165; attempts to upset Manica concession, 168; arrested by Forbes, 169; statement regarding arrest, 170

Anglo-German agreement, 219

Anglo-Portuguese Convention, 157; failure of, 159

Angoni tribe, foundation of, 32 n.; rebellion of, 388

Angra Pequena, annexed by Germany, 17, 19

Arab slave-traders in N.E. Rhodesia, 382, 385

Arnot, Frederick, founder of mission in Garenganze, 244

Awemba tribe in N.E. Rhodesia, 385; raids checked by Company's officials, 386

Babbs, Richard, pamphlet on gold discoveries in Mashonaland, 4

Babyana, Matabele envoy to England, 80

Baden-Powell, Col. R. S. S., 365

Baines, Thos., expeditions by, 5 et seq.; concession, 6, 7; his book, 175

Banyailand, Boer designs on, 266 et seq.; Boer trek described, 266–275

Barotse boundary question, 392; award, 395

Barotse concession, Lochner's, 219, 220; Coryndon's, 391

Barotseland, expedition to, 129; sketch of history, 204 et seq.; social system, 207; physical characteristics, 209; slave trade, 395

Base metal deposits in N.W. Rhodesia, 399

Batoka tribe, 204, 205, 212

Beal, Robert, commanding Salisbury relief force, 361; returns with column, 371

Bechuanaland, importance of, in relation to northern expansion, 10, 12 et seq.; proclaimed a protectorate, 20

Bechuanaland Police, ordered to advance on Matabeleland, 304, 313; strength of force, 313

Bechuanaland Protectorate, transfer of administration to Company, 343

Beira, importance of, as port, 180; railway communication with, 336

Beit, Alfred, supports Rhodes' schemes, 86; joint letter with Rhodes regarding proposal for Charter, 100; original director of Chartered Co., 103; visits Mashonaland, 281

Belingwe, defence of, in rebellion, 359

Bent, Theodore, expedition to explore ancient ruins, 278

Berlin, Conference of, 10

Biscoe, E. C. Tyndale-, at Umtasa's, 168

Boers, repel Matabele in Transvaal, 32; organise trek to Mashonaland, 269

Boggie, Mr., throws in lot with Rhodes party, 67